COMHAIRLE CHONTAE ÁTHA CLIATH THEAS
SOUTH DUBLIN COUNTY LIBRARIES

COUNTY LIBRARY, TOWN CENTRE, TALLAGHT
TO RENEW ANY ITEM TEL: 462 0073
NLINE AT www.southdublinlibraries.ie

ꞁed on or befo⸴   ꞁast date below. Fines,
⸴ibrar⸴   ꞁarged on overdue items.

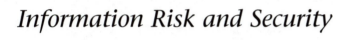

Information Risk and Security

Information Risk and Security

Preventing and Investigating Workplace Computer Crime

EDWARD WILDING

GOWER

We also acknowledge that Chapters 18, 19 and Appendix 4 are based on articles originally prepared for the *Computer Fraud & Security Bulletin* published by Elsevier Advanced Technology (with permission) and that Chapters 2 and 11 are (significant) updates of chapters in *Computer Evidence: A Forensic Investigations Handbook*, by E. Wilding published by Sweet & Maxwell (with permission).

Published by
Gower Publishing Limited
Gower House
Croft Road
Aldershot
Hants GU11 3HR
England

Gower Publishing Company
Suite 420
101 Cherry Street
Burlington,
VT 05401-4405
USA

British Library Cataloguing in Publication Data
Wilding, Edward
   Information risk and security: preventing and
   investigating workplace computer crime
   1. Computer crimes – Prevention 2. Employee crimes 3. Computer
   crimes – Investigation
   I. Title
   364.1'68

   ISBN 0 566 08685 9

Library of Congress Cataloging-in-Publication Data
Wilding, Edward.
   Information risk and security: preventing and investigating workplace computer crime / by Edward Wilding.
     p. cm.
   Includes bibliographical references and index.
   ISBN 0 566 08685 9
   1. Computer crimes--Prevention. 2. Employee crimes--Prevention. 3. Computer crimes--Investigation.
I. Title.

   HV6773.W55 2005
   658.4'78--dc22

                                                       2005022770

Typeset by Owain Hammonds, Ceredigion.
Printed and bound in Great Britain by TJ International Ltd, Padstow, Cornwall.

Contents

List of Figures

List of Tables

Foreword

Mad Magazine used to publish a cartoon strip about two 'spooks', one dressed in black, the other in white – a parody of the Cold War mentality. The threats were obvious as were the counter-measures: standing air patrols, ICBMs, massed forces and, appropriately, Mutually Assured Destruction. Even Joe Citizen prepared his emergency shelter stocked with food and fuel. Computers? Well, we only needed about five, according to IBM – as large as houses and located in strong, temperature-controlled vaults with a few trusted acolytes to tend them. Crime? Well, that was self-regulated by the likes of the notorious Kray twins and other gangland figures. The police knew where the villains lived and could 'feel their collars' should a crime be planned or suspected. But that was 40 years ago! A very non-PC world.

Today, those editions of *Mad* are collectors' items and the spooks have joined forces, or gone into syndicated crime, or both. The Cold War has 'chilled out', and many households have two or more computers. Nowadays, anyone can commit major crime from the comfort of his or her home.

This familiarity with how to scam, con, defraud and otherwise cause digital mayhem has grown through popular exposure to film, TV and the resources of the Internet. At the same pace, a sharp decline in personal integrity, loyalty and honesty has become accepted as the norm. Little wonder, then, that there is so much apathy in corporate management about these risks – the three 'wise' monkeys never had it so good!

This intriguing, entertaining exposé about the dubious company we sometimes unwittingly keep will open your mind to the threats that now face all organizations, both great and small. Its solid advice on controls and counter-measures is not an auditor's dry scratching in the margins. Rather, it is a remarkable tribute to the skills, patience and values of a small band of forensic experts who, time and again, have unearthed the truth to help prosecute, or defend, those unfortunate enough to be caught up in bad company.

Enjoy – but learn.

Phil Phillips, FBCS
President, BCS Information Security Specialist Group

Acknowledgements

This book is a synthesis of a two-day training course 'Investigating Computer Crime and Misuse', which Noel Bonczoszek and myself have presented over eight years and which constitutes part of the post-graduate diploma in Information Security, Royal Holloway, University of London. Noel, formerly a detective with New Scotland Yard's Computer Crime Unit, has always sought practical and efficient solutions to problems, an approach with which I wholeheartedly agree and which I trust is reflected in this manuscript. My colleagues at Data Genetics International Limited (DGI) provided technical assistance throughout and shouldered the considerable burden of investigative casework during this book's preparation. I am particularly indebted to Patrick Madden, Richard Bultitude and Aaron Stowell who checked the technical accuracy of several chapters. Phil Phillips, President of the British Computer Society's Information Security Specialist Group, refereed the text, provided a vital steer on the 'bigger picture' and kindly agreed to write the Foreword. Professor Anthony Sammes of the Centre for Forensic Computing, Royal Military College of Science, Cranfield University, made a number of helpful suggestions relating to the chapters on computer evidence and investigations, as did Jim Bates, President of the Institute of Analysts and Programmers. Professor Mich Kabay, Associate Professor of Information Assurance at Norwich University, Vermont, USA, provided several case studies of systems sabotage and extortion that appear in Chapter 7. Didi Barnes of First Base Technologies provided significant input to Chapter 6. John Webb critiqued the manuscript, bringing to it his particular expertise on fraud and audit procedures, as did Tim Jilani who also proffered many valuable insights into commonplace financial and accounting control failures. David Browne, Questioned Document examiner at London-based Berkeley Security Bureau (BSB Limited) kindly checked my occasional references to the evidential and forensic processing of documents and paper. The London law firm Philippsohn Crawfords Berwald provided valuable assistance with certain aspects of the law in the United Kingdom, as did Kasra Nouroozi, a Senior Partner at Mishcon de Reya. Mark Nova and Alex Bonczoszek imposed grammatical discipline and saved me from many embarrassing typos. Jonathan Norman, my commissioning editor, kept the faith, despite a cascade of unmet deadlines. I am grateful as always to the computer forensic community, to several hundred clients who brought with them a variety of puzzles and conundrums, to those lawyers, barristers, police officers, defendants, suspects and criminals who have taught me many indispensable lessons over the years, to my colleagues in the investigation and security professions and to my friends and relatives in the outside world, who haven't a clue what I do but have humoured me nonetheless. As per convention, any factual mistakes in this book are entirely my own.

Introduction

It is sometimes said that you are at the greatest risk of being attacked when you are at home and your front door is locked. Your nearest and dearest, according to this received wisdom, are those most likely to stab you to death, beat you unconscious, or otherwise cause you grievous injury.

The analogy of a house is helpful for explaining the rationale of this book.

Imagine, if you will, a large house set in an estate. The doors, windows and skylights of the house are securely locked and bolted. The walls to the property are high and dangerous for a would-be intruder to climb, the gates are guarded around the clock; all of the approaches and exits are floodlit, monitored and alarmed; guard dogs are on patrol, and the police will react instantly should an alarm sound.

Seemingly, the house and its surrounding estate are impregnable, which is most reassuring to you, the owner.

But you now find yourself bloodied, bruised, bound and blindfolded, utterly vulnerable and very, very frightened. A deranged man is holding a knife to your throat and demanding the combination to the safe. If you resist, he will kill you.

How on earth did he get in? The answer is simple: you employed him. He came in through the front door with your express permission and consent.

The locks, the walls, the guards and the paraphernalia of perimeter control in this house and estate are analogous to the firewall of a business or organization. A huge amount of IT security effort is expended here. When I last checked central London's bookstores I counted more than fifty titles on firewalls – what they are, how they work, who makes them, how to implement them, how not to implement them, how to configure them, how not to configure them, how to break through them and what to do if some miscreant does so. There is plenty of informed literature on the subject of firewalls and little excuse for any ignorance on the part of the IT professional responsible for safeguarding the corporate network.

But what about the man with the knife? He is analogous to the fraudulent, aggrieved, deranged, bloody-minded, thoughtless or otherwise deeply unsatisfactory employee, contractor, associate, temporary worker or other insider who places your organization at potential risk. Curiously, there is precious little written about this person or, indeed, about how to tackle him and defeat him. Many IT security regimes are completely oblivious to his existence, or regard the risk he poses as far-fetched, marginal or irrelevant. Similarly, many organizations are reticent even to contemplate the very real threat he represents.

This book looks at risks such as these to which your firewall offers no defence.

Over the last 12 years I have observed corporate clients at close quarters contending with a variety of emergencies. Invariably, the greatest panic ensued when 'trusted' insiders turned hostile, or when employee negligence or criminality threatened the organizations concerned with regulatory censure, embarrassment or collapse.

Many organizations, beyond seeking external assistance quickly, have failed to respond with any skill or dexterity to employee fraud or other wrongdoing. Profound and irreversible mistakes have been made because the initial actions taken by those at the scene were fundamentally wrong and ill advised. These people – the first to arrive – are sometimes referred to as 'first responders'. In a corporate environment, the first at the crime scene tend to be IT professionals, auditors, corporate security and risk specialists and others engaged in security, investigation and incident response. The success or failure of an investigation into workplace computer misuse or fraud is heavily dependent on what these first responders do, or fail to do, in the immediate aftermath of an incident.

The attendant business risks inherent to the Internet, computer networks and e-commerce make it incumbent on all businesses to take a proactive approach to crisis management. Many security breaches and other crises known to the author would have been resolved far more swiftly, or at all, had the crime scene been processed more effectively.

Computer security and fraud incident response are now very much on the agenda primarily because governments, led by the Bush administration in the United States, are insisting they should be. The Sarbanes-Oxley Act was enacted in the United States in August 2002 in the wake of the Enron scandal. The Act mandates that chief executive officers (CEOs) and chief financial officers (CFOs) of US public companies, foreign filers in US markets and privately held companies with public debt must implement internal controls and certify, annually, that all frauds are reported. Severe penalties apply, including fines of up to $5 million and imprisonment, should any executive deliberately falsify this certification.

Although Sarbanes-Oxley is directed principally at financial supervisors and auditors, its stipulations directly affect IT managers, computer auditors and security staff. A key aspect of the Act is the requirement for the control and security of the computer systems and IT infrastructure that supports this financial reporting. Specifically, effective internal controls are mandated by the Act to assure the confidentiality, privacy, availability, controlled access, monitoring and reporting of corporate or customer financial information. When the CEO and CFO sign off on their company's annual reports, they affirm that the organization's financial systems and the supporting IT infrastructure are appropriately controlled and secured and that the financial statements produced in this environment are reliable. The security and control of an organization's IT systems and their resilience to fraud and other criminality is clearly pivotal to compliance with Sarbanes-Oxley.

In the chapter entitled *Perception of Risk*, I argue that contrary to the precept of Sarbanes-Oxley et al, many IT security regimes are too fixated on external risks that emanate from beyond the firewall, that organizations are hopelessly unprepared to tackle internal fraud and criminality and often lack the resolve to do so.

Having asserted that the security effort is skewed, argued the need for a reappraisal of where the greatest risks actually reside, and questioned the state of corporate preparedness to confront them, the book proceeds by looking at some severe risks and provides guidelines on now best to mitigate and combat them.

It focuses particularly on internal IT risk, workplace computer crime and the preservation of evidence because it is these areas that are generally so badly mismanaged. The text ventures beyond the firewall and out onto the Internet or into the territories of third parties only where these impact upon or are relevant to internal crime or wrongdoing.

Anyone responsible for IT security or investigation should be conversant with the basic mechanics of computer fraud and misuse. When fraud is suspected, the investigator should seek to identify the method of its execution, which will often be surprisingly simple but ingenious also. Where computer fraud is encountered in the field, it will be executed as a variation on one or more of the attack profiles illustrated in the chapter entitled *Computer Fraud*.

Chapters follow on the associated risks represented by information theft, industrial espionage, social engineering and confidential information scavenged from trash, both commercial and domestic. Information theft is predominantly an insider risk, with vastly more confidential information removed from the workplace by employees than by hackers or external parties. Employees with direct access to sensitive systems and processes are also obvious targets for industrial spies, criminals and hackers. Understanding the techniques by which the employee may be subverted, coerced or entrapped is critical to defending an enterprise. The methods, which rely on trickery and deceit to ensnare the employee, are insidious and difficult to prevent as they usually bypass the firewall and perimeter defences altogether. It is essential that employees and others associated with the organization are on their guard.

A short chapter is included about wireless LAN interception, which is currently de rigueur for hackers and spies. This is not an insider threat, but is included here because so many networks currently in use are exposed to intrusion due to improper configuration. As ever, the drive towards new technologies outpaces attendant security considerations.

The unnerving issues of IT-based sabotage, blackmail and extortion are examined in a dedicated chapter. These threats, when realized, have often engendered blind panic, precipitating a wholly inappropriate, ineffectual and often counter-productive response. Sound procedures and a suitable incident response plan are clearly indicated, yet in practice are seldom devised or implemented.

There is a discourse on passwords and why they provide only limited value as a control. Misappropriated passwords have featured in many cases of network shenanigans. From a forensic perspective, breaking passwords on many systems has been child's play and yet the uninitiated – amongst them many senior managers – persist with the delusion that password-protected systems are secure.

Businesses must respond to the insider threat in a timely and coordinated fashion. A short keystone chapter covers the basic rules of incident response when tackling internal fraud and employee computer crime. Planning and preparation are paramount, and in our efforts to regain control we must always act within the law. Where fraud and serious malpractice occurs and a corporate response is planned to combat it, the appointment of a specialist lawyer or law firm to advise on the proposed strategy and tactics is mandatory.

Business is increasingly litigious. Electronic disclosure, where computer evidence is routinely introduced in litigation, is a burgeoning practice in the United States, and is set to gain a foothold in other countries. In the United Kingdom, for example, the Civil Procedures Rules define 'anything in which information of any description is recorded' to be subject to disclosure, which clearly includes computer documents and e-mails. In this environment, prudence dictates that selected staff should understand the practicalities of securing such evidence. To date, only a handful of corporate organizations have invested in training IT staff in evidence management, while many auditors and security personnel admit to being ignorant in this respect.

Guidance is provided for the processing of computer evidence to a criminal prosecution standard. This is the most stringent standard with which computer evidence is judged and the technical and procedural methods to ensure its admissibility reflect current best practice. If you obtain evidence to a less rigorous standard, you may find the police or a relevant law enforcement agency will reject it as unusable and your options for legal redress will be severely curtailed.

The book also introduces a proven methodology for investigating security breaches and incidents. This comprises ten analytical methods and applies to any investigation, technical or otherwise. This methodology purposefully avoids reference to specific platforms, configurations, protocols, operating systems and software. All computer systems share certain fundamental characteristics and once the methodology shown is grasped, it may be applied equally to any system or process regardless of its technical configuration.

Computer crime is usually resolved by asking questions and in this respect its investigation is no different from any other enquiry. It differs only in so much as the investigation is conducted in an unfamiliar and evolving technical environment. This book aims to assist the non-technical investigator to approach an electronic 'scene of crime' with confidence, while at the same time acknowledging their own limitations and knowing when to seek expert assistance. It is never shameful to profess ignorance, and usually it is wise to do so, particularly in complex technical environments. Things go wrong when people claim competence or knowledge that they do not possess. Should investigators need clarification or specialist assistance, they should not hesitate to obtain it.

Investigating computer network misuse is often dependent on the accuracy and scope of audit trails and event logs. These records are vital in helping the investigator to trace those computers that have been used to commit an offence. In practice, when determining the cause and epicentre of a computer network intrusion, the quality and quantity of audit and event logging available for analysis is often so deficient as to be of little or no value. Guidelines to expand the coverage of this logging, sharpen its focus and lengthen the period that records are retained are provided in a chapter that also outlines some other key resources that have proved invaluable to the investigator.

A chapter is devoted to covert investigations and in particular the surreptitious imaging of a suspect's computer hard disk. This chapter is not written as a 'how to' for people wishing to snoop into the private affairs of their employees or co-workers. Rather, it outlines the operational considerations that bear upon a proven tactic to tackle serious crime and wrongdoing. Forensic analysis of the suspect's computer has proven to be a 'quick kill' on many investigations.

Of the material published and available to date, little attention or thought appears to have been devoted to the effective presentation of computer evidence in a court of law. A chapter, *Computer Evidence in Court*, provides some guidance on testimony and evidence in the courtroom based on the author's experiences combined with those of other expert witnesses, police officers, private investigators, barristers, solicitors and, crucially, jury members.

On an administrative note, with a few exceptions, this book adopts the male gender throughout the text. This is done not on a discriminatory basis, but simply to save time, space and ink. That said, with a few notable exceptions, the fraudsters, extortionists, saboteurs, deviants and pranksters that I have encountered have been predominantly male. However, there is little empirical evidence to suggest that men are more or less devious than women and the investigator should keep an open mind. Where I refer to a suspect, victim, investigator or other member of the cast as 'him' or 'he', or discuss 'his' actions, the reader should also consider the female equivalent.

This book is not an encyclopaedic resource or an off-the-shelf contingency plan to deal with any and every eventuality – the world of business is too complex, diverse and dynamic to be that predictable. It provides, instead, guidance to deal with some common contingencies in the workplace that are frequently overlooked or mismanaged. It is my hope and my intention that the following chapters introduce practical strategies and tactics to prevent these threats, or to react to them appropriately should they occur.

EW

1 *Perception of Risk*

It doesn't work to leap a twenty-foot chasm in two ten-foot jumps.
Proverb

The premises of this chapter are:

- The perception of risk in many organizations is often biased, ill-focused or based on unfounded presumptions.
- Security efforts are disproportionately expended on combating *external* threats.
- The gravest potential risks to business continuity reside *within* the firewall.
- Inadequate controls are presumed to be effective.
- Risk assessment methodologies fail to identify catastrophic risks because they rely upon generic formulae that are of marginal value when applied to highly specialized industries, sectors and operating environments. As a result, the corporate 'jugular vein' (or Achilles heel) is rarely identified or defended.
- Rules-based risk assessment methodologies, checklists and conventional audit strategies reflect the experience and prejudices of their authors, often ignore fraud or under-emphasize its potential impact, and often fail to address the risks associated with emerging technologies, products, methods or operations because they are neither current or updated.
- Organizations are ill-prepared to detect or respond to deviance or serious criminality within the workplace because so much emphasis is nowadays placed on trust and 'empowerment' of the workforce, rather than on vigilance and control.

A biased perception

Understandably, senior management's perception of risk across all industries and sectors was massively influenced by the terrorist attacks on the World Trade Center (WTC) in New York on 11 September 2001. This event galvanized the business world, engendering a massive global investment in disaster recovery planning, effort and expenditure.

Having listened to IT security and risk managers across a range of businesses, I have been struck by how often these professionals seek to impress upon their audiences how proactive they are in regard to 'DR' (disaster recovery). The somewhat limited definition of DR adopted in these instances has tended to focus on recovering data processing operations and IT capability in the event of bombs, fires, floods, power failures, or force majeure. In the wake of 9/11 there has undoubtedly been a wide-scale reassessment and overhaul of methods, procedures and capabilities should these potential disasters strike, and this endeavour has clearly been significantly driven at the most senior levels of management.

Most mature businesses worldwide have now implemented baseline contingency planning to survive even the most extreme physical disasters.

By 2001, fires and explosions were in the forefront of the contingency-planning consciousness of those in the twin towers, due to the previous bombing of the WTC on February 26, 1993. The impact of that bomb caused businesses within the WTC to re-assess their procedures. Backup and restoration operations were vigorously tested and businesses availed themselves of both hot and cold standby processing facilities. The beneficial result of this was that many operations were technically up and running within hours of the planes hitting the towers on the morning of September 11. However, many skilled people who operated these systems, such as the trading specialists in firms like Cantor Fitzgerald, died in the attack. As a result, widespread distribution of key operations and personnel, rather than their more common centralization within a single building, is a key tenet of current disaster recovery philosophy.

The range of other man-made and natural disasters that features in the textbook disaster-recovery programme are familiar to most IT managers and are, by and large, suitably accounted for. Most of these potential contingencies have been known about and considered over many decades, which largely explains why no major company located in the WTC went out of business following 9/11.

Figure 1.1   The terrorist attack on the World Trade Center (EMPICS/PA)

This is a fact and it is worth re-emphasizing:

• No major company located in either of the twin towers went out of business as a result of the terrorist attacks of September 11, 2001.[1]

Businesses understand physical risks and have prepared effective contingency plans to mitigate them – even more so in the aftermath of 9/11. However, there are many business risks that are rarely contemplated, or addressed at all by contingency plans.

---

1   Smaller business, however, did collapse. The New York City Partnership stated that 707 small businesses in the proximity of the towers were destroyed or suffered extensive damage and that lost sales at 3400 inaccessible businesses in the immediate area totalled $795 million.

It is instructive to compare and contrast the successful disaster recovery strategies put into action in the immediate aftermath of the WTC attacks with another spectacular business disaster, which happened some six years earlier.

Nick Leeson: a threat from within the firewall

The collapse of Barings Bank in February 1995 is a quintessential tale of risk management gone wrong. Astonishingly, the failure was caused by an individual, operating alone, and without supervision.

Nick Leeson was appointed as a general manager at Barings Securities (Singapore) Limited in 1992. Upon arrival Leeson was not qualified to trade on the Singapore Money Exchange (SIMEX) but he quickly set about gaining the necessary qualifications to do so.

Due to a lack of managerial supervision and non-existent controls, Leeson soon assumed three roles that should strictly have been mutually exclusive. In addition to his official role as general manager, he soon became head trader and, concurrently, head of the back office. This was a fundamental conflict of interest that ran contrary to the most basic rule governing trading and settlements operations, which stipulates that control of the front office and back office should be strictly segregated.

The story of Leeson's subsequent unauthorized trading on the Japanese Nikkei and its disastrous consequences is well documented, not least by Mr Leeson himself in his book *Rogue Trader*.

Using a trick seen in many accounting frauds he hid the extent of his unauthorized trading position and losses in a suspense account, numbered 88888. Leeson claims that he originally used this 'lucky' account to conceal a modest loss accumulated accidentally by one of his traders. However, the enormity and extent of his trading indicates that he was actually speculating, but with virtually no success. Leeson was devoid of luck and lost money almost from the outset. In increasingly desperate attempts to balance the books he increased his bets but this only served to increase his losses. In 1992, his accumulative loss amounted to approximately £2 million. A year later, this had risen to £23 million and by 1994 Leeson had defaulted to the tune of £208 million.

On February 23, 1995, Nick Leeson and his wife fled Singapore for Malaysia leaving a massive £827 million deficit in the Barings balance sheet. By the time he was arrested in Frankfurt, Leeson had bankrupted Barings, which was subsequently sold to the Dutch bank ING for the nominal transfer value of £1.

Nick Leeson, acting alone, destroyed Barings Bank. Nobody in London or Singapore had foreseen the impending disaster, or sounded the alarm. Control failures apparent in the Barings fiasco included:

- The initial failure to establish controls when the Singapore office was inaugurated.
- The consequent failure to segregate the trading floor from the back office, which provided Leeson with the opportunity to conceal his losses.
- The lack of local management, experience, knowledge or oversight, which enabled Leeson to act autonomously.
- A confusing, ill-defined and opaque reporting structure, which obscured Leeson from view and protected him from effective scrutiny.

- His willingness to lie, misrepresent, obfuscate, forge and falsify in order to gain funds from Barings and its subsidiaries to support his losses.
- Management in London was ignorant about the specific operation of the Singapore office, emphasizing profit to the exclusion of all else.

In *Rogue Trader* Leeson identified ignorance as a key factor:

> People at the London end of Barings were all so know-all that nobody dared ask a stupid question in case they looked silly in front of everyone else.

This is a compelling observation. Few people at the time really understand what Leeson or his team of traders actually did – the mechanics and functioning of the derivatives market being relatively technical and specialized. The complexity of the trading operation in Singapore explains, in part, why nobody within senior management wanted to assume ownership of the operation or oversight of Leeson and his team. To compound the problem, nobody senior within the bank would admit their benightedness, for fear of ridicule. Fraud and incompetence thrive when management is uninformed, wilfully ignorant or just disinterested.

London empowered the Singapore office, which, for a period, became ostensibly the most profitable division of the entire bank. In this heady atmosphere, control and oversight were deemed irrelevant. As laissez-faire prevailed, Leeson went berserk.

Figure 1.2   Nick Leeson – inside the firewall (EMPICS/AP)

To return briefly to some of the premises with which this chapter began:

- The perception of risk in many organizations is often biased, ill-focused or based on unfounded presumptions.

At no time, until he went on the run in February 1995, did senior management at Barings perceive Nick Leeson to be a risk. In fact, quite the opposite; for most of his career in Singapore, Leeson was considered to be a star performer.

- Security efforts are disproportionately expended on combating external threats whilst the gravest potential risks to business continuity reside within the firewall.

Leeson was a trusted employee of Barings Securities (Singapore) Limited and had uninhibited access to systems and processes. As a result he had the opportunity to commit devastating and irreparable damage.

- Risk assessment methodologies fail to identify catastrophic risks because they rely upon generic formulae that are of marginal value when applied to highly specialized industries, sectors and operating environments. As a result, the corporate jugular vein (or Achilles heel) is rarely identified or defended.

Undeniably, the bank's derivatives trading operation in Singapore was both novel at the time and highly specialized. The specific risks relating to the derivatives market were insufficiently analysed, assessed or understood. The detailed minutiae of the trading operation fell outside the parameters of any established risk assessment matrix or methodology. The catastrophic risk posed by Leeson was never identified, flagged or prioritized, and this jugular vein remained exposed until Leeson severed it and the bank bled to death.

- Rule-based risk assessment methodologies, checklists and conventional audit strategies reflect the experience and prejudices of their authors, often ignore fraud or under-emphasize its potential impact, and often fail to address the risks associated with emerging technologies, products, methods or operations because they are neither current or updated.

In this instance, a rule-based risk assessment of the front and back office in Singapore should have identified and flagged the conflict of interest in Leeson's various roles. Had such an exercise been undertaken the ensuing disaster might have been averted. It is, after all, an unassailable rule that the back office and the front office should be segregated. That said, very few organizations actively search for catastrophic risk. In any event, the fraudster will usually find a way to bypass or circumvent established controls and procedures. Leeson, for instance, obtained unauthorized funding for his losses in direct contravention of SIMEX rules. He also continuously evaded detection through falsifying records, fabricating letters and engaged in deliberate obfuscation to deflect awkward questions from management, internal and external auditors and even representatives of SIMEX. Significantly, Leeson's deceptions and misdemeanours occurred in an emerging and evolving environment, which lacked proprietary controls specific to the operation.

- Organizations are ill-prepared to detect or respond to serious criminality within the workplace because so much emphasis is nowadays placed on trust and empowerment of the workforce, rather than on vigilance and control.

Leeson was certainly empowered, perceived by Barings' management as 'the goose that laid the golden egg'. This empowerment was permitted and tacitly encouraged upon the false premise that Leeson was highly profitable. In fact, the entire edifice was built on clay with Leeson recording false profits in three arbitrage trading accounts, numbers 92000, 98007 and 98008, accomplished through fraudulent cross-trades with the increasingly indebted account 88888. At no time during his career with the bank was any emphasis placed on vigilance or control. As an example, in 1992 Leeson's application to the UK's Securities and Futures Association (SFA) was withdrawn after Barings discovered that he had lied on the application about County Court Judgements issued against him for debt. When he subsequently moved to Barings Singapore and applied to SIMEX to trade, he again did not disclose his bad debt record. Unbelievably, his application was approved and the rest is history ...

When comparing and contrasting the impact on business continuity caused by the terrorist attacks of 11 September 2001 with the damage wrought on Barings by Nick Leeson, two inescapable facts must be acknowledged:

- Businesses based in the World Trade Center survived despite the thousands of deaths, injuries and colossal damage inflicted.

Conversely,

- Barings Bank was destroyed by the action of just *one* of its employees, acting alone.

From the perspective of business continuity, the people inside the firewall must be considered to be potentially more dangerous than those beyond it. Paradoxically, and in the face of empirical evidence, established information security doctrine has consistently highlighted the risks posed by external parties and agents – computer hackers, viruses, worms and other comparatively manageable irritants. These risks, known and understood for years, have been emphasized virtually to the exclusion of the threat posed by trusted insiders. This disregards an important fact – hackers, unassisted by trusted insiders, cannot commit catastrophic fraud because they do not have the requisite knowledge or the access to do so.

Of course, hackers can and do commit fraud as well as other types of damage. They download unencrypted credit card databases, intercept and decrypt passwords, defraud on-line banking systems, 'phish' and perform all sorts of Internet-assisted deceptions. With a few exceptions the frauds committed to date have been relatively unambitious, low value, rectifiable and in most cases were only made possible by deplorable computer security. The technology to defend against most of these external threats is available off the shelf. Ultimately, Internet fraud and deception is a marginal risk to most corporate organizations. Banks and financial institutions are clearly suffering at the hands of Internet and payment card fraudsters, and personal users, in particular, are most definitely inconvenienced by these practices, but they do not constitute catastrophic risks.

Breaches of IT security occur, but in the author's experience these have been detected only in networks and systems that were poorly administered or configured incorrectly. Moreover, the majority of these attacks, although launched from beyond the firewall of the victim organizations, were instigated by former employees, contractors or aggrieved parties who formerly had been given authorized access to the systems under attack and thereby gained inside knowledge of the targeted systems and networks.

There have also been a few exceptionally damaging attacks launched from beyond the firewall, particularly through the use of denial of service (DoS) attacks. An example was the Cloud Nine ISP, which went out of business in 2002 following a prolonged and relentless denial of service attack launched by an unknown hacker or team of vandals. It is not known whether the attacker(s) had any inside knowledge, or if the attacks were entirely responsible for the subsequent closure of the company, or whether other business factors also played a part. The closure of Cloud Nine caused something of a sensation, being one of the very few occasions in which a hacker or hackers were blamed for inducing a business failure. The denial of service attacks known to the author have been hugely disruptive and inconvenient, but not catastrophic.

It would be irresponsible and misleading to downplay, denigrate or dismiss the external hacker threat, but it is equally misleading to prioritize the risks presented by outsiders above those posed by insiders, particularly respecting the severity of the damage that can be inflicted by these respective groups. No hacker, virus writer or other cyber deviant has even come close to causing the commercial or organizational collapse of any major institution. By contrast, Barings, Daiwa,[2] BCCI,[3] WorldCom,[4] Enron,[5] Tyco,[6] Xerox,[7] Orange County[8] and Allied Irish Bank[9] (to name but a few high-profile disasters) were all the result of internal fraud, corruption or unsupervised speculation committed by trusted employees, and in most cases these comprised senior managers or directors. It is a paradox, therefore, that so much IT security effort is expended on preventing external breaches when so many latent and potentially catastrophic threats reside internally.

Every business or organization has a potential Leeson – a human 'time-bomb' ticking away, or a completely unidentified and potentially disastrous exposure in systems or processes, which awaits malevolent or avaricious exploitation. This is not pure conjecture, but an observation derived from investigating frauds, computer crimes and other unexpected and seemingly intractable problems in different businesses worldwide.

It may be tempting to reject this Leeson hypothesis out of hand, as some people have done when presented with it. Senior management have in the past asserted that a repeat of this catastrophe was impossible within their respective organizations. With the benefit of hindsight, the profound control failure to segregate the back office from the trading desk that featured in the Barings case has now been corrected in most if not all institutions. However, risk can reside in all sorts of places and in many guises, many of which are quite shaded, camouflaged, or concealed from view. It is simply foolhardy, therefore, to assert absolute and impregnable surety.

2   A single trader, Toshihide Iguchi, lost $1.1 billion of the bank's money over a period of 11 years, the losses only coming to light when Iguchi confessed to his managers in July 1995.

3   Bank of Credit and Commerce International (BCCI) was a major international bank that operated in 78 countries with 400 branches and claimed assets of $25 billion. It was found to be involved in money laundering, bribery, 'support of terrorism, arms trafficking, and the sale of nuclear technologies; ... the commission and facilitation of income tax evasion, smuggling, and illegal immigration; illicit purchases of banks and real estate'. The bank was also found to be worthless. $13 billion was unaccounted for. Investigations revealed that BCCI had been organized 'to avoid centralized regulatory review ... [with the objective] to keep their affairs secret, to commit fraud on a massive scale, and to avoid detection'. The Bank of England shut BCCI. Around a million investors were affected.

4   In March 2005 Bernard Ebbers, the former CEO of WorldCom, was found guilty for his role in the accounting scandal that led to the largest bankruptcy in US history. A federal jury in New York convicted Ebbers on all nine counts that he helped mastermind an $11 billion accounting fraud at WorldCom, now known as MCI.

5   In October of 2001, Enron officials announced that the company had fraudulently overstated its value by $1.2 billion. Enron was one of the nation's most prominent energy traders. As a result of the resulting bankruptcy, thousands of people lost their jobs and their life savings.

6   Tyco's former CEO, CFO and chief legal officer took over $170 million in loans from Tyco without approval. In addition, seven and a half million shares of Tyco stock were sold for $430 million without investors' knowledge. Formal charges were made by the US Securities and Exchange Commission (SEC) on September 12, 2002.

7   In April 2002, the SEC filed a civil suit against photocopy giant Xerox for exaggerating profits, resulting in an overstatement of close to $3 billion.

8   In December 1994, Orange County in the United States announced that its investment pool had suffered a loss of $1.6 billion, which led to the bankruptcy of the county. This disaster was the result of the unsupervised investment activity of Bob Citron, the County Treasurer.

9   Trader, John Rusnak, based in one of AIB's subsidiaries in the United States, Allfirst, ran up losses of $691.2 million. The losses were a result of unsuccessful foreign exchange speculations. The trader's losses were covered by a mixture of fictitious and genuine options positions.

An accurate evaluation of risk only emerges through a detailed and profound understanding of each individual business and its precise operations and functioning. This breadth and depth of understanding is rarely achievable without extensive study and hands-on experimentation. It is certainly beyond the resources of most managers, who must concentrate on the day-to-day running of the business. In contrast, the Leeson, wherever he or *it* resides, usually has all the time in the world to perfect his methods and plans – unless, that is, the markets are running disastrously against him.

Another problem with the Leeson is that nobody, it seems, wants to take responsibility for identifying him (or *it*) or controlling his actions (or *its* shortcomings). Security and risk professionals rarely see it as their responsibility to identify the potential causes of catastrophic business failure, nor to respond to potentially disastrous risks when they are discovered. IT security specialists, for example, prepare for foreseeable disasters and lesser contingencies that may impact upon machines and processes. They do not generally regard controlling the likes of Nick Leeson as within their remit or duties, despite the fact that computers and software featured so centrally in his wrongdoing.

Whose responsibility is it, then, to identify catastrophic people-based risk and to respond to it? Compliance? Audit? Group Legal? Operations? Departmental managers will quite often eschew responsibility for tackling serious risk, or find reasons to avoid taking corrective action. The following are typical of the evasive delaying tactics that have been used by management in response to tackling serious fraud, criminality and wrongdoing:

Chief executive:	'It's obviously a false allegation. Everyone in this company is completely committed to our ethics, visions and values.'
Group legal:	'You can't tap his telephone – it is totally illegal under EU directives.'
Group finance:	'There is absolutely no loss shown in the books, so it can't be a fraud. Anyway, how much will this investigation cost?'
Human resources:	'Your proposed methods will destroy trust within the company.'
Group audit:	'It complies with the procedures manual and anyway his department's been given a clean bill of health by Arthur Andersen.'
Operations:	'His department generated two-thirds of the group's total profit last year. The man's a genius – get off his back!'
IT security:	'He hasn't downloaded porn, spread a virus or hacked into anyone's computers, so it's not our problem.'

The tendency to equivocate, pass the buck, defer or deflect difficult decisions reinforces the necessity to formulate clear and precise departmental duties and responsibilities regarding employee fraud and malpractice, to formulate and test a contingency plan to tackle internal wrongdoing and to establish an agreed chain of command. To avoid confusion and departmental 'grandstanding', a company director responsible for risk and security and answerable to the board should be appointed to run internal investigations.

Another tendency is whenever the Leeson spectre is raised, people tend to become defensive. 'That couldn't happen here!' they protest. 'We have controls, guidelines, audits, contingency plans, segregation of duties.'

But things can and do go badly wrong, even in the best controlled environments. Compliance with ISO 17799, COBIT[10] or whichever security standard happens to be in

---

10   Control Objectives in IT.

vogue provides a psychological comfort blanket, but is of only limited value in combating bloody-mindedness, fraud and deceit. The deviant employee or determined criminal is not impressed by standards or controls, and is rarely, if ever, constrained by them. Testament to this fact was the finding of the interim report[11] into the fraud(s) perpetuated by rogue trader John Rusnak against the Allied Irish Bank's US subsidiary Allfirst:

> Mr. Rusnak circumvented the controls that were intended to prevent any such fraud by manipulating the weak control environment in Allfirst's treasury; notably, he found ways of circumventing changes in control procedures throughout the period of his fraud.

Chief Executive Michael Buckley's description of Rusnak was representative of the classical fraudster:

> It's very clear now that this guy targeted every control point of the system and systematically found ways around them, and built a web of concealment that was very sophisticated.

The following fraud reported from Australia[12] in 2003 reaffirmed that audit inspections and control points are completely useless if they are not properly devised, focused or enforced:

> Sitting at a keyboard in the Commonwealth Bank of Australia, manager Kim David Faithfull gambled on horses with stolen money, a theft that would eventually total a staggering AUS$19 million. Over a period of five years, Faithfull, 36, used the bank's computer to transfer the stolen funds into an IASBet online betting account with the Commonwealth Bank in Darwin. He took the money from term deposit accounts and foreign currency notes. But Faithfull seldom won. He also had very little luck. A compulsive gambler, he stole to feed an addiction, not to gather wealth. He didn't stash away one cent of the AUS$18 998 309.36 that he stole. He blew it all on slow horses. The fraud went undetected despite the frequency and size of the thefts, which on occasions amounted to AUS$500 000 stolen in a week, and in the face of regular audits.

Mr Faithfull was apprehended only after he wrote a confessional note to his colleagues. The auditors then confirmed his losses. The audit inspections and controls alluded to in this case were demonstrably and spectacularly ineffective, having had no effect whatsoever in deterring or restraining the perpetrator, or alerting the bank to the long-term, systematic plundering of its funds.

When tested or scrutinized, it is often the case that the checklists, guidelines, audit procedures, contingency plans, reconciliations and the other apparatus of control are founded on false premises; they work in theory but not in practice. The following case study is, again, representative:

---

11 *Report to the Boards of Allied Irish Banks, plc, Allfirst Financial Inc. and Allfirst Bank Concerning Currency Trading Losses*, March 12, 2002, published by Allied Irish Banks plc.

12 http://www.theage.com.au

FALSE PREMISES

The bank's AS/400 was the hub for processing SWIFT transactions, which frequently valued several million dollars daily.

The internal audit report stated that the AS/400 was 'exceptionally well administered and controlled' and that the risk of computer fraud was 'negligible'. This report was a great comfort to the bank's oversight committee, as had been the conclusion of the external auditors who described the control environment as 'exemplary'. Reviewing these reports, the investigator concluded that they were derivative – a 'cut and paste' job with a few phrases amended here and there to conceal the fact.

The problem, of course, was that a fraud was now suspected, albeit of marginal value.

The investigator's independent review of the access control regime substantially confirmed the auditors' findings. Profiles and functions were clearly defined and controlled – the entry, approval and release of all SWIFT payments were forcibly segregated in strict accordance with the rulebook. Ostensibly, the risk of fraud did indeed appear 'negligible'.

Unfortunately, neither set of auditors had thought to establish the *connectivity* between the AS/400 and other systems or processes on the network, nor, critically, had they traced the *transactional flow* of data between them. It transpired that the AS/400 communicated with an open access server elsewhere within the building. Approved transactions on the AS/400 were released into a payment queue on this insecure server prior to being encrypted for onward transmission over the SWIFT network. Anyone with access to this server and a knowledge of SWIFT message formats could change the plaintext messages in the queue using a standard ASCII editor to reroute a payment, inflate it, otherwise amend it, or insert a completely unauthorized instruction and thereby commit a potentially massive fraud.

The security loophole in this instance was known throughout the IT department – the transmission queue messages were often edited to facilitate error correction at the behest of the settlements office! Wrongful system configuration or implementation, and ill-conceived processing methodologies, have consistently featured in computer frauds perpetrated against electronic payment systems. In this case, the potential to exploit this loophole fraudulently was widely understood by the technicians and the settlements staff, but it was never reported to senior management. Laziness, the collective desire for an easy life, was discernable amongst the settlements staff, the IT department and even the auditors who parroted each other's findings, and affirmed the mistaken consensus.

The habitual fraudster will search for this type of exposure assiduously. He knows the holes in the system because he has *actively* bothered to look for them. His close relative, the opportunist fraudster, discovers these exposures by accident or through experimentation.

Fraud and computer system manipulation flourish in environments where:

- There are no controls.
- The controls are presumed to be effective, but are flawed.
- Controls are subject to autonomous modification or amendment.
- Controls are applied for cosmetic purposes, for point scoring, only to comply with regulation, or to obtain accreditation.

The presumption that controls are effective, common in many instances of fraud and catastrophic loss, leads to some ludicrous practices. A common mistake is to reconcile printout with the data stored on the system as a sole method of control. By and large, this is a pointless reconciliation because the printout will necessarily reflect the data from which it was generated, and no anomalies will appear, regardless of the veracity, or otherwise, of the data. During a recent treasury review, the futility of this reconciliation was apparent to processing staff, but had remained in practice because 'it's always been done this way'.

Flawed technology may also be presumed effective:

> Access to the payment system was controlled through the use of authentication diskettes. Each user's diskette was programmed with a unique authentication code. At a terminal, the user would insert the authentication diskette into the floppy drive and type in his password, thereby gaining access to the electronic payment system. The payment system was thus protected by something that the user owned (the diskette) and knew (the password). The diskette was a standard 3½ inch 1.44 megabyte format available from any computer retailer. The system administrator stated that each diskette was uniquely assigned to each user and that they were not interchangeable. He further assured the auditors that the diskettes were copy-protected and were, therefore, impossible to duplicate. A simple experiment proved otherwise. The 'protected' authentication diskette and its entire functionality could be duplicated in less than two minutes using DOS Diskcopy.

The other presumption is that people *actually* follow the rules and comply with procedures, or that they properly understand the reasons for doing so, as evidenced by an 18-year-old input clerk who possessed all of the authentication tokens and a spreadsheet with PINs for the entire payments department. Her response:

> People keep losing them [the tokens] and forgetting their passwords [the PINs], so it was decided it would be safer if I kept them all. Also, managers and supervisors are often not here when urgent payments need processing, so it's more convenient if I can do them without having to bother anyone else.

In the AIB case, Rusnak manipulated spreadsheet models that were relied upon by the bank's internal risk control staff. These spreadsheets, over which Rusnak had complete autonomy, were erroneously *presumed* to be accurate, and, therefore, reliable for control purposes:

> Rusnak manipulated the principal measure used by Allfirst and AIB to monitor his trading: Value at Risk (VaR)[13] ... by directly manipulating the inputs into the calculation of the VaR that were used by an employee in Allfirst's risk-control group. Thus, while that employee was supposed to independently check the VaR, she relied on a spreadsheet that obtained information from Rusnak's personal computer and that included figures for so-called 'holdover' transactions – entered into after a certain hour toward the end of each day. But these transactions were not real and were not even entered on to the bank's trading software. They were simply a way to manipulate the spreadsheet used to calculate the VaR.[14]

---

13 VaR is a calculation of the maximum range of potential loss in a given portfolio. Allfirst treasury risk control developed a VaR calculation program, into which Rusnak's data was presumably fed.

14 *Report to the Boards of Allied Irish Banks, p.l.c., Allfirst Financial Inc. and Allfirst Bank concerning Currency Trading Losses*, March 12, 2002.

Rusnak thus fabricated and disseminated false data, to support his unauthorized positions. The same applied to daily foreign exchange rates, which should have been derived from an independent and proven source but were downloaded from Rusnak's Reuters terminal to his PC, subsequently altered and then fed into a database used by the front and back office to validate his trades. This enabled Rusnak to engage in price manipulation at will.

The belief that Rusnak was under control was based on the premise that his trades were independently checked, which they were. The profound failure was that this scrutiny relied on control data that was not independently verified and which was provided by Rusnak, who was the subject of the control exercise in the first place.

A careful assessment of many operating environments will expose this type of absurdity, and yet management continues to assure itself that it is in control and that nothing can go wrong. This faith is largely based on audit reports, but audit, whether internal or external, rarely has the time or the resources to investigate at the level of depth necessary to expose serious or fatal flaws in each and every system. As one treasury supervisor declared to the author, 'I know you're not an auditor, you've been here for three weeks whereas they stay with us for only a morning.'

Risk is also unlikely to be assessed accurately through the use of generic risk assessment templates or methodologies, which may be helpful when applied to 'vanilla' businesses, but are ill-suited to more complex operations and environments, such as those encountered in banking and finance. The complexity of many business operations may also instil unwarranted fear. Nick Leeson's assertion that nobody asked him questions for fear of looking stupid validates the precept that there really is no such thing as a stupid question.

Perhaps the most common presumption of all is that a disaster recovery or contingency plan will actually work when put to the test. Incident response plans and other contingency measures may fail because they are never rehearsed or tested; as a result inherent weaknesses or shortcomings are not identified and corrected until it is too late. Many serious security breaches investigated by the author fomented blind panic and near chaos within the teams initially tasked with responding to them. The epithet 'Success has many fathers, but failure is an orphan' is apposite, as the buck was passed and responsibility for failure was denied.

To conclude:

- Question your perception of risk to determine whether resources are correctly allocated, and your efforts proportionately expended. There is a world of difference between being bitten by the Love Bug virus or falling prey to the Melissa virus on the one hand, and discovering that your stock valuation has been fraudulently inflated by $3 billion, or that your backside is seated upon $500 million worth of unauthorized trades.
- Regarding external threats, remain vigilant, assess your defences and enhance them if necessary. This chapter is not intended to dismiss or under-estimate the threat posed by hackers, saboteurs, vandals, fraudsters, virus writers and the other deviants who dwell beyond the firewall, but rather to put the damage these people may inflict into perspective.
- The gravest potential damage to your business may be wrought by those employees who reside within your firewall, or those associates, allies, consultants or contractors who have legitimate access to your systems and processes. They have the requisite access, the knowledge and the skill to seriously undermine you and potentially to destroy the business or its reputation. Do they have a motive or a method to wreak such havoc?

- Remember also, that the people who may cause severe damage to the business may not do so intentionally, but may in delusion believe they are acting in the interests of the business. There is little evidence that Leeson or Rusnak deliberately sought or intended to inflict damage on their employers; they acted instead to mitigate their losses, albeit with disastrous consequences.
- Be sceptical. We are taught to trust from an early age, a characteristic that the fraudster and the criminal will exploit mercilessly. Criminality and deception in the workplace are commonplace, a fact that is not taught at most business schools, nor considered in many contingency plans.
- If you haven't done so already, prepare now to respond effectively to criminality or wrongdoing by an employee or other trusted insider. In preparing your incident plan it is important to establish an agreed chain of command, to identify technical resources and personnel to assist the investigation, and to determine which investigative methods and tools may be required. Legal opinion should be sought on the judicial acceptability and propriety of these methods and tools. It is also extremely important to prevent those instinctive, counter-productive and ill-considered actions that often feature where internal fraud or wrongdoing is suspected and which so often compromise the chances of a successful resolution. Above all, do not confront the suspect until the time of your choosing when the available evidence has been assembled.
- Continue to use off-the-shelf risk assessment methodologies and generic control templates as they will identify prosaic exposures and will save time and effort in the process. However, they are unlikely to identify specialist risks in differing industries, which are potentially often far more insidious. Identifying, assessing and mitigating specialist risks usually involves prolonged investigation, extensive interviews with key staff, hands-on experimentation with systems and processes, brainstorming, war gaming and developing and evaluating risk models. The point here is that when assessing industry- and sector-specific risk you will often be entering new and uncharted territory, without the benefit of a map or compass.
- Identify the corporate jugular vein. This is the undiscovered exposure, which could be exploited to catastrophic effect, or the subversive process, which if left undiagnosed will bleed the business to death. Look also for the corporate 'temple': the critical nerve ending or body part which if struck with sufficient accuracy and force will paralyse the business. Critical Point Auditing is a risk assessment methodology designed specifically to identify catastrophic and high impact risks (see Appendix 1).
- Do not assume that your plans for disaster recovery, fraud response, business continuity or whatever else it is that you are trying to prepare for will actually work when needed most urgently. Test, test and test again. And then test some more.
- Never presume that existing controls and safeguards are in any way effective. Systems are frequently misconfigured, and procedures blithely ignored or not followed correctly or with any real comprehension. Remember also, that the fraudster or deviant employee may be responsible for devising the controls, managing them, implementing them, enhancing or upgrading them. He may also feed false data to the control systems or suppress or amend reports generated by them.
- Do not underestimate the determination of the fraudster or hacker to subvert or circumvent the control environment. The quote about Rusnak, 'This guy targeted every control point of the system and systematically found ways around them', should be to the fore when devising a defensive strategy.

- Emerging technologies, procedures, methods, products, versions and alliances bring with them new and often unexpected risks. Risk management is an evolving discipline. Sudden changes, and periods of rapid uncontrolled growth and expansion, are especially dangerous.

Above all, avoid complacency. Two years before Nick Leeson wrecked his family's bank, Peter Baring infamously declared, 'The recovery in profitability has been amazing following the reorganization, leaving Barings to conclude that it was not actually terribly difficult to make money in the securities markets.'

2 *Computer Fraud*

It is impossible to make anything foolproof because fools are so ingenious.
Ralph Waldo Emerson, writer and speaker, 1803–1882

The fraudster in the workplace has an operational, day-to-day knowledge of his employer's systems and processes and, more often than not, unobstructed access to them. For these reasons, he is in a better position to execute his crime and conceal it than the much-hyped hacker. This chapter looks at some common computer frauds, and provides advice on investigation.

Some of the fraudulent methods described pertain to Internet fraud and retail banking fraud – they are included because the similar deceptions, or adaptations thereof, may be adapted for use within the firewall. Employees have been known to commit a range of Internet and banking frauds using their workplace computers.

The popular media tend to portray computer fraud as complex and sophisticated, and its perpetrators as ranking amongst the technocratic elite. Generally, this is a misrepresentation that can be ascribed to lazy journalism. In fact, the modus operandi of the computer fraudster is rarely complex or sophisticated. Indeed, the reverse is often true; the most effective computer frauds are simple, yet ingenious.

Often, the means to defraud is discovered entirely by accident. Although not a computer fraud, the following incident is instructive:

> A young man was at the cigarette vending machine. He inserted his money into the slot and made his selection; the machine ejected a packet of Marlboro cigarettes. The man then pressed the reject button on the machine, which promptly regurgitated his cash. Having discovered this malfunction, the man re-inserted the ejected funds into the machine and stole a further packet of cigarettes. He commenced, systematically, to plunder the machine of its entire stock.

As can be seen, no manipulation of the vending machine's hardware, no fiendishly clever software programming or reverse engineering, no exhaustive research, no split-second timing – just a straightforward hardware malfunction, opportunism and, significantly, no effort.

Computer programmers and those intimately acquainted with computer systems are not necessarily the right people to examine the systems from a security perspective or during an investigation. In the case of the stolen cigarettes, the instinctive response of many programmers to solving this mystery would be thorough and systematic, but wide of the mark. They would disassemble the vending machine, test its circuitry, examine any gearing or internal components, debug and test any installed program code, verify the integrity of the source code, question the manufacturer about all of these and a raft of other matters, and then write a wholly inconclusive report. On a real investigation, where the stakes were not individual packets of cigarettes but misappropriated millions, this approach could prove disastrous.

In most cases of corporate computer fraud, misuse and technical mischief, the methods adopted by the perpetrator will be straightforward, and neither complex nor convoluted. The investigator should always strive to identify and test the simple, ingenious explanations first – it is clearly advisable to find and test the metaphorical 'reject button' prior to disassembling the machine.

This is not to say that highly technical frauds never occur, but rather to advise the investigator to seek a simple explanation for a fraud before resorting to more elaborate lines of enquiry.

The extent of the problem

Caution is advised when surveying statistics about the prevalence and cost of computer fraud to business and industry. For what they are worth, the following statistics indicative of the extent and impact of fraud in general are culled from the Internet:

- Employees commit 82 per cent of computer fraud, a third of whom are managers (Ernst & Young Fraud Survey 2001).
- Frauds committed by employees cause median losses of $60 000, while frauds committed by managers or executives cause median losses of $250 000. When managers and employees conspire in a fraud scheme, the median loss rises to $500 000 (Association of Certified Fraud Examiners).
- The cost of employee fraud in the UK was estimated at £13.8 billion in 2000, more than half of which resulted from the misuse of computer systems (Fraud Advisory Panel).

Workplace computer fraud is relatively difficult to detect and prosecute, and it is reasonable to suspect that the majority of it goes undetected. Robert P. Campbell, former head of computer security with the US Army, has estimated that only one in 22 000 computer frauds is detected, reported to the authorities and prosecuted. The true extent of computer fraud remains imponderable.

Computer frauds attempted in the workplace may be parasitic and debilitating where the funds or assets are regularly misappropriated over many years, or high impact and high value crimes that may jeopardize the survival or continuity of the business. Fraud in many business and industry sectors exposes the victim company to regulatory or legal censure, which may have a far graver impact on the business than the direct financial losses incurred. The US Sarbanes-Oxley Act 2002 places an onus on company directors to file accurate accounts – an obligation which is clearly disqualified should any latent fraud exist in the financial reporting systems.

COMPUTER FRAUD OR COMPUTER FORGERY?

It is helpful to distinguish between:

- fraud that is *facilitated* using a computer; an example is a forged letter of credit created using computer software;

and

- fraud where a computer is *intrinsic* to the crime; an example would be a fraudulent electronic funds transfer.

The latter category is generally regarded as computer fraud.

Before looking at the ways in which computer systems may be misused to defraud, it is helpful to describe the typical control environment for transactional processing, because it is these controls that the computer fraudster variously subverts or circumvents.

Controls in typical systems

A number of technical and procedural safeguards have been developed or have evolved to protect computerized transactional processing. Technical safeguards, if properly implemented, are foolproof while others – principally those designed to control people – are prone to failure. Not surprisingly, people and those processes requiring human intervention have consistently proven to be the weakest links in the processing chain. People, not systems, defraud.

The safeguards for most automated data processing systems that transact payments or high value goods or services are summarized here:

- *Verification* – the initiating instruction to transact is verified.
- *Segregation of duties* – to prevent an individual, acting alone, from initiating and executing a transaction to the point of completion.
- *Access control* – to ensure that transactional systems and processes are accessed only by those authorized to do so.
- *User authentication* – to confirm the identity of the user of the system and to assign each transaction that is processed to an operator.
- *Message authentication* – to confirm the sender and the integrity of any transaction that is transmitted to another party.
- *Encryption* – to protect data from fraudulent amendment, in storage or transmission.
- *Logging* – to record all transactions and the identity of the operators responsible for them.
- *Reconciliation* – to ensure that all transactions are accurately accounted for from initiation to completion and that any errors or omissions are identified.
- *Confirmation* – the transaction is reported, by the system or the counter-party.

VERIFICATION

It is clearly desirable to prove that any instruction to transact is real, accurate and has been requested by an authorized party.

Many organizations use 'call back', whereby instructions to transact are confirmed with the instructing party by telephone.

A fraudster may seek to initiate a transaction by submitting forged documents to support it, by impersonating the instructing party on the telephone, by telex or by other means.

When investigating a computer fraud it is always advisable to identify at which point in the processing chain the fraud commenced. It is important to check that the initiating instruction, be it a document, a fax, an e-mail, a telex, electronic funds transfer (EFT) message or other format, is a genuine instruction and not a forgery.

SEGREGATION OF DUTIES

It is a fundamental principle of control that no individual should be able to process a transaction from initiation to completion. In electronic funds transfer systems, for example, two or more individuals are involved in the input and execution of a payment.

A system profile with permissions is allocated to each person:

Table 2.1   Input, verify and release

| | | Segregated permissions | |
Profile/authority	Input clerk	authorizer # 1	Authorizer # 2
Input or amend data	✓	✗	✗
First verification	✗	✓	✗
Second verification	✗	✗	✓
Release payment	✓	✗	✗

These profiles are mutually exclusive. Theoretically, this segregation reduces the risk of fraud because the individuals necessary to transact an unauthorized payment could only do so in collusion.

Figure 2.1   Segregated duties

In busy treasuries and accounts payable departments, the enforced segregation of duties often dissipates due to pressures to complete processing on time:

> We all know each other's passwords. If we default on payments the bank is responsible for any loss of interest incurred by the counter-parties. If any one of us isn't here and the payments can't be executed this can amount to a huge amount of money. I've raised this as a control issue but the management have other priorities.

USER AUTHENTICATION

Many transactional systems employ static passwords to authenticate users.

Computers process *indiscriminately*. An impostor using a misappropriated password will not be challenged by the system. The potential for fraud materializes when the impostor is in possession of all the relevant passwords necessary to raise, verify and release a payment or execute a transaction.

Passwords are notoriously ineffective (see Chapter 4) and as a result new authentication methods and technologies have emerged. Many systems authenticate the user by a combination of factors (Figure 2.2):

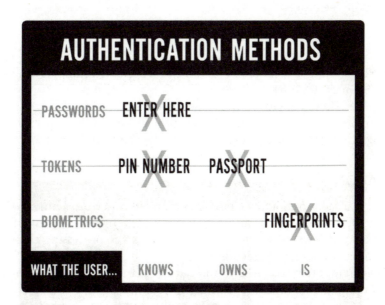

Figure 2.2   Authentication methods

Token-based authentication systems and biometric access control methods are generally far more secure than simple password-based systems (see Chapter 4).

ACCESS CONTROL

Access to transactional systems is usually restricted to those permitted to use them.

Only authenticated users who have been granted access to transactional systems will be able to use those systems. They will only be able to use them in the particular way specified by the system's administrator. For instance, a user may be able to input data but not verify it.

MESSAGE AUTHENTICATION

Message authentication verifies that a transmitted message and its sender are genuine. Many banking systems use public key encryption (see Glossary) to authenticate transactional instructions and notifications between banks.

The fraudster may seek to send a false instruction to initiate a transaction. Public key encryption, if properly implemented and supervised, is an intractable defence against such forgery. However, security is dependent on proper key management. Control fails when keys are divulged, or compromised.

ENCRYPTION

Many transactional systems use strong encryption to protect messages from fraudulent amendment. Encryption is used to protect standing data and transmitted traffic.

Strong encryption and tamper-proof authentication provide a profound level of security. Controls fail when keys are divulged or compromised, or when weak encryption is used that can easily be broken.

LOGGING

Every transaction should be recorded in full on the system, including its time and date and the operator's identity (USERID).

Funds transfers should appear in the ledger, as debits or credits.

Many computer frauds feature the falsification or suppression of entries within the transaction log, the ledger, operator event logs or other audit trails.

RECONCILIATION

Each and every transaction should be identified uniquely and consistently to ensure that all are accurately accounted for from initiation to completion. Reconciliation makes transactions traceable backwards and forwards through the processing chain, and should identify erroneous or missing transactions.

Transactions are often reconciled too late for fraud to be prevented. Next-day reconciliation is standard within the banking industry, providing the opportunity for the successful execution of sizeable funds transfer frauds and the opportunity for the fraudster to flee the scene.

In many businesses, the objective of reconciliation is simply to balance the books, rather than to detect latent fraud. Moreover, the focus of reconciliation may be too narrow, with checks between particular stages in the processing chain, but not globally.

The reconciliation of transactions is sometimes suspended temporarily due to pressures to complete processing. The fraudster may await such an opportunity to strike.

CONFIRMATION

The details of transactions may be acknowledged by a confirmation report, which shows the time and date of the transaction, the parties involved, the transaction itself, and other details considered pertinent. This report may be a printout, a fax, an e-mail response, an EFT message or other format. It may be issued by the processing system itself or by a counter-party, typically a correspondent bank.

The processing environment in which confirmation reports are processed requires control, because the details reported are central to the reconciliation and checking process.

Many computer frauds feature the interception and destruction of the confirmation report, or its falsification so that no discrepancy will be evident between the fraudulent transaction that was executed and the falsified data subsequently entered on the processing system to conceal it.

Exploiting the weakest links

If a particular method of fraud becomes difficult and challenging to commit, the fraudster will usually migrate to easier pickings elsewhere.

Fraud tends to occur at the interfaces between disparate systems and processes. These interfaces are the chinks in the armour through which the fraudster inserts his deceptions. The interfaces are inherently easier to subvert than the ensuing transactions or funds transfers in transmission, because these tend to be protected by very strong encryption and authentication mechanisms. Consequently, there is negligible opportunity to intercept, decrypt or manipulate them in any way.

The opportunist fraudster shuns the complex cryptanalysis and exhaustive code breaking efforts shown in Table 2.2 because he instinctively knows that there are simpler and easier ways to achieve his objective.

Table 2.2   Public code breaking efforts[1]

Date	Key length	Time to key disclosure	Number of computers	Maximum rate (keys tested per second)
August 1995	40-bit	8 days	120 + 2 supercomputers	0.5 million
January 1997	40-bit	3.5 hours	250	27 million
February 1997	48-bit	13 days	3500	440 million
June 1997	56-bit	4 months	78 000	7 billion
February 1998	56-bit	39 days	22 000 people	34 billion
July 1998	56-bit	56 hours	1 with 1728 processor chips	90 billion

The encryption schema shown in Table 2.2 have been replaced in most banking and financial systems by a 128-bit key or stronger:

 It has been calculated that a crypto-attack to assure the disclosure of a 128-bit key within one year of commencing analysis would require the use of 1 trillion computers, each with a processor capable of testing 900 trillion keys per second.[2]

1 *Information Warfare and Security*, Professor Dorothy E. Denning, Addison-Wesley, 1998.
2 *Hiding Crimes in Cyberspace*, Dorothy E. Denning and William E. Baugh, Jr., July 1999.

There is no potential whatsoever to subvert such a mathematically intractable defence; the only practicable alternative for the fraudster is to bypass the encrypted data stream altogether and to focus his attention instead on the weak links in the processing chain; namely the people, systems and processes that feed into it (see Figure 2.3).

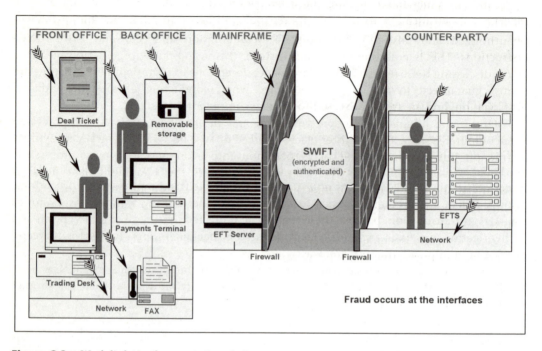

Figure 2.3   Weak links in the processing chain

Logical or physical breaks in the processing chain are clearly a risk. It is often the case, particularly where legacy systems are not integrated with newer systems, that printouts, tapes, disks and spreadsheets are used to transfer data between them and these transmission media introduce the opportunity for fraudulent amendment or input. Clearly, errors are also likely to occur as data is transferred between systems in disparate formats.

Preferably, there should be no breaks in the processing chain at all; once the data has been entered into the system it should be processed in sequence, transacted and reconciled using the same software and platform. If data must be transmitted between different platforms, processes or networks, then it should be encrypted in transit and made tamper-proof using a suitably secure cryptographic checksum.

From an audit and control perspective, the interfaces between systems and processes should be flagged as high risk, meriting careful inspection and control.

Likewise, any computer fraud investigation should commence by mapping the systems and processes involved and analysing the transactional flow of data between them. This *transactional analysis* (see Chapter 16) will identify the exposed interfaces and vulnerable points where false data could be inserted.

From a systems development perspective, straight through processing (i.e. without breaks) obviously reduces the risk of fraud or error, is efficient, relatively easy to monitor and facilitates error correction. Strategically, organizations should aim to migrate to straight through processing for all significant operations.

Pre-processing fraud

The overwhelming majority of forged documentation in the industrialized world is produced using computer software, typically word processing and graphics packages, and this is not generally regarded as computer fraud per se.

The commonplace frauds in business are perpetrated through the submission of unauthorized and false invoices, forged documentation and 'cut and paste' faxed instructions. This is not computer fraud. Instead, this is computer forgery. However, it is worth discussing these relatively mundane paper deceptions in some depth because they are almost guaranteed to feature at some stage when conducting a corporate audit or investigation, and are frequently used to initiate computer transactions.

Many frauds originate in the pre-processing area prior to being entered and processed on a computer system. The fraudster places a forged or false document, typically a payment instruction, into the 'in-tray' and this is then input into a computer for onward processing. The operator or input clerk who subsequently enters the fraudulent data does so unwittingly. The fraudster has no direct access to the processing computer but succeeds in feeding it fraudulent raw data. Pre-processing fraud is a variant of false input fraud (see below).

Controlling the documentation and processes by which transactions are initiated is fundamental in preventing this type of fraud.

PRINT, SIGN AND SUBMIT

The fraudster typically creates false invoices on his workstation or laptop. Once initialled by the authorized approver, they proceed through the accounts payable department without further scrutiny. The authorized approver is the fraudster, which illustrates yet again the need for two tiers of approval on any significant transaction.

Businesses often delegate the authority to approve transactions of less than a certain amount to a single signatory, usually a manager or senior member of staff. The signatory can thus approve low-value purchases. Fraud arises when the signatory approves invoices submitted by his own company or by a crooked supplier and submits them for settlement. The goods and services shown will be non-existent, or below the specification, quantity or quality stated in the invoice. By necessity, the total sum payable in each invoice will always fall short of the approver's authorization limit.

There is a variation to this:

> A senior sales manager produced a series of false invoices addressed to a customer with whom he conspired. The invoices involved the bulk sale of specialist equipment which had been heavily discounted without approval. The discovery of these invoices on the suspect's laptop was suspicious because genuine sales were invariably recorded on the central ledger and bona fide invoices were generated on pre-printed, perforated and sequentially numbered stationery bearing the official company logo. The fraud completely bypassed this central billing system. The fraudster thus supported the unauthorized sale of hundreds of thousands of dollars worth of equipment using Microsoft Word. The fraudulent invoices were payable to a company that the sales manager had incorporated under his directorship. His co-conspirator gained by receiving the equipment at significant discount.

This was an *off-book* fraud – the invoices and the corresponding payments bypassed the company's ledger completely. Only an inspection of inventory (a stock control) would reveal that something was seriously amiss.

RED FLAGS

For investigators and internal auditors, there are a number of tell-tale clues as to whether an invoice is genuine or fabricated. Most of these tests can be applied when scrutinizing printed invoices but some also apply when searching computer data:

- Is the invoice produced on pre-printed stationery? Larger organizations use pre-printed, sequentially numbered stationery to conduct billing runs.
- Is the invoice printed on standard A4 or letter stationery? Is it produced using a laser printer, inkjet or bubble printer? This may indicate forgery using a home PC.
- Has the invoice been photocopied or faxed? This may be an attempt to prevent an inspection of the original, which might reveal a crude and unprofessional appearance.[3]
- Does the invoice bear a full postal address including a postcode? The absence of an address may be an attempt to conceal the fact that the purported supplier does not operate from genuine offices. Check also for a corresponding website.
- Does the invoice bear a residential (non commercial) address? A residential address is not necessarily suspicious when paying a sole trader but should raise eyebrows if settling the bill for the purchase of heavy plant, or major goods or services.
- Are contact telephone numbers shown? If so, is the number a fixed landline or for a mobile handset? Invoices from businesses or suppliers 'of no fixed abode' should be treated with particular scrutiny.
- Is a PO box or accommodation address shown in the business address? Fraudulent suppliers often hide behind accommodation addresses.
- Is the description for goods or services shown in the invoice vague? This may be an attempt to make the delivery or completion untraceable or difficult to quantify. 'To consultancy services' is a prime example.
- Does the invoice bear a round figure payment, i.e. $6000.00 or £3000.00? Even if a set fee has been agreed, disbursements and other costs will usually feature in an invoice and round figure payments are unusual.
- Is the invoice marginally below the authorization level? A series of such invoices is obviously suspicious. In Figure 2.4, data mining software is used to search all invoices between £4000 and £5000. Company 1022 clearly merits more detailed scrutiny.
- Is the payment to be remitted to an offshore jurisdiction or tax haven? Any such transaction requires investigation.
- Have a series of invoices been issued bearing sequential numbers? Invoices numbered 31, 32, 33 and 34 issued in the same week from the same supplier suggests an attempt to bypass the authority level, and may also indicate that the supplier has no other

---

3   Fax headers can provide significant clues. As the Barings Bank fiasco reached its climax, the bank's external auditors received a fax purporting to come from New York trading house Spear, Leeds & Kellogg. The fax acknowledged an $86 million receivable due to Barings Futures Singapore, which partially filled the hole in the accounts. The address header on the fax read, 'From Nick and Lisa'. Nobody noticed.

```
Rec #  SUPP NAME        INV1         INV2    INVAMNT      INVDATE PAYDATE PAYAMNT
-----  ---------------  ----------   ------  -----------  ------- ------- ------+
    1  COMPANY    461   68           500129     4761.00 080293  180294     476
    2  COMPANY    751   9210165      501063     4163.28 301092  241194     416
    3  COMPANY    951   2967         601258     4201.13 190892  020994     411
    4  COMPANY    951   2969         601260     4201.13 190892  020994     411
    5  COMPANY    951   343          500104     4543.38 240192  060294     445
    6  COMPANY   1022   2010         600153     4960.00 200693  191294     456
    7  COMPANY   1022   2012         601423     4991.18 300793  201294     400
    8  COMPANY   1022   2013         500111     4960.00 300893  211294     456
    9  COMPANY   1022   2014         602084     4980.00 070993  211294     460
```

Figure 2.4   Breakpoint clustering

customers. Check always for multiple invoices submitted on the same date or in close proximity.
- Has the invoice been folded? An unfolded invoice suggests that it has not been received in the mail and may have been printed internally.
- Does the invoice bear an incorporation number and a valid sales tax code? The absence of either may indicate fraud. The total charge should include applicable sales tax.

Invoice-based fraud is very common, simple to perpetrate, but it is also relatively easy to detect. Accounts payable data can be interrogated using audit and data interrogation tools such as IDEA and ACL.

FORGED SIGNATURES AND FAXES

Many organizations rely upon written signatures to authenticate documents, transactions and payment instructions. Typically, a specimen book of signatures is maintained, which serves as a reference to authenticate signed documents or instructions. Specimen books fail as a control because:

- Personnel believe themselves to be so familiar with the authorizing signatures that they never refer to the specimen book.
- Access to the specimen book is not controlled and is open to unregulated inspection, and, therefore, to potential misuse.
- Documents are readily available elsewhere in the department which bear the signatures of authorized signatories and which may be misused to commit fraud.
- People arrogantly believe that they can always detect a forged signature.

Fraud frequently occurs when signatures have been forged. A written signature may be traced, manually copied, digitally scanned, photographed or photocopied to effect forgery. The potential losses caused by forged signatures can be severe. In 1988 a £60 million fraud at Hill Samuel Bank was attempted using forged signatures on instructions fraudulently entered into the payments cycle. More recently, a forged signature submitted into the settlements department of a London bank on a Friday afternoon resulted in the loss of £14.5 million.

It is not generally understood that a written signature, when digitized and transmitted by fax or scanned into an electronic document, cannot be verified, even by an expert forensic document examiner or handwriting expert, and that an electronic copy of a written signature has no inherent legal validity.

A simple 'cut and paste' of a genuine signature that has been photocopied, or a tracing of the signature, serves as an effective deception. Written authorization signatures are an extremely weak method of imposing control, particularly when used in conjunction with payment instruction forms that are easily forged. Banks generate an array of pre-processing documentation to initiate payments – between 20 and 30 different formats is not untypical. Often this documentation is produced using standard word-processing software and is easy to forge:

> An unauthorized payment to an offshore bank account had been spotted during a routine reconciliation. The funds involved were not huge, but merited an enquiry. The 'control environment' within the treasury alarmed the investigators. Payment instructions were raised using a Microsoft Word template for subsequent transmission to the trustee bank by fax. This template was stored on an uncontrolled group access network drive accessible by a large population. The fax instructions were authenticated with written signatures. It was evident that there was no effective control over this template or the specimen book. The settlements department was strewn with transfer instructions, many of them photocopied, or typed in an arbitrary format and even written by hand. The culprit could easily have forged the instruction using scissors, glue and correction fluid. It transpired that faxed payment instructions were regularly amended with Tipex™ after they had been approved. Amid this chaos, the investigators concluded that the company had been fortunate not to suffer a far greater loss.

As can be seen, safeguarding the input tray is as important as securing the computers and processing systems. Organizations that transmit or execute faxed payment instructions are especially at risk. If the accounts to be debited have high or unlimited payment thresholds, the penalties can be severe.

Faxed documents should not be relied upon as proof of anything:

> In 2003 the author observed a gentleman in the business centre of a hotel in Dubai amending a photocopy of a cheque to show a significantly inflated value. It was a carefully prepared forgery necessitating the use of a computer, scissors, glue, a ruler, correction fluid and a photocopier and was unwittingly assisted by the helpful woman on the desk who supplied these tools. Presumably, the resulting forgery was subsequently faxed to some hapless lender as proof of collateral.

The number on the fax header provides no authentication of the sender's identity and the ready availability of computerized typefaces, digitized logos on corporate websites and professional graphics has made the fraudster's task far simpler when forging documentation.

Modern fax machines are shipped with programmable memory, the contents of which can be altered at will. Fax header information is easily amended to forge the transmission number and sender. Fax initiated frauds may be committed by an impostor masquerading as a legitimate client transmitting a payment instruction to the bank, or by a bank employee with direct access to documentation, specimen signatures and the bank's fax machine instructing a counter-party to transfer funds to an unauthorized beneficiary.

Incoming letters of instruction that outline changes to beneficiary account details should be verified. Typically, the fraudster will purloin or forge a client or supplier letterhead and use this to issue a false letter of instruction to the effect that the organization has changed its bank account details. If acted upon without checking, the data amended on the computer system will route any subsequent payment to the fraudulently controlled account.

An input fraud, commonplace in the UK, is for the fraudster to write to a company requesting its annual prospectus, enclosing a personal cheque bearing a nominal payment. Since the document is supplied free of charge, the company is obliged to refund the fraudster, which it will normally do with a company cheque. The fraudster, now in receipt of company letterhead (covering letter), a bona fide finance department signatory name and signature and a company cheque with corporate account number, sort code and cheque signatory, has everything necessary to send a forged fax to the bank with instructions to redirect payments. As stated, the fax header information may be forged so that it purports to come from the bona fide sender.

The simplicity of cut and paste fraud is attractive to criminals who traditionally favour minimal-effort, maximum-gain ventures.

Faxed and posted payment instructions are inherently insecure. However, banks and their customers often elect to use faxes, and even electronic mail, to accept payment instructions due to the flexibility and convenience of these methods.

The following extract from a corporate bank mandate is representative:

> *It was and is hereby resolved that you should pay cheques or accept other written instructions to make payments by any means (including electronically) from any of the company's accounts, even if this causes an overdraft or increases an existing overdraft.*

This mandate is all-encompassing and effectively absolves the bank of all liability, even for faxed payment instructions where the only control is signature verification.

CONTROLS

Fax initiated payment instructions and specimen signatures are high risk. Strategically, settlements and treasury departments should migrate to secure, authenticated electronic funds transfer.

- If faxes and specimen signatures remain in use, additional authentication is necessary. Faxed instructions may be verified by a telephone call-back to the instructing party authenticated by a password or simple test key. Call-back verification should be expressly stipulated in any bank mandate where instructions may be placed by methods other than electronic funds transfer.
- Documentation bearing authorizing signatures, corporate letterhead and other paperwork must be kept secure or shredded.
- Payment instructions should not be produced using standard software. Payment instruction forms should be stored securely. Watermarks, holograms, barcodes and intaglio printing may be used to deter forgery.
- Requisitions, purchase orders and payment instruction forms should be numbered sequentially and recorded in a central log.
- Many bank mandates indemnify the bank against erroneous or fraudulent faxed or e-mailed payment instructions. Mandates should be amended to remove this caveat.

- The acceptance of payment instructions 'by any means including electronically' should be prohibited; the methods by which payments may be initiated should be clearly defined.
- If faxed payment transfers, telexes or other written instructions are never issued, they should be specifically excluded from the mandate.

Types of computer fraud

FALSE INPUT

False information is input into the computer to cause a fraudulent output. The computer processes indiscriminately – as long as the data is viable it will be processed regardless of the consequences. The dictum 'garbage in garbage out' may thus be paraphrased 'false input false output'.

The false data may be input directly by the fraudster at the keyboard of the computer terminal or, alternatively, a false instruction is placed in the input tray to be entered on the computer system by an unsuspecting data entry clerk or operator. False input is intrinsic to pre-processing fraud (see above).

False input usually occurs at the interfaces between systems and processes, with fraudulent instructions inserted when transactional data is transferred between disparate processes, computers, and networks. The transfer of transactional data between systems on diskettes, tapes and other storage media is a particular risk:

> A fraud occurred when an accounts payable batch process was raised within an accounts department. The raw payments file was then sent on a diskette to a BACS payments terminal, which was located in another part of the building. The file, which was not encrypted or in any way tamper-proof, was amended on the diskette whilst it was in transit.

Data is increasingly transferred between processing systems on memory sticks:

> A finance manager believed this to be a safe practice on the basis that he always deleted the payroll batch file from his memory stick once the transfer from the payroll system to the BACS terminal was complete. This unprotected ASCII text file contained the company's bank account and BACS routing details, as well as the National Insurance numbers, sort codes and account details for the entire workforce. If the memory stick were stolen or intercepted, the file could be undeleted in seconds using the appropriate tools, and edited to re-route payments, inflate them, or otherwise defraud. The finance manager admitted that he regularly left the device unattended and had, on occasions, mislaid it.

The widespread use of unprotected spreadsheets to transfer transactional data between systems, or as a source of control and audit data, is also high risk.

Spreadsheets introduce opportunities for deliberate falsification and significantly increase the risk of data input errors. In one such case, commission payments were calculated on an Excel spreadsheet for automatic onward processing – the threshold at which the commission became payable had been fraudulently reduced in the calculating formula.

This emphasizes the important control value of end-to-end (straight through) processing (without breaks) and reconciliation of each and every transaction from initiation to completion.

False input may also be used to feed false control data into audit systems and processes in order to conceal fraud or unauthorized transactions.

Rejected and failed transactions are also a risk. Transactions may be rejected at any point in the payments process and are vulnerable because the re-entry of the data and re-execution of the transaction may be exploited fraudulently. Rejected or failed transactions should always be flagged in the transaction report, and enquiries conducted as to the reasons for any failed transaction.

It is also advisable to check and control any free-format transactional processing capability. The potential for a fraudster to transmit a free-formatted instruction – typically, to transfer funds – using a computerized or telex system, is a high risk. It is a mistake to assume that any free-formatted payment instruction will be rejected by the counter-party. Treasury personnel often presume this to be the case even when counter-parties and trustees are mandated to act upon free-formatted instructions. At minimum, any free-format instruction should be verified by telephone call-back. Preferably, every free-format facility should be identified and disabled.

An unusual variation of input fraud was seen on a case in the mid-1990s:

OFF-BOOK FRAUD

A waste paper recycling plant was suffering from delivery shortfalls. The tonnage of waste delivered to the plant fell far short of the readings at the weighbridge. The data from the weighbridge was audited and it was confirmed that the tonnage of waste paper recorded by the control system reconciled with the cash payments made to the various drivers and companies that supplied the plant. The books balanced and showed abundant supplies, which contrasted starkly with the meagre volumes of scrap and waste to be seen in the delivery yard.

The internal auditors suspected that the data logs on the computerized control system were being fraudulently edited, or that the software was being manipulated in some manner. Investigators were instructed to test these theories by examining the control system. After some thought, they proposed an alternative strategy. It was decided instead that the weighbridge itself should be recorded using covert video cameras.

When the video surveillance tapes were reviewed, the method of the fraud was immediately apparent. On the approach to the weighbridge, a delivery truck halted. Its driver approached a standpipe at the kerb and attached a hosepipe. He then doused the waste paper and cardboard loaded on his truck until it was saturated. He then drove his vehicle onto the weighbridge and a reading was taken. Wet paper is far heavier than dry, hence the excessive readings and the inordinate payouts.

The data that was input into the computerized control system on the weighbridge was fraudulently inflated by means of a physical process – by dousing the raw material from which the software reading was taken.

A fundamental concept that the investigator must also grasp is that many of the most ingenious frauds will never be discovered through examining the books or financial data, because the method of the fraud is chosen precisely because the associated transactions will reconcile by default, and the fraud will thus evade detection. This weighbridge fraud was an example of an 'off-book' fraud – the books reconciled, but a fraud was taking place nevertheless.

FORGERY

The computer is used to forge documentation, or to clone technology. Typically, a desktop publishing (DTP) system with image scanning software and flatbed scanner are used to forge identity cards, driving licences, certificates, cheques and other documentation.

Image scanners are available commercially with in excess of 6400 dpi true optical resolution; this output when processed using a high-resolution professional printer produces counterfeit material that is indistinguishable from the original to the unassisted eye. The use of these technologies for counterfeiting and forgery has forced the security printing industry to revise its own methods and technology.

Recruitment fraud, whereby forged educational, vocational and professional certification is presented as proof of the candidate's qualifications, are commonplace and represents a very real threat to any business where the legality and contractual viability of its transactions are based upon the bona fides of the employees that initiate or execute them. The banking industry in the UK, for example, has encountered problems with securities, equities and commodities traders operating in London without valid immigration status – in such cases, every trade transacted is technically invalid, raising the spectre of regulatory censure and bruising litigation.

- It is incumbent on Human Resources departments always to validate any certification proffered by prospective candidates.

Documentation should always be verified:

> In a longstanding, and high-value, letters of credit fraud, a bespoke software package was discovered that generated forged documentation onto pre-printed business letterheads. The documentation purported to come from several different international companies, which in combination formed a bundle showing a certificate of purchase, a bill of lading, a packing note, insurance cover and other supporting documents. The user of this software was prompted to choose a company, each of which was bogus, from a drop-down menu and then insert the appropriate letterhead to generate each forged document. This documentation, once prepared, was submitted to the bank to support the issue of letters of credit. The software, effectively a 'fraud engine', had been professionally developed and supported over a number of years.

Bespoke software and hardware is also used to forge and counterfeit an array of technologies. Multimedia piracy is a criminal industry. Similarly, forgery of swipe cards, bankcards, credit cards and smartcards is rife due to its relative simplicity. This type of forgery often necessitates code disassembly and specialist hardware, evidence of which (including source code, disassemblies and printouts) may be located at the premises and on the computers of the forgers. For example, executable code associated with smartcard piracy written in Assembler 8x86 was regularly located on the computers of satellite television pirates. Reverse engineering of smartcards often involves the 'shaving' of the embedded microchip processor, which is then studied using an electron microscope.

Credit card and bankcard manufacturers have employed hologram images in the card manufacturing process to reduce card forgery. One of the difficulties facing ATM and credit card manufacturers is that the magnetic stripe, which contains identification and verification information and transactional data, is simple to forge.

'Magstripe' read-write hardware and software is available commercially. Manufacturers of these 'skimmers' trade openly on the Internet, the asking prices for professionally engineered devices ranging from $500 to $2000 (see Figures 2.5 and 2.6).

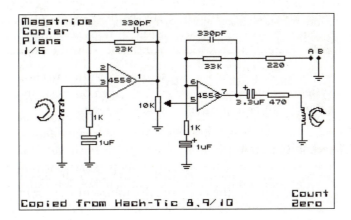

Figure 2.5   Magstripe copier plans

Instructions how to use the Portable Data Collector (PDC)

Connect the KT-2280 to the PDC.
Turn the PDC's power on (green led is now on).
Swipe a card.
The PDC's red led will flash.
This means that it received the data from the reader and it waits for new data.
If the PDC's red led stays on all the time, this means that the internal memory is full.
Connect the PDC with a PC's serial port (use the cable provided).
Start the QMODEM program by typing QMODEM and then ENTER.
Press "Shift + Tab"
Press "Ctrl + Home" to log the data into a file and type a filename.
Press the black button of the PDC to transmit the data into PC.
When finish transmiting data, press "Ctrl + Home" again to close the log file. This is a text file that you can edit with any text editor.
If you received correct the PDC's data press the PDC's red button to clear its internal memory.
The internal memory will hold at least 35 magnetic stripe cards with full data.
In most cases only part of the magnetic stripe capacity is used allowing the PDC to store more then 60 cards.

Figure 2.6   Instructions to use a portable data collector (verbatim extract)

When assessing the risk of computer assisted forgery, particularly the risk to copy-protection systems and any software- or hardware-based security mechanism, it is important to remember that any program code compiled using a computer can be reverse engineered, and its operation then subverted. For the criminal, the determining factor as to whether to embark on this challenge, which may prove 'non-trivial', will be the potential reward once it is accomplished. If the right product is targeted, the rewards can be very considerable indeed:

> (i) A master pirate who cost Sky TV millions of pounds by cracking subscriber smartcard codes and selling cheaper versions to Sky customers was jailed for four years. Broadcaster Chris Cary, 51, described as Europe's leading smartcard pirate, was sentenced at Kingston Crown Court. Judge Richard Howarth was told that Cary's Megatek company in Dublin was taking £20 000 a day until he and his accomplices were arrested in June 1996 through the undercover efforts of the Federation Against Copyright Theft (FACT) and police.

From an audit and control perspective, no security or authentication technology used to protect critical systems or processes should ever be taken on trust, and any assurances that technology is tamper proof or impregnable should be tested.

RISKS TO STANDING DATA

'Data diddling' is an inelegant phrase coined in the 1970s to describe the unauthorized amendment of standing data, or the entry of false transactions or information.

Accurate data on a computer system may be amended to defraud or deceive, typically:

- to amend standing data:
  - to inflate values (for example, sales or commissions, timesheet hours)
  - to deflate values (for example, prices)
  - to delete or suppress values (for example, stock)
  - to falsify values (for example, to feed false control data, or to re-route payments to unauthorized beneficiaries).
- to suppress or falsify logged data:
  - pre-advice reports (intention to transact)
  - transaction reports
  - non-execution reports (failed transactions)
  - confirmation reports (notification of completed transaction)
  - audit trails
  - event logs.

The amendment may be undertaken by an authorized user of the computer system or by an impostor. To thwart detection or discovery, the accurate data may subsequently be restored to its proper status. Alternatively, the fraudster may edit standing data in order to effect a fraudulent transaction and subsequently conceal it. The following case is representative:

> (i) In July 2004, Jessica Quitugua Sabathia, 31, of Vallejo, California pleaded guilty to two counts of computer fraud for using a computer to embezzle funds from North Bay Health Care Group in California. Sabathia, *formerly an accounts payable clerk for North Bay*, admitted to using a computer to access North Bay's accounting software without the authority of her employer. She issued approximately 127 cheques payable to herself and others causing losses of $875 035. *To conceal the fraud, she altered the electronic cheque register to make it appear that the cheques had been payable to North Bay's vendors.* Sabathia cashed several of the cheques, many of which were deposited into her bank account and into the accounts of others. [Author's italics]

Data may be falsified for other purposes. There have been several cases where individual customer credit limits have been raised without authorization. Falsified data has deliberately been fed into clinical trials and scientific research projects, criminal records and credit ratings have been amended, examination grades upgraded, test and engineering results have been fabricated, timesheets inflated and so on.

On networks, the level of manipulation possible will usually depend on the user's hierarchical privileges and level of access. On PCs, once the user has gained access to the computer's operating system, anything and everything on the disk is subject to editing.

> A legal discovery case centred on a series of Lotus 123 spreadsheets purportedly generated on the defendant's computer. The spreadsheets produced in evidence by the plaintiff were in exactly the same format as the spreadsheets used by the defendant, including column headings, spacing, margins, the number of columns, widths, and tab spaces. However, the plaintiff's spreadsheets showed inflated values to those of the defendant. The defendant's lawyers were at a loss to explain how these inflated spreadsheets could have been generated without leaving any trace on the defendant's computer. The probable explanation was simplicity itself: the secretary who produced the disputed spreadsheets copied the originals from the computer to a diskette, altered them on another computer using the Lotus software to show the inflation and then printed them.

Similarly, the transactional log may be edited to remove any record of the transaction, and audit or security logs designed to flag the user's activities may also be amended or deleted.

- It is a fundamental principle of control that audit and security logs that show user activity should be accessible only to the network or system administrator. Likewise, transactional logs should be protected from unauthorized amendment.

Powerful editing tools are found on many networks and are frequently used by systems developers and administrators for routine 'housekeeping' tasks, but may equally be misused. These utilities may be used to write to the physical address of data stored either in memory or on disk. Transactional data usually complies with the industry standard ASCII or EBCDIC data storage formats. Using a suitable disk editor, a lone individual could thus alter transactional data at a physical address on disk.

Such tools represent a particular threat to the integrity of standing data and message queues on payment systems. There is the potential to bypass the payments software interface with its attendant authentication and control features, and fraudulently amend raw transaction data and image files directly on disk. The Norton Utilities™ and PC Tools™ are powerful disk utilities for the PC – equally comprehensive toolkits exist for most minicomputer, mainframe and network operating systems:

> Transactional data files were stored on the bank's AS/400 in standard ASCII format, none of which were encrypted, coded or otherwise protected. A number of powerful editing tools were also present on the AS/400 including two bespoke programs, as well as Structured Query Language tools for database editing. Approximately six of the bank's employees had the access privileges and knowledge to use these tools. It transpired that the AS/400 system administrator had used these editing tools to amend the standing data in transactional files to commit and conceal a longstanding fraud with a total estimated value of £4 million.

Reconciliation checks between instructing documentation, the transaction logs and the statement of daily credits and debits should detect frauds attempted by unauthorized changes to standing data. However, checks and balances in many systems are flawed.

A common mistake is to reconcile the entries in the printout from a computer against the data stored on it. This is a pointless reconciliation because the printout will necessarily reflect the data from which it was generated. Any fraudulent entry stored in the system will be reflected in the printout – if a comparison is made no anomalies will appear between the two sets of data. During a fraud risk review, the futility of this 'reconciliation' was pointed out to the processing clerks, who conceded its shortcomings, but explained it away on the basis 'it's always been done this way'.

There may also be insufficient data when transactions are finally reconciled or approved to check whether the original data to be transacted has been entered accurately and entirely. It may be the case that key fields are never checked:

> A supervisor undertook a comprehensive check between the standing data in the payments system and a printed payments summary, a spreadsheet that showed each payee's name, the amount to be credited and the daily transaction total. This check was done immediately prior to the payments being released via an on-line payments terminal. Significantly, the printed summary did not include the bank sort codes or the account details supplied by the payees. These bank routing details were stored on the computer in an unprotected invoice registry. It was possible, therefore, for the fraudster to change the routing details in the invoice registry and re-direct the checked payments to an unauthorized account. The confirmation report showed the beneficiary account details but this was never matched against the original invoices or payment instructions, where discrepancies would have been apparent. This fraudulent re-routing went undetected until the bona fide payee(s) advised non-receipt of payment.

Ideally, the full extent of each and every transaction to be approved for execution should be checked against the original authenticated documentation or instruction that initiated it. This end-to-end reconciliation, if rigorous, will detect any fraudulent amendment of the standing data on any intermediate systems in the processing chain (see Figure 2.7).

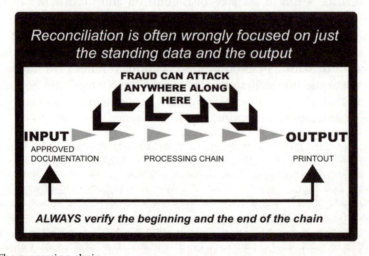

Figure 2.7   The processing chain

Particular scrutiny should be applied during this check to the accuracy of beneficiary bank account details. Ideally, the reconciliation will also encompass verification of all the routing information in the standing settlement instructions (SSIs), although dual (and preferably, tertiary) control arrangements protecting this data should suffice.

> An unauthorized transaction on an on-line credit card terminal was discovered because the fraudster had failed to tear off and destroy a paper transaction slip, which was found the next day, triggering an inquiry. It transpired that the fraudster had used a supervisor's card to authorize numerous refunds to be debited from the company's bank account and credited to the payment card accounts of friends and relatives. Realizing that these unauthorized debits would appear in the weekly bank statement, he amended the entries in the general ledger so that they were recorded as 'duplicate payments', or 'written off' transactions. The sole focus of the weekly 'bank rec' was to *reconcile* the transactions, not to identify latent fraud. 'Duplicate payments' and 'written off' entries were taken at face value and the corresponding refunds were passed as legitimate, and not investigated or audited in any way. The culprit knew this. The lack of proactive and aggressive audit in the reconciliation process meant that this fraud could have continued undetected for years – had it not been for the fraudster's careless oversight with the paper transaction slip.

In uncontrolled environments, a single operator may amend standing data. This is clearly a risk. It is advisable, therefore, to control access to standing data and the opportunity to amend it.

Where payments are regularly made to the same suppliers, employees or other counter-parties, the payment routing data can be 'locked' – protected from unauthorized changes – using SSIs. SSIs are used to route payments to client bank accounts or to transfer payments to bank accounts used by regular suppliers, employees or other payees.

Some control principles pertain to SSIs:

- SSIs should be raised on the system only when supported by complete and independently verified documentation.
- The data once verified and entered should be read-only and amendable thereafter by two independent profiles (that is, under dual control).
- Controls should be set as to the type of transaction and maximum value that may be executed for each SSI.

The insertion or amendment of a bank code and beneficiary account number to divert a payment is an obvious risk. Where SSIs are maintained under dual control, this risk is reduced. However, some cunning methods to subvert this system have been devised:

> The SSIs were carefully controlled, the standing data was read-only and entries could not be made or amended without the intervention of two people with separate computer accounts. The investigator concluded that it would be difficult, but not impossible, for a fraudster to re-route a payment by changing an SSI on the computer system.
>
> He was taken aback, however, by a forged letter sent to the treasury department by fax and post some years previously. The letter, printed on the genuine letterhead of one of the company's major suppliers, stated that it had changed its bank account and that the corresponding SSI on the system should be amended accordingly. It was a crude deception, and highly speculative, but had nearly succeeded – prevented only by the vigilance of the treasury manager, who telephoned the genuine supplier for confirmation. She retained the letter as a training aid.

PROCESSING MANIPULATION

The computer system is tampered with to defraud or deceive. This may involve unauthorized amendments to the computer system or software, the use of unauthorized software or hardware, or the fraudulent amendment of algorithms or formulae.

The use of unauthorized hardware to defraud featured in a celebrated story, albeit apocryphal, of supermarket shenanigans:

> The supermarket was suffering from unexplained stock losses. The auditors decided to spot-check the takings on the cash tills. They laboriously tallied the end-of-day takings against the sales itemization for each till. There were no discrepancies. The senior auditor felt deflated, and explained to the area manager that there was no indication of monkey business at the tills, and the explanation for the stock losses lay elsewhere. 'You're sure they tally?' said the area manager. 'Absolutely', said the weary auditor. 'We've checked all ten tills and they're all correct.' '*Ten*???' enquired the manager, 'But ... we've only got *nine*!!!'

Whether true or not, this story nicely reflects the simplicity and elegance of many processing frauds. The story serves as another gentle reminder to the investigator to seek the simplest explanations first. In all probability, the modus operandi of the criminal or fraudster will be quick, simple and easy to effect. Overly complex and contrived explanations to real world events are, in most instances, best avoided.

A well-known processing manipulation is the 'salami' fraud whereby a programmed routine rounds down, or rounds up, pennies from accounts and places the accumulated proceeds into an account controlled by the fraudster. The amounts are so small for each account that is remitted that they do not trigger enquiries by the account holders when statements are produced. Think, for example, of your own reaction should your salary cheque be short by a few pence. However, the proceeds for the fraudster may be significant, particularly if many thousands of accounts are plundered (see Figure 2.8).

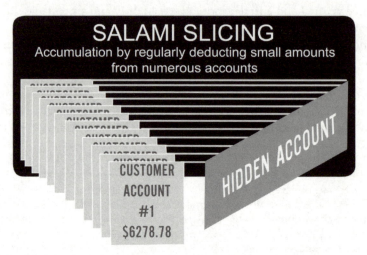

Figure 2.8   Salami fraud

The following case revealed an enthusiastic fraudster who reversed the salami principle, and prospered well, until his big mouth betrayed him:

> (i) Willis Robinson, 22, of Libertytown, Maryland, was sentenced to ten years in prison (six of which were suspended) for having reprogrammed his Taco Bell drive-up-window cash register causing it to ring up each $2.99 item internally as a 1-cent item, so that he could pocket $2.98 each time. He amassed $3600 before he was caught. *Management assumed the error was hardware or software and only caught the perpetrator when he bragged about his crime to co-workers.*[4] [Author's italics]

The salami fraud may be used to particular effect in systems that process calculations to several decimal places beyond the customary two places used in most financial records. If these fractions are channelled using a salami technique, a sizeable hidden fund can grow with little or no warning to the victim organization.

The salami technique may also be applied in committing weights and measurement frauds, where volumes of physical stock or commodities are sold. A classic example was reported from Los Angeles in 1998:

> (i) District attorneys charged four men with fraud for allegedly installing computer chips in gasoline pumps that cheated customers by overstating the amounts of petrol pumped. *The problem came to light when an increasing number of consumers charged that they had been sold more petrol than the capacity of their gas tanks.* The fraud was difficult to prove initially because the perpetrators programmed the chips to deliver exactly the right amount of gasoline when asked for five- and 10-gallon amounts – precisely the amounts typically used by inspectors.[5] [Author's italics]

A variation on this theme involved the manipulation of software to artificially inflate the volumes of petrol recorded in a billing system.

> (i) In January 1993, four executives of a rental-car franchise in Florida were charged with defrauding at least 47 000 customers using a salami technique. Prosecutors claimed that the defendants modified a computer billing system to add five extra gallons to the actual gas tank capacity of rental vehicles. From 1988 to 1991, every customer who returned a car without refilling the gas tank ended up paying excess rates for a fraudulently inflated total of gasoline. The thefts reportedly ranged from $2 to $15 per customer.

As Mich Kabay who reported this particular fraud noted, these are *very* thick slices of salami.

The salami fraud and other types of creative accounting often deliberately deploy *flawed logic*:

> (i) Bob, Ted and Alice each contributed £10 towards a television set. They went to the shop and bought a TV for exactly £30. As they left the shop, the shop assistant ran after them and stopped them. The TV, she explained, was on a special discount and had been reduced to £25. Bob, Ted and Alice were very pleased to hear this and Alice gratefully took the refund of £5. The three of them agreed that they should give the shop assistant £2 for being so honest and helpful. They then split the remaining £3 equally between themselves. Bob then said, 'That's really good, we each paid £9 for the TV, rather than £10.' But Ted looked confused, 'There are three of us, and we each paid £9, which totals £27. We then gave the shop assistant £2, which totals £29. There is £1 missing.'

4,5   Case studies of salami fraud reported by Professor Mich Kabay and Peter G. Neumann in *Risks Digest* 18.75, January 1997.

Flawed logic may be included in a program, a calculation or a formula and is why a consistent 1-cent or other small discrepancy may prove pivotal in detecting fraud.

It is important to investigate anomalies and to appreciate that errors and discrepancies produced by computer-based financial and accounting systems, however seemingly trivial, have a logical cause, and do not occur independently.

Processing manipulation may also involve the suppression or circumvention of audit trails, transactional logs and control reports. An old and simple trick to conceal the theft of stock, for instance, was used to suppress inventory records from appearing on printouts. A piece of stiff card was placed between the printer ribbon and the paper printout (see Figure 2.9). This technique is unlikely to be encountered nowadays, but the principle of suppressing the reporting function remains valid.

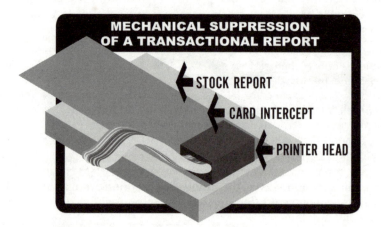

Figure 2.9   Mechanical suppression of a transaction report

Computer fraud routinely entails false entry, modification and *suppression*, typically:

- the suppression or diversion of information so that it is not written to audit trails, transaction logs or report files;
- the interception or alteration of confirmations;
- the deletion of audit trails or logs, or the destruction of the data recorded in them;
- bypassing the record-keeping process altogether by using an unauthorized and unrelated system.

Typically, the fraudster copies the transactional log or audit trail from the system, executes a transaction, which is recorded to the resident log, deletes it and restores the unaltered copy thus leaving no trace of the transaction.

A variation on this is for the fraudster to rename the transactional log upon discovering that the software generates a new one by default in the event that it fails to detect the presence of an existing log.

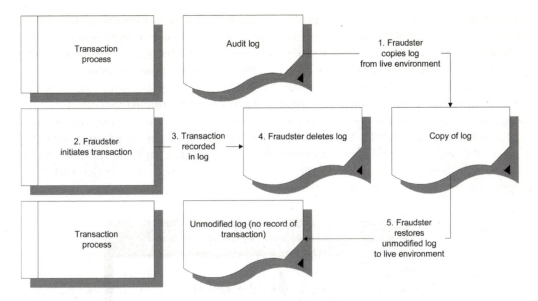

Figure 2.10   File manipulation

A batch of high-value pay-TV cards had been activated illicitly and released to the pirate community. These smartcards were genuine and appeared to have been programmed using official software. Accordingly, suspicion fell upon the broadcaster's subscription centre and focused therein on the IT department that controlled card activation and distribution.

Viewing cards subsequently recovered from circulation bore official serial numbers, none of which corresponded with those itemized in the production logs. The manufacturers could not explain how the pirates had generated these numbers. They feared that the programming software had been stolen, or reverse engineered.

The security team at the subscription centre was adamant that no technical manipulation had occurred on any of the activation machines on the network domain. Controls were described as 'watertight', and consequently they concluded that the fraud could not have originated within the subscription centre.

External consultants examined the production logs, which were generated for each and every activation session. Each log itemized the unique serial numbers assigned to the cards in the activated batches. The production logs were write-protected so that the entries listed within them could not be amended or deleted.

Seeking an explanation for the phantom cards, one of the investigators suggested that they rename the production log and then activate some cards. Astonishingly, the renamed log did not record the serial numbers of this batch, nor did it indicate that anything untoward had occurred. As a profound oversight, the programmers on the system had not considered or discovered this critical loophole.

People unfamiliar with the mechanics of fraud tend to invest a misplaced confidence in computer-generated records and logs. In the example above, the production log became something of a sacred cow – the accuracy of its reports was never questioned or tested despite the fact that unauthorized cards had been activated.

Processing manipulation is often made possible due to simple oversights when control processes are designed, developed or implemented. A control weakness in many mechanical mileometers, for example, is that they can be 'clocked' to zero and beyond by the fast rotary action of an electric drill – a trick that is well known to the vehicle resale trade.

Change control is also critical – many frauds have been abetted when systems were upgraded and previously installed controls divested, or not re-configured:

 A control incorporated in the payment module version 3 was not included in versions 4 and 5. A free-format payment raised in version 3 required the intervention of two approvers. The same transaction in versions 4 and 5 required the intervention of a single approver.

IMPERSONATION

The fraudster impersonates the legitimate user of a computer system to defraud or deceive. He may use software and hardware tools to assist this impersonation. Impersonation is frequently accomplished using misappropriated passwords or through the misuse of authentication technology.

The fraudster may thus conceal his identity and gain the systems access and rights of the user that he impersonates. Impersonation is mostly used to circumvent computer access controls, to gain unauthorized access and user privileges.

Impersonation features prominently in cases of computer hacking and systems misuse as well as fraud. The misuse of passwords to access systems, applications and networks accounts for most instances of impersonation in the workplace.

One of the commonest causes of password disclosure occurs due to visual scrutiny of the keyboard as the password is entered. This phenomenon is known as 'shoulder surfing'. In an attempted fraud against a London-based bank, for example, the culprit was authorized to enter SWIFT instructions but did not have the password to release them:

 When interviewed, he admitted having seen the password – 'BOT' – partially entered at the keyboard by his colleague. Knowing his colleague to be a keen cricket fan, he successfully guessed the rest.[6]

Written passwords are another liability:

The auditor asked to see the instruction manual to the payment system. After some delay it was delivered to him. However, he failed to notice that the manual started at page 2 and that the first page had been torn from the book. Had he seen this and enquired vigorously as to why, he would have discovered that the password to the payments terminal had been written on the missing page – a serious control violation by the manager of the department.

In most cases, the fraudster impersonates people to access systems and processes to which they have no permission. However, the criminal may also choose to impersonate an *organization*, such as a bank, or a *computer system*, such as a website, in order to garner

---

6   Ian Botham (born 1955), former England cricket captain.

confidential information, passwords and account details. As an example, the banking industry is bedevilled by 'phishers' who pose online as genuine banks or online traders in order to scavenge customer credit card details and on-line banking passwords. The deception is usually executed using electronic mail to contact potential victims and is often supported by a fully operational website that masquerades as the official on-line banking or customer service facility. The victims are fooled into entering their credit card details, account information and passwords and other information that is subsequently used to defraud.

-----Original Message-----
From: Customer Support [mailto:support@citibank.com]
Sent: 05 October 2004 19:53
To: Info
Subject: NOTE! Citibank account suspend in process

Dear CustomeZ:

Recently there have been a large number of cyber attacks pointing our database servers. In order to safeguard your account, we require you to sign on immediately.

This personal check is requested of you as a precautionary measure and to ensure yourselves that everything is normal with your balance and personal information.

This process is mandatory, and if you did not sign on within the nearest time your account may be subject to temporary suspension.

Please make sure you have your Citibank(R) debit card number and your User ID and Password at hand.

Please use our secure counter server to indicate that you have signed on, please click the link below:

http://211.158.34.250/citifi/

!! Note that we have no particular indications that your details have been compromised in any way.

Thank you for your prompt attention to this matter and thank you for using Citibank(R).

Regards,

Citibank(R) Card Department

(C)2004 Citibank. Citibank, N.A., Citibank, F.S.B.,
Citibank (West), FSB. Member FDIC.Citibank and Arc
Design is a registered service mark of Citicorp.

Figure 2.11   A 'phishing' trip (verbatim extract)

Impersonation should always be considered when investigating fraud or misuse in the workplace, as it is the most common way in which the perpetrators of computer crime seek to conceal their identity. For this reason, it is inadvisable to confront an individual solely on the basis that his USERID or profile is shown as having committed an offence.

Impersonation and the methods and tools used by intruders are discussed in more detail in Chapter 4.

SUBSTITUTION

The fraudster causes a computer system to misinterpret the data that is presented to it, typically using false or incorrect barcodes.

> A supermarket chain was suffering from 'shrinkage' at one of its stores. CCTV recordings of the tills showed nothing untoward, an inspection of the goods inward area was inconclusive and no significant escalation in shoplifting had been reported.
> The supermarket instructed a private investigator who checked the till records. Every item for sale was barcoded and scanned at the tills and he believed that these records might show an anomaly, or reveal a pattern. Sure enough, one of the operators regularly rang up between 30 and 40 boxes of matches at once – an unusual occurrence that merited investigation.
> It transpired that this till operator had cut the barcode from a box of matches and fixed this to her wrist using double-sided tape. When her friends in the neighbourhood came to her till, she would pass the items over the scanner, cover their barcodes with her hand and register a box of matches instead, courtesy of the substitute barcode attached to her wrist. The sleight of hand was not discernible from the CCTV recordings.

Barcode frauds are difficult to detect without rigorous inventory controls and careful stocktaking. The barcode reader will process data *indiscriminately*. There is no independent verification, other than the barcode presented for processing, that the tin of beans recorded by the system is not, in fact, a high value television set or car.

The swapping of barcodes between high-value and low-value merchandise (see Figure 2.12) is a well-known scam in the retail trade and it is difficult to detect because the books will *balance* – the cash receivable will reconcile with the recorded value of the products sold. In one such case high-specification computers were swapped systematically into the boxes of lower specification machines – the price differential between the PCs was marginal but the extent of the fraud was such that significant losses were incurred.

Figure 2.12   Substitution fraud

The essential deception of barcode fraud is that different items of stock impersonate or masquerade as each other. The key lesson here is that the investigator should always question and test the validity of recorded information – is it *really* a tin of beans?

Conclusion

It is important to appreciate the illusory nature of computers and that deception using them is often easier than deceiving by other means. In some respects, computers are ideal instruments with which to commit fraud. If the fraudster is astute and uses the correct tools, data may be copied, altered and eliminated without trace. Tampering with paper documents invariably leaves trace evidence. This is not necessarily the case when computer records are amended. If a software spreadsheet is altered to reflect false data and is subsequently restored to show accurate data, it is unlikely that any evidence of this process will be recorded.

Common control failures and other factors that consistently feature in cases of computer fraud have included:

- *Static passwords* – easy to intercept and open to misuse (see Chapter 4).
- *Written signatures* – easy to forge, photocopy, or cut and paste; faxed signatures have no forensic or inherent legal value.
- *Faxed instructions or confirmations* – as above.
- *Transactional instructions* raised using standard software applications and templates.
- *Partial or late reconciliation* – reconciliation should be global, that is, from initiation to execution, and in sufficient time to suspend or rescind an unauthorized or inaccurate transaction.
- *Insufficient segregation of duties* – all critical functions should be overseen and independently checked.
- *Unauthenticated call-back* – the party seeking verification does not confirm the identity of the party verifying the transaction.
- *Unprotected standing data* – standing data is subject to unauthorized amendment; transmission queues are particularly vulnerable.
- *Manual input* – operations revert to faxes and telex – systems that are easily subverted, or other systems with which staff may be unfamiliar.
- *Spreadsheets* – have featured in many cases of fraud – values are fraudulently amended or formulae adjusted.
- *Breaks in end-to-end authentication* – fraud occurs at the interfaces between systems and processes, and where there are incompatible formats which necessitate re-keying or transferring data.
- *Breaks in the processing chain* – as above.
- *Falsified control data* – audit relies upon control data, which is deliberately falsified so that no anomalies occur in transactions.
- *Uncontrolled documentation and operating instructions* – operating manuals and other documentation should be kept under close supervision and always locked away when not in use.
- *Redundant systems* – these may be re-activated and misused. Telex systems are vulnerable to this misuse.

- *Inadequate screening* – temporary workers, contractors and agency appointees may gain access to sensitive systems and processes without any checks being made as to their identity or background.
- *Inadequate fraud response planning* – inadequate planning often leads to panic and chaos. See Chapter 13 (Incident Response).
- *Open bank mandates* – payments are ordained 'by any means', without further verification.

The fraudulent potential of technology has led to a misconception in some quarters that the computer is the *perfect* criminal tool, *guaranteed* to leave no evidence, thus ensuring the fraudster anonymity. This is not the case. Computer forensic tools and techniques, combined with commonsense and tenacity, often suffice in exposing fraud and deceit.

Specific to investigating and resolving computer fraud, some key factors merit consideration:

- Anonymous communications (letters, faxes and e-mails) are often used to alert management that fraud is occurring. Any such allegation should be thoroughly investigated, the author identified and interviewed (see Chapter 11).
- Identify a lawyer experienced in preparing and executing freezing orders and injunctions. In sizeable frauds it may be necessary to freeze bank accounts and assets at short notice.
- What are the organization's priorities? To prosecute the offender or to recover misappropriated funds? To claim on fidelity or computer crime insurance? Different objectives require different legal strategies and approaches.
- Is it fraud or human error? Errors are often misinterpreted.
- If it is fraud, what has the fraudster *gained*?
- Most computer frauds are explained by mundane failures in controls (passwords and Post-its and so on).
- Other computer frauds are simple, ingenious and, sometimes, imaginative.
- Some computer frauds are extremely technical in their execution, involving programming, reverse engineering and other complex processes. These are the exceptions.
- Seek the simplest explanation as to how the fraud was committed.
- Escalate the probable complexity of the method used only after simple explanations are discounted.
- People lie – do not assume that you are being told the truth by *anyone*.
- Never interview witnesses in groups – always interview people separately.
- Obtain written witness statements as soon as possible, otherwise relevant details may be forgotten and facts may be distorted over time.
- Think like the fraudster – identify all existing controls and devise methods to circumvent or subvert them. Having done so, check your methods to see whether they would be effective to commit the fraud.
- With computer frauds, there is invariably a documentary trail of some description, elements of which may subsequently be destroyed by the fraudster, but many elements may remain intact, or be retrievable. Different parts of the trail may exist in different locations under diverse control. Recreate as much of the trail as possible and follow it.
- The missing pieces of the trail are key – they tell us much about the fraudster, his method, his knowledge and his level of access to the systems and processes involved. Identify the missing pieces.

- Computer output, whether printed or on-screen, is *illusory* – can you rely on *any* of the information that you see? Verify the pieces of trail that are recovered.
- A false instruction, once successfully fed into a system, will proceed through the processing chain undetected – it is, therefore, advisable to verify documentation at source and confirm the validity of the initial instruction to transact.
- Transactional data, control input and audit reports may also be forged and should never be presumed accurate or genuine.
- Do not assume that because the accounts balance that no fraud is taking place – many frauds are not recorded in the books, or are suppressed or amended as entries to ensure that no anomalies are evident.
- Fraud often occurs at the unprotected interfaces between systems, processes and formats – these interfaces should be identified and inspected. Locate and check the weak links in the processing chain. Unprotected standing data, data in transit on removable media, and plaintext data in buffers and pre-transmission queues are particularly vulnerable to fraudulent amendment.
- A computer fraud may feature several themes (forgery, impersonation, processing manipulation) incorporating disparate elements and systems. It is necessary to understand the unity of these themes, elements and systems and how and why they relate in order to understand the mechanism of the fraud.
- Draw a picture. This will show the relationships between the themes, elements and systems (see 'Relational analysis', Chapter 16).
- Chart the flow of data or information between systems, processes and people (see 'Transactional analysis', Chapter 16). This will identify all of the components in the processing chain, will help identify the location of misappropriated funds or assets, and clarify the identity of witnesses and possible suspects.
- Identify the epicentre of the fraud and all the data processing and storage devices involved in its commission.
- All of the computers and any other data storage and processing devices utilized in the fraud require forensic investigation. This includes the computers and devices to which the fraudster had no direct access but through which fraudulent transactions were routed, or processed remotely.
- Determine the sequence of events. It is important to understand when things happened and in what order. See 'Chronological analysis', Chapter 16.
- After determining the probable method, prove your hypothesis by recreating the fraud.
- Learn from the control weaknesses that have been exploited and apply corrective measures to all exposed systems.

In our efforts, an incident response plan is clearly indicated. The fundamental principles of contingency planning and incident response are discussed in Chapter 13. It is also necessary to secure and preserve all possible sources of evidence as soon as possible. Audit trails, transactional data, network events logs and other records will require retrieval and examination. Paper documents and printouts are also likely to feature at some stage, and these require appropriate management and handling. The correct management of evidence, its processing and analysis, will underpin the investigation. These issues are discussed in Chapters 14, 16 and 17.

3 Espionage, Intellectual Property Theft and Leaks

Good swiping is an art in itself.
Jules Feiffer, cartoonist, novelist and playwright (b. 1929)

Knowledge and information are amongst the most valuable assets that an organization owns. These assets, referred to as intellectual property (IP), are vital to the wellbeing of commercial operations but are often poorly protected.

IP may be in the form of a prototype or a research paper, a model, a formula or recipe, a manufacturing process, a trademark or design, a database, or anything that has potential commercial value that has been developed. IP may be stored as data recorded electronically or on paper; it may comprise a physical object, or even a concept or an idea.

Intellectual property is vulnerable to disclosure, to hostile interception, to solicitation and to theft and requires safeguarding. Commercial ventures are exposed to the risks of:

- employee theft
- information brokering
- industrial espionage
- deliberate or unintentional information disclosure.

Most thefts of confidential information involve employees; sometimes acting alone, but often because they have been manipulated or coerced by people outside of the company.

Ignorance or carelessness may also play a significant role in the loss or leakage of sensitive information.

Knowledge is also stored in people's minds and for obvious reasons it is very difficult to control or prevent the transfer of knowledge between employees and others connected with any given business. People may leave an organization but retain significant knowledge about its methods, operations and processes and this is a very real danger, not just because this knowledge may be proffered to third parties, but also because it may be misused subsequently to defraud the organization, to blackmail, sue or embarrass it.

This chapter looks at some of the risks to IP and confidential information and suggests some managerial and technical strategies to mitigate these risks.

Industrial espionage

The American Society for Industrial Security (ASIS) conducted an intellectual property loss survey of Fortune 1000 companies and the 300 fastest growing companies in the United

States. Of a 12 per cent response rate, companies reported $44 billion in known or suspected losses over a 17-month period during 1996–97.

Pacific Northwest National Laboratory in the United States has developed a methodology to determine the scope of economic loss resulting from the theft of IP. Its economic loss model was initially applied to a known case involving the theft of IP from a US corporation by a foreign competitor, which subsequently captured the market. The misappropriation of the IP in this case was estimated to have resulted in over $600 million in lost sales, the direct loss of 2600 full-time jobs and the consequential loss of a further 9542 jobs for the US economy as a whole over a 14-year time frame. The analysis determined that the US trade balance was negatively impacted by $714 million and lost tax revenues totalled $129 million from this single instance.

In the last decade there have been several high-profile cases of industrial espionage and information theft. The commercial impact on the victim organizations in reparations, loss of business and reputation has on occasions been staggering:

> After a long-running dispute, General Motors finally won a $100 million settlement against Volkswagen, after a senior GM executive headhunted by the German car manufacturer allegedly revealed confidential plans for an advanced assembly line (Plant X) to his new employer. In 1992 20 cases of confidential documents belonging to GM were shipped to Volkswagen headquarters in Wolfsburg, Germany, many of them allegedly transported aboard a Volkswagen corporate aircraft, via the Spanish residence of J. Ignacio Lopez de Arriortua, a Vice President at GM, later hired by VW. According to the court complaint filed by GM, Volkswagen equipped a facility with computers, copiers and shredders, and entered the information into its systems before destroying the paper copies. In addition to the settlement payout, VW agreed to purchase $1 billion of components from GM in restitution.

This case illustrates the colossal damage that may be wrought by a dishonest employee with high-level access to sensitive information. However, where the stakes are sufficiently high, external parties may be hired to scavenge information or cause disruption, as the following report suggests:

> In March 2002 the French pay-TV company Canal Plus Technologies sued NDS, a UK-based technology firm that provides encryption services used by satellite television companies to prevent access to subscription broadcasts that have not been paid for. Canal Plus used a rival encryption technology, which it claimed NDS hacked and published on a website used by satellite TV pirates. According to Canal Plus, NDS employed a 'sophisticated and well-funded' team of technicians to reverse engineer smartcards that protected the company's pay-TV systems. Following the publication of its smartcard codes on the Internet, pirates produced systems to access pay channels for free, depriving the French company of millions in lost revenues. ITV Digital, a user of Canal Plus encryption technology, also blamed piracy for the loss of £100 million revenue, which ultimately contributed to the firm's collapse in 2002.

Hostile intelligence gathering efforts by external parties have been mounted in several cases, many of which have featured the recovery and analysis of corporate and domestic rubbish (see Chapter 5).

Covert methods by external parties reported by the FBI in its annual reports to Congress include:

- agent recruitment and the placement of agents within companies
- the coercion of current and former employees
- surreptitious entry to offices, laboratories and manufacturing plants
- the theft of computers, equipment and documents
- computer intrusions into corporate networks.

Overt intelligence gathering methods have included:

- the aggressive pursuit of joint ventures, mergers and acquisitions
- the use of temporary research students with access to the target site's facilities
- scientific or technological exchanges
- direct requests for information
- contrived visits to sensitive facilities often on the pretexts of potential custom
- targeting exhibition stands and visitors at international conventions, seminars and trade or technology exhibitions
- the acquisition of technology or entire companies
- the exploitation of overseas distribution agreements.

Unsolicited requests for information via electronic mail, telephone, facsimile and post from foreign companies, 'front' companies, individuals, government officials and non-commercial organizations have all been reported.

Interestingly, the FBI describes the Internet as the 'vehicle of choice for unsolicited requests, providing an international, low-cost, anonymous medium to contact cleared contractor employees'.

> Do you have advanced/privileged information of any type of project/contract that is going to be carried out in your country? We hold commission/agency agreements with many large European companies and could introduce them to your project/contract. Any commission received would be shared with yourselves.

Figure 3.1   Advert: *Asian Wall Street Journal*

At international conventions, conferences, seminars and exhibitions US participants have reported that telephones have been monitored, rooms bugged or filmed and that baggage, possessions and equipment have been searched covertly. The risk associated with technical experts and scientists sharing their research and expertise at international forums has also been raised. These requests are usually benign, but others provide the cover 'to press US experts for restricted, proprietary, and even classified information'. Additionally, agents with technical backgrounds offer their services to commercial and government research facilities, academic institutions and defence companies. Agents have also fabricated their work experience and qualifications to gain employment with cleared companies.

Economic and industrial espionage is a strategic concern to many governments, and there have been instances of extraordinarily aggressive and concerted efforts to subvert markets, scupper product launches and other commercial ventures, or to purloin advanced technologies and 'know how'. Government eavesdropping efforts, for example, are pervasive and all embracing, as testified by Mark Lowenthal, a foreign policy specialist at the US Congressional Research Service:

> *The NSA is a big vacuum cleaner, capable of intercepting any kind of communications through the air. You just aim it at a region, and you pick up a lot of stuff. Any long-distance telephone call is likely to be picked up. If Toyota Japan wants to talk to Toyota Singapore, they're liable to be intercepted.*

It would be a mistake, however, to marginalize this sort of espionage as pertaining only to national security or to the most cutting-edge high-tech industries. At a mundane level are those everyday leaks and thefts of commercially sensitive information that afflict businesses in all sectors and at all levels. The misappropriation of data and the unauthorized disclosure of confidential information can have a devastating impact on the viability and the reputation of a business. As we shall see, employees and other trusted insiders are misappropriating vast quantities of corporate data for a variety of nefarious purposes.

APPLICABLE LAWS

In the United States, the Economic Espionage Act (EEA) was approved by Congress and became law in late 1996. The EEA contains two separate provisions that outlaw the theft or misappropriation of trade secrets. The first provision, codified at 18 U.S.C. § 1831(a), is directed towards foreign economic espionage and requires that the theft of the trade secret be done to benefit a foreign government, foreign instrumentality or foreign agent. The second provision, 18 U.S.C. § 1832, makes criminal the theft of trade secrets from any US company or operation for purely economic or commercial advantage.

Whilst many businesses are well aware that their own IP may be stolen and misused, few consider the grave legal risks arising from being in *receipt* of misappropriated information, whether wittingly or inadvertently. If a business solicits proprietary information, or turns a blind eye to employees who have misappropriated data, technology or research materials, it is in jeopardy of punitive litigation and may also be breaking the law. The EEA, for example, makes it a criminal offence to solicit or receive commercial information misappropriated from US companies.

Another risk is that material, the copyright and property of a third party, is secreted into products under development or due for release without the company's permission or knowledge:

> A software development company suspected that a programmer had assisted a competitor in the development of a new time management system. It investigated the programmer's activities and it soon became clear that the programmer's code, presumed to be the company's copyright, had itself been stolen from the programmer's *previous* employer, another major software house. The company was about to launch its own time management system but now faced the possibility of bruising litigation. As a result, the code had to be completely re-written. The product launch was delayed by many months and thousands of dollars spent on the planned promotional campaign were wasted.

In English law there is no criminal offence of data theft. The person who misappropriates electronic data does not permanently deprive the rightful owner of his data – instead he copies it, which is not an offence under the Theft Act 1968. Similar loopholes exist in other jurisdictions. The Computer Misuse Act 1990 applies, but only if the data that is misappropriated has been accessed without the permission or authority of its rightful owner. Data protection legislation also applies where personal data is misappropriated. Under Section 55 of the Data Protection Act 1998 it is a criminal offence for a person to knowingly or recklessly obtain personal data without the consent of the data controller. Ironically, the data controller also commits an offence should such unauthorized misappropriation or disclosure occur.

Cases of IP theft, data misappropriation and misuse are usually pursued in the UK through the civil courts. A number of powerful search and seizure measures exist under the civil process to remedy data misappropriation and IP theft including the search order (formerly known as the *Anton Piller order*), the freezing order (formerly known as the *Mareva injunction*) and the 'delivery up' order. These orders are granted by the courts and have been described as 'nuclear weapons', because, if granted, they bestow sweeping powers of search, inspection and seizure to the victim of fraud, IP infringement or data misuse against the perpetrator. In the most serious cases, the power to search, inspect and seize evidence is granted *ex parte*, that is, in the absence of the alleged perpetrator and without forewarning him that action is imminent. Guidance about the technical aspects of search orders is provided at Appendix 3.

Fundamentally, the key points are:

- IP theft and data misappropriation to gain commercial advantage is illegal in the United States and certain other countries such as Germany.
- Data protection laws apply in many jurisdictions and it is usually the *custodian* of the data who infringes these laws when information theft or data misappropriation occur.
- There are very powerful injunctive tools for legal redress available in the civil courts in many jurisdictions.
- The punitive costs of soliciting proprietary information, or being in receipt of it whether wittingly or otherwise, can be onerous in the extreme.

PREVALENCE

As reported in the *Computer Fraud & Security Bulletin*,[1] the computer investigations consultancy DGI noted that the single most prevalent computer misuse in the year 2002–3 was the theft of IP and proprietary data by trusted *insiders*.

Of 70 investigations completed in the year by DGI, 26 comprised the theft and misappropriation of IP by employees. Data was often transmitted out of the victim organizations using corporate e-mail systems, although instances of information being burned to CDs and DVD or copied to Iomega Zip disks and other external devices were also apparent. In one case, the perpetrator printed out a database for selective re-entry. There were several cases where proprietary client databases were mail-merged and letters posted in order to solicit custom for competitive businesses.

The trend was reconfirmed in the operational year 2003–4.[2] From a breakdown by category, the theft of IP remained the most prevalent risk. Of 78 reactive investigations,

---

1   May 2003.
2   The DGI Annual Report on Computer Risk and Response 2003/4, 29th April 2004.
    http://www.dgiforensic.com/pdf/Annual%20Review%202004.pdf.

there were 18 cases of IP theft, of which 13 involved hostile defections by individuals or groups.

Of 130 investigations conducted by DGI in the operational year 2004–5, there were 47 cases of IP theft, all perpetrated by employees.

This threat is clearly prevalent but it is almost completely ignored by the IT security industry. The unwavering focus on external computer threats is totally at odds with the simple reality that it is overwhelmingly those *inside* the firewall that steal the vast majority of data.

IP THEFT AND DEFECTIONS

The risk that key staff will defect to competitors taking proprietary data and intellectual property to a new employer or venture is ever present. The employee may offer misappropriated information as an unsolicited gift, or a predatory competitor may stipulate it as a tacit or explicit condition of the employee's contract. Companies sometimes recruit individuals not for their skills or talents but for the information they bring with them.

> A group of employees in a publishing house in London defected, unexpectedly and at short notice, to set up a competitive business. A forensic examination of each of their PC's disk drives resulted in the recovery of several hundred pages of e-mail correspondence between the team and its external backers. They had all used Microsoft Hotmail in the belief that their communication would be anonymous and hidden. In fact, a large number of their messages, which proved breach of contract and conspiracy, were recorded in the Internet caches of the computer drives examined.

The extent of IP theft and data misappropriation has on occasions been potentially calamitous:

> A hostile defection by a team of core technical specialists was suspected. Investigations revealed that technical specifications, operations manuals, market analyses and contractual data had been misappropriated – transmitted to a nascent competitor via the victim organization's e-mail system. Several CDs of information had also been copied and removed. The investigators located the rival business plan and an array of documentation to support the proposed venture. The conspirators were brazen – e-mail traffic located on their company laptops and on the network indicated that they had even used their employer's video conferencing facilities to discuss their plans. As one investigator observed, 'The victim company was raped – virtually every item of commercial value was stolen.'

Scientists, technicians and process engineers are likely targets for competitors seeking information because these professionals have unfettered access to confidential methods, systems and processes and a working knowledge of them. The following cases were all prosecuted under the EEA in the United States:

- In November 1997 Harold Worden, a 30-year veteran of Eastman Kodak Corporation, was sentenced for his part in misappropriating and brokering the company's secret 401 process that produces a clear plastic base used in camera film. Prior to his retirement as a senior process engineer, Mr Worden took confidential Kodak documents relating to this process and was alleged to have recruited his successor to continue providing him with confidential information. His own firm brokered the consultancy services of more than 60 former Kodak employees, some of whom consulted for Kodak's competitors. A Kodak spokesman claimed that the drawings, plans, manuals and documentation removed by Mr Worden were worth billions of dollars to Kodak in potential lost market share. Mr Worden reportedly received a meagre $26 700 for selling the company's information.

- In October 1997 Steven Louis Davis was indicted for stealing and disclosing confidential information relating to the Mach 3 shaving system developed by Gillette. Mr Davis was employed by Wright Industries, a Tennessee designer of manufacturing equipment contracted by Gillette to assist with developing the new shaving system. Mr Davis was originally the lead process control engineer for the Mach 3 project but was removed from this position at Gillette's request. He was alleged to have sent engineering drawings for the new razor to competitors including Warner-Lambert, Bic and American Safety Razor Co.

- In September 1997 Mr Pin Yen Yang and his daughter Hwei Chen Yang were arrested in Cleveland, Ohio and charged with the theft of trade secrets from Avery Dennison Corporation, a large US manufacturer of adhesive products. The Yangs were convicted in 1999 for having paid an Avery Dennison scientist, Dr Ten Hong Lee, upwards of $160 000 for proprietary manufacturing information and research data over a period of approximately eight years between 1989 and 1997. Payments were made via Dr Lee's family members in Taiwan.

- In June 1997 Hsu Kai-lo, Chester Ho and Jessica Chou were arrested by the FBI and charged with attempting to steal the process for cultivating Taxol from plant cells. Taxol is a complex drug used in the treatment of ovarian cancer and pharmaceutical giant Bristol-Myers Squibb had invested $15 million to develop a process to manufacture it. The front company for which Chou ostensibly worked, offered to pay a Bristol-Myers Squibb scientist $400 000 in cash plus shares and royalties on future sales resulting from the commercial exploitation of the processing technology.

Proactive and aggressive audit of all major research and development projects is clearly indicated. In a case from 1995, management had consistently ignored warnings about a scientist in charge of engineering research, which proved to be a costly mistake:

> The investigators had been assured that the audit team had searched the office properly and found everything and anything that might be relevant. Except, that is, for the diskette in the bottom drawer of the suspect's desk. The TIF files on the diskette showed a series of faxes to a number in Japan. The transmission logs showed dozens of communications to this number, the relevance of which soon became clear. The top secret manufacturing specifications and process for the company's flagship product had been transmitted directly into the office of the Director of Research at the company's principal competitor.

Ultimately, however, it is impossible to control the transfer of *knowledge*. Those employees or contractors intimately acquainted with the design and implementation of key manufacturing processes or the development of a product may, if so minded, convey this information without recourse to documentation. As such, the control and security of IP is fundamentally a *people* issue. Alarmingly, this risk does not appear to have impacted on the consciousness of most human resources managers at all.

DATABASE THEFT

Historically, the contract between employer and employee involved an exchange of 'loyalty for security'. Today's rapidly changing business environment has made the promise of job security a thing of the past. This has resulted in a growing lack of loyalty amongst many employees. With a transient workforce and a breakdown in traditional loyalties, many employees regard the proprietary data belonging to their employers as currency with which to barter in the jobs marketplace.

In the case of simple database theft, the thief will often be the person responsible for administering the database. Marketing and data input personnel often have unrestricted access to commercially valuable databases, as do travelling sales personnel who maintain databases of clients and prospects on laptop computers, and are granted significant autonomy in their day-to-day dealings. The point, again, is that those with authorized access to information commit most data theft.

Typically, employees steal databases to sell to competitive companies, or will take databases or other information with them as they move on to their next place of work, offering the database as an 'added bonus'.

> A DP operator admitted to selling his employer's database on a regular basis. The database contained technical information that could be exploited by hackers and pirates. His standard charge was £500 to prospective purchasers and most of his deals were struck on-line. This individual worked in a business that had a high turnover of staff due to the modest remuneration it offered. The culprit had fallen heavily into debt and believed his skills and ability were undervalued.

A more audacious case took place in August 2005:

> A former America Online employee was sentenced to 15 months in prison for selling AOL members' details to spammers. Jason Smathers, 25, allegedly sold a database of 92 million screen names and e-mail addresses to various spammers for $28 000. As a result, about seven billion unsolicited spam e-mails flooded the inboxes of AOL members. AOL said Smathers' act had cost the company at least $300 000. AOL fired Smathers in June 2004. He was said to have used another employee's access code to steal the list of AOL customers in 2003 from its headquarters in Dulles, Virginia.

The illicit use of client and marketing databases may be policed using 'seeding'. Certain unspecified names and addresses within the database are in fact monitors – agents acting for the database owner – with instructions to forward all unsolicited mail shots for investigation. Seeded names are distributed evenly across the database, typically every 250th, 500th or 1000th address. Any mailing from a source unknown by the data controller is thus brought to his attention and may be investigated. Seeding also enables database managers to monitor contractual compliance, where, for instance, a marketing list is rented for an agreed 'one-off' mailing but is then mailed a second time without permission.

New technologies facilitate IP theft

TECHNICAL EXPOSURES

There are some key technical factors that serve to undermine the protection of IP and corporate data, principally:

- the IT profession's continuing obsession with external threats outside the firewall;
- the ease with which information can be copied seamlessly and undetected using a range of data storage devices and transmission methods;
- unsupervised employee access to electronic mail, the Internet and high-speed communications;
- poor IT security with inadequate audit trails and network and firewall monitoring.

Technology that facilitates the storage and sharing of IP also makes it easier to steal. The range of highly portable devices by which information may be transferred between locations and systems has expanded in recent years, and the capacity of these devices is rapidly increasing. A single DAT tape, the size of a small matchbox, can store the entire IP of many small and medium enterprises while an LTO tape, half the size of a standard VHS videotape, can store 400 gigabytes of compressed data. The data storage capacity of these devices increases as their physical size decreases. Memory sticks, the size of a small cigarette lighter, with over a gigabyte of storage capacity, can be purchased for less than £60. Available, also, are wristwatches capable of storing 256 megabytes of data, downloadable using a standard USB port (see Figure 3.2).

Figure 3.2 USB memory data watch (reprinted with kind permission of www.rememberus.co.uk)

The technologies to store and process data have also converged with a range of multi-functional devices now hitting the market. These and similar developments such as solid-state memory for digital cameras, have caused some major revisions in the training of law enforcement officers in search and seizure procedures.

As well as holding thousands of music tracks, for example, the Macintosh iPod can also act as an external hard drive, with the attendant risk that this entails. In July 2004, the UK Ministry of Defence added the popular Apple music accessory to a list of devices banned in most sections of its UK headquarters and offices abroad. The Australian Department of Defence has also banned the use of iPods in specific defence areas, stating, 'The threat from iPods is considered the same as for all other forms of easily portable storage media; their presence within defence areas is strictly controlled and in some cases prohibited.'

Other portable devices include smart-phones and handheld computers such as the Pocket PC and Palm PDAs. Newer versions of portable devices transfer data at significantly enhanced speeds. USB 2.0 and Firewire (IEEE 1394) have much higher transfer rates than the equivalent technology of a few years ago, significantly increasing the opportunity to steal large databases using connected hard disks. These devices are 'plug and play', with the Windows 2000 and XP operating systems mounting them as drives for immediate use.

The prospect of sensitive information, equipment or facilities being photographed and transmitted using the latest mobile telephones, copied to websites or mailed electronically to unauthorized parties has already prompted Intel, Samsung, the UK Foreign Office and the US Lawrence Livermore National Laboratory to ban camera phones from their premises. Schools, health clubs and strip clubs have also banned the devices. Regardless of bans and clampdowns, the popularity of camera phones seems unlikely to wane. Experts predict that by 2007, almost half of the mobiles sold worldwide will include a camera.

Even where portable data storage devices are banned or controlled, individuals intent on transmitting illicit data may bypass the corporate firewall with its attendant monitoring by using a rogue modem and an analogue telephone line:

> On searching the suspect's office for evidence of data theft and collusion, the investigators discovered a standard BT RJ11 telephone jack had been professionally installed in the skirting board. The IT department had ordered it and paid for it at the suspect's request. Nobody ever asked him why he needed this archaic communications link in preference to the company's digital broadband services.

Without resorting to spot checks and searches of people and their possessions and computers, it is extremely difficult to monitor or prevent the misuse of external data storage devices. Due to their portability, these devices are also easily mislaid or lost, which introduces another risk should the information stored on them be confidential or sensitive.

The information on memory sticks and other portable data storage media may also be *copied* quickly and *surreptitiously*, which re-emphasizes the need for encryption or biometric access control when sensitive data is in transit (see Figure 3.3).

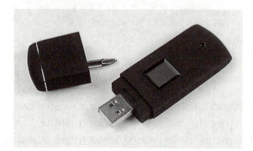

Figure 3.3   The BioDisk (reprinted with kind permission of Cardmedia (Europe) Ltd., www.card-media.co.uk)

Forensically, it is possible to determine that USB memory sticks, CD drives or other devices have been attached to a specific computer. The registry of the operating system will record devices that are connected to the computer (see Figure 3.4). The problem, however, is that there is rarely any indication at all of *which* files have been copied to (or from) these devices. The misappropriation of data using memory sticks is thus *traceless*.

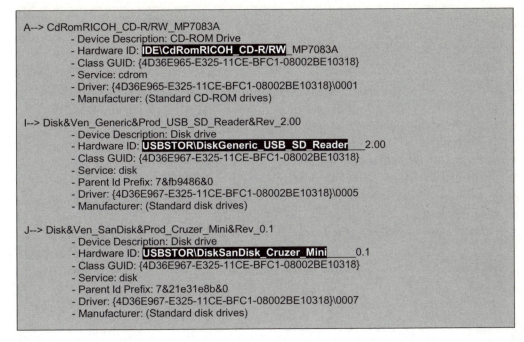

```
A--> CdRomRICOH_CD-R/RW_MP7083A
        - Device Description: CD-ROM Drive
        - Hardware ID: IDE\CdRomRICOH_CD-R/RW_MP7083A
        - Class GUID: {4D36E965-E325-11CE-BFC1-08002BE10318}
        - Service: cdrom
        - Driver: {4D36E965-E325-11CE-BFC1-08002BE10318}\0001
        - Manufacturer: (Standard CD-ROM drives)

I--> Disk&Ven_Generic&Prod_USB_SD_Reader&Rev_2.00
        - Device Description: Disk drive
        - Hardware ID: USBSTOR\DiskGeneric_USB_SD_Reader___2.00
        - Class GUID: {4D36E967-E325-11CE-BFC1-08002BE10318}
        - Service: disk
        - Parent Id Prefix: 7&fb9486&0
        - Driver: {4D36E967-E325-11CE-BFC1-08002BE10318}\0005
        - Manufacturer: (Standard disk drives)

J--> Disk&Ven_SanDisk&Prod_Cruzer_Mini&Rev_0.1
        - Device Description: Disk drive
        - Hardware ID: USBSTOR\DiskSanDisk_Cruzer_Mini___0.1
        - Class GUID: {4D36E967-E325-11CE-BFC1-08002BE10318}
        - Service: disk
        - Parent Id Prefix: 7&21e31e8b&0
        - Driver: {4D36E967-E325-11CE-BFC1-08002BE10318}\0007
        - Manufacturer: (Standard disk drives)
```

Figure 3.4   Examination of a computer's registry

The misuse of write-enabled CD-ROM drives is usually easier to investigate as many of the software packages that enable the user to burn data to a CD generate audit trails, which, in some cases, provide comprehensive details of the files and folders that were copied, when and from which location.

Data thieves often leave tell-tale traces of their misdeeds. Figure 3.5 shows a WinZip log file of misappropriated files being decompressed and extracted from the suspect's computer to an undisclosed network drive (Z:). The thief destroyed the files on his PC but overlooked the log.

Webmail services such as Hotmail and Yahoo are also used by thieves illicitly to export data from corporate computers. It is generally impracticable to block the use of all available web-mail services at the firewall and there are no quick and easy solutions to preventing insiders from exporting data by these services. However, by virtue of the Windows operating system, evidence of these messages and any related mail attachments are frequently recorded in the Internet cache of the host computer or in other locations of the local hard disk and may be identified and extracted using forensic tools (see Figure 3.6, an email recovered from the slack space on the suspect's computer disk).

DGI has successfully investigated numerous cases where 'anonymous' web-mail services have been misused. In several instances the mail messages and the transmitted attachments have been recovered from the perpetrator's workstation, having been recorded by default within the Internet cache. Evidentially, such evidence has immense probative value.

Unencrypted backups that are sent for archive are also a potential risk that is often overlooked. In April 2005, Iron Mountain, a company that manages corporate data storage, acknowledged that it had lost track of four sets of customer backup tapes since the beginning of the year. In other instances, trading firm Ameritrade stated that the company that handles its backups had lost a tape containing information on about 200 000

```
"D:\WINDOWS\Temporary  Internet  Files\Content.IE5\S5U7GDQ7\5  -  budget  and
projection [ 1] .zip"
Extracting to "D:\WINDOWS\TEMP\"
Use Path: no    Overlay Files: yes
cl:
"Z:\Project_Alpha\Specs\Contract final.zip"
Extracting to "Z:\Project_Alpha\Specs\5 - budget and projection\"
Use Path: yes    Overlay Files: no
cl:
"D:\WINDOWS\Temporary  Internet  Files\Content.IE5\ZERQKYSV\5  -  budget  and
projection[ 1] "
cl:
"Z:\Project_Alpha\Zipped_stuff\4 - Calibration.zip"
Extracting to "Z:\Project_Alpha\Zipped_stuff\4 - Calibration\"
Use Path: yes    Overlay Files: no
cl:
"Z:\Project_Alpha\Zipped_stuff\3 - Planning.zip"
Extracting to "Z:\Project_Alpha\Zipped_stuff\"
Use Path: yes    Overlay Files: yes
cl:
"Z:\Project_Alpha\Zipped_stuff\Contract Final.zip"
Extracting to "Z:\Project_Alpha\Zipped_stuff\Contract Final\"
Use Path: yes    Overlay Files: no
cl:
"Z:\Project_Alpha\Zipped_stuff\1 - Specification.zip"
Extracting to "Z:\Project_Alpha\Zipped_stuff\1 - Specification\"
Use Path: yes    Overlay Files: no
cl:
"Z:\Project_Alpha\Zipped_stuff\2 - Design.zip"
Extracting to "Z:\Project_Alpha\Zipped_stuff\2 - Design\"
Use Path: yes    Overlay Files: no
```

Figure 3.5   An incriminating WinZip log

```
target="_top">spirit@hotmail.com</a>
&gt;To: <a href="/cgi-bin/cframes/compose?disk=207.165.130.65_d586&login=joker&f=33793&
curmbox=ACTIVE&_lang=&mailto=1&to=joker@hotmail.com&msg=MSG16842292.28&start=23440&len
=3267&src=&type=x" target="_top">joker@hotmail.com</a>
&gt;&gt; Cc: <a href="/cgi-
&gt;&gt; Subject: meeting
&gt;&gt; Date: Wed, 20 Jan 1999 01:41:25 PST
&gt;&gt; Mime-Version: 1.0
&gt;&gt; Content-type: text/plain
&gt;&gt;
&gt;&gt; Ray
&gt;&gt;
&gt;&gt; They've said yes but want more samples –
&gt;&gt; particularly the
&gt;&gt; CAD/CAM
&gt;&gt; and test-bed stuff – if OK we could be talking
&gt;&gt; 200K per
&gt;&gt; release. Suggest meet usual place. D
&gt;&gt;
&gt;&gt;_____
```

Figure 3.6   Hotmail correspondence indicative of a collusive IP theft

customers, while Bank of America told US government officials in February 2005 that it had lost a backup tape containing data about government credit card holders. Richard Reese, CEO of Iron Mountain concluded, 'Companies need to reassess their backup strategies and seriously consider encrypting sensitive data to prevent a potential breach of privacy.' All the more so when low-level IT staff, disparagingly referred to as 'tape monkeys', process backup tapes. These menial workers have the access and the information to help potential thieves target specific tapes. As Jon Oltsik of Enterprise Strategy Group says, 'The process is totally insecure. You put your most junior people on this job, who are the most likely to be bribed and look for another way to make money.' Oltsik's firm surveyed 400 companies, of which 60 per cent admitted to never encrypting offsite backups.[3]

Another major concern is data leakage from improperly secured wireless networks (see Chapter 6).

TECHNICAL COUNTER-MEASURES

In response to the threat of localized data theft from workstations using memory sticks, CDs and other portable storage devices, there is currently a move amongst some security-minded organizations towards centralized network configurations, where sensitive data is processed in one place, rather than being distributed on laptops, desktop PCs and other distributed systems.

Blade technology puts the data and processing guts of desktop computers into rack-mounted processors locked safely inside a central server room. Blades – processor, memory and storage on a card – reside in rack-mountable enclosures that supply power, ventilation and other support components. Like most cluster-based systems, blade servers can be configured to include fault tolerance and redundancy – should a blade fail another blade can automatically step in to take its place. Individual blades are usually hot-swappable, which makes it easy to replace a board with a new one in the event of system failure. Blade technology clearly makes the network support function far easier and has been shown significantly to reduce maintenance hours.

However, the key security benefit of blade technology is that the user has no access to any local ports or drives through which unauthorized data may be misappropriated or uploaded – instead, he is presented with a simple receiver box, the size of a video cassette, with no onboard data storage capability or external communication channels.

In effect, we have come full circle with blade technology, which in many ways replicates the central mainframes and dumb terminal processing environment of old. The Pentagon, Los Alamos National Laboratories, the US Coastguard, NASA and several federal agencies and defence departments in the United States have implemented blade networks (also known as extended bus networks), largely in response to the US national infrastructure protection directive.

There are also network-based software solutions that can detect the unauthorized utilization of USB and Firewire devices on a network and which can prevent localized data misappropriation by centralized control. Using these software systems, administrators can disable specific types of storage device such as CDs, diskettes, USB memory sticks, iPods and other MP3 players, digital cameras and flash memory while enabling local USB and Firewire ports for other services. An example is the GFI LANguard Portable Storage Control system (see http://gfi.com).

---

3   http://www.securityfocus.com/news/11048.

A further option is a hardware lockdown of each workstation connected to the network, as described in Chapter 9.

Software and source code may be protected using a variety of copy-protection mechanisms. 'Dongles' – independent hardware devices that authenticate the installed software licence without which the software will not execute – have proved particularly effective in preventing software piracy and theft. It is also recommended that valuable source code be removed from network drives or workstations, and maintained on standalone development computers that are suitably secured, physically and logically.

The circulation of documents may be controlled through the vigorous enforcement of procedures, and, increasingly, through the use of digital rights management – a Microsoft technology to control the distribution of electronic files and access to their contents.

Backup tapes and data in archive may be encrypted to prevent unauthorized disclosure, and wireless networks should be secured.

Leaks

LOW-TECH LEAKS – CARELESSNESS AND IGNORANCE

Predictably, many information leaks and disclosures of confidential data occur not through the misuse of hi-tech gadgetry or espionage but through people's carelessness and ignorance.

It is ironic that many organizations take great care to secure their computer systems and electronic data but fail to safeguard printout and hard-copy documents. In many offices, highly sensitive documents and files are frequently left unattended in open areas. Cleaners and other temporary shift staff may steal or photocopy this material with impunity.

Hard copy, illicit photocopying, fax transmissions and even the post room have featured in several cases where information has been misappropriated or leaked. One such case that impacted on Prime Minister Tony Blair's government was reported in October 2004:

> A woman working as a temp at the Cabinet Office in London was arrested following a Special Branch investigation into a series of damaging leaks of confidential government papers to *The Sunday Times*. Police detained a 23-year-old on suspicion of stealing documents. Revelations in *The Sunday Times* included private concerns within Whitehall about America's post Iraq war strategy and the cabinet split over the decision by the former Home Secretary, David Blunkett, to introduce national ID cards. A Cabinet Office spokesman said: 'An agency worker was arrested on suspicion of theft from Cabinet Office premises. The individual concerned was assigned to the Cabinet Office through an employment agency and the assignment was terminated immediately following the arrest.'

Temporary staff agencies are an obvious means through which to plant agents, where qualifications and bona fides are often taken on trust, and never checked, either by the agencies or their clients.

Tape recordings, voicemail, digital answer-phones and other audio formats have featured in several cases of information leakage and disclosure. Mini-cassettes, as used in Dictaphones, are also easily overlooked. Memoranda, for example, often originate on tapes, before being forwarded for transcription.

Confidential information also leaks, not through malicious intent, but through simple oversights, or in unexpected ways that are difficult to anticipate or predict:

> (i) A defensive briefing strategy had leaked during a hostile takeover bid and investigators were called in to find out how the leak occurred and to identity the culprit. During the course of their investigation, notebooks were retrieved from the company's rubbish. The source of the leak was one such notebook – a PA had annotated the leaked briefing paper in Pitman shorthand before transcribing it on her computer. She had thrown the notebook away, failing to appreciate its significance. Agents contracted by the hostile bidding group had discovered it while scavenging through the company's waste.

Whiteboards and flip charts such as those used in seminars and at strategy meetings can also prove hazardous. A huge amount of information will be generated during a typical brainstorming session, all of which may be retrieved by an opponent, particularly if left in a public place such as a hotel conference suite.

Discarded hardware, equipment, tapes and disks are clearly a potential risk (see Chapter 5), as are typewriters:

> (i) The computer forensic expert journeyed across London with instructions to back up the suspect's PC, but when the door to the suspect's office was unlocked, no computer could be found. A wasted journey, it seemed. In the corner of the room under a plastic dust cover was a large electric typewriter. He reported this to the case manager who instructed that the machine be secured and delivered to a forensic laboratory. An examination of the strike indentations on the typewriter ribbon revealed 24 fraudulent invoices.

Microphones, concealed or overt, are also hazardous. In April 2005 HRH Prince Charles infamously described the press as 'these bloody people' within range of a battery of microphones, whilst in 2000 George W. Bush decried a journalist as 'a major league asshole from the *New York Times'*. It is also technically easy to intercept broadcast transmissions outside of seemingly enclosed forums where public announcement systems are used. Telephone tapping, bugging and covert recording are all realistic threats – particularly during mergers and acquisitions, where there is boardroom infighting, impending product launches, proposed joint ventures, or during periods of industrial unrest and upheaval. A qualified and trusted electronic counter-measures team should sweep boardrooms and other sensitive meeting areas accordingly.

Remember also that computer screens may be observed through windows either at street level or from adjacent buildings using binoculars or a telescope. Turn screens inwards!

HAZARDOUS METADATA

One of the more oblique and unexpected routes by which sensitive information may leak is through *metadata*. This is a little understood risk that pertains to any individual or organization that transmits electronic documents as it can result in the unwitting disclosure of data that is embarrassing or potentially litigious.

Microsoft Word files contain within their coding significant information (called metadata) about each document's origin, history and provenance. Much of this metadata is not apparent through the Microsoft Word software interface and can only be seen using specialist software.

Word 97, in particular, was notorious for the wealth of information that could be gleaned from its metadata. In February 2003, for example, the Blair government published a dossier entitled *Iraq – its Infrastructure of Concealment, Deception and Intimidation*, which was subsequently quoted by the US Secretary of State Colin Powell in an address to the United Nations as proof of Saddam's brutality and mendacity. It was soon discovered, however, that much of the material in this dossier was plagiarized from a research dissertation written by one Ibrahim al-Marashi, a postgraduate student.[4] In its introduction the dossier claimed to have been derived from official intelligence sources, but was quickly ridiculed as the 'dodgy dossier', due to its obvious plagiarism and dubious origin.

Prime Minister Blair's government made an additional blunder by releasing the dossier as a Microsoft Word file on the number 10 Downing Street website. An interested reader, Richard M. Smith, downloaded the file and examined its metadata.[5] Mr Smith extracted the file's revision log (see Figure 3.7), which recorded the previous ten iterations of the document.

Rev. #1: "cic22" edited file "C:\DOCUME~1\phamill\LOCALS~1\Temp\AutoRecovery save of Iraq - security.asd"
Rev. #2: "cic22" edited file "C:\DOCUME~1\phamill\LOCALS~1\Temp\AutoRecovery save of Iraq - security.asd"
Rev. #3: "cic22" edited file "C:\DOCUME~1\phamill\LOCALS~1\Temp\AutoRecovery save of Iraq - security.asd"
Rev. #4: "JPratt" edited file "C:\TEMP\Iraq - security.doc"
Rev. #5: "JPratt" edited file "A:\Iraq - security.doc"
Rev. #6: "ablackshaw" edited file "C:\ABlackshaw\Iraq - security.doc"
Rev. #7: "ablackshaw" edited file "C:\ABlackshaw\A;Iraq - security.doc"
Rev. #8: "ablackshaw" edited file "A:\Iraq - security.doc"
Rev. #9: "MKhan" edited file "C:\TEMP\Iraq - security.doc"
Rev. #10: "MKhan" edited file "C:\WINNT\Profiles\mkhan\Desktop\Iraq.doc"

Figure 3.7   The revision log of the 'dodgy dossier'

The revision log listed the last ten edits of a document, showed the names of the people who worked with the document and the various filenames that the document went under.

A reporter soon identified the names shown in the revision log. It transpired that Paul Hamill was a Foreign Office official, John Pratt was a Downing Street official, Alison Blackshaw was the personal assistant to the Prime Minister's press secretary and Murtaza Khan was a press officer for the Prime Minister. The 'cic22' referred to in the first three entries of the revision log was identified as the Communications Information Centre, a department of 10 Downing Street run at the time by Alastair Campbell, Blair's press secretary. This was proof that the dodgy dossier never originated from the intelligence agencies. The Word version of the dossier was hurriedly removed from the 10 Downing Street website and reissued in the more secure PDF format. Mr Campbell, however, was brought before a parliamentary committee to explain his role in the dodgy dossier, its plagiarism and the tell-tale revision log.[6]

---

4   http://www.casi.org.uk/discuss/2003/msg00457.html.

5   Mr Smith's article is at www.computerbytesman.com/privacy/blair.htm.

6   This blunder was not an isolated incident. The US Army and the Multi-National Corps-Iraq released an official report on the shooting of Nicola Calipari, the Italian military intelligence agent shot by US troops at a roadblock in Baghdad in March 2005. The report was posted in PDF format to the coalition's website. The Italian press quickly discovered that the redactions in the report – which blacked out about a third of the text – were done insecurely and that the text, including that 'hidden' by the attempted redaction, could be cut and pasted from the PDF document in its entirety thereby revealing the identities of all the soldiers involved and other classified data.

Metadata also records the user and affiliation to which the software was originally registered, the created, modified, saved and printed times and dates of the file, the make and model of the printer used to print the document, and (in Word 97) a record called the PID_GUID, which shows the Network Interface Card inserted in the computer at the time that the document was created, and a unique document reference. The PID_GUID has proven useful in tracing the common genealogy of documents as this identifier is transferred from a previous document to a subsequent iteration derived from it when the 'Save As' option is invoked.

Editorial amendments to documents may also be recorded. In this respect, the 'Track Changes' and 'Fast Save' options within Word are particular risks.

For the security minded, metadata may be stripped from a wide range of data formats automatically using tools such as the BEC LegalBar Metadata Scrubber (http://www.beclegal.com/lsy/lsylegspeclegbarmetadata.asp) and Workshare Protect (http://www.workshare.com/products/wsprotect/default.aspx). It is no coincidence that the legal profession was the most vocal in demanding such protection.

Information security versus IT security

In recognition of the diversity of ways and channels by which information may leak or be misappropriated, many organizations have appointed an information security manager (ISM). The ISM is responsible for the safeguarding of *all* information within the company, regardless of its format.

There is clearly little point emphasizing IT security in an environment where printed documentation is not controlled, or conversely, introducing a clear-desk policy where the computer network is wide open to intrusion or misuse.

- It is vitally important to protect information in all of its various formats; IT security is essential, but it is only one building block in the defensive wall.

The ISM manages the information security department, which coordinates and oversees the IT security function, as well as being responsible for all aspects of counter-espionage and non-technical information security, document and archive control and information security training and awareness.

POLICIES AND PROCEDURES

The erosion of employee loyalty, when combined with managerial complacency or inattention, greatly exacerbates the risks of data theft and the deliberate leaking of information.

Commonplace managerial failings include:

- lack of managerial understanding, awareness or interest about the gravity of these risks;
- failure to screen job applicants to ensure their identity, qualifications and suitability;
- contractual weaknesses for employees and others with access to systems, processes and data;
- failure by organizations explicitly to assert the ownership and copyright of their intellectual property;

- the absence of clear reporting lines, written disciplinary procedures and guidelines outlining acceptable employee behaviour and computer use;
- ineffective people management skills, which can lead to perceived or justifiable grievances that may fester and manifest themselves in acts of sabotage or subterfuge;
- poor or non-existent exit procedures when employees depart the workplace.

It is necessary, therefore, to promote a culture of good practice and to signal the types of behaviour that the organization deems unacceptable. Ensure that the organization's written employment contract carries clauses covering the use of computers, software, the Internet and electronic mail. This policy is the keystone that underpins all other protective measures, whether technical or procedural (see Appendix 2).

It is essential that the employment contract is unequivocal and explicit in defining and asserting the organization's IP and its copyright. Likewise, contracts with third parties engaged in the development of IP should be clear and incontestable. Contracts should be drafted by qualified lawyers and enforceable by law.

Reporting lines for all employees should be clearly defined, so that any concern or suspicion of espionage, information theft or other impropriety is conveyed to the appropriate department.

Pre-employment screening is an effective control to identify undisclosed personnel factors that may pre-dispose an individual to criminality, dishonesty or fecklessness. It is a truism that the best way to avoid being a victim of fraud, theft and dishonesty is not to employ the fraudulent and the dishonest, or to do business with them. Pre-employment screening should uncover:

- past criminality
- falsified and exaggerated qualifications
- concealed bankruptcy
- debt and poor credit rating
- conflict of interest, that is, undisclosed business and commercial interests elsewhere
- civil litigation involving the candidate
- drug and alcohol problems
- dismissal from previous places of employment
- disciplinary hearings
- dishonesty or fecklessness in previous employment
- County Court judgments and small claims against the candidate.

Background checking of candidates seeking employment and those already recruited and with access to sensitive information or processes should be undertaken where practicable. The intensity of this checking should be commensurate with the sensitivity of the position sought or occupied, and the level of access to critical information or processes that is envisaged.

Regular performance appraisals are useful because they may highlight minor grudges, which if left unattended, may escalate into serious grievances and wilful acts of sabotage or subterfuge. Managers should be on the lookout for unusual behaviour by individuals, which may indicate incipient problems.

Some businesses, notably airlines and other safety critical operations, have introduced random alcohol and drugs testing. The relative benefits and jurisdictional legality of such testing should be assessed and established, as this control has proved effective in identifying high-risk employees.

In high-security facilities it may be advisable to conduct random searches of personnel and their possessions entering and leaving the premises. In many jurisdictions, personal searches are considered an infringement of civil liberties and human rights. Any proposal to conduct searches will therefore require the assent of legal counsel.

All employees should be formally notified of any items specifically banned from the premises such as cameras, mobile telephones, data storage devices and other prohibited items. Prominent notices to this effect should be exhibited at the entrances to the premises concerned.

Exit procedures should be devised and implemented to ensure that departing employees are forbidden access to corporate data, systems and processes. HR and IT should have formal notification and advisory procedures to ensure that exposed systems and processes are secured against misuse by departing employees (see Chapter 19).

Conclusion

The objective is to ensure the security of all sensitive and confidential information, in whatever format, whether static or in transit. This is a broader and more complex requirement than is evident in most IT security regimes, and requires a distinct mindset and enhanced perception about where risk actually resides. This requirement is not new – it has been known for years – but many businesses persist with the conventional model where IT security operates in isolation of other protective efforts.

In enhancing information security, relatively simple measures, such as a clear-desk policy, enforced password changes and the mandatory use of shredders, have been shown to have a disproportionate impact. They have the additional benefit of being relatively cost effective, easy to implement and to enforce. Additional recommendations to enhance information security and mitigate the risks of hostile espionage efforts appear in Appendix 5.

In the next chapters we will look in more detail at some of the relatively low-tech exposures that account for many real world information security breaches. By mitigating these common threats – trash scavenging, password misuse, wireless LAN interception and old-fashioned trickery and deceit – we may begin to impose a semblance of good order.

4 *Password Misuse*

Your password must be at least 18770 characters and cannot repeat any of your previous 30689 passwords. Type a password that meets these requirements in both text boxes.
Microsoft knowledge base article 276304, November 2003

This chapter illustrates the shortcomings of password-based authentication systems and explains some of the tactics that may be used by an intruder to gain access to systems.

The mundane nature of most computer misuse is not widely appreciated by people outside of the IT industry. Many instances of unauthorized systems access and impersonation are caused by common password theft or misappropriation.

Case studies

As the following case studies show, passwords are often misappropriated by guile, through simple deceit or by the use of commonly available software tools.

THE 'SOPHISTICATED HACKER'

'My client is the chairman of a stockbroking firm in the city. His electronic mail has been broken into and messages opened and read. My client was skiing at the time and he has no remote access to e-mail. The only other person with legitimate access is his PA who raised the alarm this morning. I suspect a sophisticated hacker is at work. You and your Tiger team are to conduct a thorough investigation and report back to me urgently.'

The investigator smiled wryly at the term 'Tiger team' and the pompous reference to 'a sophisticated hacker' – he doubted it.

The network event log had recorded the intrusion. The investigator searched for the chairman's account activating on the days when he was known to be on holiday and without access to the system. Sure enough, the account activated shortly after midday on the day of the intrusion and logged off approximately 30 minutes later. The workstation address of the login was also recorded. Notable, also, was the activity of another user at the same workstation at the time of this intrusion. The investigator observed a USERID – 'JONESC' – log out immediately prior to the chairman's log in, and log in again after the chairman's subsequent log off.

The workstation address was assigned to a computer located in a Mr Jones' office. When interviewed, Jones confessed to hacking into the chairman's mailbox by misusing his boss's password. He was unaware that he could have logged on with the chairman's

USERID while simultaneously active on the system in his own right. As a 'sophisticated hacker', this particular culprit was in a league of his own.

It transpired that a temporary PA to the chairman had disclosed the password while drinking in a local pub. She had since left the company, but nobody thought to change it.

As in this case, people, in writing or in conversation, often disclose passwords. The information is sometimes wilfully volunteered to expedite a particular task or for the sake of convenience. Revoking redundant computer accounts and changing passwords to remote access systems is fundamental to security. This failure frequently results from inadequate communication between human resources and IT when an employee leaves the company. The consequences can be commercially onerous:

SOMEONE ON THE INSIDE

The managing director was clearly agitated and perplexed: 'Our major competitor must have someone on the inside – they know our every move. Within hours and even minutes of us posting new prices on the stock control database they have updated their own prices to undercut us. We think that someone's stealing the database and selling it to them, or forwarding the price changes to them somehow.'

The cause of the leak was, in fact, elementary. The former MD of the company had left eighteen months earlier to set up in direct competition. No one had revoked his remote computer access, the password to the stock control system had never been changed and there was no audit trail of who accessed it. During a sting operation, investigators covertly filmed the departed MD online to the stock control database, flaunting its lack of security from the privacy of his new office.

Early misdiagnosis of the symptoms of computer crime and a failure to seek obvious routes by which passwords may be divulged have, on occasion, frustrated investigative efforts:

'IMPACT'

A chemical plant suffered a succession of debilitating network intrusions. Someone had broken into the plant's Shiva LAN Rover dial-in port and disabled remote access accounts, thereby denying certain users access to the network.

The IT manager had monitored network traffic to determine whether the intruder was using packet-sniffing software to intercept and decrypt passwords as they were broadcast over the network. These tests were inconclusive. He was at a loss to explain the attacks and eventually the plant's management team sought external assistance.

Investigators ascertained that the Shiva LAN Rover was controlled by a password – 'IMPACT' – and that this had not been changed since the system's installation.

Members of the IT team were interviewed separately. Each interviewee was asked whether he could recall any other strange or seemingly unrelated incidents on the network. A number of interviewees volunteered that clusters on the network had crashed intermittently, causing major disruption. These crashes were attributed to power outages. When pressed on the issue, however, many of the interviewees admitted that this explanation was improbable. As a result, the investigators inspected the controller software for the Cisco routers. Significantly, the administrative password for the routers was also 'IMPACT' and it too had not been changed since installation.

Two independent and unrelated systems had been attacked and both shared a common factor – the same password. This was no coincidence.

The investigators now asked selected IT staff whether the password 'IMPACT' was widely known or used, or whether it was written in any electronic or printed document. Later the same day, a Microsoft Word document was found in an open access directory on the server. It read:

Router configuration password = IMPACT

The date on which this document was last accessed corresponded with the date of the first network cluster crash. The hacker, it seems, read the document that morning and hacked the network in the afternoon.

In this case, the IT manager concluded, wrongly, that passwords were being 'sniffed'. Similarly, the network crashes were incorrectly attributed to power failures. This diagnosis, doubted by many, was not challenged. Crucially, the IT staff overlooked the causative link between disparate attacks on dissimilar systems.

The availability of hacking software on the Internet further undermines password security. Amateur computer hackers or 'script kiddies' as they are patronizingly referred to, may avail themselves of a plethora of password 'crackers'. Computer professionals also use these tools, primarily to recover passwords forgotten by users.

Official pronouncements from manufacturers about password protection are often misleading or disingenuous in this respect. Here, for example, is what Microsoft says on the subject:

Microsoft support engineers cannot help you retrieve passwords that have been lost or forgotten and applied to files and features in Microsoft products. Some third-party companies claim to be able to circumvent passwords that have been applied to files and features that Microsoft programs use. For legal reasons, we cannot recommend or endorse any one of these companies. If you need help to break or to reset a password, you can locate and contact a third-party company for this help. You use such third-party products and services at your own risk.

In fact, Microsoft Office software remains extremely vulnerable to cryptographic attack (see Figure 4.1):

Despite claims that Office XP documents are protected by better passwords than those of earlier versions, AOXPPR [a password recovery suite from Elcomsoft Inc.] can recover XP's passwords even more quickly than ever. [...] Whether you're dealing with a user who forgot their password, a file that was created by an employee who left the company, a document that was password protected by a disgruntled employee, or a file that is part of a legal investigation, AOXPPR provides the tools to recover it.

Government Technology magazine

Password successfully recovered !	☒
Advanced Office 2000 Password Recovery Professional statistics:	

Total passwords	2097935
Total time	1m 53s 563ms
Average speed (passwords per second)	18473
Password for this file	Silvia
Password in HEX (unicode)	5300 6900 6C00 7600 6900 6100

☐ Save in unicode

✓ OK   💾 Save...

Figure 4.1   A dictionary attack

Password-protected Word documents and Excel spreadsheets regularly feature in investigations and the proven technical capability to decrypt these files is immensely valuable to investigators. Conversely, the inherent weakness of the encryption deployed in these products renders them ill-suited for protecting highly confidential information, a vulnerability unappreciated by many users:

FALSE SENSE OF SECURITY

The finance director had spent several weeks closeted in his office in the penthouse suite of the building. It was the financial year-end and a series of reports and projections were nearing completion including the much anticipated calculation and discretionary allocation of annual bonuses to the workforce. Speculation and gossip were rife. The FD had taken defensive measures to prevent any leaks. He worked throughout the period in an isolated office that was locked at all times when vacant. Furthermore, the Excel spreadsheets he used to calculate the bonuses were password protected on his computer and the backups were stored on diskettes in a safe. Unbeknown to the hapless FD, however, his computer ran on a network with Windows for Workgroup installed and contained a hard disk that was flagged as a *shared drive*, accessible from *any* other computer attached to the network. Predictably, the IT department had downloaded the confidential spreadsheets via the network and had long since broken the corresponding passwords using commercially available recovery software. They downloaded and decrypted the spreadsheets daily to monitor the FD's progress.

A proportion of 'cracker' tools employ 'brute force' attacks that systematically try every possible password combination and length to decrypt or authenticate. Others, such as LC5, compare hash values generated from millions of *known* passwords with the hash value of the *unknown* password, which is revealed once the hash values are matched. Many tools exploit known cryptographic weaknesses in specific software packages or operating systems. There is a vast array of user-friendly and extremely effective hacking software available on the Internet.

Passwords that rarely or never change feature regularly when computer misuse occurs. On a recent investigation the administrator password to an AS/400 system had not been changed for six years and was common knowledge throughout the IT department – not surprising then that someone misused the account to obtain access to confidential information. The problem persists: a series of fraudulent EFT transfers investigated by DGI in May 2004 occurred because the attacker knew the passwords necessary to raise and release unauthorized payments.

Because password compromise and subversion is so prevalent it is incumbent upon the investigator and security personnel to understand the many ways in which password-controlled authentication systems may be compromised or subverted.

Access control

Passwords in conjunction with a 'USERID' are the common prescription to secure logical access to computer systems and networks. Users, it is assumed, will select secure passwords and will willingly and unfailingly comply with good password discipline. Unfortunately, this is rarely the case.

The choice of password will determine its value. A weak password is one that is easy to determine. Dictionary passwords and names are best avoided. Some security experts extol the virtues of obscure acronyms or meaningless word associations. As usual, the security vulnerabilities often arise due to people, who generally resort to the familiar and the memorable.

Survey of commonly chosen passwords, City of London (*Source*: Compaq)

- sexual or abusive swearword or term (30%)
- partner's name or nickname (16%)
- favourite holiday destination (15%)
- favourite sports team or sports personality (13%)
- object on the person's desk (8%).

Even when they are compelled to choose non-dictionary passwords, a variation on words or names will usually be adopted. A handful of people can recall numeric or alphanumeric combinations more readily than words. However, the overwhelming majority of people find numeric passwords above five digits difficult to remember. The banking world is accustomed to the ATM cardholder who commits his PIN to paper, or even those who write it on the ATM card itself (see Figure 4.2).

Figure 4.2   Stupidity accounts for many security breaches

DGI encounters plaintext passwords written down in diaries or other paperwork within the vicinity of approximately 3 per cent of the computer systems that the company investigates. The ubiquitous Post-it™ note is the most common culprit.

Mainframe, minicomputer and microcomputer network operating systems enable system administrators to impose a relatively rigorous password regime.

Table 4.1   Typical access control configuration

Control	Access control parameters Value
Power-on password	Activate on PCs and laptops
Network password	Configure
Dictionary words	Disallow
Minimum password	6 characters
Maximum password	8 Characters
Alphanumeric/symbol password	Yes
Alphanumeric/symbol password fixed position	Yes
Consecutive characters	2 characters repeatable
Prohibited characters	All keyboard characters permissible
Fixed position repeated character between old and new password	Allowed
Reused passwords	Prohibited
Password expiration	30 days
Intruder lockout	After 3 failed login attempts
Disable device and user profile upon lockout	Activate
Concurrent logins with the same USERID	Disallow
Administrator device access	Administrator login is fixed to a dedicated workstation in a secure area
Time-out	Activated after 5 minutes of user inactivity elapse
Dynamic IP addressing	Disable where practicable
System diskette or CD boot-up	Disable (except for administrator)
User availability	07:00 – 01:30

Through the enforcement of strict logical access control regimes the user is strait-jacketed into using alphanumeric, case sensitive, non-dictionary passwords that expire every thirty days, that allow (or disallow) consecutive characters, forbid the use of real names or places and so on. Unfortunately, it is a universal truth that the more complex the criteria necessary to formulate the password, the greater will be the temptation for the user to write the password down – a veritable vicious circle. Again, enter, stage right, the humble Post-it™ note.

Even though the more sophisticated operating systems enable a relatively high degree of access control, experience has consistently shown that intruders continue to gain access to systems and networks to which they have no authorization.

Password disclosure matrix

The reliance upon static passwords to authenticate users makes computers and interface software vulnerable to intentional or accidental password disclosure. Passwords may be written down, disclosed verbally, observed when entered at the keyboard ('shoulder surfing'), obtained by deception ('social engineering') or disclosed using software and hardware tools. For these reasons, static passwords should *never* be used to authenticate electronic funds transfer systems or any other form of high security processing.

Table 4.2   Methods of compromising passwords

	Non-technical attacks and exposures	
Methods	*Indications*	*Prevention and detection*
1. Guessing		
Tedious, inefficient but occasionally successful way to crack a system	Repeated intruder lockouts shown in network activity logs or audit trails	Repeated guessing ('three strikes and you're out') should trigger a system lockout, disable the user account or workstation
The word 'password' is commonly used to access computers, as are sequential numbers, typically 123456 and so on		The event log should record all logins and logouts on the network, and this may be reviewed for intruder lockouts or other signs that the system is compromised
On many poorly administered systems the USERID is the same as its corresponding password		
2. Observation		
The keyboard is observed as the password is entered – directly or with a telescope, binoculars or video camera	The hacker may act suspiciously near the user and his workstation	A heightened user awareness to the risk of 'shoulder surfing' may be instilled as part of an ongoing computer security training and awareness campaign
		Turn computer screens and keyboards away from windows
3. Verbal disclosure		
Passwords are often divulged on the telephone, typically to expedite processing when the custodian is absent	Unless someone confesses, there is rarely any evidence that a password has been disclosed, other than a compromised system	Ongoing security training and awareness
Passwords are often shared for the sake of convenience		Users should be instructed never to tell anybody their passwords – easier said than done!
4. Written disclosure		
Written passwords are seen within the proximity of 3 in every 100 workstations	Written passwords are frequently seen in diaries, on Post-it™ notes and scraps of paper, in	Commonsense applies – the passwords to a BACS payments terminal and its software was

Unsuspecting users may also transmit passwords via e-mail

documents and instruction manuals, and in software configuration files

Spreadsheets are a particular risk – with departmental or processing passwords being recorded in a central registry

recently seen written on the front page of the BACS instruction manual, left unguarded in an open office!

Known plaintext passwords on systems that have been compromised may be searched for on associated servers, workstations, backup tapes and so on

5. Duress

The attacker may force the user to disclose a password or PIN – in extreme cases at gunpoint

Subjecting victims to duress is more common in ATM and street robberies, than to intrude into networks

People under duress usually show clear signs of distress

Some systems have 'duress passwords' – if the user is threatened, he enters the duress password instead of the assigned password, which automatically triggers an alarm at a monitoring station, thereby alerting central services of the security violation

6. Deception

The intruder obtains the password by deceiving the unsuspecting user into revealing it, either in person, by telephone, or more commonly using an e-mail pretext

Typically the intruder masquerades as an authorized user requiring urgent access

Favoured method of master hacker Kevin Mitnik. See Chapter 8, 'Social Engineering'

Computer security training and awareness campaign

7. Trash Search

Rubbish trawling, also known as 'dumpster diving', is commonly used by hackers to obtain USERIDs, passwords, organization charts, printouts, discarded hardware and software and other materials that will assist them

Rubbish trawling is believed to be the most common method of conducting industrial espionage

The unexplained disappearance of waste from commercial or residential premises

The theft may be recorded on CCTV

Users should never discard tapes, diskettes, CDs or storage devices that appear to be faulty. These devices can usually be read using specialist forensic or data recovery software

Redundant or malfunctioning computer storage devices, including hard disks, CDs, diskettes and so on should be referred to the appropriate IT department

All waste and documentation

should be destroyed using cross-cut shredders

Technical attacks and exposures

---

8. Embedded password

The password to an application is embedded or hard coded into its login or activation interface

This is a common threat with remote access software installed on laptop computers – the dial-in password is embedded and if the machine is connected to the network, the software will dial-in and be authenticated by default

Embedded passwords are usually shown in the login script in half-duplex

Typically a row of asterisks is shown in the password field, that is, *******, with each asterisk representing a single character of the password

Embedded passwords should be audited and removed from systems – particularly from laptops and mobile systems with remote access software installed

---

9. Phishing

The user is deceived into entering his password, account or credit card details into a false website that mimics a genuine online banking or customer services website, or corporate technical support service

Phishing is a form of host emulation – see 14

The deception is usually initiated by an inbound e-mail from the fraudster masquerading as a legitimate operator

Phishing is a significant threat to online banks and their customers

Users should be wary of responding to any request sent by electronic mail from an unknown sender, and should never respond to an unsolicited request for confidential information or passwords

---

10. Spyware

Spyware may record and transmit keystrokes from a compromised computer to the attacker who may reap a host of application and on-line access passwords as a result

Remote system monitoring may be conducted using commercial programs such as Red Hand, or may be accomplished using Trojan horse programs such as Back Orifice that install and execute without the user's knowledge

The user may notice degraded system performance

The compromised computer may also crash due to memory conflicts

A software audit should detect keyboard-monitoring programs, Trojan horses and other spyware

There are several commercial and free spyware detection and removal tools available on the Internet

Google search: 'spyware detection'

Virus detection software will also detect many strains of malicious 'spyware'

For comprehensive protection, it

is recommended that several detection programs are used

11. Hardware interception

Keystrokes are intercepted and recorded using a hardware based I/O device

This is the simplest and easiest way to guarantee password disclosure

The latest I/O devices transmit intercepted keystrokes to a remote receiver

The Keyghost™ can intercept the first 2 million keys input at the keyboard and costs less than $200

A hardware inspection should detect any unauthorized device

Note that these devices may be hard-wired *inside* the keyboard, which makes them more difficult to detect

12. Packet interception

On some legacy systems and networks the authentication session is transmitted in plaintext

USERIDs and passwords may thus be intercepted using 'sniffer' software executed on a 'promiscuous' computer attached to the network

Encrypted passwords intercepted in transmission may also be decrypted using utilities found on the Internet such as LC5 (see www.atstake.com)

A diagnostic analysis of network traffic using a monitoring tool such as LANalyser will determine whether or not login sessions are encrypted

This type of attack may be prevented by one-time password generators such as SecureID from RSA Security, or biometric authentication

Switched Ethernet LAN configurations are less vulnerable to packet interception than broadcast Ethernet configurations

13. Decrypt utility

Software is used to decrypt the master password registry

The SAM password registry on Windows NT may be decrypted using LC5, as may be passwords that are transmitted via NT networks that are encrypted using the standard LANMan hash issued by Microsoft

LC5 is commonly found in IT departments and is distributed as an audit tool

A software audit should detect both authorized audit software and unauthorized hacking utilities

The master SAM file is always located on the server and the attacker can only compromise the file by gaining direct access to its host

Fileservers should always be located in restricted access areas to which only authorized staff have access

14. Host emulation

This is a false user interface that masquerades as a genuine login screen and captures USERIDs and passwords as they are entered by the user

False login screens are commonly found in older non-Windows networks and in some Unix, VAX and mainframe environments

The user may notice a delayed or interrupted login, and may be informed that his first login attempt failed and be prompted to re-enter his password

A software audit should detect host emulation programs

---

15. Unrestricted utilities

The hacker is granted administrator privileges by running a program assigned administrator privileges located in an area of the system accessible at a lower level

High level diagnostic, editing and maintenance utilities are found on AS/400, Unix, VAX and mainframe systems; these require careful control and supervision

Powerful editing utilities have been misused to commit many computer frauds where standing data has been amended

In such cases, these utilities should be suspected and searched for

A computer audit should identify unrestricted utilities and executables, and those assigned administrator privilege

---

16. Generic, dormant and default accounts

User accounts remain valid on systems after the assigned users have left the organization

Temporarily assigned accounts may remain active beyond the required period

Generic, dormant and default accounts are frequently encountered on AS/400 systems, older versions of Unix, VMS and IBM mainframes

These computer accounts are often redundant, or are the default accounts shipped by the manufacturer of the operating system, which have never been changed

A computer audit of assigned users and privileges will identify accounts vulnerable to misuse

Exit procedures should include the immediate removal of the ex-employee's assigned computer account and remote access account and the return of any authentication tokens

---

17. Unix root password

On older Unix networks the Supervisor (SU) password is transmitted in plaintext when a Telnet or FTP connection is

This vulnerability can be tested using a network traffic analysis program such as LANalyser

Telnet and FTP should be configured to deny root access on Unix systems

established and this may be intercepted using a sniffer program		All login sessions should be encrypted

18. Covert surveillance of keyboard

Video cameras may be hidden in ceiling space above workstations Security CCTV may overlook sensitive computer operations such as Finance or R&D	Security CCTV and video surveillance may inadvertently record users working at computer keyboards	Covert cameras should be detected during a counter-surveillance inspection A CCTV audit should be conducted to ensure that coverage is appropriate, and that pictures are properly lit, in focus and correctly time-stamped

19. Forensic analysis

Plaintext passwords processed in RAM may be inadvertently copied to disk slack space Plaintext passwords can be extracted from file slack space using forensic tools Embedded passwords may be extracted and login and application passwords decrypted from computers that are examined forensically	If conducted professionally, there will be no indication on the target computer that any forensic image copy or analysis has occurred	The use of forensic disk-purging tools can destroy residual data remnants in slack space Computer audit should identify and invalidate embedded passwords Total disk encryption on laptops will thwart forensic efforts

Many IT professionals have encountered 'host emulation' programs that mimic the operating system login screen, store the USERID and password as they are entered, and then broadcast an error message before terminating and restoring control to the genuine operating system. The user, believing he has mistyped his password or USERID, proceeds to login without further thought and is entirely unaware that the dummy interface has intercepted his password for subsequent retrieval and misuse (see Figure 4.3).

Ignorance also leads to a false sense of security. Many Microsoft Windows users live under the false premise that the screen saver password is secure. They are unaware that Windows can be revoked by soft booting (Ctrl-Alt-Del) the computer twice in succession or by booting the machine from a system diskette.

Having gained access to the DOS prompt the attacker has full access to every file or directory on the computer. On many versions of Windows total access to the system may be gained simply by switching the machine off and restarting it. One hapless individual, angry at evident tampering on her computer, entered the screen saver banner 'DO NOT TOUCH – PASSWORD PROTECTED!' Upon arrival the next day, she was dismayed to see her intended admonishment flickering across the screen: 'DO NOT TOUCH – PASSWORD PROTECTED – NOT!'

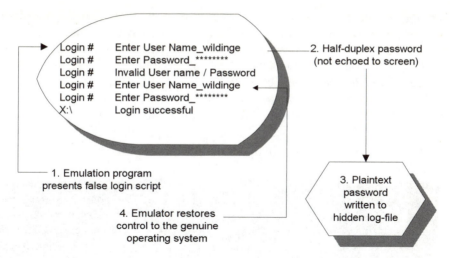

Figure 4.3   Host emulation

Similarly, many network users mistakenly presume that the network login screen will prevent a potential intruder from gaining access to the information stored on their local hard disk.

Network administrators may neglect password controls by failing to set up policies (see Figure 4.4). With the default configuration shown, passwords may be re-used *ad infinitum*, blank passwords are permitted and accounts subjected to consistent failed logins are not disabled.

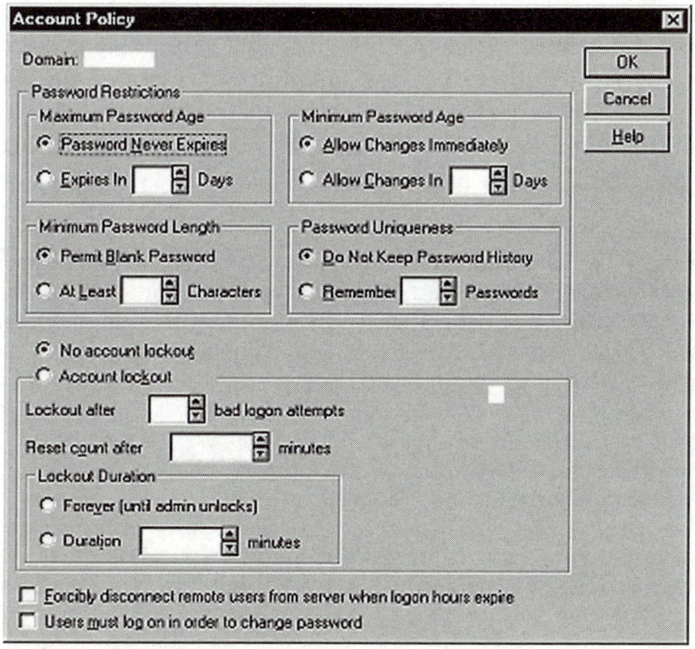

Figure 4.4   Windows NT Account Policy

The 'top ten' list of commonest computer passwords in use varies somewhat between surveys, cultures and generations. There are dozens of password libraries available on the Internet. The Internet worm program that propagated itself so successfully in 1988 used a password library consisting of the 600 most prevalent Unix passwords to gain unauthorized access to approximately 6000 host computers. Many older operating systems were shipped with default user accounts that were never subsequently removed or properly safeguarded by a change of the shipping password. These default accounts, which are generic and widely posted and known within the hacker fraternity, are a particular threat to systems security (see Figure 4.5 – passwords shown here in full duplex for clarity).

```
LBL>telnet elxsi
Elxsi at LBL
login: root
password: root
incorrect password, try again
login: guest
password: guest
incorrect password, try again
login: uucp
password: uucp
WELCOME TO THE ELXSI COMPUTER AT LBL
```

Figure 4.5   Password hacking

Imposing password discipline is fraught with difficulties. One of the most profound threats to password-based security and authentication systems is posed by the widespread availability of 'cracker' software tools and utilities. Password cracking tools (euphemistically described as 'audit utilities') such as John the Ripper, Crack and Satan will be only too familiar to many of this book's readers. These tools are shockingly effective at decrypting USERIDs, passwords and registries, as systems administrators around the world will testify.

Many legacy computer systems and networks remain inherently vulnerable to password interception and compromise. In 1996, for example, a computer hacker waged a war against a utilities company that lasted for many months:

> The company ran a distributed Sun Solaris network. The hacker intentionally induced network crashes and caused random havoc by destroying data. He covered his tracks by disabling audit trail generation and by purging the network event logs. These attacks persisted despite repeated changes of the Supervisor (SU) password. The evidence suggested that the hacker was using packet 'sniffer' software on a promiscuous computer attached to the network to intercept passwords in transmission. Solaris is a Unix system and SU logins at the time were not encrypted. This critical exposure permitted the hacker to compromise the SU password with impunity. The attacks became increasingly brazen, assured and aggressive and profoundly undermined confidence in the system's integrity. The network administrator urged the company to implement authentication technology across the network to generate non-reusable authentication passwords, knowing this would defeat the hacker. His urgent request was resisted on budgetary grounds and only acted upon at the insistence of external security consultants.

Network traffic transmitted in plaintext is vulnerable to interception and enables a potential intruder to reap passwords with relative ease. There is a range of hacking programs that are effective at packet interception, particularly using the standard TCP/IP network transmission protocol. Encryption over the network reduces the risk of interception, depending on the strength of the encryption used. Most network traffic is broadcast in plaintext, and the majority of users are unaware of how easy and straightforward it is to intercept and read transmitted data and passwords.

L0phtCrack, a Windows NT password cracker originally released by the hacker group L0pht Heavy Industries, earned a formidable reputation amongst hackers due to its ruthless efficiency in breaking Windows NT passwords (see Figure 4.6), whether stored *in situ*, or intercepted in transmission over a network. The product, now called LC5, has since been acquired by Symantec Corporation. It is widely used to audit the security of networks.

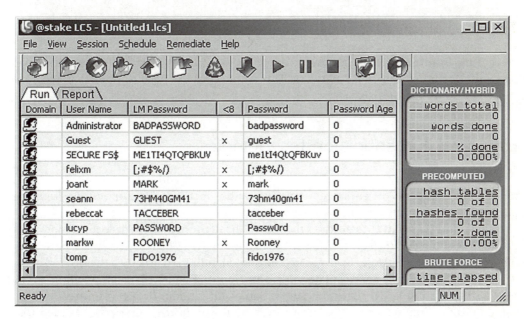

Figure 4.6   USERIDs and passwords decrypted using LC5 on a PC

LC5 includes an option called SMB Packet Capture which is used with a network card in a PC set to 'promiscuous mode' to intercept passwords sent across broadcast Ethernet networks (see Figure 4.7). Once a transmitted password has been intercepted, LC5 can be used to crack the hash in the normal fashion.

LC5 and other utilities such as John the Ripper exploit the cryptographic weaknesses of IBM's LanMan hash used to encrypt the Security Accounts Manager (SAM) file on Windows NT servers. The SAM file contains a list of all the USERIDs and passwords for the network domain. If an intruder can access the SAM file, and then uses a tool such as LC5, he can obtain unrestricted access to a list of valid USERIDs and passwords, including the Administrator account.

The SAM file is located on the server drive in the following paths:

```
c:\winnt\system32\config
c:\winnt\repair
```

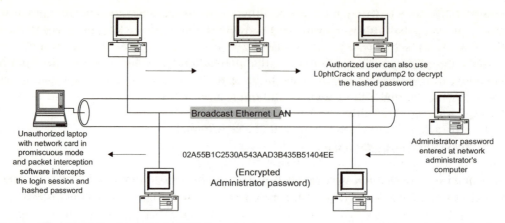

Authorized user can also use
L0phtCrack and pwdump2 to decrypt
the hashed password

Broadcast Ethernet LAN

Unauthorized laptop
with network card in
promiscuous mode
and packet interception
software intercepts
the login session and
hashed password

02A55B1C2530A543AAD3B435B51404EE

(Encrypted
Administrator password)

Administrator password
entered at network
administrator's
computer

Figure 4.7   L0phtCrack used on a LAN

Preventing an intruder from gaining access to the SAM file is clearly necessary to prevent password disclosure on any NT network. This emphasizes the need to physically secure the file server from unauthorized access.

Enhanced authentication technologies

The vulnerability of many networks to packet interception and password 'sniffing' has led to the development of enhanced authentication methods, incorporating 'one-time' password generators and biometric access controls.

A one-time password authenticates the user to the network for a single login session. When the login session ends, the one-time password expires, never to be reused. Expired passwords if intercepted cannot, therefore, be re-entered to gain unauthorized access to the network.

One-time passwords are calculated using an algorithm stored on a chip within a hand-held authentication token that processes variable and random data transmitted by a host computer or central server. A PIN known only by the authorized user protects each token from misuse.

Token-based authentication is widely used to secure corporate networks as it mitigates the risk of password interception when logging in to the network. RSA Security is an industry leader in this field (http://www.rsasecurity.com). The company's SecureID token is a 'two factor' authentication system based on something the user *knows* (the PIN) and something he *owns* (the token).

Even though the network login is protected using one-time passwords, any subsequent passwords to hosted or online applications, drives or files may still be intercepted using key-logging technology (see below). Bespoke solutions such as those offered by RSA Security are indicated to protect such resources. There remain, also, procedural risks with token-based authentication. PINs may be divulged and associated tokens stolen, lost, mislaid or pooled. In one instance, an 18-year-old input clerk had all of the SWIFT smartcards for the entire settlements department. Her response: 'People kept losing them, so it was decided it would be safer if I kept them.'

Biometric methods offer an alternative solution. Biometric authentication verifies the user by unique physical or behavioural characteristics, typically by comparing fingerprints or written signatures or through the use of retinal scans or voice recognition. 'Live and well' sensors pre-empt the misuse of amputated body parts while 'duress' sensors detect anxiety or fear, as would be expected should a user be forced to access a system at gunpoint.

Some biometric systems offer only marginal reliability or utility with a propensity for false-positives (incorrect user authentication) and false-negatives (incorrect user rejection). User-acceptance of this technology remains ambivalent.

Keyboard interception

The *guaranteed* way to intercept passwords in plaintext is to trap them during transmission through the input/output (I/O) ports of the computer itself, that is, *before* any process can be used to encrypt the password. This interception takes place before the computer is logged in to the network and before the operating system, other software or on-board firmware has executed, or interacted, with the data entered at the keyboard. Everything entered at the keyboard is captured, including BIOS[1] passwords, network login passwords, application passwords and ISP and on-line service passwords as well as any other text or keyboard instructions entered by the user. The USERIDs and passwords are captured exactly as typed, before any layer of encryption can be added. Key logging is not impaired by access control software or biometric authentication systems.

In early 2005, reports broke about two bank frauds where key-logging devices were used. In the first case, personal banking passwords were intercepted on a public access Internet banking workstation in South Africa. The second case reported in March 2005 was sensational:

> A criminal gang successfully hacked into the computer system of the London offices of the Japanese bank Sumitomo Mitsui in an audacious bid to steal £220 million. The gang reportedly tried to transfer funds electronically to ten bank accounts after breaking through the bank's computer security system using key-logging devices to obtain passwords. According to one theory, contract staff working in the evening attached the devices to computers in the bank's treasury department.

The interception of plaintext passwords in transmission has been a longstanding computer security exposure. IT security professionals are well aware of the short-comings of password-based regimes but are often prevented from introducing safer forms of user authentication due to budgetry restraints, managerial ignorance or indifference. In this respect, a demonstration of the KeyGhost[2] is guaranteed to dispel complacency, ignorance or obduracy.

- This device provides a cast-iron guaranteed method by which passwords may be intercepted – not via a network or on the server, but between the keyboard and the console.

KeyGhost does not impair or affect the resident system's functionality and it is invisible at the user interface. It cannot be detected using security software and its presence is

---

1   (Basic Input Output Services). These are power-on (hardware-based) passwords.
2   See www.keyghost.com (KeyGhost) and www.microspy.com (MicroSpy).

transparent to the user. The key-logging hardware can be connected to a target computer in seconds without the need to install any software or adjust any of the computer's hardware settings. The device has no moving parts, no settings or switches and it requires no batteries or external power supply (see Figures 4.8 and 4.9).

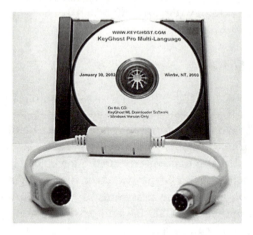

Figure 4.8   KeyGhost

2 million keystrokes are recorded – all passwords are captured

Figure 4.9   KeyGhost connected to a computer

The software to analyse the captured keystrokes is installed on to a designated inspection computer and extracts the intercepted data to a readily intelligible log file. The device is capable of storing up to 2 000 000 keystrokes. Versions of the device are available that provide 128-bit encryption, rendering the recorded log files secure against unauthorized browsing.

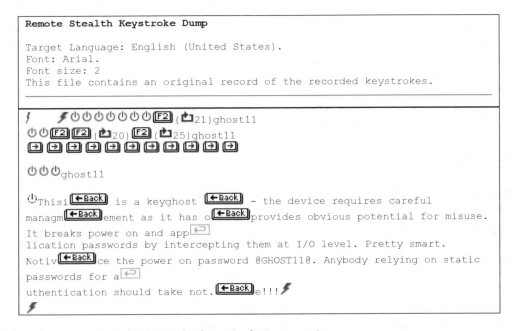

Figure 4.10 Remote stealth keystroke dump (verbatim extract)

KeyGhost is shipped as a module that is placed between the keyboard plug and the computer. However, the technology can also be placed *inside* the keyboard. The manufacturer states that it is developing a version capable of transmitting the captured keystrokes on a target computer in real time to a remote receiver.

Keyboard monitoring has an obvious role within law enforcement, security, audit and control to investigate suspected cases of electronic mail harassment, Internet misuse, computer fraud, the misappropriation of confidential data and IP and other computer crimes. The admissibility of evidence obtained using key-logging devices has not yet been determined in a UK court. In June 2002, however, a New Jersey court set a US legal precedent, when a district court judge ruled that the evidence obtained using a key-logging device against Nicodemo Scarfo for his role in an illegal gambling operation was admissible:

> In January 1999 FBI agents surreptitiously entered Mr Scarfo's office, but were confounded by his use of PGP encryption to protect computer files they believed would prove incriminating. The agents returned having obtained a search warrant that permitted them to install a key-logging device into his computer, which enabled them to obtain his password in plaintext when Mr Scarfo entered it at his keyboard. The search order from a federal magistrate judge stated that the FBI could:
>
> '...install and leave behind software, firmware, and/or hardware equipment, which will monitor the inputted data entered on Nicodemo S Scarfo's computer in the target location

> so that the FBI can capture the password necessary to decrypt computer files by recording the key related information as they are entered.'
>
> Defence lawyers argued, unsuccessfully, that keystroke logging was akin to a telephone wiretap, which the FBI never obtained.

KeyGhost is an extremely effective tool for conducting covert computer investigations and should dumbfound and unnerve anyone complacent or foolish enough to believe that a simple password-based authentication regime is secure.

On the flipside, these devices are potentially extremely dangerous if they fall into the wrong hands. Armed with this technology, a computer fraudster or criminal may cut through many networks effortlessly.

Conclusion

Password-authenticated systems and networks will deter opportunist or casual misuse. However, reusable passwords offer no profound control value and should never be used to authenticate any network, system or application through which high-value funds transactions may be executed, or where highly confidential data is processed or critical processes are developed or used.

A risk assessment is necessary to identify those network systems and applications which merit higher levels of security and in these cases the implementation of one-time password generators, biometric authentication or an alternative accredited authentication technology should be mandatory.

5 *Trash Risk*

The idea of strictly minding our own business is mouldy rubbish. Who could be so selfish?

Myrtle Barker, American journalist (b. 1910)

In seeking to exert control over a vulnerable employee, external parties may adopt a variety of simple but effective methods to obtain intelligence, access and influence. One of the most insidious and unnerving methods that is widely used is the surreptitious analysis of the contents of people's trash.

Intelligence collection

The collection and analysis of trash is the method of choice by those engaged in industrial espionage, providing intelligence not only about the targeted organization but also about its employees, key staff, managers, directors, shareholders and associates. Any intelligence gathered may subsequently be used to subvert or coerce key people considered to be malleable. The determined opponent will 'lift' commercial waste, and may also target the trash of designated individuals at their residential addresses.

The 'trash lift' is a method also used by hackers, fraudsters and other criminals, journalists and investigators from a variety of agencies and with differing agendas. It is essential that all concerned, and particularly those in sensitive positions or with privileged access to confidential information, are aware of these tactics and the necessity to defend themselves and their organizations from this subterfuge. Instances of trash scavenging have been particularly evident during corporate mergers and acquisitions and high-stake product developments and launches.

Domestic and office rubbish will often contain confidential and personal data while factory waste, such as packaging, off-cuts and by-products, can provide clues about manufacturing capacity, shipment volumes, processes and formulae. For example, the chemicals, or packaging, disposed of by a pharmaceutical plant may indicate the types of drug currently under development. Similarly, even the disposal of journals, periodicals, newspapers and other material in the public domain may assist an opponent in determining current projects, research and development, or the organization's commercial focus or strategy.

Trash scavenging is not limited to factory and office premises. Directors, senior executives and other key staff should be aware that their homes may be targeted and should exercise due caution when disposing of documents and data.

> (i) Perhaps the most widely publicized instance of trash analysis took place in 2000. Microsoft's rival, Oracle, was reported in the *Wall Street Journal* to have been behind attempts to bribe janitors into selling Microsoft's trash. Oracle admitted in statements that it had hired IGI, a private investigation firm that made two attempts to purchase office trash from the Association for Competitive Technology, a Microsoft-backed group. While not admitting direct involvement in the 'cash for trash' scheme, Oracle admitted it had hired IGI to investigate the ACT as well as other groups. A statement released by Oracle claimed that the groups 'were misrepresenting themselves as independent advocacy groups, when in fact their work was funded by Microsoft for the express purpose of influencing public opinion in favour of Microsoft during its antitrust trial'.

Some other publicized examples of compromised trash lifts have included:

- In 1991, two rubbish bags were removed from the house of Roger Carr, Chief Executive of Williams Holdings, when his company was trying to take over Racal Electronics, now Vodafone.
- In 2001, Procter & Gamble admitted that a company working on its behalf went through rubbish put out by Unilever, its fiercest rival, in an attempt to find out more about its hair care business. Procter & Gamble denied that its contracted company had misrepresented themselves to Unilever as market analysts.
- During a prolonged and acrimonious commercial spat between British Airways and Virgin Atlantic in the 1990s, BA hired detectives who rifled through various executives' domestic waste.

An invidious aspect of rubbish scavenging is that the criminal or spy may assemble a picture of the target's lifestyle in order to determine potential personal vulnerabilities. Credit information and evidence of indebtedness, excessive consumption of alcohol, lifestyle indicators and patterns of activity, indications of drug misuse, medical history, undisclosed criminality, sexual orientation or predilection may all be assessed from what is disposed of in domestic rubbish. This information may be used to coerce, blackmail or compromise the individual into disclosing confidential information, steal intellectual property, commit fraud or otherwise cause damage.

The hacking community refers to trash scavenging as 'dumpster diving' – a reference to the high capacity dumpsters used for waste collections by large organizations. Hackers scavenge though corporate waste in order to retrieve discarded computer equipment and software, which they can utilize, and to obtain information about their intended targets.

Many hackers regard dumpster diving as an essential preparatory step in conducting a computer intrusion. By analysing recovered trash the hacker gains significant intelligence about the target organization, sufficient to map out its structure, operations and activities with some accuracy. Significantly, the hacker may also be able to determine the interpersonal relationships within the organization, which he may attempt to subvert or manipulate. He may also glean technical details about the IT infrastructure, the computer and communications equipment that is installed and details about maintenance contracts and service agreements. Crucially, he will also attempt to harvest telephone numbers, passwords and account names.

When dumpster diving, hackers look for:

- Telephone lists – contact details
- Memos – background and developments
- Faxes and letters – correspondence
- Post-it notes – passwords and other scraps
- Organization charts – reporting lines and departments
- Staff lists – key personnel and job functions
- HR information – residential addresses, private telephone numbers, personnel records
- Work schedules – roles and assignments
- Shift rotas – predicted attendance, where, when and why
- Maintenance contracts and service agreements – useful for establishing a 'pretext' approach, masquerading as an engineer or contractor
- Company financial data – corporate bank accounts, electronic payments systems and so on
- Payroll data – private bank accounts
- Bonus payments information – useful background information
- IT security and policy manuals – incident response – how will the organization react to being hacked? What are the installed defences? Where are the weaknesses in its defences?
- Diaries and calendars of events – itineraries of key personnel, when they are on holiday or away
- Printouts of e-mails – intelligence
- System manuals – systems in use and their connectivity
- Equipment packaging – new systems being installed
- Printouts – source code, USERIDs, access privileges, passwords, database dumps
- Disks, tapes, CD-ROMs and memory – computer media with recoverable information. Hackers will often use discarded hard disks for their own storage purposes.

All of this information will be assembled in order to develop a convincing 'pretext' approach to an unwary computer user. This type of approach, known as 'social engineering', will usually be made by telephone but may also be initiated using e-mail. The hacker will pretend to be a member of staff, a contractor or a service engineer working for the victim organization. The hacker's knowledge of the organization will be comprehensive and thorough, enabling him to convince his target that he is a genuine insider with rights of access and authorization. Using subtle deception he will elicit passwords and authentication codes from unsuspecting users.

Source code is also often found in commercial waste – thrown out as part of the natural software development process.

If you don't look after your rubbish, someone else will! When it comes to waste, some very devious (and ingenious) practices have been noted:

> An information brokerage incorporated a waste reclamation company with the sole objective of obtaining competitive research data for its client. The company's trucks collected sacks full of microfiche and other confidential waste from the client's principal competitor on the supposition that it would be recycled or incinerated. Unbeknown to the victim company, the waste was delivered to the information brokerage for commercial, financial and technical assessment. For the privilege of having its waste processed so meticulously, the victim of this deception was invoiced several thousand pounds.

It would be a mistake to assume automatically that dumpster diving is illegal. Sentencing a private detective convicted of theft for removing rubbish from residential properties, Justice

Bernard Marder declared his distaste for this practice, declaring, 'An Englishman's rubbish is part of his castle and if his black bag is violated he has the right to bring theft charges against the culprit.' In the author's experience, however, reclaimed documents and other data have been ruled admissible in civil courts, provided that no trespass occurred during their collection. At the time of writing, domestic refuse left on a public highway in the United Kingdom is the property of the local Council. The intention permanently to deprive the Council of its property is a criminal offence under the Theft Act. If, however, discarded documents and data are copied, and the originals returned to the Council's waste ground, no offence has been committed. Many countries have not legislated on the privacy issues arising from discarded waste. The US Supreme Court has stated that there is no expectation of privacy once an item is left for garbage collection, but individual states, notably Hawaii (in *State v Tanaka*), New Jersey (in *State v Hempele* and *State v Goss*), Vermont (in *State v Morris*) and Washington (in *State v Boland*) have all ruled that their constitutions prohibit searches of garbage without a warrant.

As part of a security audit or review and having first obtained legal advice it may be worthwhile to hire an investigation company to lift corporate waste or the domestic refuse discarded by senior management and other personnel likely to be targeted by competitors, hackers, journalists, fraudsters et al. This exercise can provide a rare insight into the type of information that a determined hacker, journalist or spy could assemble about the organization and its key staff.

---

i   The security expert commenced the review by walking the perimeter of his client's premises. Peering through a ground floor window, he observed a report marked 'COMMERCIAL IN CONFIDENCE'. He photographed the top page, which was legible. He continued his inspection and halted outside an anteroom to the computer centre. The word 'MAGIC' was written in large letters on a whiteboard – evidently a password. This was a second significant finding in the first five minutes of the inspection.

Progressing towards the reception area, he took a look at the contents of a rubbish bin. Amid the discarded drinks cans, sweet wrappers, newspapers and other detritus, he found a bundle of printouts. Someone had thrown out a directory showing the name, job title, telephone extension, pager, mobile number and the USERID for every employee in the company. Breaking into the company's computer network would be simplicity itself.

Try this exercise yourself; you may be surprised at what you discover.

Disposal of documentation

It is always recommended that confidential documentation should be shredded. The use of line shredders is considered sufficient to deter all but the most determined opponent, but this method is by no means guaranteed.

David Browne of Berkeley Security Bureau is one of the UK's leading forensic document examiners. He spends a fair proportion of his time reconstructing shredded documents. This is what he says:

> *Line shredders are presumed secure but I have been able to reassemble shredded output from some makes and models. The fragments are typically 2 or 3 millimeters wide.*

Printed or handwritten characters are therefore intelligible or interpretable and there is just enough leverage to reassemble the text. Of course, some hapless folk rely on 'Mickey Mouse' shredders, which cut documents into strips an inch wide – need I say more?

Cross-cut shredders, which slice documents into minute fragments, offer a far higher assurance than line shredders that paper has been disposed of securely. Even they, however, are not infallible.

In 2002, following the Enron debacle, ChurchStreet Technology Inc., of Houston, Texas announced the imminent release of its software to automate the digital reconstruction of cross-cut waste. The company states that shredded remnants as small as 0.25 mm × 0.25 mm can be reassembled (see Figure 5.1). Should the ChurchStreet process be as effective as it is claimed, then it is a spectacular testament to the old adage, 'Where there's a will there's a way.'

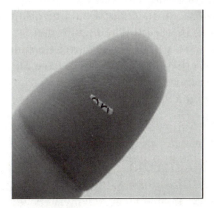

Figure 5.1   Cross-cut remnant. Photograph courtesy of ChurchStreet Technology Inc. (www.churchstreet-technology.com)

The hobby or practice of dumpster diving is not without its attendant risks. The websites that proffer advice on this activity warn of the extremely unpleasant nature of what often resides in the trash – particularly discarded food, sanitary items or human or animal waste. Disposed 'sharps' (syringe needles), razor blades, broken glass and other hazards are an ever-present risk to health and safety. Commercial waste, such as that thrown out by banks, law firms and accountants, is usually more palatable than domestic garbage, and often requires little or no sanitary processing – an altogether better class of rubbish as one would expect from such august institutions.

For obvious reasons, veteran dumpster divers advise against scavenging inside compactors or incineration chambers.

In implementing a defensive strategy, perhaps the most difficult task is to convince people that this threat even exists, which is strange because it is generally far easier to steal rubbish than it is to break into computer networks, tap telephones or bug conversations. A continual education and awareness effort is needed in this respect.

Practical defensive measures include:

- Encourage the shredding of all waste paper, regardless of its relative sensitivity.
- Purchase shredders appropriate to your needs.

- Cross-cut destruction is more secure than line shredding, but is not infallible.
- Computer printout and large volume waste may require a bulk shredder.
- Destroy all obsolete documents.
- Do not unreservedly trust confidential waste disposal and recycling companies. Such companies can be targeted or used to gather intelligence. If a third party is used for secure waste disposal, check that it carries out its duties properly.
- Shredders should be available at the homes of directors, senior management and key personnel.
- Do not discard any sensitive material in hotel rubbish bins or waste paper baskets, at airports, conference centres and so on
- If interesting or sensitive articles are removed from open source publications such as journals, magazines or newspapers, do not dispose of the remainder of the publication using a waste bin. Otherwise the original publication can be located and compared to identify precisely which article was removed and retained.
- Industrial or development scrap materials should be destroyed in a controlled manner where their destruction can be observed and confirmed.
- Cleaners are often targeted to gather intelligence. Consider using in-house, company-employed cleaners and security guards. They will have more loyalty and accountability and you have control over them.
- Periodically spot check commercial premises to evaluate the security of trash and waste disposal.

Disposal of computer media

Computers and data storage media clearly require secure disposal. The inadvertent disclosure of company confidential information or personal information is embarrassing, undermines client confidence and in many jurisdictions is unlawful – in the EU, for example, this is an offence under data protection laws. The failure to destroy data prior to the disposal of computers has on occasions led to severe embarrassment:

> In February 2000, an obsolete personal computer sold on by a bank contained 108 files relating to Sir Paul McCartney's private cash dealings. The PC was released for second-hand sale without first being wiped securely of financial data relating to the former Beatle. Merchant bank Morgan Grenfell Asset Management had 'simply failed to erase the memory contained on the computer's hard disk'. Other client details reportedly found on the PC included a 'large charity for the blind, the Cancer Research Campaign, the International Association of Odd Fellows and a duchess'. Deutsche Asset Management (as Morgan Grenfell Asset Management is now called) issued an unreserved apology to any clients embarrassed by the incident and promised an urgent review of its disposal procedures.

It is not sufficient simply to delete files on computers – the data remains *in situ* and may be restored using forensic software. Information is recovered every day from hard disks that have been subjected to concerted attempts at data elimination:

A suspected paedophile had taken steps to destroy incriminating video clips and stills from his computer. It was evident to the forensic examiner that the disk, seized during the execution of a search warrant, had recently been formatted, repartitioned and that a new operating system had been installed. No incriminating pictures could be seen on the freshly installed system. However, by running an EnCase[1] script that searched for graphics files in unallocated clusters on the disk, more than 11 000 photographs were recovered, many of them clearly illegal.

The recommended procedure for wiping data from hard disks, diskettes and magnetic computer media is that it is purged using dedicated data cleansing software. Positive erasure involves overwriting data stored on magnetic disk so that its polarity is changed. There are data recovery consultancies that claim that they can recover data that has been erased positively. The author has seen no proof of these claims – highly specialized laboratory equipment would be required to locate and read residual magnetism on disk and the costs to do this appear to be prohibitively expensive. For most practicable purposes, the content of a file or disk that is erased positively is irretrievable.

Positive erasure options may be specified to varying degrees of security (see Figures 5.2, 5.3 and 5.4), including:

- A quick, single-pass sanitation method that overwrites all data with zeros. This type of sanitation prevents the use of software data recovery tools. This is the US Department of Defense's approved method for cleansing disks but it is not suitable for sanitizing disks with secret information.
- A high security but slower sanitation method, matching US Department of Defense standard DOD 5220.22-M, that overwrites the targeted data with seven passes. This method prevents the use of software and hardware data recovery tools.

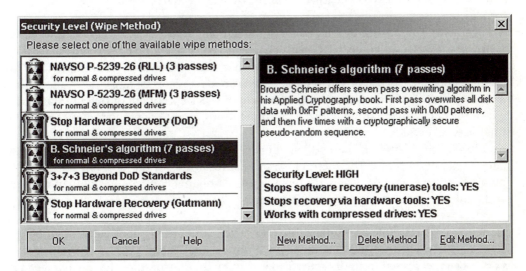

Figure 5.2   CyberScrub™ data purging software tool

---

1   EnCase is an industry standard forensic software suite manufactured by Guidance software.

Figure 5.3   Positive erasure of data with a repeated character

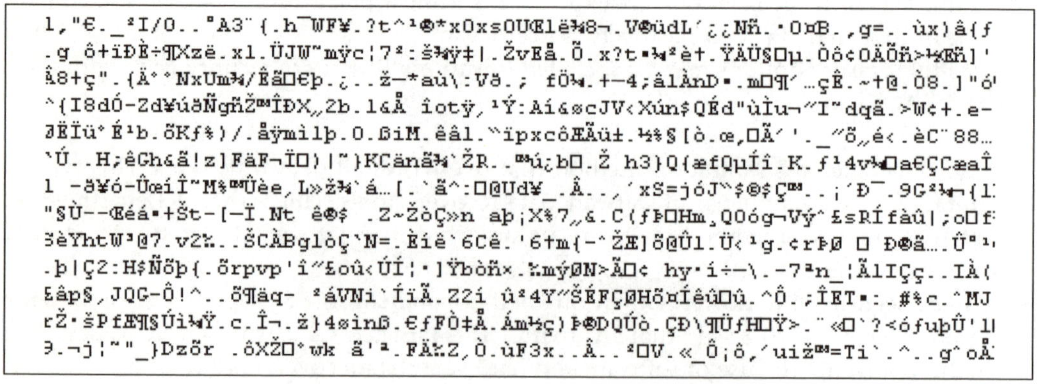

Figure 5.4   Pseudo-random output generated by the Gutmann erasure process

- An overwriting algorithm developed by Bruce Schneier in his book *Applied Cryptography*. A first pass overwrites all disk data with character FFh, a second pass with character 00h, and then five further passes are completed with a secure pseudo-random sequence. This method prevents the use of software and hardware data recovery tools.

- A secure but slow sanitation method, exceeding the US Department of Defense standards, where the data is overwritten a total of 13 times, using a mixture of random patterns. The final pass is verified.

- An ultra secure sanitation method based on Peter Gutmann's paper[2] that overwrites the data a total of 35 times. The method erases data regardless of the disk raw encoding by purging electromagnetic magnetic remanence. Gutmann combats all known software and hardware data recovery tools and methods.

Diskettes become unstable and suffer from bad sectors and are frequently discarded on the mistaken assumption that the data on them is unreadable. Valuable or incriminating data has often been recovered from diskettes disposed of by their owners, or that are damaged or seemingly unusable. The following remarkable story appears definitive in this respect:

---

2   'Secure Deletion of Data from Magnetic and Solid-State Memory',
    www.cs.auckland.ac.nz/~pgut001/pubs/secure_del.html.

> In February 1991, Julie Snodgrass was stabbed to death outside Clark Airbase in the Philippines. The prime suspect was her husband, Joseph. During questioning by USAF Office of Special Investigations agents in his office, Snodgrass suddenly pulled a pair of pinking shears from a box next to his desk and began hacking apart two 5.25 inch diskettes that he kept in his desk. The agents confiscated the shredded diskettes, but not before Snodgrass had cut them into 24 pieces. Experts, including the National Security Agency, the FBI and the diskette's manufacturer, told the Air Force investigators that the information was irretrievably lost. However, Special Agent Ed Cutchins and Technical Sergeant Dave Tindall succeeded in splicing pieces of the two diskettes and recovered more than 85 per cent of the data on them. The diskettes stored love letters to a mistress, a database for a black-marketing operation and, most damaging, a letter asking the mistress to hire a contract killer to murder his wife. This information proved pivotal in the conviction of Snodgrass for first-degree murder.

As Mr Snodgrass must now appreciate, diskettes should be erased using appropriate software or shredded.

An alternative method of erasing data from magnetic media is to use a degaussing wand, which produces a magnetic signal strong enough to obliterate any data or data traces (see Figure 5.5).

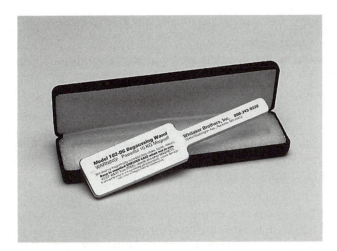

Figure 5.5   Whitaker Brothers 102-DG degaussing wand (reprinted with kind permission of Whitaker Brothers, www.whitakerbrothers.com)

Non-magnetic media, such as CD-ROMs, DVDs, optical disks and solid-state memory of the type found in memory sticks all require secure disposal.

- Deleted files on memory sticks may be recovered relatively easily with forensic methods. Data on memory sticks may be positively erased using secure erasure software.

Commercial garbage may contain larger numbers of discarded CD-ROMs. The CD-ROM burning process is sensitive, and can lead to failed disk writes. The disks, which are cheap to buy and are often perceived as valueless, are simply thrown away. However, the information on these disks may still be readable using specialist tools, allowing the hacker to read a partially completed backup or other sensitive information.

CDs, DVDs, WORM drives and optical disks that cannot be overwritten and which are to be disposed of require physical destruction. A number of commercially available shredders can destroy CDs, DVDs, credit cards and other 'plastic', Iomega Zip disks, DAT tapes and even LS 120 super disks.

It is also necessary to secure information on any computer, device or media with onboard memory that is sent to a manufacturer or servicing centre for repair, routine maintenance or upgrade, to ensure that information is not unwittingly divulged. Strong disk encryption provides a profound defence against information leaks. Another option is to remove the hard disk of any computer prior to its despatch.

An example of unwitting disclosure, albeit one that was clearly in the interests of justice and decency, led to the downfall of British pop star Gary Glitter when, in 1997, a member of staff at PC World in Bristol, England, spotted photographs of children being sexually abused on the singer's computer.

For control purposes:

- The disposal of data storage media should be designated the responsibility of a specific individual, for example, the IT security manager or the information security manager.
- A department, typically from IT, should be stipulated operationally to dispose of data storage media.
- Tools and techniques to destroy data on computer media should be evaluated and approved by this department.
- All concerned should be notified that media intended for disposal should be reported to and collected by this department.
- Media should be logged, inspected to ensure that all data is purged, and approved for disposal.

In a highly secure operating environment it may be advisable to forbid or prevent the localized use of portable data storage media. This may be achieved through the technical measures described in Chapters 3 and 9.

6 *Wireless Risks*

With the development of inventions like the radio and the wireless telephone, the whole world is becoming, in a very literal sense, a whispering-gallery.
Irving Babbitt, scholar and author, 1865–1933

The proliferation of laptop computers, notebooks, PDAs, Blackberrys and other portable devices has significantly added to business efficiency, portability and flexibility. To augment and enhance data communications and maximize the utility of these devices, wireless networks of various kinds have gained widespread acceptance and popularity.

However, the added convenience and cost benefits of wireless access have brought with them some attendant risks, particularly relating to the security exposure inherent in broadcasting data over radio waves.

Wireless networks

Wireless networks are far more susceptible to compromise than hardwired computer networks. Wireless LANs (WLANs) are by their very nature 'promiscuous', and difficult to secure against interception. Wireless traffic is transmitted via radio waves, and as such, it is clearly vulnerable to eavesdropping through the use of suitable receiver equipment and software.

Personnel who have implemented wireless networks are often loath to admit the inherent security vulnerabilities that this technology imposes upon the company network, offsetting the known risks against its perceived benefits. Unfortunately, and as a disarmingly simple demonstration can prove, an intruder armed with suitable equipment and software can compromise or intercept the traffic on an unprotected wireless LAN near effortlessly.

Over three days in December 2004, a *Sunday Times* reporter accompanied by three IT security consultants discovered that he could:

- access potentially sensitive data being sent from departments at the Frenchay Hospital in Bristol;
- snoop on guests using wireless networks at the Intercontinental Hotel near Hyde Park and the Knightsbridge Hotel, London;
- intercept communications between two people logged on to a wireless network operated by PricewaterhouseCoopers (PwC);
- snoop on 70 unencrypted wireless networks in three of London's most affluent residential areas, including Eton Square, Belgravia;
- identify 2222 wireless networks during a four-hour 'war drive' across London, of which 64 per cent were unencrypted and open to eavesdropping.

Wireless interception is legal in many countries – the attack is completely passive and does not tamper with systems or software, or cause any damage or denial of service. That said, in the United Kingdom, Section 1(2) of the Regulation of Investigatory Powers Act 2000 makes it a criminal offence to intercept intentionally and without lawful authority, at any place in the United Kingdom, any communication in the course of its transmission by means of a private telecommunication system – which seems applicable in the case of wireless networks. In addition, if the eavesdropper causes a computer to perform any function with the intent to secure access to any program or data held in any computer, he may be in breach of the Computer Misuse Act 1990.

Of major concern is that an intruder, having successfully intercepted wireless network traffic, leaves no trace whatsoever of his activity. Without recourse to specialist tools there are no tell-tale signs of this interception, and the intrusion is not recorded in audit trails or event logs.

This is not to say that wireless networks cannot be protected and safeguarded. However, wireless network security is entirely dependent on the implementation of suitable encryption and authentication mechanisms, and it is a lamentable fact that the original standard encryption protocol – WEP (Wired Equivalent Privacy) – that has known security flaws, is frequently still being deployed in wireless networks, despite the fact that there are now other, far more secure, methods of encryption and authentication available.

Wired Equivalent Privacy

WEP is a security protocol for wireless local area networks (WLANs) defined in the 802.11b standard. WEP was designed to provide the same level of security as that of a wired LAN. WEP aimed to provide security by encrypting data over radio waves so that it is protected as it is transmitted from one end point to another. However, it has been found that WEP is not as secure as once believed and currently implemented versions of the standard are no hurdle at all to the seasoned intruder.

A recent study by Nikita Borisov, Ian Goldberg and David Wagner at the University of California at Berkeley, highlighted the following vulnerabilities of WEP protected networks:

- passive attacks that decrypt traffic based on statistical analysis;
- active attacks to inject new traffic from unauthorized mobile stations, based on known plaintext;
- active attacks to decrypt traffic, based on tricking the access point;
- dictionary-building attacks that, after analysis of about a day's worth of traffic, allow real-time automated decryption of all traffic.

Borisov, Goldberg and Wagner demonstrated that all of these attacks are practical to mount using inexpensive off-the-shelf equipment and applied equally to the 40-bit and 128-bit versions of WEP running 802.11 or the enhanced 802.11b network standard. The vulnerabilities that they noted followed hard on the heels of a groundbreaking paper by Fluhrer, Mantin and Shamir, the original team to study weaknesses within WEP. They recommended at the time that anyone using the 802.11 standard protocol for wireless networks should not rely on WEP for security and that other measures should be taken to protect wireless networks.

As any communications security expert will vouch, wireless networks can be detected, identified, intercepted and cracked, regardless of whether or not they employ WEP encryption. All that is required is a laptop computer, notebook or PDA running software such as Kismet, NetStumbler and AirSnort and a wireless network card usually with an antenna attached.

War driving

There is a misconception amongst some people that data transmitted on wireless networks is of little or no interest to intruders. In fact, potential intruders and hobbyists are known to drive in vehicles around built-up urban and industrial areas with their wireless enabled notebooks intent on hunting down unprotected wireless networks.

This activity is called 'war driving' and is conceptually similar to old-fashioned 'war dialling' when intruders systematically ran through all the telephone networks in search of a dial tone indicating the presence of an unprotected dial-up node, which they could subsequently exploit. Nowadays, intruders drive around built-up areas with receiver equipment, intent on locating a signal indicating a wireless network. The following websites provide an insight into what people are actually doing:

- http://www.dis.org/filez/openlans.pdf
- http://www.netstumbler.com/

To raise awareness of just how many wireless networks are unprotected, a group of security professionals and hobbyists organized an annual 'WorldWide WarDrive' (http://www.worldwidewardrive.org/). On their last drive in July 2003, which covered four continents, they identified a total of 88 122 wireless networks, 67 per cent of which were unencrypted, with 28 per cent broadcasting the access point's SSID (Service Set Identifier), the packet header that identifies the network. If the SSID is broadcast, it makes it far easier for the network to be identified, thereby signalling 'low hanging fruit' to a potential intruder. If the SSID hasn't been changed from its default, then it follows that the default password may also not have been changed. Equally, where a non-default SSID is broadcast, this may indicate that the rest of the security layers in that network may be sufficiently derelict as to enable an intruder easy access. Even if the SSID is not broadcast, an attacker can still log on to the network if security is poor – but this requires more skill and patience than is the case when the SSID is actively broadcast.

If WEP encryption isn't enabled, intruders can use a packet analyser (or 'traffic sniffer') program such as Kismet or AirSnort to eavesdrop on network traffic. They don't even need to have associated or authenticated with the wireless network to do this; they can just select a channel on which to capture traffic and that's that! And as stated, even if WEP is enabled, many tools can break it. A Google search on the expressions 'WEP' and 'crack' returns a wealth of information about the freeware and intruder tools available to break this encryption. AirSnort is one such tool but many other wireless traffic sniffers these days also incorporate a WEP cracking function into their software.

Due to the known weaknesses of WEP, the more secure WEP+ and WEP2 encryption standards have been implemented in many access points. A further and significant enhancement was WPA (Wi-Fi Protected Access), a subset of the IEEE's 802.11i wireless security specification that was ratified in June 2004. WPA provides more sophisticated data encryption than WEP via the use of TKIP (Temporal Key Integrity Protocol) and also incorporates 802.1x and EAP authentication based on a central authentication server, such as RADIUS (remote access dial-in user system). However, because the easiest way to implement WPA is not to use the stronger 802.1x authentication that is provided, many WPA systems end up using the simpler authentication system instead – Pre-Shared Key (PSK) – called 'WPA-PSK'. Unfortunately, if this is used with weak passwords then it can be easier to break than WEP! 802.11i provides better security than WPA because, in addition to TKIP, it provides the US government standard of encryption, AES (Advanced Encryption Standard). However, AES requires hardware upgrades for existing Wi-Fi network devices.

Risks with portable devices

In addition to the vulnerability of unsecured access points is the exposure posed by portable devices with wireless access when they are not connected to the corporate network.

Many coffee houses, airports, train stations, hotels, and fast food chains such as McDonalds now offer either free or paid-for wireless access. There are very few conditions or safeguards for use, mostly as these networks are designed only to provide access to the Internet. However, a company laptop connected to one of these public access networks could be susceptible to localized hacking by other users connected to the same wireless network.

Furthermore, an option specified in 802.11x permits ad-hoc or peer-to-peer networking. If the PCMCIA card or other type of client card in a laptop doesn't have this ad-hoc mode disabled, it could assist another person in the vicinity to connect directly to the laptop without the need for any access point at all. This is a potentially serious risk because these portable devices are not protected by the corporate firewall and may have cached copies of sensitive e-mail or contain documents, spreadsheets and other sensitive data. It is advisable, therefore, that portable devices are protected by their own software or hardware firewalls and that users are informed of the potential risks inherent in accessing public access wireless networks. They should also keep their wireless devices disabled and turn Bluetooth off when not required.

By default, most wireless cards are set up to log on to any access point they detect. This provides the intruder with the opportunity to tap into employee computers simply by installing his own access point in a location near your network. Once the user is connected to this 'spoofed' access point, his or her computer is subjected to the full range of intrusion techniques including password sniffing and hostile port scanning. Many corporate laptops and portable devices do not have strong personal firewalls, enabling the intruder to gain complete access to these systems. The USERIDs and passwords that are intercepted may then assist the intruder to access hardwired networks and intrude far deeper into the global corporate network infrastructure. In this way, the compromise of one laptop or portable device may lead to attacks on far more critical distributed systems and wider area networks.

Similarly, wireless cards are often configured for use at 'hot spots', public Wi-Fi access points available at coffee shops and restaurants. Intruders can easily spoof the SSID of a hot spot, tricking corporate users into believing that they are logging on to a recognized and controlled network.

Conclusion

In the intermediate future, wireless networking in the corporate arena requires constant vigilance and enhanced security. Business managers and security directors need assurances that they are not compromising their most valuable secrets purely on the grounds of cost efficiency, flexibility and the convenience that wireless technology offers.

RECOMMENDATIONS

- Does the flexibility and convenience of wireless LANs really outweigh the potential security risks they expose you to?
- 'Out of the box' wireless LAN configurations offer inadequate security for most commercial uses.
- Undertake a controlled self-assessment. Is the information transmitted on your wireless networks of interest to criminals, intruders, industrial spies, competitors, journalists or investigators?
- If so, you must use encryption. Secure encryption is essential if your networks transmit valuable research and development data, product launch schedules or other commercially sensitive information. It is also mandatory if the wireless network carries any personal or financial information covered by data protection legislation (for example, patient's records, credit card details, and so on).
- Be aware that the 40-bit and 128-bit versions of WEP running 802.11 or the enhanced 802.11b network standard are easy to crack and cannot be relied upon to prevent snooping. Implement, instead, the significantly stronger WPA standard but use it with 802.1x authentication, or better still, use the 802.11i protocol.
- Make sure you choose suitable equipment – preferably equipment that supports 802.11i. If you have decided to implement WPA, choose products that let you use a 64-digit hex key, not just a short passphrase – because they are easily cracked.
- Are you broadcasting the access point's SSID (Service Set Identifier)? If the hardware allows it, disable SSID broadcasting and make sure that the access point is in restricted mode. Whilst a skilled attacker can bypass this configuration it will nevertheless help obfuscate the wireless network from the more opportunistic attacker.
- Are you broadcasting any access point's SSID (Service Set Identifier)? This is a major and dangerous exposure. Turn off SSID broadcasting completely. This will help obfuscate the wireless network from hostile detection and attempted intrusion by opportunistic attackers. A persistent and skilled attacker may persevere but generally the opportunist will move on to a more visible device.
- Consider undertaking a penetration test or 'war drive' to identify unprotected access points – you may be shocked by what you discover.
- Consider using security solutions from specialist providers such as 3Com or Cisco.
- Implement a wireless network monitor so you can see attempts to sniff or access your network.
- Secure your laptops and portable devices that connect to your wireless LAN by installing personal firewalls.
- Make sure that the wireless access point(s) are on the 'dirty' side of the corporate firewall so that the internal network cannot easily be compromised and penetrated.

- If possible, use MAC filtering. MAC filtering can be implemented on most access points/routers to permit only those computers authorized to connect to the network. MAC filtering is not foolproof – the authorized MAC addresses can still be spoofed – but, again, it is a significant deterrent to the opportunist hacker.
- Make sure that access points, antennae and other equipment are kept in a secured area just as you would with any other network devices.
- Remote management interfaces on wireless network devices such as access points provide an easy way for an attacker to gain control of the network. If possible, run a port scan of the network device to find which ports are open and disable the remote management interfaces you find. It is best to administer the device using an out-of-band (serial) connection.
- If remote management interfaces are absolutely necessary, try not to use SNMP (port 161/udp) and disable this if possible. If you must use SNMP, make sure to change the public (read) community string and the private (read/write) community string from the defaults, make them non-dictionary, and change them often. If there is a web management interface, see whether you can use https rather than http, and make sure that the user/password pair is strong and changed frequently. Telnet should be disabled if practicable.
- Use antenna shielding to restrict signal leakage into areas outside the zone in which coverage is required and use directional antennae where possible, rather than omni-directional antennae which are easier for a would-be intruder to detect (this may mean replacing the antennae shipped as standard with the access point/bridge devices).
- Consider the control benefits of configuring portable devices so they will only connect to your corporate wireless LAN and nothing else.

Finally, wireless networks can be made safe but only if implemented and maintained carefully. They offer security commensurate to the knowledge and the skills of those who implement them, the administrators who run them and, crucially, the people who use them.

As an example, Didi Barnes, Head of Research and Development at First Base Technologies, points out that network security is unwittingly subverted when employees implement 'rogue' Wi-Fi access points – those that are installed without authorization, and 'out of the box' with no security turned on, to facilitate network communication. This often occurs where company policy hasn't kept pace with advances in technology. As Didi says, 'You can't discipline an employee for something they didn't know was wrong. Company policy must be kept up to date with technological advances, and employment contracts should state that unauthorized hardware and software is forbidden.' With regard to the 'human firewall' – the people, policies and procedures to protect the network – Didi makes another compelling observation:

> *I also frequently find that I can wander about both inside and outside of a client's premises, brandishing a large antenna whilst undertaking a wireless audit, but no staff question me as to what on earth I am doing! If people were made more aware of such suspicious activity and the procedure for promptly reporting it, such an attempted intrusion could be stopped in its tracks!*

7 *Sabotage, Extortion and Blackmail*

We often provide our enemies the means for our own destruction.

Aesop (c. 620–560 BC)

Sabotage

Computer systems sabotage may arise during industrial disputes, as a result of personal or ideological grievance, as a measure to generate overtime payments, contract renewals or extensions, to blackmail and extort, to conceal evidence of crime or wrongdoing, or as a political protest or prank:

> (i) According to the *Wall Street Journal* (January 29, 2001), outgoing Clinton-Gore staffers at the White House performed a range of 'pranks' including prizing the W ('Dubya') key from many White House computer keyboards, super-glueing drawers on office desks, infecting computers with viruses, recording offensive reception messages on answering machines, slashing telephone lines, loading pornographic images on printers and computers, writing graffiti on corridors and bathroom walls, turning desks upside down, and, as a valedictory sign-off, leaving a trail of trash across the West Wing. Damage was conservatively estimated at $200 000.

Sometimes, as will be seen, sabotage may be completely *inexplicable*.

Physical attacks, including bombing, arson, the use of sledgehammers and so on, *may* be an indication of a computer illiterate attacker. In a recent case the saboteur, aggrieved and irrational, used a Stanley knife to cut Ethernet cables across a network. On another case – a civil search order – the saboteur sought to destroy evidence by smashing a Philips screwdriver through a disk drive.

Hardware disablement, the physical disconnection of disk drives, circuit boards, peripheral devices, or logical attacks using software usually indicates varying measures of technical proficiency. A case of network sabotage investigated in Madrid in the mid-1990s showed the attacker on a covert video recording, physically disconnecting network cabling. Using this simple attack, he had routinely taken the network off-line for periods of up to an hour at a time – this potentially represented 150 man-hours of lost productivity on each occasion.

As with other forms of criminal endeavour, those with the greatest opportunity to cause mayhem are those with the greatest access to the victim's systems and processes:

> In September 2000, a disgruntled Federal Aviation Administration (FAA) software engineer was charged with stealing the *only* copy of a computer access code for software used by flight controllers to guide passenger jets through Chicago O'Hare International Airport. A federal grand jury charged Thomas Varlotta, 42 at the time, with damaging and stealing government property. Prosecutors said Mr Varlotta erased the code from a computer hard drive and quit the next day. The code was recovered in a search of his home in June 1998. It had been encrypted with a 14-digit password and required *six months* to unscramble. The code controlled the Automated Flight Data Processing System, which controlled arrivals and departures from O'Hare to the terminal radar approach and control facility. An FAA spokesman stated that Mr Varlotta's actions did not endanger the safety of airline passengers, but without the code, any failure of the software might have forced air traffic controllers to exchange flight information by telephone.

The case emphasizes the need for peer review over code development and software change control, and the physical and logical segregation of critical duties. As a rule, no single individual should ever have sole control over computer backups or key computer applications.

A very common case of logical systems sabotage occurs when employees, temporary workers and others who have held positions of trust but have become disenchanted, turn hostile and are fired, suspended from the workplace or resign. They subsequently cause damage remotely, misusing dial-in passwords, often misappropriated, or backdoors implanted in the victim's system prior to their departure.

> In 1997, George Mario Parente was arrested for causing five network servers at the publishing company Forbes, Inc., to crash. Parente was a former Forbes computer technician who had been terminated from *temporary employment*. In what appears to have been a vengeful act against the company and his supervisors, *Parente dialled into the Forbes computer system from his residence and gained access through a co-worker's login and password*. Once on-line, he caused five of the eight Forbes computer network servers to crash, and erased all of the server volumes on each of the affected servers. No data could be restored. Parente's sabotage resulted in a two-day shutdown in Forbes' New York operations with losses exceeding $100 000. Parente pleaded guilty to one count of violating the Computer Fraud and Abuse Act.[1] [Author's italics]

The following case reported by CNN, and repeated here in some detail, contained many of the classic elements of systems sabotage:

I WANTED TO GET EVEN

In March 1998 Shakuntla Devi Singla, 43, of Fairfax Station, Virginia, pleaded guilty in US District Court in Washington to accessing a federal computer without authorization and intentionally causing damage when she hacked into the US Coast Guard's personnel database the previous July.[2]

Singla, a former Coast Guard employee, *helped build the database that she eventually attacked*. According to court documents and Singla herself, she hacked the network

---

1   Statement for the Record of Louis J. Freeh, Director, Federal Bureau of Investigation on Cybercrime before the Senate Committee Technology, Terrorism, and Government Information, Washington, DC, March 28, 2000.

2   Report by *Laura DiDio*, CNN.com, July 22, 1998.

because she was frustrated that the Coast Guard wasn't responsive to her complaints of improper conduct by an agency contractor.

Singla said, 'I wanted to get even with them. *I was frustrated and depressed because no one listened to my complaints of sexual harassment in the workplace.* I did delete information, but I did not crash the system.' She said she regretted the incident and knew at the time that it was illegal.

On July 8, 1997, about eight people including Singla were logged on to the agency's intranet when the database server crashed. According to Dave Swatloski, the agency's chief of information resources management, it took 115 Coast Guard employees more than 1800 hours to restore the lost data, *mainly because of a faulty tape backup system.* 'Had the tape backup not been bad, we would have only suffered 36 hours of downtime,' Swatloski said.

Costs included $35 000 to *manually re-enter the personnel data* and about $5000 for a new tape backup system, he said.

Singla was able to dial in to the network unimpeded *by using the password of an unsuspecting end user, who had given it to her before Singla left the job.*

'It's been a hard lesson learned,' said Jerry Heinl, chief of systems security at the Coast Guard's Headquarters Support Command. 'We are now especially emphasizing the importance of not sharing passwords.'

The Coast Guard has always conducted *background checks* on security and systems administrators and outside contract workers, and Heinl said that policy would remain in place. Additionally, 'Workstations connected to the agency's intranet are now configured automatically to lock out usage after five minutes of being left unattended,' Heinl said.

'We've also rebuilt the entire database to ensure that we had no rogue passwords or IDs floating around,' Swatloski said. [Author's italics]

Predictably, this attack was abetted through the misuse of a password. Most significantly, the backup and data restoration regime in this case *failed*, causing extended downtime and a massive recovery effort necessitating the manual re-typing of several thousand records.

- Key backup tapes and processes invariably fail when they are most desperately needed. It is a potentially catastrophic assumption that plans for disaster recovery and business continuity will actually work when needed most urgently. TEST, TEST and TEST again. And then TEST some more.

Ms Singla attacked the very database that she had helped to create, which is significant. In identifying a systems intruder or attacker it is helpful to determine any commonality in the development or design of disparate systems, applications or processes that are targeted, as these may reveal common authorship, contribution or ownership. Clearly, it is far easier for the attacker to hit a system with which he is intimately acquainted, and has access to.

There is often a compelling reason why a particular database, program or library is targeted by an attacker in preference to other areas of the system. Access to parts of the system may be restrained by access controls, thereby forcing the attacker to concentrate only on those areas available to him. Alternatively, the attacker may operate in a heightened emotional state, target areas or data of personal significance, or, seek to undermine the status, work in progress or input of a perceived antagonist or enemy. Behavioural analysis can be extremely helpful in determining the motivation, emotional state and competence of a workplace saboteur (see Chapter 16).

Ms Singla cited sexual harrassment as the root cause for her actions, and management's apparent failure to confront or tackle her alleged tormentor as a catalyst. If this was her genuine explanation, and nothing suggests otherwise, then it is proof that grievances come in many forms, not all of which are commonplace or predictable. Grievances may be significant and have real cause, as appears to be the case with Ms Singla, or trivial and baseless but perceived as major by the aggrieved. Grievances may also be poorly articulated or undisclosed and left to fester, and, therefore, difficult for management to understand, discern or react to.

In cases of sabotage, it is clearly helpful to understand the attacker's motivation, but on very rare occasions no clear explanation is ever forthcoming. The following case of impersonation, false input and systems sabotage is exceptional because its underlying cause clearly fell beyond the boundaries of rationality:

In December 1993 the UK's *Guardian* newspaper reported the conviction of a male nurse who hacked into a hospital's computer system and modified entries, including prescriptions. The hacker:

- prescribed drugs used to treat heart disease and high blood pressure to a nine year old with meningitis. This change was spotted by a ward sister;
- prescribed antibiotics to a patient in a geriatric ward. These drugs were administered to the patient, with no apparent adverse reaction;
- 'scheduled' an unnecessary X-ray for a patient;
- 'recommended' a discharge for another patient.

The hacker gained access to the computer system after learning the password through observing a locum doctor having trouble logging in. He had been sacked for unprofessional behaviour in 1990, but was re-employed in 1992 at the same hospital. He pleaded guilty to unauthorized modification of computer records but offered no explanation for his actions and denied any malicious intent.

People sometimes behave in a manner that is inexplicable and not all crimes have a logical cause. It also illustrates how control weaknesses in computer systems can, literally, be life threatening.

Extraordinarily, this individual was re-hired by the same employer that previously dismissed him for unprofessional behaviour. Common failings in HR procedures and pre-employment screening feature consistently in the case studies of systems sabotage, fraud and other criminality.

Product contamination is another form of sabotage. The recall of defective product can be very expensive and embarrassing for the victim organization. An interesting case of computer-assisted sabotage and product contamination was reported in the *San Jose Mercury News* in September 1986:

A former employee of the Encyclopedia Britannica, disgruntled at being laid off, committed computer sabotage by altering portions of the text being prepared for updated editions of the renowned encyclopedia.

'We have uncovered evidence of deliberate sabotage in the EB computer files,' editor-in-chief Tom Goetz disclosed in a memo to editorial personnel. Goetz wrote, 'What is perhaps most distressing for each of us is the knowledge that some of our hard work has been turned into garbage by either a very sick or a very vicious person.'

A former employee confessed and helped to undo the damage. The publishing company said that the 44-million word 1987 edition was safe, but employees laboured overtime to catch deliberate inaccuracies prior to the publication of the 1988 edition.

The former employee's more vivid changes included *the transposition of Jesus Christ with Allah.*

Mr Goetz said that the company planned to pursue legal actions 'vigorously' and that *it was issuing new computer passwords to employees.* An industry executive said at the time, '*In the computer age, this is exactly what we have nightmares about.*' [Author's italics]

Yet another case, it would appear, of password misappropriation and misuse.

Locating errors within a 44-million word transcript was clearly an immense undertaking, even with the assistance of computerized spell-check, 'grep' searching and 'find and replace'. Nor can error correction of this magnitude and complexity be automated through the use of artificial intelligence. It is dependent, instead, upon patient, vigilant scrutiny using the 'mark one eyeball'.

Risks of this type are commonplace in the software industry where latent errors and bugs are deliberately introduced into source code by programmers and developers to ensure the contamination of lucrative bug fixing and maintenance contracts.

It is interesting that the attacker consistently replaced references to Jesus Christ with Allah. This may have indicated the attacker's beliefs, perceptions or values, which emphasizes again the value of *behavioural analysis* and *contextual analysis* when investigating these incidents (see Chapter 16).

Extortion and blackmail

Thieves and extortionists are increasingly aware of the fact that the computer's content may be of far greater value than the resale price of the computer itself. There have been reports from the United States of blackmailers demanding ransoms – in one case $100 000 – to return laptop computers to their rightful owners.

In another case, a database containing highly sensitive and potentially embarrassing commercial information was ransomed for £1 million, with an implicit threat that the data would be released to the regulatory authorities.

Data ransom may originate externally, or internally. There are various 'levers' available to the extortionist, who may:

- encrypt vital data using a key known only to himself who then demands payment or issues an order. The extortionist instructs the victim that the decryption key will be released only if his demands are complied with;
- threaten to sabotage systems, destroy or corrupt data unless payment is received or a demand is met;

- intimidate the victim organization by threatening to release confidential information, the disclosure of which would inflict loss of confidence, embarrassment, commercial loss, damage to reputation, legal proceedings, a regulatory enquiry or some other damage;
- threaten to spread a commercially damaging rumour via anonymous electronic mail, chatrooms or using an untraceable website on the Internet. Unsubstantiated rumours relating to managerial corruption, commercial malpractice, corporate liquidity, viability or share price can be particularly damaging;
- threaten to disclose IT security exposures, commercial vulnerabilities or a scandal known to the extortionist;
- work to rule, or slack, on the presumption that the employer is totally dependent on the extortionist's IT skills and has no recourse to alternative expertise;
- place a software routine that causes critical operations to terminate or malfunction, rectifiable only by the extortionist should his demands be met;
- deliberately sabotage or destroy data or project work, or make it inaccessible, immediately before defecting to a competitor or new venture.

Professor ME Kabay of Norwich University, Vermont, Michigan, reports several archetypal cases of attempted extortion, blackmail and ransom in his paper 'Extortion Online'[3]:

- 1971. Two reels of magnetic tape belonging to Bank of America are stolen at Los Angeles International Airport. The thieves threaten to destroy the data if their ransom demands are not met. The bank ignores the threat because it has adequate backups.
- 1973. A West German computer operator steals 22 tapes and receives $200 000 for their return. The victim organization has no backups.
- 1977. A programmer in the Rotterdam offices of Imperial Chemical Industries (ICI) steals all of the office's computer tapes, including the backups. ICI promptly informs Interpol of the attempted extortion. Police arrest the programmer and an accomplice.
- 1999. 'Maxus', a 19-year-old Russian hacker, breaks into the website of CD Universe and downloads the credit-card information of 300 000 of the firm's customers. He threatens the company, saying, 'Pay me $100 000 ... or I'll sell your cards and tell about this incident in the news.' CD Universe refuses his demand and he posts 25 000 of the accounts on a website. 300 000 cardholders are forced to change their credit card numbers.
- March 2000. Oleg Zezev, a Kazakh computer hacker, breaks into Bloomberg LP. He sends e-mails threatening to reveal confidential information unless the company pays him $200 000. Zezev is arrested, tried and found guilty of conspiracy, attempted extortion and computer intrusion. He is sentenced in 2003 to a four-year prison sentence and ordered to pay restitution of $950 000. The trial includes testimony from media mogul and New York mayor Michael Bloomberg who met with Zezev in London in August 2000 as part of a police sting operation.
- August 2000. The Creditcards.com website is penetrated and the attacker copies 55 000 credit card numbers. The extortionist demands $100 000, is refused, and subsequently publishes the card numbers on the Internet.
- 2001. The FBI targets criminal hackers in Russia and the Ukraine who copy more than a million credit card numbers from 40 sites in 20 states. The hackers blackmail the victim organizations by threatening to publish the credit card details of their customers online.

---

3   http://www2.norwich.edu/mkabay/index.htm.

These cases employed common theft and the threat to destroy or disclose sensitive data. Alternatively, the extortionist may use encryption to hold data to ransom. An audacious but amateurish attempt at extortion involved a Trojan horse program.

In December 1989, 26 000 envelopes containing 5¼ inch diskettes were posted from two locations in London.[4] Each diskette bore a label entitled 'AIDS Information Introductory Diskette Version 2.0' and contained an interactive program that asked a series of questions about the respondent's health and lifestyle. Ostensibly, this routine calculated the respondent's probable exposure to the AIDS/Human Immunodeficiency Virus (HIV). Having installed itself on thousands of computers throughout Europe, the program proceeded to print an invoice that demanded the payment of either $189 or $378 depending on the nature of which type of 'lease' the victim chose. Payments were to be sent to PC Cyborg Corporation at a PO box in Panama. A hidden routine within the program encrypted files on the victim computer but only after it had been rebooted approximately ninety times. The encryption caused significant data loss and the program's installation routine crippled a number of PCs as organizations attempted to remove the program. Scotland Yard's Computer Crime Unit arrested Dr Joseph Lewis Popp, an American citizen, for this offence. Dr Popp was extradited to the UK to stand trial but was declared unfit to plead.

At the time the AIDS diskette, as it became known, was a case of computer-assisted blackmail without parallel and the attempted extortion was instrumental in expediting the passage of the Computer Misuse Act 1990 through the British parliament.

Insider, specialist knowledge may also be used to coerce an organization, to levy demands, or, as claimed in the following case, to 'highlight security weaknesses'.

In November 2001 an encryption expert was found not guilty of attempting to extort £25 million from Barclays Bank by threatening to expose confidential security information. Graham Browne, former manager of the bank's elite cryptography team, was acquitted on a charge of blackmail by a jury at the central criminal court in London. The case centred on a series of anonymous letters that were sent to the bank's chief executive by one 'TB Shaw'. The sender intimated that he would expose the bank's alleged weak security unless £25 million was paid to himself and 13 other people. Browne maintained that the letters had been a joke and that he only ever intended to highlight alleged security weaknesses on systems used to protect the UK's eight million Barclaycard account holders. He described his demand as 'ludicrous', and did not think it would be taken seriously.

The threatened or intimated release of sensitive information will usually require intensive investigation and highly coordinated crisis management.

The danger of a malcontent in the computer department is a particular risk. The US Defense Security Service uses the acronym 'CITI' – Critical Information Technology Insider – to describe potentially the most dangerous type of saboteur:

He's extremely difficult to manage, takes offence easily, never listens to advice and is very secretive. He also works to rule, never stays after hours or at the weekends, even in an emergency. Problem is, he has us by the balls – and he knows it. He is the only one here who really understands the computer systems and he won't allow anyone near them. I never know what he's up to – he just clams up and refuses to tell me anything. I tried to enlist a second guy as his deputy, but he point-blank refused. I went to retrieve the backup tapes from him last week but he flew into a rage. He's completely out of control.

---

4   DNA was isolated on the postage stamps. The diskette was mailed to a commercially purchased database of computer magazine subscribers.

There have been cases where IT managers have encrypted master data files and destroyed backups, and then ransomed the decryption passwords.

Software bombs

The people *inside* the firewall can inflict far greater damage to an organization than the world *outside* it. Malevolent intent within an organization's IT department has on occasion resulted in devastating damage to data, critical processes and business productivity. The 'enemy within' is an insidious threat, particularly in instances where a malcontent IT worker embeds a malicious program or routine into the computer system.

Malicious software or routines may be embedded in the system:

- as a perverse form of insurance against dismissal or redundancy;
- as a means to blackmail an organization;
- as a means of extortion;
- to defraud;
- to cause deliberate malfunctions, rectifiable only by the perpetrator, as a means to enhance job security or reputation because the perpetrator is perceived as indispensable
- as an illicit method of software copy protection;
- out of sheer bloody-mindedness or deviance.

TIME BOMBS

A 'time bomb' is a simple trigger routine added to a program, a batch file or a sub-routine or contained within viral code that monitors the operating system's internal clock or the computer's hardware clock. When a certain date and/or time is reached, the trigger detonates the bomb to cause damage to data, or to produce an effect of the programmer's choosing. Time bombs often featured in early computer virus code, with the 'warhead' set to explode on an infected computer on a given date – the Datacrime virus, for example, triggered on or after October 13, 1989[5] while the Michelangelo virus triggered on March 6, any year.[6] Time bombs within computer viruses are a relatively easy threat to manage – PC virus protection software is widely available, implemented in nearly all organizations and regularly upgraded to combat emerging strains.

The time bomb planted internally within the organization is a more intractable threat. Due to their simplicity and compact coding, time bombs may easily be concealed within hundreds of thousands of lines of machine code contained in business mainframe or network systems (see Figure 7.1).

---

5   Any infected program run on October 13, 1989 or thereafter would format the first nine tracks of the infected computer's hard disk and display the message 'DATACRIME VIRUS RELEASED: 1 MARCH 1989'.

6   This is the birthday of the renaissance artist Michelangelo Buonaroti. When triggered, the virus destroyed the information in track 0 (the first 256 cylinders on the infected disk). As the File Allocation Table (FAT) and the root directory information are found in this section, the disk becomes inaccessible.

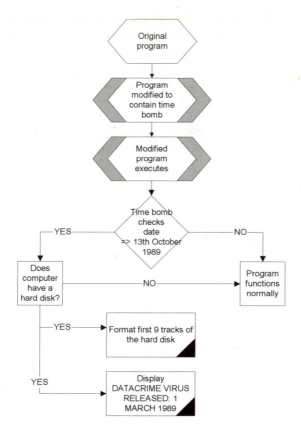

Figure 7.1   The Datacrime virus

LOGIC BOMBS

A 'logic bomb' is similar to a time bomb in that it is an embedded code routine that checks whether pre-specified trigger conditions have been met. The programmer dictates both the set of conditions that will trigger the bomb and its effect upon detonation. The warhead of the logic bomb is likely to be highly destructive and usually designed to inflict crippling damage or data loss.

More insidious (and dangerous) variants introduce random data corruption – this can cause havoc in financial and accounting data. *Significantly, the data corruption will be copied to the backups over an indefinite period.* This totally undermines confidence in the integrity of the data even in the event that the system is completely restored from backup media.

Logic bombs are the traditional weapon of the malcontent programmer, systems administrator, systems analyst or crooked IT professional, providing a method to extort or blackmail an organization, or simply to punish it for some perceived grievance. Logic bombs feature in computer virus programs, but are also encountered in specific systems where the code, activation criteria and location are unique.

The coding is usually compact and, therefore, extremely difficult to detect. A classic logic bomb will search for the programmer's payroll ID number and will trigger should that number fail to appear in consecutive payroll calculations.

Logic bombs and time bombs may be primed years in advance of triggering, thus providing the corrupt programmer ample opportunity to avoid detection – he may have left the victim organization months or even years prior to the bomb's detonation. The introduction of a time and logic element is a devious tactic – the absence of the programmer's payroll number is checked each month until a period of six months elapses, then the bomb detonates (see Figure 7.2).

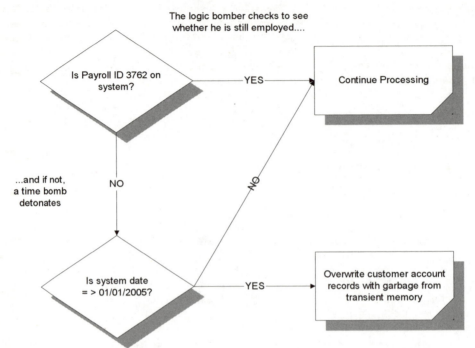

Figure 7.2 Classic logic bomb

The logic bomb is configured with its creator's instructions. Conditions that might trigger a logic bomb are limitless – the absence or presence of specific files or data, keyboard entry sequences, the activation of certain resources, a counter set to monitor the total number of database entries, a particular workstation in use at a specified time, a login by a particular USERID – these and many other possible trigger conditions may apply.

In certain cases, the extortionist will provide a keyboard input instruction to *defuse* a bomb should the victim organization submit to his demands.

Bombs may be introduced into the system externally as attachments to e-mail or in virus-infected programs. Up-to-date anti-virus software and a well-configured firewall should detect and reject known generic malware. However, the most pernicious logic bombs are usually planted by insiders who have authorized access to systems and processes.

The logic bomb threat used to be considered primarily a mainframe or minicomputer problem because the software for these environments was often developed internally whereas commercially available microcomputer (PC) software is shipped in compiled form. With most modern organizations reliant on microcomputer architecture, this is no longer the case – the author has, on occasion, encountered logic bombs on PC networks.

The following case studies have been reported in the news, and provide some insight into the motivation of the logic bomber:

> Donald Burleson, a 35-year-old programmer, was employed as a systems analyst by the USPA & IRA Company,[7] an insurance brokerage based in Fort Worth, Texas. Burleson was reportedly disciplined a number of times, on one occasion for storing personal data on the mainframe. A trivial offence, perhaps, but to Burleson this appears to have been the 'straw that broke the camel's back'. He added an illicit program routine to the company's IBM System 38 to erase database entries unless a preset value was reset. The malicious routine lay dormant on the system for two years until his employer finally dismissed him. On September 21, 1985 Burleson regained access to the system at 3 a.m. by entering the USPA building with a set of duplicate keys. He entered the password that controlled access to the secret routine and executed it. As a result Burleson destroyed 168 000 records of sales commissions owed to employees. In 1988 he gained the dubious distinction of becoming the first American citizen to be convicted of 'harmful access to a computer'.

Burleson was caught after investigators trawled through several years' worth of system files and discovered the logic bomb within the system, a painstaking process akin to finding the 'needle in the haystack'. The Burleson incident is well known and is often cited as an example of the potential devastation that the trusted insider can inflict.

There have since been a number of similar incidents that have been prosecuted in the US:

> In 1992 Michael John Lauffenburger, a 31-year-old programmer, pled guilty to attempting to sabotage one of General Dynamics' mainframe computers with a logic bomb that prosecutors asserted could have erased US national security data. The bomb targeted a database of Atlas rocket components. Lauffenburger installed the logic bomb prior to resigning from the company with the intention of being hired as a high-priced consultant to help reconstruct data erased from the billion-dollar Atlas missile space programme after the bomb detonated. But another programmer discovered the destructive code by accident in May 1991, raised the alarm and it was defused. The logic bomb had been set to explode on May 24, 1991.

Investigators said that had Lauffenburger's bomb triggered it would have cost $100 000 to restore the database maintained at the General Dynamics' Kearny Mesa plant in San Diego.

> In January 2000, John Michael Sullivan, a former employee of Lance Inc., was sentenced to 24 months' imprisonment and ordered to pay restitution of $194 609 for knowingly transmitting a destructive computer code, contrary to the US Computer Fraud and Abuse Act. Sullivan was hired by Lance in 1996 to develop a computer program to help staff to collect sales, inventory and delivery information and transmit it by modem to the company's headquarters in Charlotte, North Carolina. Sullivan was demoted on May 8, 1998 because of his alleged poor performance. On May 22, 1998 he resigned from the company. Jurors heard that ten days before resigning, Sullivan inserted a time bomb in the software he developed for hand-held computers used by the company's 2000 sales representatives. The time bomb triggered at noon on September 23, 1998 rendering the field staff's computers inoperable.

Lance Inc.'s direct loss in this cases exceeded $100 000.

---

7   The United States Planning Association, Inc. and the Independent Research Agency for Life Insurance, Inc.

> (i) In 2002 Roger Duronio, a 60-year-old systems administrator for UBS PaineWebber was charged with attempted securities fraud and violating the US Computer Fraud and Abuse Act. The indictment alleged that Duronio planted a logic bomb to delete information from workstations attached to the network at 9.30 a.m. on every Monday in March, April and May of 2002. The logic bomb, similar to a computer virus in its method of propagation, spread to 1000 PCs of the company's 1500 networked computers.
>
> Duronio left UBS PaineWebber on February 22, 2002. He had reportedly complained about his salary and bonuses. The logic bomb detonated on Monday March 4, 2002. It caused temporary chaos, but the company recovered relatively quickly due to a competent backup regime. The indictment, however, stated that Duronio's alleged logic bomb caused $3 million of costs to PaineWebber to assess and repair the damage done.

Interestingly, Duronio had previously purchased options to sell 31 800 shares of UBS AG (PaineWebber's parent company) at an average strike price of $42.91. These 'put' options make money only in the event that the stock price falls below the purchase price before the options expire. The indictment alleged that Duronio deliberately crashed the company's systems in order to cause its stock price to plummet immediately prior to his options expiring on March 15, 2002. If this was his intention it failed. The attack was not made public at the time and UBS stock did not fall below $45 at any time in March 2002.

> (i) In March 2002, Timothy Lloyd, a 30-year-old programmer with Omega Engineering, Inc. of Bridgeport, New Jersey, was sentenced to a 41-month prison sentence for inserting a logic bomb into the company's network just prior to his being fired. Twenty days later the bomb triggered and deleted the company's research, development and production software in one fell swoop. The company claimed that Lloyd's sabotage cost it about $10 million in sales.
>
> Omega, a manufacturer of measurement and control instrumentation for NASA and the US Navy suffered the loss of nearly its entire software development programme. The attack occurred on July 30, 1996. The indictment stated 'Lloyd intentionally caused irreparable damage to Omega's computer system by activating a logic bomb that permanently deleted all of the company's sophisticated software programs.'
>
> Lloyd's access rights and privileges were cancelled on July 10, 1996, the day of his dismissal. Lloyd was Omega's chief programmer and its network administrator. After 11 years with the company, he knew the network inside out and had the supervisory privileges to make the adjustments, authorized or otherwise, of his choosing. Lloyd embedded the logic bomb within the network's Novell Netware operating system and disabled the automated backup and recovery procedures.

Critically, in the Omega case, the culprit reportedly destroyed tape backups, which rendered any chance of recovery impossible.

Controls[8]

At a profound level, it is clearly vital to prevent a potential saboteur from gaining access to your computer systems, operations and processes.

The security of premises and facilities is clearly a priority. Servers, communications hubs and racks, generators, cabling and other equipment are vulnerable to physical attack and

---

8   This section is expanded from an article by the author entitled 'Be Prepared' in *MIS Magazine*, March 2002, http://www.misweb.com.

merit suitable physical protection and control. Businesses should review physical access to their buildings, the control and authentication of visitors, physical search procedures, x-ray, firearm and explosive detection, internal and street-level CCTV coverage, and fire prevention and suppression, particularly in server rooms and communications suites. Employees should be made aware that unaccompanied strangers should always be challenged – devastating sabotage can be committed with a humble Stanley knife or screwdriver if the attacker gains access to critical data cabling or disk drives. If the server door is propped open with a fire extinguisher, think again!

Servers, communications racks and key operations and processes should be housed above street level and access to internal areas should be monitored by CCTV, physical and software access controls. In the immediate wake of 9/11, banks and other companies in both London and New York deployed legions of security guards to protect their premises, but this vigilance has since lapsed.

A common and mistaken presumption is that servers and other high-end hardware or communications equipment will immediately be available for hire or purchase in the event that installed hardware is destroyed. This may well prove a false premise – particularly in the event of a disaster affecting a large number of businesses in the locality.

When conducting a risk analysis, always pay attention to the power supply – a knock-out blow of a critical generator or UPS can cause mayhem. Should national infrastructure be attacked, it is possible that power supplies may be affected and real-time processing could be seriously disrupted. Businesses should conduct a controlled self-assessment with regards to the need for critical power supply. Standby generators and UPS systems should be inspected and tested.

A critical point analysis should identify the corporate jugular vein and appropriate defensive measures (see Chapter 1 and Appendix 1).

Malicious or fraudulent programs developed in-house by IT staff with intimate knowledge of the computer systems and authorized access to them are:

- extremely difficult to prevent
- extremely difficult to detect
- extremely pernicious with the potential to cause catastrophic downtime or data loss.

Bomb programs are often implanted in complex processing environments. Logical access control to networks, routers and other critical systems is also clearly warranted. Regular housekeeping is necessary to remove or disable redundant user accounts on the network, both internally and, particularly, those that may be accessed or activated remotely. Recommended Microsoft and other software patches to protect mail servers from virus attack should be implemented and firewalls, remote access servers, dial-in ports and websites should be tested for exposures to hacking and port scanning. Intrusion detection systems should be checked and reconfigured.

Core databases, particularly those that contain confidential, financial, personal or customer records that are particularly attractive to extortionists and hackers, should be protected by strong encryption and access control, or, preferably, stored on an isolated internal network or computer with no logical connection to the Internet or other system.

Extensive and comprehensive pre-employment screening, to include the checking of character references and past employment records, will assist in clearing applicants for sensitive IT positions. Unfortunately, in practice, this rarely ever happens. Contractors and temporary or short-term employees are a particular risk.

Where laws apply, the corporate information security policy, which should be read and signed by all employees upon induction, should clearly state that unauthorized access to computer systems, programs or data, or the unauthorized modification thereof, is a criminal offence and that the company will seek to prosecute any offender.

An information security (IS) department, separate from the IT department and accountable to a head of information security, is advisable when establishing an effective corporate information security regime. It is generally recommended that the IS department employs one full-time professional for every 1000 users. The IS department should be fully supported at board level, sufficiently sponsored, and budgeted independently of the IT department.

Trained computer auditors, accountable to the Head of Internal Audit, should perform regular audits and spot-checks of systems and processes (see Figure 7.3).

Figure 7.3   IT supervision and control

Information security personnel should be trained to flag any employee who shows signs of being troubled or aggrieved, particularly if that employee holds an information-critical position. Downsizing, outsourcing and industrial unrest may foment a sabotage mentality amongst a disillusioned or dispossessed workforce, and extra vigilance is merited where traumatic change is envisaged or expected.

Audit and control software such as RACF and ACF2 in the mainframe environment is useful, but a determined and knowledgeable attacker will be able to circumvent it, particularly if he has administrator privileges.

Control can be imposed, to a limited extent, by restricting in-house software development. This requires the elimination of compilers, assemblers, interpreters, certain applications and utilities. Obviously, forbidding the development of *any* software within an organization is, for most organizations, completely impractical. Furthermore, many logic bombs are not coded within software at all but are prepared as batch files or simple instruction sets that cause the operating system or software to execute a destructive or pernicious routine. The people most likely to devise a logic bomb or Trojan will be analysts or programmers who, by definition, must have access to the system and will certainly possess powerful programming utilities and software tools within their own collections.

Networked systems are inherently vulnerable (regardless of programming restrictions) to Trojan programs transmitted via uncontrolled workstations.

In an ideal world, in-house software development should be subject to strict control including source code verification, peer review and extensive pre-implementation testing. Similarly, change control should be vigorous during system or software upgrading or enhancement.

Real-time systems, such as those used in trading and brokerage, are particularly vulnerable to bomb programs and routines. Thorough on-line monitoring, total quality assurance, software change control, segregated oversight and control of any such system are clearly indicated. A high level of redundancy must be built into real-time systems so that a failure of a primary system can immediately be augmented and succeeded by a secondary system. The saboteur, of course, will target any reserve system if allowed sufficient physical or logical access to it.

Remember that the attacker may deliberately knock out a primary system thereby forcing you to invoke a standby system. This may be because he knows of a flaw within the secondary system that may be exploited fraudulently or with criminal intent, which is absent in the primary system.

The development and maintenance of bespoke software should be subject to contract, with unequivocal copyright assigned and agreed by all parties. The implied or actual use of undisclosed copy-protection mechanisms or other coded routines within bespoke applications or hardware should be expressly forbidden by contract.

Users should be taught to recognize and report irregularities in program libraries, files and directories and computer and software functioning. Most critically, unsolicited electronic mail messages and attachments, whether executable or not, should not be opened, but reported immediately to the IS department. Under no circumstances should unfamiliar or unsolicited programs or routines be executed. In practice, of course, people will run unfamiliar software and read unsolicited e-mails. Trojan horse programs, for instance, will often mimic legitimate software and many computer users cannot resist opening unsolicited e-mail, even when the dangers presented by electronic mail viruses and worms are well known.

Commercial software can be tested for obvious bugs and virus contamination by standard software validation. However, searching for malign code (other than generic viruses and other malware in the public domain) is neither viable nor practicable for most businesses. This level of security usually applies to sensitive military or government systems where software and upgrades are supplied from the developer as source code that is painstakingly analysed, line-by-line, prior to being compiled internally.

At a practical level, the threats of systems sabotage and cyber-extortion may best be mitigated by the judicious mixture of procedural and technical controls:

- As with other mission-critical functions, the segregation of duties is essential in a controlled IT environment.
- Never become reliant on any individual.
- Key processes should also be clearly documented so an uninitiated operator can perform them. Many companies suffer from a critical over-reliance on key individuals and there is often little transference of knowledge or redundancy in the processes they oversee.
- Business continuity plans should include the sourcing of alternative telecommunications carriers, the maintenance of an emergency contact list to include home, office and

mobile numbers and – if warranted – a fully maintained off-site communications and call desk facility.

- Assign supervisory or administrative rights to at least two people, but not to a wider group than is strictly necessary.
- Backups and other key administrative tasks should always be dual or tertiary control functions. This is good practice, not just to ensure business continuity in the event of a disaster, but also to prevent those rare attempts at extortion whereby a single key operator holds their employer to ransom by encrypting critical data or refusing to share their skills.
- Backups are the single most important defence against a range of potential computer disasters and their maintenance should never be entrusted solely to an individual.
- Backup tapes must be verified and restored. Rotate backup tapes, but don't recycle them indefinitely as this may lead to media decay and data loss.
- Maintain a secure inventory of backup tapes, which should be signed in and out of storage.
- At least one current backup tape set should be stored off-site; in the aftermath of the IRA bombing of Bishopsgate in central London in 1993, firms that maintained backup tapes on site in fireproof safes were denied access to their premises and hence their tapes by the fire brigade because the targeted buildings had suffered such severe structural damage.
- This is also the reason why businesses should not rely upon a disaster recovery site that is within close proximity to their core operations – a local power cut, fire or bomb could knock out both sites simultaneously. This demonstrates the need to distribute key processes and personnel to diverse locations.
- It is recommended that data volumes and system volumes should be backed up separately. Data volumes should be backed up at least daily, and many current backup systems provide instant mirroring. System volumes may be backed up less frequently, as and when the system configuration changes. The system volume may be restored from backup, thereby avoiding time-consuming configuration, as would be the case if restored from operating system disks and software.
- Remember that a latent time bomb, logic bomb, virus, worm or other malicious routine may be transferred to the backup tapes, and that restoring contaminated tapes onto a live system may reintroduce the threat.
- Remember also that backup tapes may have evidential value, particularly if they contain a record of a malicious routine or indications of it. The tapes should be duplicated in line with forensic and evidential best practice, before being restored to the system.
- Beware of the risk that a logic bomb need *not* necessarily *destroy* data. The damage wrought may be more insidious and difficult to detect, such as the introduction of random data errors within financial and accounting systems and spreadsheets, or critical control data. 'Data diddling' of this type can literally be life threatening, particularly if it occurs in data feeds to safety critical processes. Worse still, any errors introduced into data will, by default, be reflected in the backup process, resulting in a complete loss of confidence.
- Significantly, the system or data volumes may contain critical evidence of the malicious routine, in a stable format, prior to its execution. If located and isolated, analysis of the routine will disclose its precise functionality and may indicate remedial action.
- Larger operations may use on-line data warehousing, 'hot sites' or leased line off-site mirroring for near instantaneous backup. Should this be the case, the saboteur, in all likelihood, will attempt to disrupt the backup transmission, or the backup facility. This again emphasizes the absolute priority to safeguard the physical and logical security of

the backup regime, and the importance of dual or tertiary levels of supervision for critical systems and processes.

- Audit trails, firewall logs, network event logs and other critical system monitoring and transaction records should be recorded on dedicated disks and servers, independent of operational systems and networks, and be accessible only by systems administrators with commensurate access privileges. In the event that a bomb executes, or any other security breach occurs, logs and audit trails must be secured and retained immediately for analysis. Logs and audit trails should be retained for a minimum of ten working days.
- Exit procedures must be devised and carefully coordinated in the event of suspension or dismissal (see Chapter 19).
- It is imperative that key systems and processes be restored both on site and off site within acceptable time frames. Many businesses have found that this is simply not achievable – often because backup tapes will not read due to failed data transfer, media corruption, and software and drive incompatibility. There is also the dangerous assumption that incremental backups and daily, weekly and monthly archives will guarantee that the system may be recovered. If one tape becomes corrupt, it is possible that its relatives will be equally damaged, particularly if they have been processed in the same mechanical and environmental conditions.
- Tests should be conducted using live data to ensure that tapes and tape drives (or other backup systems and processes) are functioning properly.

It is often the case with a disaster recovery programme that complacency diminishes or undermines its value. Many programmes have never been tested at all, either in anger or in rehearsal.

- The aftermath of a disaster is not the time to test the integrity of your backups!

Despite the considerable effort involved, now is the right time to shakedown emergency procedures, and to sharpen up and test the IT control environment and business continuity plans.

Response to a triggered bomb

An act of sabotage or a ruthlessly programmed time bomb or logic bomb may seriously disrupt the business and could even destroy it. Without reliable backups, the victim organization may need to resort to time-consuming and expensive data recovery efforts with no guarantee whatever of restoring the system or its data.

In all likelihood, the attacker will execute a devastating attack that minimizes the opportunity for the victim to recover. In the Omega case, for example, the culprit reportedly used the NetWare command 'PURGE' to destroy the data on the company's network. This proved far more devastating than simple deletion, because PURGE destroyed the Netware File System (NWFS), thereby erasing the indices on which most data recovery systems, including the NetWare 'SALVAGE' program, depend. Worse still, the backup tapes had been deliberately destroyed.

Figure 7.4 shows an incident response plan to deal with the immediate aftermath of a logic bomb, time bomb or other destructive routine. Successful recovery is critically dependent on the availability of reliable backups, and successful investigation will largely depend on comprehensive audit trails, event logging and other resource monitoring. Clearly, if the bomber is in charge of both the backups and the monitoring, he may inflict complete paralysis. Independent supervision and control of these functions is a must.

Evidentially, it is essential that any data storage media upon which the bomb may reside, or which has been subjected to its detonation, is processed forensically and investigated immediately.

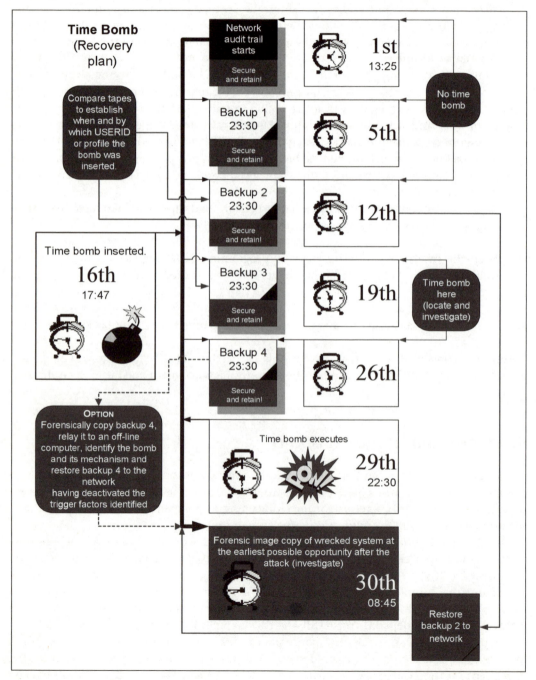

Figure 7.4   Time bomb recovery plan

8 *Social Engineering*

We are inclined to believe those whom we do not know because they have never deceived us.

Samuel Johnson, diarist (1709–1784)

'Social engineering' is a euphemism adopted by computer hackers to describe the process by which an opponent deceives, entices or otherwise manipulates an unsuspecting person into revealing confidential information, or cajoles, blackmails or otherwise coerces his victim to obey instructions. Against the odds, this strange expression has gained general acceptance.

The social engineer shares the methods if not the philosophy of the confidence trickster or blackmailer. There is little to distinguish between these groups, although their ultimate objectives may differ.

Exploiting weaknesses

Not surprisingly, the social engineer exploits people's vanity, stupidity, or instinctive trust:

User	Hi. Veronica speaking.	
Hacker	Hello Veronica, you don't know me but I'm the new guy with central support services, standing in for Jim Lake. You know Jim? My name's Bob Griffin, by the way.	
User	Of course, everyone knows Jim! He's on holiday at the moment isn't he? Anyway, nice to talk to you Bob. How can I help?	
Hacker	Jim's left a note for me to make some amendments to the reporting function in the new accounts package and he suggested I give you a call. Jim tells me you're a top gun on this system and the right person to help me.	
User	(Laughing) Flattery will get you everywhere. Actually, it's been giving me quite a bit of grief recently – your call's very timely.	
Hacker	Well, we're here to help! Anyway, Jim's left me instructions about the changes to make, which should make your life a lot easier, incidentally! Are you logged in at the moment? If so, could you log out and then log back in again as the administrator?	

It is clear where this conversation is leading – to the disclosure of Veronica's password. The call is friendly, informal and slightly flirty and the hacker sounds convincing. He has done his homework, scavenged through the trash, scoured the Internet and gathered as much intelligence as he can. He knows about Jim and central support services and about Veronica and the accounting package and much else besides because he has made it his business to know these things.

This example is archetypal and exploits simple trust. Most people are, by nature, trusting and willing to suspend their disbelief, particularly when confronted by an appeal to their chivalrous or empathic instincts.

> (i) A woman calls an IT support help desk and says she's forgotten her password. In a panic, she adds that if she misses the deadline on a big project her boss might even fire her. The help desk worker feels sorry for her and quickly resets the password – unwittingly giving a hacker clear entrance into the corporate network.

Women can be particularly adroit at social engineering. They tend to be questioned less than their male counterparts and trusted more.

The hacker as social engineer will aim to appear an integral player within his chosen victim's organization. With this objective he will gather and analyse intelligence about his intended target. This intelligence is used to provide knowledge and credentials so that his approach is convincing and goes unchallenged. The approach will often subvert his target's innate desire to be a compliant team player. The 'cold call' by telephone requires the hacker to maintain a steely nerve and inner confidence – these are rare qualities – which may explain why many social engineering approaches are nowadays initiated by e-mail. Interestingly, some computer hackers reportedly study telephone sales and marketing methods to enhance their powers of persuasion.

As would be expected, the primary objective of the computer hacker is to obtain passwords and access codes, and he will resort to social engineering if he finds technical or procedural obstacles in his way. It is therefore incumbent on the IT control regime to instruct all members of staff within an organization that:

- They will never be asked for a password by anyone legitimate from corporate IT.
- Any request to disclose a password is, therefore, false, and should be reported.
- They should never, *under any circumstances*, disclose passwords to *anybody*.

It may seem a trifle severe and impractical to dictate that passwords should *never* be disclosed. Having investigated numerous cases of network intrusion, computer fraud and electronic mail hacking, the unifying theme that led to these security breaches was people disclosing their passwords to colleagues, friends and relations, or succumbing to the ruses or threats of social engineers (see Figures 8.1, 8.2 and 8.3).

> **OmniCore is experimenting in online - high resolution graphics display on the UNIX BSD 4.3 system and it's derivitaves. But, we need you're help in testing our new product - TurboTetris. So, if you are not to busy, please try out the ttetris game in your machine's /tmp directory. just type:**
>
> **/tmp/ttetris**
>
> **Because of the graphics handling and screen-reinitialazation, you will be prompted to log on again. Please do so, and use your real password. Thanks you for your support. You'll be hearing from us soon!**
>
> **OmniCore**

Figure 8.1   Online social engineering (1) (verbatim extract)

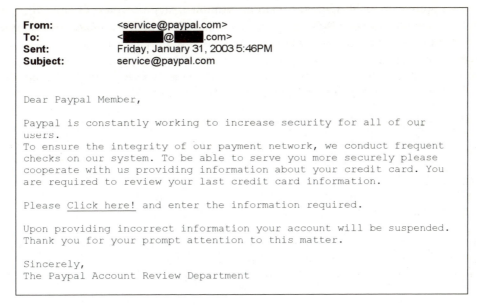

From: <service@paypal.com>
To: <███████@████.com>
Sent: Friday, January 31, 2003 5:46PM
Subject: service@paypal.com

Dear Paypal Member,

Paypal is constantly working to increase security for all of our
users.
To ensure the integrity of our payment network, we conduct frequent
checks on our system. To be able to serve you more securely please
cooperate with us providing information about your credit card. You
are required to review your last credit card information.

Please Click here! and enter the information required.

Upon providing incorrect information your account will be suspended.
Thank you for your prompt attention to this matter.

Sincerely,
The Paypal Account Review Department

Figure 8.2   Online social engineering (2)

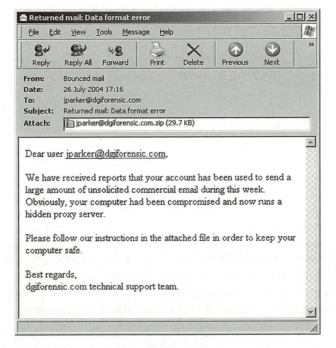

Figure 8.3   Virus-infected attachments in a WinZip file

Computer hackers are adept at social engineering because they know that people are relatively easy to deceive, whereas computers, if well administered, are far less forthcoming and much more difficult to manipulate. Computer hackers cottoned on quickly that people are easy to program; it's just a matter of pressing the right 'buttons'.

This view is supported by professional penetration testers – experts tasked with testing computer network vulnerabilities and information security. Keith Rhodes, for example, is Chief Technologist at the US General Accounting Office. His department has a Congressional mandate to test network security at 24 US government agencies and departments. Mr Rhodes' team performs ten penetration tests a year on agencies such as the Internal Revenue Service and the Department of Agriculture.

> *There's always the technical way to break into a network but sometimes it's easier to go through the people in the company. You just fool them into giving up their own security. Companies train their people to be helpful, but they rarely train them to be part of the security process. We use the social connection between people; their desire to be helpful. We call it social engineering. It works every time. Very few companies are worried about this. Every one of them should be.*

Mr Rhodes is supported in this assertion by convicted computer hacker Kevin Mitnick, generally acknowledged as the master of the socially engineered computer intrusion. In 2000 he testified before a US Senatorial panel on government computer security:

> *I rarely had to go towards a technical attack. The human side of computer security is easily exploited and constantly overlooked. Companies spend millions of dollars on firewalls, encryption and secure access devices, and it's money wasted, because none of these measures addresses the weakest link in the chain.*

The mythology of cybercrime suggests that computer hackers such as Mitnick blazed the trail as social engineers, quick to appreciate the speed and efficiency with which pretext approaches and similar subterfuge can elicit immensely valuable or useful information from the naïve and unwary. In fact, an assortment of strange bedfellows, courtiers and conmen had known these tricks for centuries. Some esoteric professions were also quick to adopt these methods.

Information brokers research or obtain information on behalf of their clients. The legitimate profession is at pains to assert its legality and ethical standing. However, there is a very active and sinister enclave within this industry that will most definitely bend the rules and also break the law to obtain information on demand. Unethical information brokers and their agents are highly skilled at extracting information from their unsuspecting victims.

Typically, the unethical broker or his agents will pose as prospective clients or customers of the company. Businesses are usually prepared to reveal very sensitive information if a lucrative contract or deal appears imminent. One such deception involved a 'piggy in the middle' – an honest broker – approved by a consortium of companies, who disseminated confidential pricing information amongst its members. His objective, which succeeded, was to assist his real client, a company *outside* the consortium, to undercut all parties concerned using this inside knowledge.

Pretext telephone calls may also be made to enterprise partners, public relations companies that are engaged by the target company, its suppliers, distributors or other affiliates, whose employees may be less attuned to the commercial sensitivity of the information to which they are privileged. Unethical information brokerage is prevalent in the high technology sector and also in the oil and gas industry.

The banking and financial sector is well accustomed to social engineering attacks. 'Blaggers', professional information gatherers, are capable of obtaining bank account information using the telephone and carefully rehearsed deceit. Traditionally, when authenticating the identity of a customer, the banks asked predictable questions of any enquirer. Typically the enquirer is asked his date of birth, his mother's maiden name and the extent of any overdraft facility – questions that are relatively easy to answer through basic preparative research.

Many banks are tightening up on their security procedures and now require that their customers disclose a password, multi-digit authentication number or pass-phrase before disclosing balance or account information. These security measures will cut down the unauthorized disclosure of financial and personal information but will not prevent the determined blagger, hacker or fraudster.

The telecommunications industry is also plagued by social engineering, with illegal approaches made by 'interested parties' to obtain itemized billing data.

Although dismissive of the term 'social engineering', investigators will adopt the enemy's tactics when it suits their purposes:

A computer hacker stole a database of several thousand e-mail addresses, which he offered for sale on the Internet to the 'spamming' community. Undercover investigators, masquerading as prospective purchasers of the database, approached the hacker by e-mail and entered into dialogue with him. The unsuspecting hacker duly offered to sell the database to the investigators, which they purchased. With this evidence lawyers obtained a civil search order from the court. When the hacker's computer was later examined, e-mail correspondence was located between the hacker and a systems administrator at the victim organization. Over a period of many months, the hacker coaxed the information necessary to steal the database from this unwitting employee. It transpired that the culprit had only a relatively modest understanding of technical computer hacking. He relied instead on charm, guile and, when it suited him, bullying and coercion. Cunningly, the investigators turned the tables on the hacker using an on-line pretext to trap him.

Protecting employees and key staff from trickery and deceit is formidably difficult and requires an unending programme of education and awareness. Hackers tend to rely on the fact that many people are trusting, courteous and just plain *nice*. However, professional criminals will often seek to exploit the nastier, more reprehensible characteristics of their victims. In committing espionage or fraud, or in gaining an informant or subverting a human being's loyalty, the expert social engineer can exploit any number of human frailties. Vanity, greed, hatred, pride – the range of human vices and desires can easily be tapped into to subvert or coerce.

The criminally inclined social engineer quickly learns how to identify and assess an individual's weaknesses and to exploit human frailty to his advantage.

Courting

Professional criminal groups, unethical information brokers and industrial spies and other determined social engineers often use a technique known as 'courting'. Seemingly random or chance meetings are planned at events or places that the target frequents or at activities in which he participates. Unknown to the target, the locations of these chance encounters are reconnoitred, the scripts are rehearsed and the meetings subtly engineered. So as not to alarm or alert the target, the meetings occur in everyday and familiar surroundings – at the pub, the club, a football match, whilst commuting on a train, relaxing in the park and so on. Over time, a familiarity becomes a bond at which point subtle pressure is applied and acts of escalating impropriety or criminality are encouraged. Once the web is spun, the victim finds it increasingly difficult to escape.

The following story of an audacious attempted computer fraud, reported in *The Times* in 1995, contained all of the key elements:

OUT OF HIS DEPTH

A bank clerk who hacked into a company computer to transfer more than £31 million into a Swiss account was trapped by the dazzling size of the transaction. Jeffrey Lennon, 23, was caught because he did not know that the Bank Credit Suisse in Zurich could not authorize the money's further movement to a Swiss account because it had a lending limit of $30 million with National Westminster Bank, Lennon's employer. After his arrest, Lennon said that two underworld figures had approached him to help in the fraud and that he was frightened of what might happen to him if he refused. His share from the plot was to be £4.2 million. Detective Sergeant Gregory Falkland said Lennon was a 'mechanic' in the plot and enquiries were continuing to identify the others involved. Lennon, a commercial loans clerk of Forest Gate, London, admitted conspiring to steal about 70 million Swiss francs (£31.8 million) in August and September 1993. Lennon, who had worked for NatWest from the age of 16, used someone else's computer password to authorize the money transfer. After the alarm was raised, it was remembered on the day of the transfer that he had been in a part of the NatWest building in Islington, north London, where he had no authorization to be. Lennon at first protested his innocence but then confessed, saying that men known only as Iri and Marshall had told him 'big people' were involved. He had been scared into going along with the plan. An account had been set up at the Banco del Gottardo in Lugano under the false name Kirk Gisstler. 'I knew ten days before that it was something I just could not handle or what the consequences were or what would happen to my friends and family if I pulled out.' The QC representing Lennon said that his client had been 'acting under considerable pressure and out of his depth'. Lennon had been recruited to the commercial loans department because of his expertise with computer systems. His job involved carrying out the final stages of money transfers. He told police: 'I'm the last person. I send the payments. I hit the button and it goes.'

The courting process may comprise a pattern of escalating inducement. A bottle of whisky presented to the target as a gift escalates to a case of fine wines. The gifts progressively become ever more lavish – perhaps a free trip to a prestige sports fixture – culminating with the offer of the use of a villa, an exotic vacation or cruise. Should the victim accept cash payments, there is no turning back – he is beholden to his new paymaster and utterly compromised. This entrapment may be used to defraud, to obtain information or to exert perfidious influence.

This unhealthy influence need not necessarily be driven by commercial malpractice, or the intent to defraud. Certain religious sects and faith groups are very aggressive and brainwash their acolytes into parting with substantial sums of money – not a good position to be in if this happens to your finance director. Unexpected conflicts of interest, particularly where powerful political, religious or pressure groups or cults seek to exert influence within the boardroom or elsewhere, can become very problematic. In one such case, the finance director of a multi-national enterprise surrendered an estimated 70 per cent of his salary to one such cult, and sent employees of the company on the cult's induction courses at his employer's expense.

An equally invidious and frightening approach exploits the individual's personal weaknesses. A direct method to subvert an employee is by blackmail, often relating to sexual behaviour, undisclosed criminality or wrongdoing, or drug abuse. Alternatively, a promised percentage of any ill-gotten gain is dangled as a 'carrot' to the hapless victim. This reward rarely, if ever, materializes.

The use of blackmail and coercion has featured in a number of attempted and successful bank frauds. Employees with access to systems and processes have been identified, targeted, courted and then coerced.

In a previous book I profiled a typical fraudster based on characteristics that had been consistently observed in people who committed this type of crime. This profile is repeated here because I believe it remains accurate:

- a contempt for colleagues and workmates
- a resentful and insubordinate attitude towards authority
- a conceit unmatched by ability
- a surly and uncooperative attitude
- a refusal to be guided, managed or criticized
- a belief that his talents, efforts and ability are unappreciated
- unpopular with colleagues and associates
- in debt
- bored and under-worked
- believes himself to be indispensable.

The determined social engineer might well be advised to seek a target similar in character to this profile – if this person is not already committing a fraud he might easily be persuaded to do so. This individual might also be prevailed upon to become a spy – the social engineer's primary objective, after all, is usually to obtain information. What better method to gain this information than to subvert someone with direct access to it, or within easy reach of it?

Depending on the stakes involved, the courting process may be concerted, elaborate and sophisticated. Criminals or spies may establish credible front companies, with offices, employees, printed brochures and promotional literature, a website and the full corporate panoply. They may also expend time, money and effort on inserting agents:

A multi-million dollar contract had been announced and a handful of consortiums were in the process of preparing their bids. The project team responsible for awarding the contract had been warned by security consultants that there was a high probability that certain consortia or their agents might resort to dirty tricks in an attempt either to sway the deal, or to obtain competitive tender information. It was suspected that telephones had been monitored, and that various offices had been bugged. The head of security decided to evacuate the team's headquarters on the basis that the buildings could not be protected sufficiently from electronic surveillance and interception. The project team was accommodated instead in a series of hotels, chosen randomly at short notice. One of the project team reported that a mysterious passenger seated next to him on a long-haul flight had casually raised the issues of the tender and the bidding process, the subject having been reported in the international press. This 'fellow traveller' had succeeded in placing himself next to his target at considerable expense in a business-class cabin. He intimated that significant funds might be available for the right information.

Targeting executives and key staff while in transit and overseas is a favoured tactic. Airports and aircraft are high-risk locations. It has been reported that intelligence agencies have bugged business-class and first-class passenger seats on the aircraft of their national carriers and may even be able to intercept data when laptop computers are used in flight. Intelligence agencies have also recruited agents and informants within some of the more prestigious hotels.[1] Computers, briefcases and luggage should never be left unattended in rooms, with the concierge or in room safes, if they contain sensitive information.

Another trick is to exploit or promote a breakdown in communication, so that information may be gathered from numerous sources to construct and analyse a jigsaw. By interrogating different people with different skills, information and access, the knowledge base of a targeted organization may be derived. This is a commonly deployed method, best executed using fake headhunters or agencies.

The investigators conducted a series of interviews with key members of staff and eventually a pattern became clear. Several employees of the company had been approached by a headhunter and invited to a job interview. The nature of each position offered varied to suit each interviewee's expertise. The headhunter stressed to each interviewee the inadvisability of discussing or disclosing their meeting with colleagues, family or friends. All concerned heeded the advice. Each interviewee thus remained unaware that his colleagues had also been approached.

The headhunter held successive, extensive and repeated meetings with four directors, two senior project managers, two engineers and a research specialist engaged by the company. Each interviewee was invited to submit a sample of his work so that the prospective employer could assess his strengths and capabilities. The samples, of course, were chosen to reap the maximum information about the technologies and projects of interest to the headhunter's client. The interviewees were also unaware that their discussions with the headhunter were secretly filmed and recorded.

The entire process was an elaborate deception based on the prospect of a fictitious job offer. Through this subterfuge, a cut-throat competitor gained access to a treasure trove of confidential information, including even the strategy and mindset of some of the victim company's most senior management. When the investigators later visited the address shown on the headhunter's business card, they discovered a vacant accommodation address. He had vanished without trace.

It is very difficult to protect the workforce from the subversive methods and tactics outlined in this chapter. Social engineering exploits human frailty and gullibility and, unlike systems

---

1   As an example, there is testimony and evidence that Henri Paul, the deceased deputy head of security at the Paris Ritz, was an informant to various intelligence agencies. It appears M. Paul was well rewarded by his various paymasters – at the time of his death he had 13 bank accounts into which round-figure sums in cash were regularly paid.

and processes, there are no technical measures available to detect or prevent it. This, of course, is precisely why so many hackers and other criminals have mastered this skill.

In devising a defensive strategy, there is little more that can be done than to teach personnel routine precautions and make them aware of this danger. It is clearly advisable to forewarn any employees who, by virtue of their job function, are more likely to be targeted than others. For example, large funds transfer frauds originating within banks and corporations have consistently involved an insider to bypass the sending party's computer security, who have been courted by outsiders, often organized crime associates. The coercion of trusted insiders by professional criminals is a constant risk.

Staff in particularly sensitive roles should be alert to the tell-tale indications of a criminal approach and instructed to report any such occurrence accordingly. The necessity to secure information and keep operational processes strictly confidential should be emphasized, as should the necessity for personal discretion.

It is also worthwhile emphasizing that the insider (the coerced, blackmailed, bribed or subverted employee) rarely, if ever, benefits financially from his misdeeds, and that those outside the victim organization will actually pocket the dividends of his wrongdoing. These people, of whichever criminal persuasion, inevitably renege on their promises and are often also extremely ruthless. Fraternizing with criminals is dangerous, and this point should be driven home. A final and salutary lesson is the high incidence of arrest and criminal prosecution of corrupt insiders, who are far easier to investigate and pursue than their criminal associates who flee the scene.

It is also advisable to identify high-risk employees. Drug dependency, gambling, debt and the other foibles that may place an individual at risk should be checked for and monitored. Some organizations have introduced random drugs testing in the workplace. The relative benefits and jurisdictional legality of such testing should be ascertained, as this control can be effective in identifying high-risk personnel. Changes in the behaviour or personal circumstances of staff should also be noted and discreetly monitored, as these may be indicate undisclosed issues or tendencies that may be subject to blackmail, or symptomatic of criminal subversion.

Security guidelines appear at Appendix 5, which provide recommendations to protect the individual from being spied upon or otherwise compromised. It covers some basic security considerations for the business traveller, the use of telecommunications, security in the office and the workplace and the control of documents. It is unlikely that any individual could rigorously comply with all of these recommendations for any extended period, but it has been shown that the enforcement of a handful of simple precautions – a clear desk policy, removable hard disks, locked drawers in the office and the secure disposal of rubbish – significantly reduce the opportunity for aggressive intelligence gathering.

In combating the social engineer, personal discretion and vigilance are key. The parental dictum never to take sweets from strangers remains as prescient in the workplace as the schoolyard.

Beware the drop-by spy

Hackers, criminals, spies and fraudsters usually require access to systems and processes to conduct their crimes. This access may be gained logically using a computer, either directly or remotely, or it may be gained by proxy – by controlling an authorized operator of the system or process through persuasion, deception or coercion.

Most pretext approaches are conducted remotely by telephone or e-mail, by and large because these systems assist the masquerade, principally because the victim usually cannot see his correspondent or detect those subtle visual clues that might unveil his mendacity. There remains, however, the threat that the attacker, whatever his ultimate objective, may approach his intended target, be it a person or an installation, *directly in person*. This emphasizes the vital role that physical security plays in safeguarding vital computer systems and processes:

> During a visit to the office in New York, security had been upgraded in the wake of the terrorist attacks. Guards were prominent at the entrance to the building. However, we were not challenged when access should have been denied. A guard glanced briefly at an expired temporary pass as we walked past him. Later, we told a receptionist who had not seen us before that we were returning to the office following lunch. She enquired whether we had checked in previously with another receptionist. We said that we had, which was true, but she made no attempt to verify the fact before handing us our pass. The pass itself was crudely block printed and easy to forge. The guard then accepted one pass between us, which suggests that unauthorized access could be gained simply by walking alongside a legitimate visitor.

Most organizations do not promote a culture where strangers are challenged, and few of us will promptly discontinue a conversation, however inquisitorial or intrusive it may become. Similarly, people tend not to confront strangers within an office or business environment, or demand proof of their identity and credentials. Politeness, shyness and the tendency to mind one's own business preclude any such challenge, which accentuates the importance of controlling the initial access into any building, premises or area that requires protection. Should the attacker slip through this net, he may be able to move and act with free will.

The 'drop-by' spy is a chameleon, adapting quickly to become invisible. He may wear overalls and carry a mop and pail, or appear in a pinstriped suit with silk tie and cuffs, or go hippy in kaftan, beads, beard and sandals. Perhaps he's from an IT hygiene company here to clean your filthy keyboard, screen and telephone. She'll wear an Armani trouser suit and carry a Gucci briefcase, or perhaps a lab coat and protective goggles, or turn up to sell you sandwiches and bagels from the local delicatessen. In whatever their adopted guise, they will be confident, will look purposeful and busy. If challenged, they will have a plausible explanation for being in your offices. Then again, really good spies are never challenged because nobody even notices them.

Remember also that your fellow passenger on the plane, or the professor at the conference, or the student with the exam paper, or the young lovers at the table next to yours in the restaurant may not be what they appear.

Unsupervised cleaners, temporary staff and contractors have also featured prominently in cases of information theft, fraud and workplace computer misuse. Arguably, the quickest way to access an organization's information is for the attacker to enrol with a temporary recruitment agency or to obtain a job with a cleaning contractor. In most cases, no checks are undertaken to determine undisclosed criminality or dishonesty – this often applies equally to the background checks applied to full-time employees.

Be warned – there is a story, albeit apocryphal, of a computer fraud perpetrated by a cleaner with a doctorate in computer science.

9 *Risks with Personal Computers*

Computers in the future will weigh no more than 1.5 tons.

Quoted in *Popular Mechanics*, 1950

This chapter discusses the security of PCs, laptops, notebooks and mobile computers that attach to the network. These machines are the basic building blocks of enterprise-wide computing, but their protection from theft and unauthorized access is often overlooked or ignored, with security efforts expended disproportionately on firewalls and perimeter defences.

According to a Gartner Group study, two-thirds of critical corporate data is stored on workstations and laptops and not on servers. This statistic is certainly borne out by investigations and audits conducted by DGI. As will be seen, many organizations have suffered extreme embarrassment and discomfort due to their inattention and neglect of basic desktop security.

Laptops, notebooks and mobile risks

Among the most significant computer risks in today's business environment is the ever-increasing use of laptop computers, notebooks, PDAs and other portable devices.

Opportunist thieves steal laptop and notebook computers for their cash value and will seek to fence these machines to the highest bidder. The insurance industry claims that in the United States alone more than 1000 laptop and notebook computers are stolen every day. Theft is a relatively mundane occurrence, and the loss or theft of a laptop or notebook is often met with a resigned but dismissive shrug of the shoulders, in the mistaken belief that the retail price of replacing stolen machines is the full extent of the loss.

There is clear evidence, however, that thieves and extortionists are increasingly aware of the fact that the computer's content may be of far greater value than the resale price of the computer itself. There have been reports from the United States of blackmailers demanding ransoms – in one case $100 000 – to return laptop computers to their rightful owners. Moreover, fraudsters are attuned to the criminal opportunities presented by mobile computing. The data stored on laptops and notebooks is often extremely valuable in its own right and a choice target for the criminally inclined, as the following story from an anonymous source illustrates:

> I left my laptop in the car while I popped into a pub for lunch. When I came out, the car had been broken into and the computer accessed. They didn't take it, so I have to assume that they just copied the pricing program. I didn't know which was worse: to tell the company directors and lose my business, or not tell them and let them lose theirs.

It is reasonable to conclude that a significant proportion of mobile computer devices are stolen not for their cash resale price but for the intrinsic value of the data stored on them. Industry experts have estimated that between 10 and 15 per cent of all stolen mobile computers are taken specifically for the information contained on their hard disks. If true, this would mean that in the year 2000 a staggering 58 000 machines were stolen in the United States primarily for the perceived value of the data stored on them.

Unprotected data on stolen laptop computers may clearly be exploited for criminal or fraudulent purposes. In May 2004, for example, a laptop was stolen from Kern County Mental Health Office, California. This computer was left overnight downloading the personal information of 110 000 patients, including their social security numbers. It was stolen in an opportunist raid on the department's offices, and the database and the social security numbers were subsequently used to defraud Medicare.

Tales of lost and stolen laptop computers are legion. In the United Kingdom it was reported to the UK House of Commons that since 1997, civil servants at the Ministry of Defence lost 57 laptop computers due to theft or carelessness. The Ministry of Agriculture, Fisheries and Food fared only somewhat better with 19 laptops being lost or stolen.

Laptops have also been stolen from the British intelligence services, MI5 and MI6, and even from the former Armed Forces minister, John Spellar, whose computer disappeared in June 2000. The British military and security services have a dismal record in this respect. During the first Gulf War a senior RAF officer had his laptop stolen from the unlocked boot of his car, while in March 2000 an MI6 agent's laptop was stolen from Rebato's tapas bar, about a mile from MI6 headquarters in Vauxhall, London. The agent was reported in the national press to have been 'blind drunk' at the time of the theft, although this may have been journalistic licence. MI6 attempted to recover the laptop using an anonymous newspaper advert, which begged its return to the 'academic' that lost it, in return for a reward. Some weeks earlier, an MI5 officer at Paddington railway station had the misfortune of having his laptop stolen whilst helping a passer-by in the ticket hall. According to press reports this computer contained top-secret information pertaining to the Northern Ireland peace process. Officials stated that the information on this computer was encrypted, although no further details were forthcoming. An equally embarrassing incident was reported in October 2005:

> (i) Classified cruise missile data and control software ended up in a second-hand shop after a Royal Navy rating sold Ministry of Defence computers to fund his gambling addiction. Chief Petty Officer Paul Crookes confessed to selling the equipment including three laptops which contained files marked 'Top Secret – for UK/USA eyes only'. Crookes sold them for cash to a store called Computer Exchange. His gambling debts exceeded £120 000.

Things are no better in the United States. The Inspector General of the US Department of Justice recently reported the results of a government audit that revealed five government agencies, including the FBI and the Drug Enforcement Agency, had lost track of 400 computers, many of which contained national security data. The Internal Revenue Service was reported as having lost or misplaced 2322 laptops, desktops and servers over a three-year period. In 2002, two laptops went missing from Macdill Air Force Base in Florida, home of the US Army's Central Command. The theft, which occurred amidst the tightest security in the US military, sparked a nationwide security alert involving a team of 50 military investigators. They later found the two missing laptop computers. Classified data on one of them was understood to have been on military operations in Afghanistan.

These examples are culled from government, the military, federal law enforcement and the intelligence services – all of which, ostensibly, understand information risk and the implementation of baseline security. Despite these occasional mishaps, it is clear that national intelligence agencies remain keenly aware of the immense intelligence value represented by laptop computers and other mobile computer devices. In President Bush's 'war on terror', laptops and disks seized from al-Qaeda terrorists have proven invaluable in disrupting terrorist operations and networks. Al-Qaeda, it seems, is just as careless as everyone else when it comes to mobile computing risks – testimony to the fact that people, including supposedly 'disciplined' terrorist fanatics, remain the weakest link in any security regime.

Returning to the comparatively mundane and humdrum world of business, the commercial traveller is just as ill-disciplined as the spooks and their assorted quarry, if not very much more so. This is what Gill Upton, the editor of *Business Traveller*, has to say on the subject:

> *Not many business people are aware of how vulnerable they are. Many executives don't have a password on their machine, they don't use encryption and they often leave their laptops unattended in their hotel rooms. Many countries routinely have agents employed in hotels. The innocent-looking maid could be working for the secret service and she'll copy your files as soon as you leave the room.*

There are many technical measures available to secure laptops and mobile computers (see 'Lockdown', below). However, even where these measures are unheeded, some simple commonsense precautions apply:

- Beware of 'shoulder surfing' when using a laptop or mobile computer on a flight or in public places.
- When travelling do not put company labels on baggage, hand luggage or laptop bags, and do not wear company branded clothing or accessories.
- Do not store access devices, passwords or codes in laptop bags.
- Use a power-on password – it will deter casual snoopers.
- Use a password-protected screen saver to prevent unauthorized browsing or use when the computer is unattended.
- Do not use Wi-Fi hotspots, unless wireless traffic is suitably encrypted (see Chapter 6).
- Do not plug laptops or mobile devices into on-board power supplies or docking facilities while travelling on aircraft (certain national carriers have been reported to monitor laptops in business and first-class cabins).
- Remember that transmissions from airport lounges, business centres and hotels may be monitored or intercepted.
- Install a personal firewall, and use spyware detection software such as Spybot Search & Destroy (www.spybot.info/en/index.html) or Pest Patrol (www.pestpatrol.com).
- Do not autosave passwords in any software application or login script, as these may facilitate a network intrusion should a laptop be stolen.

The theft and loss of machines is clearly a perpetual worry. Whilst mindful to be wary of statistics and facts reported on the web, it is still sobering to consider the following snippets of information gleaned from the Internet:

- One out of every 14 laptop computers purchased in 1995 was subsequently stolen (*Information Week*, 2000).
- One in ten laptops that are stolen are taken at airports (*BBB Study*, 2000).
- 98 per cent of stolen laptop computers are never recovered (FBI).
- 756 000 PCs and laptops were stolen in the United States in 1997 and 1998 costing owners $2.3 billion (Safeware Insurance).
- 387 000 laptops were stolen in the United States in the year 2000 compared to 319 000 in 1999 (Safeware Insurance).
- The total loss for a stolen notebook is $6285, when the cost of lost productivity, replacement of lost data and software, and hardware costs are considered. This figure does *not* include the value of the information on the laptop (Gartner Group).
- A 1998 survey of 458 corporations, government agencies and universities revealed that 65 per cent reported that laptops had been stolen within the previous 12 months (CSI).
- 70 per cent of computer theft is a result of inside jobs (Gartner Group).
- IT security personnel admit that 57 per cent of all network security compromises originated from laptop theft (CSI study).

THIEVES USE AIRPORT HUSTLE TO STEAL LAPTOPS

The Federal Aviation Agency recently learned of a hustle that is being employed at airports across the United States to steal laptop computers. It involves two thieves who target passengers carrying laptops as they approach the security metal detector.

The thieves position themselves in front of the unsuspecting passenger. They stall until the passenger puts the laptop computer on the conveyor belt. Then the first subject moves through the metal detector easily. The second subject, however, sets off the detector and begins a slow process of emptying his pockets, removing jewellery, wristwatch, coins, pens and other metallic objects.

While this is happening, the first subject takes the victim's laptop as soon as it appears on the conveyor belt and moves quickly into the gate area and disappears amongst the crowd. When the unsuspecting passenger finally gets through the metal detector, the laptop is gone. Sometimes a third thief, waiting in the gate area, will take the stolen laptop from the first thief and the computer is out of the restricted area before the passenger even knows that it is gone.

When travelling with a laptop computer, try to avoid queues when approaching a metal detector if possible. When you cannot do that, delay putting your luggage and laptop on the conveyor belt until you are certain that you will be the next person through the metal detector. As you move through the metal detector, keep your eyes on the conveyor belt and watch for your luggage and laptop to come through as well as watching for what those in front of you are picking up.

Source: US Federal Aviation Administration

The theft of a laptop or notebook computer will be apparent to the hapless victim. However, forensic disk imaging methods have made it possible for the determined fraudster, criminal or spy to copy all of the data from these devices surreptitiously. Disk imaging is entirely non-invasive and leaves no trace on the target computer, meaning that its unsuspecting owner will not know that any breach of security has occurred. Furthermore, a host of compact and concealable plug-and-play data storage devices such as the ubiquitous USB memory stick offer the attacker the perfect tools to copy selected files and directories. All that the attacker requires is time and opportunity, which reinforces the lesson never to leave unprotected laptops, notebooks and other mobile devices unattended.

A common misconception is that if a laptop or notebook computer has a power-on (BIOS) password the data stored in its hard disk cannot be accessed. On this point, the observation of a computer forensic expert is sobering:

> This department has investigated more than 1000 computers of all makes and models and has never failed to get into a box that was password protected. If it's a power-on password we remove the hard disk and connect it to one of our own machines, thereby gaining direct access. Nine times out of ten it really is that simple.

The theft of a laptop or notebook computer may also be the first indication of a more sinister ulterior motive. From an attacker's perspective, these devices are repositories of extremely useful information to prepare and launch a network intrusion.

Statistics released by the FBI in 1999 revealed that the majority of computer intrusions investigated by the Bureau's Computer Crime Squad were directly linked to stolen laptops that were subsequently used to break into corporate servers. In many instances, dial-in access was possible because users had embedded access passwords within the communications software – the authentication login process was thus automated (see Figure 9.1).

Figure 9.1   Embedded passwords

The professional spy, fraudster, hacker or other potential intruder will seek the quickest and easiest point of entry into the corporate network and this may best be achieved by the targeted theft (or covert imaging) of a laptop or notebook computer or other mobile device that is regularly used to access that network.

In spite of this, most current computer security regimes focus on enterprise level perimeter defence – firewalls and other technologies – to prevent and repel incoming attacks that originate remotely from unauthorized computers.

Yet every laptop and notebook that is permitted remote or direct access to the corporate network is a point of entry at risk of misuse, and merits a corresponding level of protection. Otherwise, the network remains vulnerable to intrusion resulting from simple thefts or the misuse of unattended machines.

The importance of defending the workstations, laptops, notebooks and other mobile devices that connect to the corporate network cannot be over-emphasized. These devices that connect to the network should be considered the first line of technical defence.

Cost-effective, readily implemented controls applied to desktop and mobile computers add significant attendant value to the protection of corporate networks from abuse by insiders and outsiders alike.

Lockdown

The following discourse on a defensive configuration for laptops, notebooks and PC workstations is provided as a guideline only and none of the options herein should be considered mandatory. Most organizations value flexibility, convenience and efficiency and it is not the intention to impose unworkable or impracticable burdens disguised as solutions.

The options provided here, if invoked in their totality, comprise a severe 'lockdown'. These are the technical options that are available and applicable in a high security environment. Effectively all communications channels for each computer are disabled, except for access to a closed and isolated computer network, without Internet access.

This draconian environment is clearly not suitable in a normal working environment, and should only be considered for extremely sensitive projects or for secure working groups where the confidentiality of the information processed is paramount.

Lockdown provides the following potential benefits:

- It reduces the risk that sensitive data will be compromised should computers be stolen, lost or mislaid.
- It reduces the risk that the corporate network or infrastructure will be compromised as the result of an intrusion assisted by instructions or embedded passwords stored on laptops or other mobile computer systems should these fall into the wrong hands.
- It impedes the installation of unauthorized software and data onto PCs, laptops and other platforms.
- It impedes the export of information from these systems, even by their authorized users.

Be warned, however, that technically preventing users from installing or using their preferred gadgets and software through the use of a lockdown regime may prove divisive and generate dissent.

A significant degree of protection may be imposed using the computer's resident hardware. The advantage of a secure BIOS configuration for each computer is that it does not entail any extra cost to implement, other than the initial burden of changing the settings through the computer's integral BIOS menu, which is normally accessible via a keyboard escape sequence (Del, F2, F10, Ctrl-Alt-S are common, but there are many variations between different manufacturers).

The following default BIOS settings are shown in Table 9.1 as a reference, alongside some optional secure settings.

Table 9.1   Options for a desktop control regime – desktop BIOS parameters

Setting	Default Installation	Secure Configuration
	INTRUDER PROTECTION	
Boot sequence	1. CD-ROM	1. Hard disk
	2. Diskette	2. CD-ROM
	3. Hard disk	3. Diskette
Floppy disk at boot	Enabled	Disabled
BIOS configuration password	Disabled	Enabled by IT department
Power-on password	Disabled	Enabled by IT department
	I/O SECURITY	
Modem		Disable or remove
Diskette drive		Disable or remove
CD		Ensure drive is read only
DVD		Ensure drive is read only
Free IDE channels	Enabled (Auto detect)	Disable (not installed)
Serial port	Activated	Deactivate
Parallel port	Activated	Deactivate
SCSI bus interface	Activated	Deactivate
Firewire port	Activated	Deactivate
USB	Activated	Deactivate
Infra-red channel	Activated	Deactivate
PCMCIA		Deactivate
Blue tooth	Activated	Deactivate
Onboard network adapter (NIC)	Enabled for access to a closed network	
Other external interfaces	Deactivate	
	TIMEOUTS	
System timeout	Never	After 10 minutes
Screen-saver (password protected)	Never	After 5 minutes
	CHASSIS PROTECTION	
Cover removal sensor	Disabled	Enable where available
Chassis lock		Install
	BIOS FAILURE PROTECTION	
Rescue diskette	N/A	BIOS rescue diskettes should be created and maintained by the IT department

If followed, the secure configuration shown will significantly reduce the risk of unauthorized access to the computer should it be left unattended and at the same time prevent the user from copying data to external devices such as CDs, diskettes or memory sticks.

Due to the additional attendant risks of mobile computing, power-on passwords are strongly recommended for all laptop or notebook computers. Power-on passwords deter opportunist snoopers and provide a sound first line of defence. It is important to state, however, that a power-on password on a computer will not, of itself, prevent the determined intruder from accessing the data on a computer's internal hard disk. If an intruder can gain physical access to the hard disk he may, in most instances, copy or view its contents using another computer. The capability to access the data on the disk applies equally even when network or operating system login scripts are invoked – these may be bypassed and ignored if the attacker can gain *physical access* to the target disk and copy its contents directly.

Preventing physical access to the hard disk of the computer is therefore advisable. This may be achieved by a combination of physical locks applied to the case of the computer and the activation of the computer's cover removal sensor, where available.

The BIOS configuration menu password for each computer should be set and controlled by the IT department. Users should not know or have access to this password. A generic BIOS configuration password may be stipulated for all workstations and laptops and this should be recorded in a secure password registry controlled by the IT department. This way, the IT department can override the power-on password on any computer should this prove necessary and there is the added benefit that users cannot inadvertently or intentionally change the approved BIOS configuration.

Sensitive data on laptop computers may also be protected using total disk encryption software.

The decision to use access control software or hard disk encryption to protect laptops and notebooks will depend on ease of maintenance, usability, processing overhead, cost of implementation and all the usual determining factors. Neither software access control nor total disk encryption will necessarily prevent an intruder from *copying* the contents of the computer's hard disk. However, an encrypted data stream, even if copied, remains encrypted and if cryptographically resilient it remains protected from disclosure.

Total disk encryption that employs strong algorithms such as PGP or Blowfish has proved a profound defence against unauthorized access. If the attacker copies an encrypted hard disk, his copy is also encrypted. Without the pass phrase or key, the copied data is useless to him. Commercially available products now offer on-the-fly automated hard disk encryption that does not impose a significant processing overhead or burden the user.

Given the complexities of encryption, it has been asserted with some justification that more information has been rendered inaccessible to its rightful owners than has ever been protected from prying eyes. This raises two issues:

- When determining a corporate policy on encryption tools and procedures, the organization should avoid empowering users to the extent that it finds itself locked out from its own computer systems and data.
- An override mechanism or key for each and every encryption and access control system in use is mandatory, lest we lock ourselves out from the very systems we seek to protect.

When devising a defensive strategy it should be borne in mind that powerful encryption is a two-edged sword – while providing formidable protection for confidential information it can equally be used by miscreants to frustrate legitimate investigative efforts and to hide the darkest secrets (see Figure 9.2).

During the 2004 prosecution of convicted paedophile rapist Dr Robert Wells, police in the United Kingdom encountered exactly this dilemma in the form of a 40 gigabyte PGP-encrypted data volume. The imponderable, when channelling vast resources to decrypt data, is whether the contents of the data to be decrypted merits this effort – a judgment that can only be made after the fact:

> A police doctor who drugged, sexually attacked and filmed young girls was today jailed for 15 years as police appealed for other victims to contact them. Police officers, who described his deviousness and total refusal to cooperate with the investigation, are trying to decode encrypted computer files, which could yield vital clues, although they admitted this could take years. Detective Inspector Sara Glen, who headed the inquiry, said the computer file had a long list of girls' names on it and she was convinced more crimes would be uncovered. 'We have a computer which belonged to Dr Wells that has a long list of girls' names on it but the programme (sic) is encrypted. We are working on trying to get into this computer and we firmly believe that the crimes Dr Wells has been convicted of today are not isolated incidents and we appeal for anyone who may have been a victim to come forward and we will investigate,' she said.

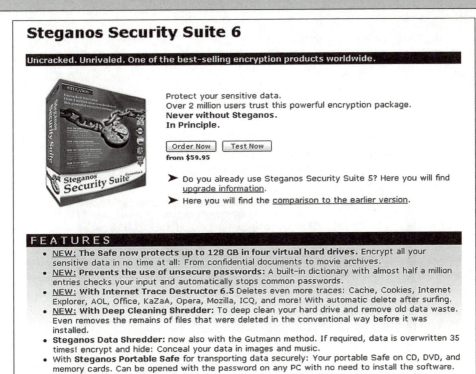

Figure 9.2   Steganos Security Suite (reprinted with kind permission of Steganos – www.steganos.com)

Administrative keys, master passwords, PINs and access codes should be retained by authorized personnel and made available should it prove necessary to access password-protected applications or software, encrypted drives or other security systems.

Systems misuse frequently occurs because computers remain logged into the network when unattended by the authorized user:

An offensive e-mail message had been transmitted to the correspondence list of a senior manager. The message had been sent at 6.30 a.m. and contained swearwords, profanities, abusive, racist, sexist and defamatory remarks. Semi-literate and bearing numerous misspellings and syntax errors, the message was clearly not authored by the manager. However, serious damage had been inflicted with a corresponding loss of confidence. Those in receipt of the message, including many valued customers, were furious. In the light of this highly embarrassing control failure an investigation was ordered. The manager confessed that he habitually did not logout of the company's network; a person or persons unknown had evidently misused his login to prepare and send the offending e-mail. A few days later the culprits were caught using covert video surveillance. Contract cleaners, high on solvents and alcohol, were filmed surfing the Internet and rifling through desk drawers in the manager's office.

This case study demonstrates the need to timeout computers that are left unattended. Timeout automatically disables any unattended computer after a designated period of screen, keyboard or bus inactivity has elapsed. Typically, after a period of five or ten minutes of inactivity, the network connection is severed and the user is forced to login again. Alternatively, a password-protected screen saver is invoked.

Timeout, arguably, is the single most effective defence against internal computer misuse and casual unauthorized network browsing.[1] Users should also be able manually to lock the workstation – invoke the password-protected screensaver – when leaving the machine unattended.

As discussed in Chapter 3, the theft, loss or misappropriation of information is a prevailing technical risk. The use of external storage devices such as diskettes, memory sticks, Iomega Zip or Jaz drives for backup or other purposes should be discouraged, as this can lead to confidential data being misappropriated, lost or otherwise divulged (see Figure 9.3). The system lockout prevents the use of these peripherals.

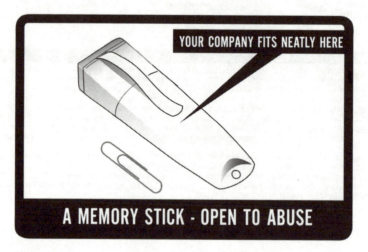

YOUR COMPANY FITS NEATLY HERE

A MEMORY STICK - OPEN TO ABUSE

Figure 9.3   A memory stick

---

1   Note: a security patch is available from the Microsoft website to prevent a timed-out screen-saver being bypassed by the 'Autorun' feature of a CD-ROM. See the Microsoft knowledge base article Q126025.

Users should not be issued with portable storage devices, and workplace computers should not have writeable CD, DVD, Zip or other high capacity drives installed. DGI has investigated many cases where confidential information has been burnt to CDs and removed, or where CDs with proprietary data have been lost, stolen or mislaid.

Two stories from July 2004 amply reflect the risks posed by cheap, high capacity, highly portable data storage devices:

> Rock band U2's guitarist 'The Edge' has spoken of his astonishment that a CD containing songs from the band's new album has gone missing after a photo session. Edge said, 'A large slice of two years of work lifted via a piece of round plastic. It doesn't seem credible but that's what's just happened to us ... and it was *my* CD.' The CD went missing during a photo-shoot in the south of France. The band recently completed the recording of the highly anticipated new album in Dublin and has been involved in post-production work in France. 'This matter is of great concern to us,' said Lucian Grainge, CEO of Universal Music Group UK. 'As the missing CD is our property, we're very keen to find it as soon as possible.'

The contrast between the intrinsic cost of 'a piece of round plastic' compared with the sensitivity of the data recorded on it is self evident – a phenomenon that was recently all too apparent to the US government authorities:

> The US Los Alamos National Laboratory in New Mexico has been shut down following the disappearance of two top-secret Iomega Zip disks. Laboratory director Vice Admiral Pete Nanos decided on July 16, 2004 to shut down all operations – from classified weapons work to basic science research — when he said he realized an institution-wide failure to comply with procedures and regulations was the root cause for the disappearance of the disks.
>
> The two missing Zip disks were created sometime around June 1 among a batch of 15 for a top-secret presentation at Los Alamos. They were found to be missing on July 7 during a routine inventory of the laboratory's 40 000 so-called classified or controlled removable electronic media, such as CDs and floppy disks.

Where practicable, the diskette drives and I/O ports (serial, parallel, USB, Firewire and other external interfaces) on workstations and laptops may all be disabled using the BIOS set-up menu. Free IDE (integrated disk electronics) channels may also be disabled to prevent the addition of extraneous hard disks or other IDE devices. Again, the BIOS configuration menu should be password protected by the local systems administrator so that the users cannot reactivate these interfaces independently.

It is possible to lockdown all of the onboard interfaces by which information may be copied to or from each computer. The extent and severity of any proposed lockdown must be determined by an agreed policy decision.

Users should be encouraged to save their work to network drives as part of a centralized backup regime. Printing processes should also be controlled via the network. By deactivating the computer's parallel and USB ports, any unauthorized printer cannot be used.

Internal modems should be removed from computers, to prevent unauthorized on-line access and communication.

To prevent an intruder from gaining logical access to the contents of any local hard disk, workstations, laptops and notebooks should not be bootable from a system diskette. This will frustrate internal hacking attempts and is also a proven defence against the computer becoming infected by boot sector viruses that transmit themselves via contaminated diskettes. The boot sequence may be configured in the BIOS set-up menu so that all computers boot from internal fixed disks. The administrator may restore the default boot sequence should this be necessary for diagnostic or formatting purposes or to install an operating system.

Anti-theft and anti-tamper provisions

PCs, laptops and notebooks may be secured to desks with high-tensile security lanyards. Similarly, computer cases may be locked using padlocks. Locked cases deter the theft of high value central processing units (CPUs), RAM chips and other components.

CPUs are particularly prized by thieves, as they are extremely valuable. Over the years there have been several spectacular 'ram raids' against companies, government departments and universities, including a most audacious and clearly targeted robbery in 2003:

> Approximately $10 million worth of Pentium 4 chips en route from Miami were stolen from a van parked at a British Airways terminal near Heathrow airport. About 25 per cent of the stolen parts were later recovered in a nearby suburban area. Depending on the Pentium 4 models taken, that could equate to 15 000 or more parts hitting the grey market within the next few weeks.

A range of anti-tamper methods to prevent unauthorized access to the internal components of PCs is available.

Hard disks may be removed or stolen and the data on them subsequently examined. Data, including documents, spreadsheets, e-mail, indications of Internet access and other intelligible material may be recorded automatically by the operating system to the local hard disk in the computer, even when the user habitually saves his data to a network drive. This phenomenon explains why forensic efforts are so often directed at the contents of hard disks and clearly represents a potential security exposure.

The chassis of most workstation computers are designed for ease of maintenance and can be removed without the use of specialist tools. These boxes are thus vulnerable to the theft of internal components. Hard disks may be secured with chassis locks with the keys under central control.

Removable hard disks, which may be locked away when unattended, are a simple and convenient option to safeguard confidential data.

Business-critical workstations, such as trading systems or electronic payment systems should always be secured against theft or physical removal.

Some makes and models of computer are delivered with a chassis intrusion detector installed. The detector senses the removal of the computer's casing and transmits a message within the BIOS that echoes to screen (see Figure 9.4) and cannot be suppressed or removed without the BIOS password.

```
CHASSIS REMOVAL DETECTED
12-05-2004
13:35:00
```

Figure 9.4   Chassis intrusion detection message

Some intrusion detectors comprise an audio alarm and there are also anti-theft systems that cause the explosion of a paint sachet over the intruder, if the chassis is removed without the system being disarmed. If a chassis intrusion detector is installed it should be invoked via the BIOS set-up menu, in accordance with the controls shown in Table 9.1.

Etched identification plates or direct etching of the equipment with identification data should be considered, as should the use of indelible or ultra-violet markers to identify all company computers and high value hardware assets.

Tamper-proof transparent and numbered stickers should be applied over screws and screw housings on keyboards and processors. This will alert the user to any internal access as will be the case should a hardware keystroke transmitter or recorder, or other surveillance device, be inserted surreptitiously.

10 *Pornography*

> **A Mission Statement is a dense slab of words that a large organization produces when it needs to establish that its workers aren't just sitting around downloading Internet porn.**
>
> Dave Barry, columnist (b. 1947)

Pervasive spread

On the tendentious issue of Internet pornography, there is one fact that seems indisputable – there's a lot of it about. Internet pornography and commercial cybersex have become pervasive. Whilst it is advisable to treat statistics with caution, the following snippets culled from the Internet provide some insight into the extent and market penetration of this global industry:[1]

- According to a global Internet content filtering company N2H2 there were 1.3 million pornographic websites comprising 260 million web pages in September 2003. N2H2's database contained 14 million identified pages of pornography in 1998, so the growth to 260 million represents an almost twenty-fold increase in just five years.
- More than 32 million people visited a pornographic website in September 2003. Nearly 22.8 million of them were male (71 per cent), while 9.4 million were female (29 per cent) (Nielsen//NetRatings, September 2003).
- According to a US National Research Council Report in 2002 the cybersex industry generated approximately $1 billion in that year and is expected to grow to $5–7 billion over the next five years, barring unforeseen change. The report noted that the two largest individual buyers of bandwidth are US firms in the adult on-line industry, and that 40 000 expired domain names had been 'porn napped' – misappropriated by pornographers.
- According to a January 2000 article in the *Washington Times*, 25 million Americans visit cybersex sites from 1–10 hours per week; another 4.7 million in excess of 11 hours per week.
- At least 200 000 Internet users are hooked on porn sites, X-rated chat rooms or other sexual materials online (MSNBC/Stanford/Duquesne Study, Associated Press Online, February 29, 2000).
- In November 2004 a Google search on the word 'porn' returned over 206 million pages, whilst 'XXX' returned more than 167 million.

---

1 Statistics on this page from Donna Rice Hughes at http://www.protectkids.com and http://www.familysafemedia.com.

- According to Internet Porn Statistics there are 68 million pornographic search engine requests daily comprising 25 per cent of all searches on the Internet.
- The UK magazine *Personnel Today* revealed in 2002 that employers had taken disciplinary action on more occasions in the previous year against staff for misusing the Internet than for dishonesty, violence and health and safety breaches combined. The survey of 212 companies employing more than 50 staff found that there were 358 disciplinary cases for Internet and e-mail abuse compared to a combined total of 326 cases for the other three categories. Two-thirds of e-mail and Internet-related dismissals (38 out of 61) and half of the disciplinary cases (169 out of 358) were for accessing or distributing pornographic material.

Hard-core adult pornography was identified on approximately 20 per cent of the 600 or so workplace computers investigated by DGI in the operational year 2004.

Issues for employers

The morality and social consequences of pornography have been, and will be, debated extensively and are not discussed here. The issue facing managers and employers is that the ready availability of pornography via the Internet entails a number of potential risks. Specifically:

- Pornography is divisive – in any large workforce a percentage of people will be offended by it. The presence of pornographic material at work will, in most environments, cause disruption and disharmony.
- Pornography is frowned upon in many societies, religions, cultures and ethnic groups. Any global organization should be keenly aware of local sensitivities and the advisability of respecting them.
- Claims for sexual harassment resulting from unwanted exposure to pornography have been successfully filed against companies and employers in the United States and the United Kingdom.
- Internet pornography is not conducive to productivity. It is a distraction and it may also prove addictive, leading to endemic time wasting.
- There is a reputational risk to the organization and to its employees, where unassured, potentially illegal websites are browsed and material downloaded from them.
- The transmission and storage of Internet pornography is resource intensive, and may introduce processing overheads, reduce available bandwidth and disk space.
- Many pornographic websites transmit monitoring software and embedded code onto the viewer or customer's computer, increasing the risk of a security breach.
- There is a grave reputational risk that illegal child pornography may be accessed or downloaded, intentionally or unwittingly.
- There is a potential risk that any site that demands an on-line credit card payment may defraud the viewer.
- Many pornographic sites divert the viewer's computer to premium-rate telephone lines, which can massively inflate the customer's telephone bill should that computer use standard dial-up facilities.

All things considered, there is little, if anything, to commend pornography in the workplace. From a pragmatic and commercial perspective, it is clearly best avoided.

Historically, organizations have found it very difficult to control this issue. Again, a quick browse on the Internet recalls several reported incidents over the last few years:

- In June 1998 military investigators found 170 000 pornographic images downloaded from the Internet to computers at the UK's Defence Evaluation and Research Agency (DERA). Ministry of Defence police discovered staff had used a special program to collect the images around the clock from sexually explicit websites. Employees used 200 false identities to collect the images, which were downloaded in three weeks. A key computer had spent 70 per cent of its online time downloading and distributing the pornography. More than 3500 DERA employees across Britain had access to the system containing the material, it was reported. Jim Bates, a forensic computer expert who carried out an independent inquiry, told *The Sunday Times*: 'The sheer amount of material is staggering. I've never seen anything with such huge quantities relayed to such large numbers of people.'
- In 2000, the biggest mass dismissal for Internet misuse in the United Kingdom occurred when mobile phone operator Orange fired 45 staff from its Darlington, Hertford and Peterlee call centres. A source close to Orange was quoted at the time that the sackings were over the distribution of images of 'severed body parts' rather than pornography. Orange did not confirm this; a spokeswoman said that the material distributed was 'most offensive' but offered no more detail. The company conducted a full audit of its Lotus Notes e-mail system across the United Kingdom, to determine the extent of the offensive material's distribution.
- In November 2001 car manufacturer Jaguar suspended a number of workers from its Merseyside plant amid a pornographic e-mail scandal. According to a report in the *Liverpool Post*, five employees were asked to leave the plant and a further 11 faced dismissal for the distribution of 'inappropriate' material. Jaguar did not comment on what kind of 'inappropriate material' had been sent, although it was understood that the mails contained pornographic images. The incident reportedly came to management's attention when the suspect mail found its way onto the company's parent network, Ford, in the US.
- In October 2002 the Virginia Department of Transportation (VDOT) in the United States fired 17 workers for surfing pornography sites during business hours. In addition, the agency fired eight contract workers and suspended 61 others for two weeks without pay, for excessive use of the Internet.
- Also in the States, in May 2004 23 Kentucky state transportation employees were fired or forced to resign or retire and 20 other workers were suspended for using state computers to look at pornography. A routine examination of Internet use on the Kentucky Transportation Cabinet's computers showed 212 computers had been used to view thousands of pornographic images during a 24-day period. The 212 computers were located at cabinet headquarters and cabinet offices across the state.

Stories of people being fired for inappropriate Internet use are myriad. Mass dismissals of the type reported here are exceptional. More often individuals or small groups of people are fired. The British Trades Union Congress (TUC) recently estimated that as many as 1000 workers in the UK have been disciplined or dismissed because of pornographic images viewed over the Internet.

Defining what exactly constitutes pornography has proved perplexing. The Oxford Dictionary defines it as 'pictures, writing, or films that are intended to arouse sexual excitement'. There is plenty of offensive material on the Internet patently *not* intended to 'arouse sexual excitement', and there are also lots of lewd sexual jokes flying around. In December 2000, for instance, the British insurance company Royal & Sun Alliance suspended 41 staff reportedly for distributing 'lewd' Bart Simpson cartoons, an act that attracted adverse criticism at the time and was regarded by some as disproportionate.

There is clearly confusion, and in setting guidelines and policies for the workforce it is advisable to contemplate and anticipate a range of material that might be deemed offensive.

The risk of being sued on the grounds of sexual harassment arising from unwanted exposure to pornography is real, and in an increasingly litigious society, is set to increase. The case of *Morse v Future Reality Ltd* heard at a London employment tribunal in 1996 set a British precedent:

> Ms Morse shared an office with several men. The men regularly accessed sexually explicit and obscene images using the Internet. Some of these pictures were shown to Ms Morse, as was a lewd toy gorilla. Ms Morse stated that these activities caused her discomfort. She resigned accusing the company of sexual harassment. She cited the pornography, foul language and the culture of obscenity in the office as the grounds for her complaint. The tribunal held that these factors did indeed constitute sexual harassment, that Future Reality Ltd was liable and awarded compensation and loss of earnings.

In the United States, 12 librarians sued the city library system of Minneapolis in 2003 for $400 000, alleging pornography on library computers contributed to an intimidating, hostile and offensive workplace that violated state and federal law.

Management may assume that the summary dismissal of an employee accessing pornography on the Internet at work to be fair, proportionate and appropriate. However, in the United Kingdom there have been some surprising judgments on this issue. In July 1998, for instance, an employment tribunal heard the case of *Dunn v IBM United Kingdom Ltd*:

> Mr Dunn had used his employer's computers to access pornographic websites. IBM concluded that this constituted gross misconduct and summarily dismissed him. However, the employment tribunal upheld Mr Dunn's complaint of unfair dismissal. The tribunal concluded that Mr Dunn's actions, to which he had confessed, were not *indisputably* a breach of IBM's policy and did not, therefore, warrant summary dismissal. The tribunal added that Mr Dunn had also been dismissed unfairly because the company's policy did not indicate that dismissal would result from his actions.

At another hearing in the United Kingdom, a tribunal judged that a summary dismissal of an employee was unfair because the company did not have a written policy expressly forbidding the downloading or transmission of pornography or a declaration that such an act was deemed to be gross misconduct. The tribunal's summation was a salutary reminder of the importance of policies and procedures:

Clearly the Employment Appeals Tribunal or any other third party will be heavily influenced by the existence of a written e-mail and Internet policy where the employer reserves the right to dismiss for breaches of policy. It is unlikely that the use of the

Internet for unauthorised purposes will amount to a sufficient reason justifying an employer from dismissing an employee without notice in the absence of a clear written statement to this effect in the company's policy. An exception to this, perhaps, would be where an employee was using the company's facilities to download obscene pornography from the Internet.

The respondent failed to have in place clear policies and a code of practice on employee use of e-mail and the Internet. The consequences of its misuse should have been made absolutely clear to all employees. After much discussion, the tribunal decided that the onus was on the employer to have a clear policy in place to deal with the use of e-mail and the consequences for its misuse/abuse. Because of this, the tribunal has to hold the dismissal unfair.

An acceptable computer usage policy similar to that shown at Appendix 2 is clearly essential. The policy will not, of course, prevent pornographic web browsing or downloads, but it does underpin the company's position, abrogates any grounds for equivocation or excuse, and provides a clear framework for a law court or employment tribunal to pass judgment.

The policy sets the standards with which employees agree to abide. The policy can be sold to the workforce on the basis that it protects not only the employer but the employee also, by forbidding activities that are potentially dangerous for all. The policy needs to be explicit and transparent, stating precisely what employees can do with their computers and those actions that are forbidden. Generic expressions such as 'offensive' and 'objectionable' should be properly defined. It should be expressly stated that anyone caught intentionally viewing or downloading pornography will be deemed to have committed gross misconduct. Employees should sign a confirmation that they have read the policy and agree to abide by it.

Technically, many firewalls incorporate content filters that are configured to blacklist or prevent the transmission of certain file types. Typically the MPEG, AVI, MOV, ASF, WMV, WAV, QT and MP3 multimedia formats and the JPEG photographic format when transmitted as mail attachments are forbidden. Specific websites and portals may also be blocked, and filters applied to screen content of a sexual nature. The problem has always been that any rules-based filtering invariably results in false positives where legitimate traffic is blocked, and false negatives where forbidden material is permitted.

Child pornography

The possession or distribution of child pornography is a very serious criminal offence in most jurisdictions.

In the United Kingdom four offences involving indecent photographs or pseudo-photographs of children were created by the Protection of Children Act 1978. (The definition was extended to include 'pseudo-photographs' by section 84 of the Criminal Justice and Public Order Act 1994.)

Under section 1(1) of the 1978 Act, it is an offence for a person:

a) to take, or permit to be taken, or to make any indecent photograph or pseudo-photograph of a child; or

b) to distribute or show such indecent photographs or pseudo-photographs; or

c) to have in his possession such indecent photographs or pseudo-photographs, with a view to their being distributed or shown by himself or others; or

d) to publish or cause to be published any advertisement likely to be understood as conveying that the advertiser distributes or shows such indecent photographs or pseudo-photographs, or intends to do so.

The maximum penalty for possession of such images is five years' imprisonment. For making, showing or distributing the material, the maximum is ten years. However, section 1 of the Protection of Children Act 1978 relates only to the taking and distribution of indecent photographs of children and has been supplemented by section 160 of the Criminal Justice Act 1988 which states: 'It is an offence for a person to have any indecent photograph of a child (meaning in this section a person under the age of 16) in his possession.'

The Sexual Offences Act 2003 amended the Protection of Children Act 1978 so that it applies to all people under the age of 18 rather than 16. In addition, section 49 of the Sexual Offences Act 2003 makes it a criminal offence to intentionally control the activities of a child relating to the child's involvement in pornography in any part of the world. Section 50 of the Sexual Offences Act 2003 makes it a criminal offence to intentionally arrange or facilitate the involvement of a child in pornography in any part of the world.

As Professor Martin Wasik, who is the Chairman of the Sentencing Advisory Panel to The Court of Appeal (Criminal Division) of The Supreme Court of England and Wales, has pointed out, the possession of child pornography is not, as some have argued, a victimless offence. Every indecent photograph or pseudo-photograph of a child is, with limited exceptions, a picture of a real child being abused or exploited. The Internet and other developments in technology have undoubtedly made these offences more prevalent.

The Sentencing Advisory Panel has produced what it calls a COPINE typology to describe varying levels of this offence. COPINE stands for *Combating Paedophile Information Networks in Europe*, and is a project founded in 1997, originally based in the Department of Applied Psychology, University College Cork, Ireland, and since transferred to Interpol.

The COPINE levels recommended for sentencing by law enforcement are shown in Table 10.1.

The COPINE levels are helpful in specifying what illegal child pornography is. The problem, which is well appreciated by law enforcement officers, paediatricians, computer forensic practitioners and other experts, is that it is sometimes very difficult to determine the age of a person from a photograph or video. This imprecision is compounded by the pornography industry itself, which plies 'teen', 'Lolita' and 'Barely legal' websites featuring young-looking models who are, in fact, adults. For this reason many prosecutions are based on material that demonstrably features children, and in some extreme cases even infants and babies.

The paedophile sub-culture is vile. Professor Max Taylor of the COPINE project reported in March 2003 that more babies and toddlers are appearing on the Internet and that the abuse of children is getting more torturous and sadistic than it was before. The typical age of children featured is between six and twelve, but the profile is getting younger.

The discovery of child pornography in the workplace merits immediate attention at the highest management level.

The author has been advised on two occasions by senior management figures in blue-chip companies that they regarded it as purely a 'business decision' as to whether or not the police would be informed in the event of child pornography being discovered in the

Table 10.1   COPINE typology

COPINE level	Equivalent UK Police level
Not an offence (1)	
1 Non-erotic/non sexualized pictures of a child	–
Subject to dispute (2–3)	
2 Nudist (naked or semi-naked pictures of a child in legitimate settings/sources)	?
3 Erotica (surreptitious photographs of a child showing underwear/nakedness)	?
Offences (4–10)	
4 Posing (deliberate posing of a child suggesting sexual content)	1
5 Erotic posing of a child (deliberate sexual or provocative poses)	1
6 Explicit erotic posing of a child (emphasis on genital area)	1
7 Explicit sexual activity by a child or children not involving an adult	2
8 Assault (sexual assault on a child involving an adult)	3
9 Gross assault (penetrative assault on child involving adult)	4
10 Sadistic/bestiality (sexual images of a child involving pain or an animal)	5

workplace. This argument is fatuous and specious. Child pornography in the workplace is a potentially catastrophic risk; if an incident were mismanaged, the reputation of the organization and its management team could be destroyed. The inclination might be to fire any employee engaged in making, exchanging or trading this material in the hope that the problem might go away. Such a decision would, in fact, automatically render the organization a hostage to fortune. Published psychological assessments indicate that paedophiles tend to be obsessive and addictive personality types and the idea that by dismissing these people from the workplace, an organization can divest itself of all culpability for their misdeeds is utter folly.

Should child pornography be discovered in the workplace, its correct evidential management will be critical. If substantiated, the evidence will in all likelihood be required in a criminal prosecution. There will be an onus on the organization to isolate and protect the evidence but not to process it or analyse it, as this will be a job for the police. All the rules to prevent contamination and to ensure the continuity of the evidence as outlined in Chapter 14 will need to be scrupulously observed.

Where this offence is suspected, it is advisable to isolate the computer from the network, but not to conduct any further investigation, unless trained and officially authorized forensic experts are present. The machine should be placed in safe storage under lock and key to which only authorized personnel have access.

There is a clear risk that evidence will be compromised through its discovery. The person who discovers what he suspects to be illegal material may proceed to open all the incriminating pictures and view any videos and by doing so fatally damage vital evidence. The 30-minute rule (see Chapter 14) clearly applies. He may also invite others to look at the material which, of course, is a criminal offence.

Proportionality is also important. The court will find it questionable should the person discovering the material proceed to view tens, hundreds or even thousands of illegal pictures for no reason other than curiosity. There are forensic methods to determine the dates and times that pictures were last accessed, or whether 'thumbnails' have been expanded.

A clear reporting line for this offence and all other forms of computer misuse is clearly indicated. Users should know precisely to which department they report their suspicions or discoveries.

Remember also, that should material be discovered using a browser over a network, the material will be copied to the hard disk of the computer used to view it. There is a very real risk of causing the further contamination of machines in the organization. Similarly, it is a mistake to assume that the extent of the problem will be limited – illegal images may be found on other computers, servers and data storage media, and backup tapes, all of which will have to be audited.

As always, do not mistake the user with the activity on his assigned machine – careful forensic analysis is always required in any case involving pornography to ascertain the precise circumstances by which material came to reside on a disk, its provenance and any evidence to identify the culprit. As stated, in cases of child pornography, the police or an approved sub-contractor will undertake this analysis.

Similarly, do not automatically assume that the offending material was downloaded from the Internet or transmitted via e-mail. There is a possibility that it may have been uploaded directly from a digital camera, camera phone, memory stick or other storage media. If the pictures or videos have been uploaded, there is a distinct possibility that they were recorded directly by the offender himself, that is, your *employee*, and that the children depicted may be in imminent danger. The police's forensic investigation will link any such images to a particular make and model of camera, should this be the case.

Finally, any suspicion or allegation that an individual has been accessing child pornography or is in any way engaged with it must be investigated thoroughly but with extreme tact and sensitivity. These cases should be judged at official trial and not by kangaroo court. Do not under-estimate, either, the mass hysteria surrounding this issue, nor indeed the appalling ignorance of some sections of the public about it. The following incident, from 2000, shamefully reflects the deplorable state of education in the UK:

> (i) A hospital *paediatrician* has hit out at vandals who forced her to flee her home after apparently taking her job title to mean she was a *paedophile*. The 30-year-old trainee consultant at the Royal Gwent Hospital, Newport, South Wales said she planned to move home after returning to find the outside of her property daubed with 'pedo' (*sic*).

Lives and reputations are at stake. Of the 7272 potential UK offenders ensnared by the UK police's crackdown – codenamed Operation Ore – 35 had committed suicide by July 2005. In this climate, it is essential that only probative, cogent and compelling evidence is brought before the courts and that people resist jumping to conclusions.

11 *Anonymous Letters*[1]

> **Anger is one letter short of danger.**
>
> Anon.

Anonymous letters are surprisingly common in business. The motivation for sending such letters varies. Typically, an employee is aware of internal fraud but is too intimidated to raise the issue openly. Instead, the employee sends an anonymous letter to the chairperson or management of the company, outlining their suspicions. Alternatively, the writer may be a whistle blower who disagrees with company practices and sends a letter, often with supporting evidence, to a journalist or regulator.

Sexual indiscretion, jealousy or resentfulness may also prompt the sending of anonymous letters. Soured office romances have featured in many cases.

Threat letters are also often sent anonymously.

Investigation

It is very important that anonymous letters are investigated thoroughly. False allegations can blight an individual's career without foundation, while true allegations, if ignored, may place an organization in a perilous legal, regulatory or operational position. In one instance, an anonymous letter was ignored for ten years before its allegations were finally exposed as truthful. In another, a series of letters intimating dire retribution for perceived injustices was persistently dismissed as the work of a crank – until, that is, the perpetrator threatened devastating computer sabotage along with the technical proof of exactly how and when this could be achieved with total impunity.

Upon receipt of an anonymous letter, the targeted organization should endeavour immediately to retrieve the document from whoever received it. If the letter has gone to a third party, its receipt may never be acknowledged. However, if the recipient is associated with the victim organization, it is probable that they will raise the issue if only to establish whether the allegations raised are true.

In managing this potential threat the following guidelines are advised:

- The mailroom should be instructed always to retain envelopes, and supporting documentation should be attached to incoming correspondence using paper clips. Envelopes and other documentation should not be discarded at the point of receipt.
- The original letter, its envelope and any attachments should be recovered from the recipient.

---

1   This chapter is an update from *Computer Evidence: A Forensic Investigations Handbook*, Wilding E., ISBN 0 421 57990 0, Sweet & Maxwell 1997, and is published with permission.

- Whoever handles the correspondence should wear cotton (not rubber) gloves. This will preserve potential fingerprint evidence on the document.
- Do not remove staples, fasteners, tags or pins from the suspect letter or documents – these may be of evidential relevance.
- Do not write on the documents, underline anything or use highlighter pens. It is essential that exhibits should not be altered in any way. *Never write on, or annotate, original exhibits.*
- The letter and its envelope should be photocopied and placed in a large paper envelope. Do not use plastic wallets.
- A photocopy of the document should be stuck to the containing envelope so that its context may be seen without having to examine the evidence directly. Do not write on the containing envelope – this may indent the letter or documents within.
- Photocopies only may be annotated and circulated to the relevant people.
- The original letter, envelope and other documentation should be sent for forensic examination by a qualified Questioned Document examiner.

At the laboratory the document will be subjected to various tests. The ESDA[2] test has often proved the origination of anonymous correspondence, the sender's home address or other information discernible as an indented impression from a letter written on a previous page of the writing pad or on a separate piece of paper.

Similarly, fingerprints are retained in paper for many years and documents may be treated to determine who touched them. It is possible to conduct DNA analysis on documentation – this may involve the analysis of hair, fibres and saliva. The careful preservation of any such evidence must be considered.

The paper and style of envelope may match the victim organization's own standard stationery. The analysis of the paper stock is important, as examples from the same manufacturer may be located in a suspect's premises or work area. In the following case, which involved evidential printouts (none of which were anonymous), the paper stock proved crucial:

AUTHENTIC PRINTOUTS?

In September 1999, the author was asked to investigate the provenance and authenticity of a number of printed electronic mails, which had been produced by a female defendant charged on a single count of solicitation to murder. The electronic mails were purportedly produced during 1994 and 1995 on a system administered by a supermarket chain, the defendant's former employer.

The prosecution asserted that the electronic mail correspondence was forged and had produced a crude forgery of its own, hastily typed in Microsoft Word, as evidence of how easily this could be done. In fact, it was soon evident to the defence team that the capability to forge correspondence was inherent within the electronic mail system and it proved easy to produce perfect forgeries between *any* and *every* correspondent registered on the system. Ostensibly, this finding did not bode well for the defence case, as it appeared to support the prosecution's allegation.

---

2 Electrostatic Detection Apparatus. A forensic test that reveals indentations in paper imperceptible to the naked eye.

The printouts were produced on a distinctive stock, a coarse-grained and cheap paper used for internal correspondence and reports. Significantly, the supermarket chain had discontinued ordering or using this paper stock in late 1995 or early 1996, which corroborated their authenticity.

Notable also, was the defendant's use of Tipex correction fluid to conceal a number of paragraphs and sentences in the correspondence on the basis that she considered their content too personal and embarrassing. Tipex had also been used to hide the dates of some of the e-mails, which the defendant stated were inconsistent and could not be explained. This concealment was significant, because the defendant was highly computer literate, worked as a systems analyst in the company's IT department and almost certainly knew of the COPY command in the e-mail system that enabled the user to adjust the date, sender, recipient, subject and text within any existing electronic mail. This being the case, why had she not used COPY to produce the alleged forgeries having first edited out any personal and embarrassing entries and corrected the anomalous dates?

A contextual analysis also supported the defendant's assertion that the printouts were genuine correspondence. She consistently referred to 'e-mail', while her correspondent always used the expression 'email'. In combination, these individual strands of evidence – the paper stock, the Tipex, the COPY command and the spellings – combined as a compelling indication of the printouts' authenticity.

The laboratory will determine whether a printer or typewriter was used to create the correspondence and, if so, which type of printer, which typeface, and point size.

If a typewriter was used to create the letter, typeface comparison may be undertaken on typewriters identified within the organization. The strike pattern of the keys on every typewriter is unique which makes typeface comparison an exact science. Typewriter ribbons may also be examined forensically for key strike indentations and sequences – entire documents have been recreated using this technique.

Laser-printer copy cannot be traced so easily because it has no clear differentiation. Use of a laser printer and a standard font virtually guarantees typographic anonymity, unless there is a fault on the printer. There have been rare cases where a toner cartridge has leaked or become unstable, where the precise printer used could be identified from output alone.

It is possible, however, to differentiate between laser copy, inkjet, bubble-jet and dot matrix output. This may ascertain print-queue routing and help identify the potential computers from which a suspect document was printed. The print drivers installed on a suspect's PC may be significant. A document printed on a laserjet, paintjet or bubble-jet will obviously require a computer with an appropriate software driver to generate it.

Handwriting is unique and distinctive and is much less likely to be used by the sender of an anonymous letter. It is very difficult for the individual to suppress idiosyncratic traits. One individual, for example, consistently wrote the letter 't' with a double cross bar – upon attempting to disguise his handwriting by back-sloping it he failed to correct this characteristic.

If a document has been photocopied, it may be possible to identify debris, in the form of dust, dirt and other microscopic residue, on the glass of the photocopy machine, which is reflected on the subsequent photocopy. Inspection of photocopied documents may, therefore, determine whether seemingly unrelated documents have been photocopied on the same machine. It may even be possible to identify the photocopier used, by comparing its output with the suspect documents.

The envelope requires attention. Franking marks or the presence of a stamp will reveal whether the communication was sent by the organization's internal post or via the public postal system. If sent internally, it is probable that the letter was typed on site. If sent externally, the envelope will bear a postal mark, which will help identify where and when it was posted. Furthermore, electrostatic indentation detection will determine whether the suspect letter was actually delivered inside the envelope it was purported to have been sent in, because the franking machinery should leave an impression on the letter within the envelope.

The franking mark will identify the postal area in which the letter was posted. Larger post offices maintain CCTV recordings for security purposes. With the cooperation of the postal authorities, a review of the security videos might reveal a known face in the area of the surveillance on the day that the letter was sent.

Content and context

In determining the author of an anonymous letter it is necessary to analyse the content and context of the letter.

- Is a named individual attacked or derided in the letter? This person will probably be intensely disliked by the writer whose animosity may well be known.
- Is anyone mentioned in the letter praised? This person may be the letter's author or friend.
- Does the letter contain any swear words or obscenities? Women generally swear less than men and avoid using a particular subset of profanities.
- Are there any consistent spelling mistakes? These may occur in other readily available documents on site and may reveal common authorship. If it is suspected that the letter was generated internally, a text search for consistent misspellings or unusual expressions on fileservers, mail servers and electronic gateways and user directories and archives should be considered.
- Are there any consistent syntax or punctuation errors? These will be inherent and will be present in any other documents produced by the writer. Again, a search of computer servers, electronic gateways and archives is recommended.
- Is the grammar and spelling correct or does it demonstrate a degree of illiteracy? It is difficult for an educated individual to fake illiteracy or poor education.
- Is the letter formatted in a distinctive style that might be recognizable in other documents or computer templates?
- Are there any unusual or distinctive phrases?
- Is there any sign that the writer's native language is foreign?

By analysing the content of the document, therefore, it may be possible to determine the identity of the writer. On a past investigation, a series of anonymous letters stated that a salesman was inflating prices for his own benefit. One of the letters described the salesman as 'a naughty little boy'. A male writer would be unlikely to use such an expression, which indicated that the writer was female and probably older than the salesman. Another letter in the series praised a woman who worked in the same man's department, stating that she might confirm the allegations. The writer used a clumsy attempt to disguise her identity by consistently misspelling the surname of this woman. It transpired that she and the salesman were ill-disposed towards each other. Two of the anonymous letters were subsequently found on the woman's computer. Contextual analysis of this type is often more revealing than forensic investigation.

In another case, an anonymous fax, its author consistently misspelled the place name 'Hampshire' as 'Hantshire'. When subsequently asked to compose a business letter addressed to Hampshire, this habitual misspelling was immediately evident.

```
Rather than poking about in accounts you should concentrate
on Gary Sumner in purchasing. The bastard is ripping you
off. Check out his involvement with Telik Contracts - he's
taking backhanders from John Mayall at Telik. You must have
done at least £100K with them in the last six months. Look
into it.
```

Figure 11.1   The writer's motive

The motive behind the letter in Figure 11.1 may be genuine, or it may be intended to slander a colleague, or even divert the focus of an ongoing investigation. In one such case, the recipient of a similar letter was also its sender! Intuitively, the sex of the writer is discernible. A consistent and overwhelming majority of seminar audiences have correctly identified the writer of this communication as male. It should be remembered, however, that people's intuition is often wrong.

If a communication has been faxed, the investigator will attempt to ascertain the time of the transmission and the sender's number. This may be determined by reference to the transmission report produced by the recipient's fax machine, although it is comparatively simple to mask and even forge the sending machine's number. The fax header may show the transmission machine's number – amateurs will use a fax bureau, copy shop or other commercial fax service and the area code and location shown on the header will be relevant to the enquiry. Analysis of transmission logs may reveal the time, date, duration, destination or origination of the transmission.

If the identity of the sending fax machine is established, along with the time and date of the transmission, reference to access control logs and CCTV recordings will help determine who was in the building, and possibly the immediate area, at the time. This analysis will be more revealing should the transmission take place outside of normal business hours.

The composite letter shown in Figure 11.2 is typical of threats sent to businesses. The total information set (the report titles, IP addresses, passwords and other data mentioned) known to the writer should be ascertained as this may identify his, her or their identity. A risk assessment should be conducted as to whether the declared information set is accurate and, if so, what the business and operational impact is likely to be, should the writer(s) follow through. Disaster recovery processes should be tested vigorously in the face of such a threat. In this case an ESDA test has come good – the writer(s) never intended to give us the handwritten telephone number![3] The surname 'Caruthers' is misspelled. The date

---

3   Bear it in mind, however, that the ESDA impression may have occurred in the mailroom or since the receipt of the letter.

Mr Paul Caruthers
Chairman
ACME Oil (International) Limited
Langham House
20-22 Gresham Street
London
EC1 2NN

5-12-2001

Mr Caruthers,

If the enclosed letter signed by yourself and your Board does not appear in the national Press within the next ten days we will:

- Destroy computer networks, databases and communications systems worldwide
- Release detailed information about ACME Oil to the Tax authorities in the U.K., U.S. and E.C.
- Release your confidential reports:

"Political torture in Africa – ACME guideline 615"
"Inducements for contract – Nigeria"

THIS IS NOT AN IDLE THREAT.

Some passwords for you:

7342694

192.168.0.116 - Heathrow – Beckham10
192.168.0.170 - Park Avenue – NyjEts222
192.168.0.90 - Kuwait – AcMe%stanDby1

Yours sincerely,

The Committee for Ethics in Business

Figure 11.2   Typical composite letter

format is a Microsoft Word default. There are plenty of other clues here. First stop, perhaps, is to conduct a Google search on 'The Committee for Ethics in Business'.

If a computer is suspected of being used to prepare such a letter it should be processed forensically, and searched for distinctive phrases found in the letter (see Figure 11.3).

Figure 11.4 shows EnCase finding the string 'political torture' in the letter in an unallocated cluster. EnCase searches through the entirety of the disk, including deleted files, file slack space, unallocated clusters and other areas ignored by the operating system. Searches are not case sensitive and matches are displayed in context for immediate analysis. This software (from Guidance Software, Inc.) is ideal for searching for ASCII text. The difficult part of the investigation, as ever, is identifying precisely which computer to examine.

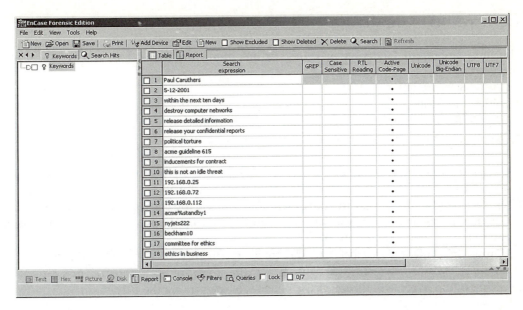

Figure 11.3 Search criteria for checking a suspect's hard disk using EnCase software

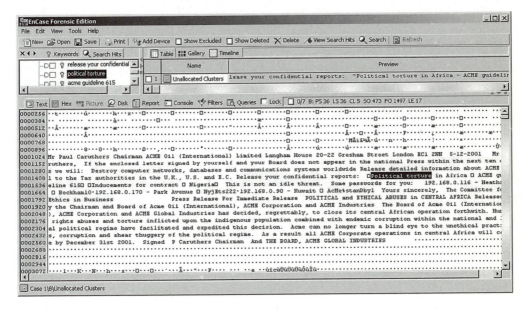

Figure 11.4 Locating a letter on a suspect's computer

Conclusion

The most important factor when trying to determine the identity of the writer of an anonymous letter is that he or she is:

- highly motivated;
- acquainted with the victim organization, its staff or processes;
- bearing a grudge, the nature of which will usually be evident in the text.

These factors serve to intensify the focus of the enquiry. The problem is not, therefore, akin to looking for a needle in a haystack. The heightened motivation in sending such a letter often goes hand in hand with an aroused emotional state, the consequence of which is that the writers of such letters frequently lose control, and by doing so, reveal much about themselves and their circumstances.

From an evidential perspective, the forensic integrity of the source documents is paramount. Mismanagement, particularly in the form of excessive or inappropriate handling of the paper, will diminish the chances of identifying the perpetrator.

12 *Press Leaks*

I learned a lovely new acronym today: 'Law Enforcement Agency Key'.
Charles H. Lindsey, mathematician and cryptographer

Leaks to the press abetted by insiders have proved extremely embarrassing and detrimental to many commercial and government organizations.

Motivation

The motivations to leak information to the press vary. Journalists are often assisted in their reporting by the deliberate connivance of senior figures within the organizations that they report. Many civil service departments and ministries leak confidential information deliberately, to alert the public to proposed budgetary cutbacks, or otherwise obstruct or influence central government plans deemed undesirable. Top-secret papers, proposing sweeping cuts or traumatic overhauls, tend to be mislaid in public places only to be discovered by 'passing' journalists.

Governments tend to leak like sieves, but again they often do so intentionally – typically to test public opinion on proposed policies, but also for more nefarious purposes. Politicians and journalists are bedfellows by necessity.

The point, of course, is that many press leaks originate at the highest levels, or are officially sanctioned, albeit tacitly. Agendas are seldom what they seem and the investigator should bear this in mind.

Many of the most sensational leaks are by civil servants or others with access to secret government information. Examples are legion; in the United Kingdom they have included:

- Sarah Tisdall, a Foreign Office clerk, was jailed in 1984 for six months for passing documents about the stationing of American cruise missiles in the UK to *The Guardian* newspaper.
- Clive Ponting, a senior civil servant, was acquitted in 1985 having pleaded not guilty to breaching the Official Secrets Act for leaking documents about the sinking of the Argentinian battleship *General Belgrano* during the Falklands war.
- Cathy Massiter, a former MI5 officer, revealed that the agency bugged anti-nuclear campaigners and told Channel 4 television that MI5 bugged the telephones of politicians and human rights campaigners. She was not prosecuted.
- Peter Wright, a former MI5 officer, claimed in his 1987 book *Spycatcher* that MI5 officers plotted to undermine Harold Wilson, the former Labour prime minister.
- Richard Tomlinson, a former MI6 officer, was jailed for 12 months for the unlawful disclosure of information under the Official Secrets Act.

- David Shayler, a former MI5 officer, was jailed for six months in 2002 after selling top-secret documents to a newspaper for £40 000. He claimed he was a whistle blower trying to expose corruption in the security service.
- Katharine Gun, a former translator for GCHQ, the security service's main monitoring centre, faced prosecution in February 2004 for leaking a memo to a newspaper on an alleged American 'dirty tricks' campaign to tap the telephones of UN delegates in the run up to the Iraq war. She confessed to having leaked the memo but the case against her collapsed after the prosecution offered no evidence.

There are many motives to leak information to the press, some of which could be considered noble; others selfish, indulgent and ill-advised:

- to whistle blow and make public confidential information that the informant considers to be in the public interest;
- to disclose institutional corruption, incompetence, wrongdoing or illegality;
- to disclose commercial malpractice;
- to embarrass individuals or organizations;
- to influence policy or strategy, or to manipulate situations;
- to undermine management and usurp;
- for payment or other reward;
- to pass the buck – 'See what they're up to! It's nothing to do with me!'

Activists and pressure groups are always keen to gain informants and access to information within the organizations they target.

As in the cases of Massiter, Ponting, Tisdall, Gun and Shayler, conscientious objection is often cited as the catalyst behind many leaks.

When investigating a press leak, two key questions are germane:

- What is the motive for the leak?
- Who benefits by it?

The underlying motive may be self-evident. Alternatively, it may be discerned by a careful contextual analysis of what is reported.

Investigation

In a sizeable enterprise employing several thousand people, the investigation of a press leak needs to be focused so that time, energy and resources are not wasted on unproductive lines of enquiry.

The victims of damaging leaks often seek overly complex and contrived technical explanations for them:

The chairman of the board was adamant that his telephone was tapped and that the office was bugged. How else could information leak to the press? He ordered an electronic counter-measures team to survey the company's offices.
Had the chairman compared the text of the offending article with the confidential memoranda prepared by his PA, he would have noticed several striking similarities, which

clearly indicated that this memo was the source of the newspaper report. The sweep team reported no taps, bugs or other surveillance devices. It had found instead dozens of photocopies of the memo. No longer a restricted document, this memo had slipped out of control, thence into the public domain – a fact which was later confirmed by the journalist.

As in all investigations, it is advisable to seek the simplest explanation first, prior to escalating the complexity of the enquiry. Typically, the investigation will avail itself of a range of methods, foremost amongst which will be the examination of data and correspondence on computers, electronic mail traffic from and to the targeted organization, itemized telephone bills, both landlines and cellular, and fax logs.

Telephone interception has proved extremely effective in these instances but, legal considerations aside, this is a resource-intensive method, as succinctly summarized in the 1973 film *The Day of the Jackal*. The Interior Minister, presiding over an emergency committee to find President De Gaulle's would-be assassin, congratulates Police Commissioner Lebel for identifying a mole within their midst:

> 'One thing. How did you know which telephone to tap?'
> 'I didn't. I tapped you all.'

Telephone interception is an immensely powerful investigative method but is best deployed only once a list of suspects has been clearly defined. Telephone interception is also illegal in many countries, and even where this method is legal in certain circumstances, as in the United Kingdom, the admissibility of any evidence accrued is not guaranteed.

The investigator has one distinct advantage when investigating a press leak – the journalist or newspaper that has published a story will often reveal significant clues as to its sources.

Let us examine the imaginary story published in '*The Daily Despatch*' (Figure 12.1).

It is advisable to break down the story into its constituent sentences. For reference it is helpful to number the sentences in the story, and then to comment on each, as to whether:

- statements made are substantively correct, or are inaccurate;
- probable sources for the statements and quotations that are reported:
  - e-mails
  - documents and reports
  - conversations
  - tape recordings;
- source material shown in the report that is in the public domain (this will be eliminated from the enquiry);
- inaccuracies or mistakes, which reveal not only the journalist's ignorance of specific areas, but also the ignorance of his source (but accounting for the possibility that the source will use 'double bluff');
- clues as to the hidden agenda or motivation of the source;
- restricted information known only to a few;
- witnesses to any of the events or conversations reported;
- confidential information known by people outside of the organization, or by former employees.

The analysis is shown in Figure 12.2.

Fisticuffs at Ingot
<u>Ray Higgins, City correspondent</u>

A blazing row between the principal shareholder of Ingot Enterprises and the non-executive directors of the company erupted last week as the Board sought to suspend dividend payments for the third consecutive quarter. Sir James McNeal, who holds 20 percent of the group's stock, was said to be "incandescent with rage" over the decision by the Board of Ingot Holdings to defer dividends, following a bleak assessment for the company's growth and prospects.

An internal memorandum seen by *The Daily Despatch* forecasts "a downturn in all commercial operations" and predicts a trading loss for 2005 - the first recorded - in Ingot's lucrative telecommunications and broadband sectors. Market analysts have described Ingot's performance in recent months as disappointing, despite the recruitment of John Bannister as Chief Executive in 2003. Insiders say that the failure of Ingot's retail electronics division in May 2004 is regarded by the Board as "a cataclysmic blow" and a "psychological low point" set to accelerate the decline of other under-performing sectors.

In the board meeting last Monday, Sir James described Bannister's non-interventionist approach as a "gross dereliction of duty" and stated that the collapse of the retail division resulted from "breathtaking incompetence". The markets are now keeping a close watch on Ingot's US chemical and pharmaceutical subsidiary IngoPharm, also said to be in severe difficulties, following the reported failure of its anti-depressant L102 to receive a rating from the US Food and Drug Administration.

Figure 12.1 The story

The contextual analysis reveals a possible motive for the leak at sentences 4 and 6. Bannister's alleged poor performance as Chief Executive of the company is the underlying message in this report, with Sir James McNeal as the main antagonist. An ambitious insider or a self-serving outsider appears intent on usurping Bannister as the Chief Executive. Sir James McNeal, of course, is an obvious candidate.

From the contextual analysis sheet in Figure 12.2, it is evident from sentences 2 and 5 that Mr Bannister's confidential correspondence has been compromised. The quotations are from the board meeting but may have leaked from the minutes. Let us suppose that the minutes contained other information that was even more contentious than reported here – has this not been reported because the journalist does not have the minutes? If so, he may be relying on the quotes 'gross dereliction of duty' and 'breathtaking incompetence' from someone who witnessed them being said. However, journalists have a nasty habit of retaining information for future stories, and the minutes may be destined to appear as a different story or a follow-up to this report.

Sentence 7 indicates that the journalist may have another informant in the United States, either within IngoPharm, or possibly the FDA. It is more likely that an informant in London has discovered this information second-hand.

Having conducted a contextual analysis by sentence, the investigator should have a better grasp of how and why the story was constructed and this may give him an insight into the people most likely to have assisted with the story.

It is now necessary to itemize precisely the information that we are searching for. It is also advisable to assess whether any or all the documents or memoranda indicated could have been photocopied by a temp or a cleaner, or scavenged from rubbish, retrieved from

1. A blazing row between the principal shareholder of Ingot Enterprises and the non-executive directors of the company erupted last week as the Board sought to suspend dividend payments for the third consecutive quarter.

*A substantively accurate report. Present at the meeting on Monday 8 November 2004 were Bannister, Barker, Collins, Jameson, Jones, McNeal, Smith, Phillips and White (**minutes**).*

2. Sir James McNeal, who holds 20 percent of the group's stock, was said to be 'incandescent with rage' over the decision by the Board of Ingot Holdings to defer dividends, following a bleak assessment for the company's growth and prospects.

*McNeal holds 15 per cent – is the reported figure an intentional mistake? 'Incandescent with rage' is a quote from McNeal in a letter to Bannister dated Tuesday 9 November 2004 (**Letter 1**).*

3. An internal memorandum seen by *The Daily Despatch* forecasts 'a downturn in all commercial operations' and predicts a trading loss for 2005 – the first recorded – in Ingot's lucrative telecommunications and broadband sectors.

*A confidential memorandum containing the exact quotations published has been identified as **Memo 1**, dated 25 October 2004.*

4. Market analysts have described Ingot's performance in recent months as disappointing, despite the recruitment of John Bannister as Chief Executive in 2003.

A possible motivation is to undermine Bannister as Chief Exec.

5. Insiders say that the failure of Ingot's retail electronics division in May 2004 is regarded by the Board as 'a cataclysmic blow' and a 'psychological low point' set to accelerate the decline of other under-performing sectors.

'Insiders' – more than one?

*The quotations are from a confidential letter sent from Collins to Bannister dated Friday 21 May 2004. (**Letter 2**).*

6. In the board meeting last Monday, Sir James described Bannister's non-interventionist approach as a 'gross dereliction of duty', and stated that the collapse of the retail division resulted from 'breathtaking incompetence'.

Again, an attack on Bannister.

*A substantively accurate report of the board meeting, which was **minuted** on Monday 8 November 2004.*

7. The markets are now keeping a close watch on Ingot's US chemical and pharmaceutical subsidiary IngoPharm, also said to be in severe difficulties, following the reported failure of its anti-depressant L102 to receive a rating from the US Food and Drug Administration.

***FDA verdict on L102** was only notified to IngoPharm last week (Thursday 11 November 2004) and has not yet been made public. How does the journalist know about it?*

Figure 12.2   Contextual analysis of the newspaper report

discarded computer disks, or compromised due to other technical or procedural flaws. If we can eliminate these possibilities or classify them as unlikely, we should do so.

To do this we use an information set (Table 12.1), showing the entirety of the information that the journalist used to construct his story. All of the documents, memoranda and other information necessary to compile the story are itemized.

The security provision for each document and memoranda in the information set is then assessed. Documents that have restricted circulation are assessed as high security, those with wider but limited distribution are medium security, and those in general circulation are categorized as low security.

Table 12.1   Information set and assessment of security provision for each item

Item	Date	Number of copies (known to be in circulation)	Security level (assessed)
1. Letter 1	9/11/2004	2	HIGH Filed with Bannister and McNeal
2. Memo 1	25/10/04	4	MEDIUM
3. Letter 2	21/5/04	2	HIGH Filed with Bannister and Collins
4. Minutes/Board meeting	8/11/04	9	MEDIUM
5. FDA verdict	11/11/04	4	HIGH Filed with Mason and Gold (US)

The information set in Table 12.1 indicates that this leak is unlikely to have occurred due to simple mishaps or carelessness with the handling of the documents or computer files. Significantly, three items (1, 3 and 5) are assessed as HIGH security with a restricted circulation.

Two executives in the United States, Mason and Gold, have received the FDA's report (item 5). However, the information in the newspaper article provides no detailed findings; only the fact that the anti-depressant drug L102 has failed its certification. This fact could easily have been discussed between the parties shown and others in the company.

The informant may have made unauthorized photocopies of the HIGH security documents 1, 3 and 5 or he may have copied or accessed them in electronic format, or printed them. A forensic investigation into these possibilities is now indicated. The documents should be examined for fingerprints and other residue.

Photocopier memory should be inspected at this stage.

Computers will also require examination. Letter 1 will probably be located on a computer owned by or used by Sir James McNeal, who is not an employee of the company. His permission to examine this computer will be needed. Letter 3 should be located on a computer to which Collins had access.

At this point, a distribution matrix should be prepared (see Table 12.2). By using such a matrix, we identify the people most likely to possess, or have access to, the information set, either in part or as a whole. A tick indicates that the individual in the left-hand column has access or ownership of the document or memoranda indicated in the top row.

Table 12.2   Distribution matrix

	Board meeting (attended?)	Letter 1	Memo 1	Letter 2	Minutes	FDA verdict	SCORE
Bannister	✔	✔	✔	✔	✔	✔	6
Barker	✔				✔		2
Collins	✔		✔	✔	✔	✔	5
Jameson	✔				✔		2
Jones	✔		✔		✔		3
McNeal	✔	✔			✔		3
Smith	✔		✔		✔		3
Phillips	✔				✔		2
White	✔				✔		2
Mason						✔	1
Gold						✔	1

As should be expected, Bannister, as Chief Executive, has access to all of the information set, but Collins comes a close second, having access to five of the six items necessary to compile the article. In this instance, a thorough investigation of Collins appears justified.

Is Collins leaking information to McNeal? Between them, they have the entire information set necessary to construct the story.

Additionally, the analysis of telephone calls or faxes to or from IngoPharm in the US, and calls to or from *The Daily Despatch*, and Ray Higgins, its City editor, from any line or mobile phone operated by the company are clearly indicated. Likewise, a search for electronic mails and other correspondence between these parties should be prioritized.

Contextual analysis and information matrices help to sharpen the focus of the enquiry, but they should not dictate our actions to the exclusion of other possible explanations. The possession of, or access to information, which has leaked, does not automatically infer guilt. Instead, the methods shown identify where leaked information may originate or currently reside, so as to expedite forensic analysis and determine whether there is any indication of unauthorized access or disclosure.

13 *Incident Response*

> **There cannot be a crisis next week. My schedule is already full.**
>
> Henry Kissinger, diplomat and statesman (b. 1923)

As stated in Chapter 1, many incident response plans fail to tackle the issue of employee malevolence and criminality; an alarmingly high percentage of banks and financial institutions, for example, do not have an incident response plan for internal fraud or computer misuse. Given the volume and value of daily transactions processed by the typical back office, this lack of preparation could arguably be construed as wilful negligence.

In several emergencies observed at close hand by the author, a committee assembled, and a heated discussion ensued which quickly degenerated into a full-blown row as senior and departmental managers pointed the finger of blame at each other and sought to absolve themselves of all responsibility. The danger here is that as the clock ticks by, no action is taken to mitigate the damage, recover the loss or to identify and prosecute the culprits.

Where action has been ordained, it has often been ineffectual or misguided. Evidence has been mishandled and remedial opportunities – investigative and legal – have been squandered or overlooked.

The resulting inertia and general chaos clearly benefits the perpetrator, providing him with the opportunity to cover his tracks and escape.

This 'headless chicken syndrome' is the result of two things:

- lack of foresight and planning
- blind panic.

Panic is to be avoided at all costs, as it results in irrational and ill-advised actions, which cannot later be reversed or rectified.

What is clearly needed is a tried and tested incident response plan to tackle the insider threat in whichever form it may manifest itself. For those organizations that have implemented preventative measures and are smug in the belief that as a result a serious emergency will never arise, I reiterate that the determined fraudster or computer criminal will find a way around your controls.

The methods to tackle employee wrongdoing are for the most part very different to the methods used to respond to other business emergencies. For example, a business continuity plan designed to mitigate the effects of a fire or a flood will be of limited assistance in the event of a fraud, extortion attempt or suspected IP theft. The incident response plan to tackle the insider threat should be seen, therefore, as a specific element of a much wider business continuity strategy, coordinated by a corporate incident response committee and sanctioned by the board and reporting to it.

Incident response plans should be subject to constant review and regular testing.

Fundamental rules

ESTABLISH A REPORTING LINE

It is essential that all employees and departmental managers know *where, how* and *to whom* to report their suspicions of fraud, computer misuse or employee crime. If there is any confusion, serious wrongdoing may go unreported.

Many organizations have established a security and investigations department as a central reporting function, which is also responsible for investigation and incident response.

Confidential fraud hotlines and anonymous whistle-blower schemes have also proved effective in encouraging the reporting of suspected fraud and other criminality.

Fundamentally, if fraud and other malpractice is not reported it is unlikely to be investigated.

DO NOT PANIC!

Panic leads to mistakes – the most common mistake is for a manager to confront a member of staff with an accusation based purely on hearsay and where there is no supporting evidence. The suspect vigorously denies any wrongdoing and subsequently obliterates all traces of his guilt. Typically, the suspect is confronted late on a Friday afternoon, and is then left unattended to destroy or amend computer files and shred incriminating documentation and other evidence over the weekend.

- Do *not* confront any suspect until all of the available evidence is gathered. If the suspect is forewarned of an investigation, he will take precautionary measures and destroy or conceal evidence.

Other symptoms of panic include:

- inadvertently alerting the suspect(s), often when secretive meetings are held by the investigating team on-site to discuss the suspected fraud or wrongdoing;
- ill-advised probing to test the evidence or to attempt to ascertain the validity of rumours;
- unwittingly tampering with the evidence as the result of hasty and amateur examination – this applies particularly to computer evidence;
- seeking the wrong advice – when fraud is suspected or discovered, the organization may first consult its external auditors despite the fact that these same people may have been negligent in failing to identify the problem in the first place.

GET A GRIP!

It is necessary to take *control* of the situation and to do so quickly – otherwise, there will be chaos. In responding to fraud and computer crime it is necessary to control not only systems and processes, but also people. A clear, concise command structure is vital so that the response is coordinated and managed to the best effect.

Investigating fraud, workplace crime and computer misuse usually requires the deployment of unconventional tactics and methods; it is advisable, therefore, to approve these in advance and test them accordingly.

- The actions taken (or not taken) in the first few hours of an investigation will determine the relative chances of its success or failure. These hours should not be wasted.

As with all endeavours, planning and preparation are key.

Incident response plan

CHAIN OF COMMAND

Who is in charge?

When a serious incident occurs someone must take charge. A Controller must be designated and appointed.

The established chain of command will be a matter for each individual organization. It is essential, however, that there is no confusion as to the command and control of the operation. In many larger companies, it should be the director of security and investigations who controls incident response. Whoever is appointed to be the Controller must be invested with total authority.

Things go wrong when the Controller and the chain of command are not clearly stipulated and there is infighting for control – typically between HR, audit and group legal, none of which is necessarily qualified to conduct investigations or an incident response. Similarly, individuals or departments, which act independently of the Controller and outside of the chain of command, may jeopardize the operation.

The chain of command must be short. The incident response team should report directly to the Controller, without having to consult or confer with intermediate stages in a hierarchy:

- The Controller commands and controls the incident response team and its operations.
- All actions must be agreed and approved by the Controller.
- No independent actions are permitted.
- All investigative findings, intelligence, evidence and exhibits are recorded and filed with the Controller, or his appointee(s), to be assessed and graded, and with no other person.

To expedite and optimize the decision-making process, the incident response effort should be commanded locally. It should not depend on decision making or approval at arms length or by management with no direct experience of the contingency being responded to.

INCIDENT RESPONSE TEAM

Who will be involved?

A range of different skills is required to respond effectively to the insider threat. Tasks need to be assigned to the appropriate person or department and coordinated to the best effect in an ordered chain of command.

The precise composition of the incident response team will vary between organizations, but typically will include representatives of:

- group security and investigations

- IT
- HR
- group legal.

It is *not* necessary for each of these departments to be consulted or to express an opinion on every aspect of the operation. The Controller is in charge and should seek input from departmental representatives of the team only where their specialist skills or knowledge are apposite. This is not the right forum for 'talking heads' or a debating society.

RISK ASSESSMENT

How serious is the incident?

The scope and intensity of the investigation and the resources allocated to it will depend on the gravity of an incident in terms of its potential impact on the commercial viability and the reputation of the business.

A fully blown response is usually necessary only for those incidents that are assessed as *high impact*, that is, having the potential to cause significant damage to the business or to induce its failure.

A less comprehensive response may be required in cases assessed as *medium* or *low impact*, but the same evidential standards and operational methods and procedures to resolve them apply.

There is a always a risk that a seemingly minor incident may be dismissed as trivial or marginal, when, in fact, it may be symptomatic of a more serious underlying problem. The onus is on the Controller and his assessors to determine the relative significance of all issues and incidents that are reported.

The risk assessment should be completed swiftly and need not utilize formal methods – most business managers, once they are made aware of a risk, are capable of assessing its relative gravity without complex software or formulae. If this is not the case, then formal methods should be implemented as part and parcel of the incident response plan.

A risk assessment will help to quantify the skills and resources needed, and set the timetable by which actions must be completed.

STRATEGIC OBJECTIVES

In responding to this incident, what are your goals?

The Controller, in conjunction with the corporate incident response committee and the board, will determine the organization's strategic objectives, specific to each contingency that arises.

The strategic objectives of the operation will vary depending on each particular incident. For example, the prosecution of the culprit may be the priority in one case, but the recovery of stolen funds and assets may be judged a more critical concern in another. The strategic objective of the organization may be to sue a culpable or negligent third party. Alternatively, the objective may be fundamental to the survival of the business. Where regulation applies, as in the airlines, a serious fraud or employee misdemeanour that impacted upon flight safety would jeopardize an operator's licence, thereby threatening the afflicted carrier's viability in the industry. Retaining the operating licence in such a case would clearly be the airline's overriding concern.

Whatever the objectives, it is always advantageous to identify the perpetrator(s). The investigation, therefore, should not await the setting of any strategic objectives, or be dependent on them. However, the strategic objectives of the organization must be agreed and formally stated. Things go wrong, where there are numerous, often conflicting agendas and no clearly defined strategic goals.

LIAISON

Who do you need to help you?
The incident response team will need to consult with internal departments, but may also call upon external specialists and law enforcement, including:

- professional investigators
- technical surveillance contractors
- forensic experts
- accounting experts
- lawyers – specialists in employment law, fraud, intellectual property and so on
- police and specialist law enforcement – fraud, computer crime
- regulators (where applicable).

The Controller has the executive power to appoint and instruct external specialists as he sees fit. Specialists should be identified and approved before a crisis happens. That way you will avoid a time-consuming approval process when an incident does occur.

The full contact details for all departments, external agencies, lawyers and regulators should be logged in a central spreadsheet and disseminated to the incident response team.

Mobile and home telephone numbers for all key individuals should be maintained.

The contacts log should be regularly updated.

Informal but regular liaison with external experts, specialist contractors, lawyers and law enforcement agencies will expedite and facilitate the incident response, should it become necessary.

REPORTABLE AND REGULATORY MATTERS

Are you required by law to report the incident? If so, to whom, how and when?
The incident under investigation may comprise a heinous crime, and if this is the case it is advisable that the appropriate law enforcement agency be notified without delay. For example, offences involving child pornography, national security or terrorism fall within this category. Qualified legal opinion is required as to which types of offence require immediate notification to the authorities. In the United Kingdom fraud and computer misuse are not, by default, reportable offences.

For organizations that are subject to regulation such as those in the banking and financial services sectors, the incident may require immediate notification to the regulatory authorities. For example, the incident may be reportable under the money laundering regulations or for SEC compliance in the United States, or FSA and SFA compliance in the United Kingdom. Many industries are also regulated by health and safety watchdogs, which have their own reporting and enforcement schemes.

The prompt establishment of facts is mandatory in this respect.

OPERATIONAL SECURITY

Who should know?

The incident response team should comprise only those who 'need to know'.

- If the suspect is made aware of the investigation, he will take precautionary measures and destroy or conceal evidence.
- Under criminal and regulatory law in many jurisdictions, 'tipping off' – informing an individual that he is under investigation – is a serious criminal offence.

Maintaining the secrecy of an investigation is referred to as operational security (OpSec).

OpSec is essential if a covert investigation is to be undertaken where an employee is suspected of a serious crime or misdemeanour. The overriding principle of OpSec is the 'need to know'.

How many people really need to know that the investigation is taking place?

The number should be kept to a minimum. In large organizations it often applies that everybody from junior management level upwards believes that they have a divine right to know about everything and anything, however remotely it may touch upon their respective domains. This happens because rights and responsibilities are not properly assigned and understood. OpSec is only achievable if the director (and it should be a board-level appointment) responsible for security and investigations is assigned powers commensurate with his role. These powers include the irrefutable right to withhold information about operations, unless specifically instructed otherwise by the board.

OpSec is compromised in the same ways as confidential information. Disclosure may occur through word of mouth, on-line gossip, the careless handling of documents and computer disks or simply being overheard. Gossip spreads like wildfire in most companies. The secret to success is to keep this mischievous and potentially dangerous genie well and truly corked in his bottle.

- Do not discuss the investigation, or any aspect of it, using e-mail or on-line chat facilities and do not prepare memoranda, file notes or reports on corporate computers readily accessible to the suspect(s).

As stated in Chapter 4, password-based authentication to electronic mail systems is easily subverted and there have been many cases where suspects have engaged in their own monitoring of electronic mail exchanges between the very people conducting, or party to, the investigation. There is a real risk that the hunters become the prey.

In establishing and maintaining OpSec, commonsense applies. Ideally, all meetings that concern the investigation should take place off-site, preferably at a remote location not commonly used by employees of the organization. In practice, this often tends to be a hotel conference room.

Meetings or briefings should not be scheduled in any appointment system, diary or daybook accessible by the suspect or his colleagues or associates.

- To reiterate, if a suspect is aware of the investigation, he will cover his tracks, which will make the investigation significantly more difficult, complex and protracted. He may also disperse and hide his assets, transfer and conceal bank accounts and prepare other counter-measures, which will impact upon the effectiveness of freezing and seizure orders.

LEGALITY

Is what you propose to do legal?

- Always obtain written legal advice before commencing a covert investigation and ensure that your proposed tactics and techniques are legal within the jurisdiction where the incident has occurred.

Evidence obtained using illegal methods is inadmissible in many jurisdictions and may expose you to litigation, prosecution, regulatory censure and adverse publicity.

- The investigation is always conducted under the strict obligation to act within the law.

The incident response plan should include a written legal opinion from a qualified attorney on the jurisdictional legality for any of the following investigative methods that are envisaged:

- telephone and fax interception
- telephone call log analysis
- surveillance
- covert audio and film recording
- on-line monitoring of computers
- desk searches
- copying personal correspondence and documents located in company premises
- searching personal property within company premises
- pretext calls and visits
- computer forensic examination of suspects' computers
- downloads from mobile telephones, PDAs, memory sticks and data processing devices which may belong to the suspect and *not* to the organization
- audit trail, firewall log and transactional analysis
- reviewing access control logs and CCTV recordings
- targeted trash lifts
- Internet research
- sting operations
- interviews with witnesses
- interviews with the suspect(s)
- other.

In the United Kingdom, companies must comply with the *Regulation of Investigatory Powers Act* and the directives of the *Telecommunications (Lawful Business Practice) (Interception of Communications) Regulations 2000*, collectively referred to, hereafter, as 'RIP'.

RIP provides a framework with which companies must comply when monitoring electronic data processing equipment and telecommunications. This legislation entitles an organization to monitor systems owned and operated by the company, including computers, networks, firewalls and telephones, and data transmitted and stored on these systems may be produced as evidence in disciplinary hearings, civil proceedings, criminal prosecutions or to resolve disputes. Recordings and monitoring may also be made for regulatory purposes, in arbitration, for quality control, for training and other purposes that an organization deems necessary.

RIP imposes a number of expectations and stipulations, summarized briefly here:

- Monitoring may only take place on privately operated data or telecommunications networks. It is, therefore, illegal to intercept a public telephone system, such as the BT or Mercury network. Where a conversation is intercepted on an extension line within an office or company (that is, within a private telecommunications system), there is no breach of the law. When assessing the legality of such interception, it is necessary, therefore, clearly to delineate the boundary between the public telephone system and any private network that interfaces with it.
- Monitoring may only take place with the express authority of the lawful owner and operator of the private network.
- Reasonable steps must be made to inform employees and users that the organization's systems and networks are subject to monitoring. Preferably, this should be stipulated in the employment contract. Many organizations also remind users that systems may be monitored using login banners and screen messages.
- Monitoring must take place for a specified purpose:
  - to establish facts necessary for the conduct of the business;
  - to prevent or detect crime;
  - to detect unauthorized use of a system, or misuse.

Broad-brush monitoring of the workforce for no specific purpose clearly constitutes a transgression. There is also an expectation that any monitoring should be proportionate to the intensity and gravity of the threat or risk being investigated.

- Make sure that you have in place a company policy permitting the monitoring of company data processing and communications systems to detect and prevent fraud and other serious wrongdoing. See Appendix 2, 'Acceptable usage policy'.

Data protection, privacy law and human rights statutes will also impact upon any proposed investigative methods. These laws are evolving rapidly; ensure that the legal advice obtained is up to date and applicable.

Human resources and corporate lawyers may be reticent to endorse any action that could be perceived as intrusive against the person, for fear of transgressing data protection, privacy and human rights statutes. Advice from professional fraud and employment lawyers is likely to be far more robust as to which methods are, in fact and precedent, permissible.

Be aware, also, that HR and corporate lawyers have, on occasions, wilfully misinterpreted or misconstrued data protection, privacy and employment law out of a misguided loyalty to suspected colleagues, or simply to avoid the nuisance, inconvenience and disruption that an investigation often causes. This is a real phenomenon, observed on many occasions.

It is highly advisable, therefore, to obtain formal, independent advice from specialist external lawyers with extensive practical experience of corporate fraud and employee criminality and wrongdoing in the workplace.

- A specialist external lawyer should always be retained and consulted before a dedicated investigation into an individual or group commences. All proposed methods should be cleared in writing before deployment.
- In cases of fraud or serious malpractice it is advisable to retain a specialist external lawyer immediately. Injunctions and freezing orders may be needed at very short notice to prevent the suspect from departing the jurisdiction, concealing funds or assets, or from misusing misappropriated IP or confidential information.

The investigation is conducted under the umbrella of legal privilege. All communications between the appointed lawyer and the Controller and his team regarding the strategy, tactics, findings or evidence obtained pertaining to the case are protected from being disclosed to the suspect or his legal team.

CONTROL REGIME

What current monitoring and logging takes place? Can it be improved?

Investigating fraud, computer crime and misuse in the workplace is critically dependent on the quality of firewall and network event logging, application monitoring and accurate transactional recording.

A review of audit trail generation, coverage, granularity and retention to determine whether potential breaches of security, particularly those assessed with a severe or catastrophic impact, could be resolved to the point of locating the computers and individuals responsible, should be conducted. If not, then the scope and focus of system and process logging and monitoring requires urgent revision. This should be done before an incident occurs (see Chapter 17).

- Investigating computer misuse is heavily dependent on appropriate audit trails and logging.

Conduct a review of CCTV coverage and access control logging within company premises.

Critical systems and processes should be identified and controls assessed and where necessary improved. Access should be appropriately assigned and logged. As with all mission-critical functions, supervision and segregation is essential.

- Recovery from computer misuse may prove impossible without a proper backup regime. TEST, TEST and TEST AGAIN.

In larger organizations, key infrastructure may fall within different jurisdictions and under diverse operational control. Some networks may also be outsourced or managed in partnership with other companies.

- The incident response plan must account for this fragmentation. Procedures should be devised and tested to harmonize the collation of intelligence and evidence from disparate networks, systems and processes, some of which may not fall under the organization's direct control. When contemplating an approach for logs or other potential evidence in the possession of third parties, operational security must be considered.

CRIME SCENE MANAGEMENT

Who will obtain the evidence and how?

Crime scene management and the preservation of evidence are vital to incident response. First steps are crucial and it is advisable to train in advance all members of the incident response team in evidence handling and management.

All evidence, whether documentary, digital or other, must be gathered and preserved in accordance with best practice (see Chapter 14).

- A checklist of all available sources of evidence should be prepared and incorporated in the incident response plan to ensure that no potentially evidential material is overlooked (see Chapter 17).
- Evidence should be processed according to criminal prosecution standards to ensure its admissibility. In the UK, for example, computer evidence will accord with the *Association of Chief Police Officers (ACPO) Guidelines on Rules of Evidence for Computer Based Crime.*

The Controller may call on external forensic consultants, or, if available, an in-house computer forensic team – a decision matrix as to these options is at Appendix 4.

- Only authorized and trained personnel approved by the Controller may process evidence.
- If no local expertise is available, forensic specialists should be retained immediately – they have extensive knowledge and experience of incident responses.

The Controller will appoint an Exhibits Manager to record all evidence in a central log (spreadsheet) with each exhibit's unique reference, a description of the exhibit and its relevance, where, when and by whom it was found. The Exhibits Manager is responsible for the chain of evidence, preserving evidential integrity and the secure custody of all evidence (see Chapter 14).

INTELLIGENCE

What access and IT skills will be needed?

It is always preferable to gather intelligence covertly, without the knowledge of the suspect(s). The incident response team or its designated agent will need access to corporate network user accounts and the contents of directories, electronic mail boxes, hard disks and other data storage media located in the vicinity of the suspect's desk or workplace. It may also be necessary to restore backups, or to employ real-time on-line monitoring of the suspect's workstation.

- A senior member of corporate IT will advise the Controller on how best to achieve this objective without compromising operational security.
- Where the IT department is itself the subject of an investigation and there is no recourse to its personnel, the Controller will consult with external forensic IT specialists or other technical experts to assess how best this objective may be accomplished.
- Covert investigations will only be conducted by qualified personnel or contractors who are trained and experienced in this field.
- An attorney will assess and approve all proposed covert methods in advance.

Intelligence gathering may also involve the installation of hidden cameras, audio monitoring, localized telephone interception or on-line software or hardware surveillance – all of which must be done without the knowledge of the suspect, or indeed anyone else who might jeopardize the operation. These technical surveillance methods may require specialist assistance from expert contractors, and should only be implemented once approved by the Controller, in accordance with qualified opinion as to the legality of the proposed methods.

- Intelligence obtained during covert investigations should be processed to criminal prosecution standards. In the event that it is demonstrably impossible to accord with this standard, any shortcoming will have to be accounted for in court.

SECURING EXPOSED SYSTEMS AND PROCESSES

What about control failures that are discovered during the investigation?

Where systems and processes have been compromised, it will be necessary to close any loopholes that have been exploited.

However, very careful consideration is required as to how and when these loopholes are closed, as this may alert the suspect to other covert investigative efforts. It may, for example, be possible covertly to monitor the loopholes and record their exploitation by the suspect and use the resulting logs as evidence.

- A 'knee-jerk' reaction is to close loopholes immediately. However, this may be counter-productive and deny the incident response team the opportunity to trap or ensnare the perpetrator. A risk assessment should be conducted to determine the potential extent of the damage – commercial or otherwise – that might result should any exposure remain until further evidence is gathered. If the potential impact is assessed as limited or marginal, there may be relative advantages in leaving the loophole exposed but monitored.
- Beware of entrapment – enticing someone to commit a crime is clearly inadvisable. Setting a 'honey pot' – a lure that will attract the suspect – may fall within the category of entrapment. Take legal advice if such a tactic is contemplated.
- Clearly, if a loophole exposes the organization to a high impact fraud, theft or information leak, immediate corrective measures may be mandated.

Depending on investigative and evidential considerations, any loophole should always be closed at the earliest possible opportunity. An investigation as to how and why the loophole occurred, its subsequent exploitation and the appropriate corrective procedure should be disseminated to all relevant departments and an audit undertaken to ensure that the loophole is closed, throughout the organization.

REACTIVE INVESTIGATIONS

What happens if the incident has happened and the culprit is known?

If you are responding to an incident which is disclosed within the workplace, that has already taken place and where the identity of the suspect or the culprit is known, the priority is to safeguard all of the available evidence as quickly as possible in order to prevent it from being tampered with, overlooked or lost, intentionally or otherwise.

- Secure the scene of crime and prevent any unauthorized access to it at the earliest opportunity.
- Identify and close any loopholes (see 'Crime scene management' above).

In securing the evidence it may be necessary to cordon off work areas or offices, to impound computers and other material and to change locks and post guards at entrances and exits. Grid searches should be conducted in the areas to which the suspect or culprit had access and all potential evidence that is found should be logged in an inventory. Speed is of the essence.

- Legal advice should be taken to ensure that all searches of company property, personal possessions or people are conducted lawfully.

Decisions will have to be made quickly as to whether the police should be called in and strategic objectives will have to be determined. If the police attend and commence an investigation then all operational decisions will necessarily pass to them. The disadvantage, here, is that you lose control.

Alternatively, if it is decided that an internal enquiry will be conducted, it may be necessary to call upon external specialists to assist with the investigation or to review particular systems or processes.

INTERVIEWS

What rules apply should you interview witnesses or the suspect?

If the investigation is covert, interviews with witnesses should only be conducted when all the available evidence has been secured and, preferably, assessed.

If the investigation is being conducted overtly, interviews may commence immediately provided that the interviewer is competent in the strategy, tactics and procedure of investigative interviewing, fully briefed and appraised of all relevant facts and evidence.

Interviews with witnesses and the suspect (or suspects) will usually be necessary.

- In the UK, the police will interview in accordance with the *Police and Criminal Evidence Act* (PACE) – the statutory framework governing police procedure and the admissibility of evidence in court. An early decision is, therefore, advisable as to whether the police should be involved, as they will interview the suspect under caution.
- If a person is interviewed without being cautioned and admits culpability for a crime or misdemeanour, his statement is likely to be admissible in civil proceedings. However, it is highly unlikely to be admissible in criminal proceedings unless the interview and the statement are conducted strictly in accordance with PACE.
- If a decision is made not to include the police and to interview under formal caution, legal advice should be obtained to ensure that interviews are conducted in accordance with employment law, privacy law and human rights legislation and in accordance with the civil procedures rules. In most cases, the suspect will have the right to have legal representation and/or a witness present during the interview.

Never interview suspects or witnesses in groups. Ideally, interviewees should be segregated and always spoken with individually. Committees are usually steered by the most dominating personality appointed. Meeker individuals, many of whom may have greater insight and better judgement than the appointed chairperson, may remain mute, even when preposterous recommendations or conclusions are promoted. By interviewing witnesses separately, interviewees may proffer useful information and observations that would otherwise not be expressed.

A simple, effective way to prevent rumours, theories and inaccuracies from establishing themselves as facts is to obtain detailed written accounts of what happened from those who witnessed the events being investigated. When challenged to provide a written account, most people are more conscientious, more precise and more detailed in the reconstruction of the events than when asked to provide a verbal recollection, particularly so if they are required to sign their testimony. Interviews should be conducted individually and not in groups and each witness statement should be as detailed as possible and include:

- the date and time of the incident(s) described;
- when, where and by whom the incident was first discovered;
- what was observed, what happened, or was believed to have occurred;
- the names of any witnesses present;
- proposed remedial actions taken at the time, or subsequently;
- conversations or meetings relating to the incident and where and when they occurred;
- forensic or other evidence introduced by the witness;
- reference to logs, memos, diaries, e-mails, documents, printouts, computer data or any relevant information or item;
- other relevant details that the witness can recall.

A statement can never contain too much detail, but can often contain too little. Discrepancies between statements should be investigated and resolved.

Start any enquiry with a clean sheet of paper and establish what *actually* happened, as opposed to what people believe or wish to assert happened. The investigator should remain vigilant to hidden agendas, infighting and personal vendettas. Where possible, interview first-hand witnesses and always corroborate hearsay evidence. Rumours, Chinese whispers, contrived explanations, speculation and theories should never cloud or unduly influence the investigator's judgement.

- Interviewing is a minefield, and not to be entered into by the unwary. It is clearly incumbent on the incident response team to define and agree its proposed strategy in advance, after consulting at the highest levels and having obtained qualified legal opinion on all aspects of the process.

LEGAL RESPONSES

Having obtained the evidence, what are our options?
Once all of the available intelligence and evidence has been assessed, it is necessary to determine an appropriate legal or disciplinary response, if any, to the incident that has occurred.

If legal action is envisaged, it is imperative that qualified lawyers, highly experienced in the matters at hand, are appointed. Fraud, computer misuse and workplace criminality require the attention of specialist lawyers who are intimately acquainted with applicable statute and procedure.

The appropriate qualifications and experience of the lawyer(s) that are retained should be established in advance as an integral element of incident response planning.

At this stage, it will be necessary for the Controller, the incident response committee and the board to assess a wide range of issues and options.

The lawyers will advise on the following:

- the probative value and admissibility of the evidence;
- the options for restitution under civil law;
- the suspect's rights;
- any legal obligations within the company's disciplinary procedures;
- compliance with employment law, privacy law and human rights legislation;
- interviewing the suspect employee;
- pursuing negligent or implicated third parties;
- whether the police should be notified or involved;
- the option of a private prosecution;
- whether civil proceedings and a criminal prosecution can proceed simultaneously;
- disclosure;
- any necessary further actions;
- other.

Ultimately, the advice given at this stage and any decisions taken will be at the highest levels.

Fundamentally, whatever decisions are made and whatever conclusions are reached will be entirely dependent on the integrity of the evidence obtained, and the legality of the techniques and methods used to obtain it.

Coordinated incident response planning and preparation ensures that this evidence, in all respects, is solid.

DISCIPLINARY RESPONSE

If the decision is taken to deal with the matter using the organization's disciplinary code, detailed legal advice will be necessary to ensure that any interviews, requests for information or searches of the suspect or his property are undertaken strictly in line with applicable jurisdictional laws and conventions.

- It is highly inadvisable to dismiss an employee solely on the basis of unsubstantiated allegations or suspicions. This effectively relinquishes control over the suspect and exposes the organization to a potential claim for wrongful dismissal.

Having secured the evidence covertly, a decision may then be taken to suspend the employee, pending further investigations, during which time the evidence accrued is analysed and interpreted. Control over the employee is maintained during this period, and he may be recalled to account for his actions.

EXIT PROCEDURES

Should the decision be made to suspend or fire an employee, suitable exit procedures must be in place to:

- preserve evidence;
- safeguard critical systems and processes from sabotage;
- secure and account for company assets assigned to the departing employee.

Many devastating acts of sabotage and other subterfuge have occurred due to poor or non-existent exit procedures. This is a very serious control failure in many organizations. See Chapter 19.

FIDELITY AND COMPUTER CRIME INSURANCE CLAIMS

It may be necessary to quantify any direct and consequential financial losses resulting from the incident for a proposed insurance claim, or to seek restitution or compensation through the courts. Computer evidence and other records seized may be needed in order to calculate this loss.

Any major claim on insurance is likely to be vigorously contested, through the appointment of loss adjusters and experts. The quantification of loss will have to be supported by detailed evidence.

- What documentation and other evidence will be needed to make a claim?
- Were operating procedures and guidelines in place and adhered to? Control failures may adversely affect any claim.
- Is the insurance cover sufficient to cover the losses sustained?

There will be an expectation that any evidence to support a claim will have been gathered in accordance with approved standards.

PRESS AND MEDIA MANAGEMENT

Mismanagement of a crisis makes for very bad publicity, and it is necessary to prepare in advance a strategy to handle press enquiries.

- All media contact should be directed to a single point of contact, preferably a director trained in PR and adept at liaising with journalists.
- A statement, agreed by the Controller, the incident response committee and the board should be prepared.
- There should be no deviation from the agreed statement without the express agreement of the board.

FOLLOW-UP AND LESSONS LEARNED

It is advisable to conduct a post-incident investigation and circulate the ensuing report to all relevant parties. Any exposures or procedural failures that have been discovered must be notified.

14 *Ground Rules on Computer Evidence*

First I shall do no harm.
Hypocratic oath

When processing a crime scene, care must be taken to ensure that potential computer evidence is secured so that its integrity is guaranteed.

Figure 14.1   Comer's axiom – preparation is key to incident response[1]

Digital evidence is inherently unstable and difficult to protect and preserve. There are a number of factors that impact upon the evidential processing of computer data, many of which arise due to the *intangible* nature of electronically stored information.

- Data is easily *changed*. It is very easy to modify computer data, intentionally or otherwise, and computer evidence is often contested on this basis. There is an onus to prove beyond question the *integrity* of evidential data, not just at the point of seizure, but at all times during its subsequent custody. Conversely, in the absence of reliable log files or audit trails, it may prove a formidable challenge to prove that a fraudster has amended a field in a database or accounting system. Computer fraud may flourish

---

1   First articulated by fraud and security expert Mike Comer in 1998.

undetected in an environment where data may be changed and where this alteration goes unrecorded.

- Data may be *disguised* or *concealed*. There are many techniques by which data may be hidden from discovery. As examples, data may be hidden in areas of a disk that are inaccessible by the operating system, or the illegal content of a file may be camouflaged to reflect an innocent-appearing file using a process called steganography.
- Data may be *encrypted*. The fact that data has been encrypted should be evident, but breaking the encryption without the password, pass-phrase or key may prove an intractable problem, depending on the strength of the encryption algorithm and the complexity and length of the password.
- Data can be *destroyed*. Positive erasure software may be used to over-write files, directories, data partitions or entire disks. This destruction is irrevocable. When planning to seize computer evidence it is vitally important to deny the suspect or any associate the opportunity to destroy the evidence.
- It is difficult to prove the *authorship* of data. Proving beyond doubt that a particular person wrote a computer document, or created a digital photograph, or amended a field in a database can prove difficult. For example, I am writing this book using Microsoft Word software. To the inexperienced eye, an inspection of the Word 'Properties' field of this chapter might suggest otherwise as shown in Figure 14.2.

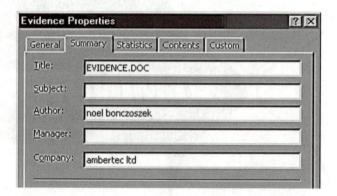

Figure 14.2 The author?

The table tells us who the *registered user* of the software is but does not reveal the *actual* author of the document, which leads us to another observation...

- Data is easily *misinterpreted*. Careful thought and consideration is required when attempting to determine: what data means; how, why, where and when it was created; whether it is the result of an automated process or human intervention; whether it is accurate, truthful or incorrect or false. Before any hypothesis is promulgated, theories need to be tested, preferably in an emulated environment and proved. Interpreting the ways in which differing categories of computer data are created, amended, transmitted, stored and processed often requires extensive experimentation and is a process which can be subject to error, as many expert witnesses have found to their cost.
- Data may be *unintelligible*. We may overlook significant computer evidence because we neither understand it nor appreciate its function, or its relevance.
- It is difficult to prove the *ownership* of data, and for this reason hackers, paedophiles and

other miscreants continue to assert that the incriminating evidence found on their computers is not actually their property or responsibility.

- Data may be *copied*, without trace. Microcomputer operating systems do not by default maintain logs or records of files or directories that have been copied from their host computers. This transparency explains in part the spiralling escalation of intellectual property theft and data misappropriation. Forensic investigation of a computer may determine that data has been copied, but this cannot be guaranteed.
- The *time* and *date* when data was created, amended, saved, transmitted or printed may be falsified, or just wrong. Clocks on computer systems may be adjusted at will and the dates and times indicated in computer files, audit trails and logs must always be treated with caution. International time zones must be accounted for, as must seasonal time adjustments.
- Data may *degrade* or be *corrupted*. This is particularly true of data stored on magnetic media, which, obviously, may be corrupted by exposure to magnetic fields or electro-magnetic pulses. Environmental factors such as heat, dust, exposure to sunlight, damp and humidity can also cause damage, as can the mechanical wear and tear that occurs from successive read and write operations. User error can also cause data loss or corruption. The stability and reliability of different data storage media should be considered when determining the most suitable method to preserve computer evidence.
- Data may be *unreliable*. The information in databases, documents and other computer files may simply be incorrect, or out of date.
- Data may be difficult to *access* or *read*. Obsolete or discontinued hardware or outmoded computer programs may be necessary to read the data in the storage format presented, and this equipment and software may not be readily available. Alternatively, data may be protected by access control systems or software protection measures.
- Data may be stored in a format that makes it difficult to understand or interpret.
- Data may be stored in *significant volumes*. Laptops and desktop computers are currently shipped with hard disk capacities exceeding 80 gigabytes, and data archiving exercises frequently run into terabytes of data. These huge volumes of information impact upon the time it takes to process computer evidence and to analyse it.
- Data may fall beyond the jurisdiction of a local court or judiciary. It may be stored overseas, interstate (in the United States) or offshore. This is a particular problem where virtual drives are encountered on a computer that has been seized – the machine lies within the ruling of the court but the virtual drive accesses information stored overseas and outside of its jurisdiction.
- For all or any of these reasons, data may be difficult to *process*.

It should be clear by now that electronic data requires very careful evidential management.

Right of seizure or inspection

The bedrock of any successful computer forensic investigation is that it should comply with the jurisdictional law in which a prosecution or legal action is anticipated. If the law is broken during the course of the investigation the evidence may be contested and found inadmissible.

A clear threat to evidential admissibility may arise should the investigator trespass, *physically* or *logically*, into premises or systems under investigation. Trespass is an ever-present risk to the computer investigator. The following judgment in November 2001 caused consternation to law enforcement and child protection professionals:

> A man accused of being a member of the world's biggest known Internet paedophile ring walked free from court on a technicality. Andrew Aspinall, 42, was alleged to have had more than 7500 pornographic pictures of children on his computer and disks in his home and office. He was arrested in September 1998 during a police operation to break up the notorious Wonderland Club. But a Scottish sheriff ruled a police search of his home in Livingston, West Lothian, illegal because the police took a civilian worker along to unplug and remove the equipment. Sheriff Peter Gillam ruled the presence of John Cherry, a civilian forensic expert with the police team, breached the *European Convention on Human Rights* because he had not been named in the search warrant. He refused to allow the computer or the disks to be entered as evidence, ruling that Mr Aspinall was denied the opportunity to refuse entry to Mr Cherry into his home. Mr Aspinall's counsel, Alan Mackay QC, told the court: 'The whole search was rendered illegal by the active participation of Mr Cherry.' With the computer evidence ruled inadmissible, the case was abandoned. Mr Aspinall had denied charges of possessing child porn with intent to supply.

In most corporate investigations, the systems to be investigated are clearly the property of the company and there is no doubt about the right of access, either by the company or its agents. Difficulties arise when employees, or others, use their own computers or hardware in the conduct of their day-to-day business and a right of audit or inspection is not expressly stated in their employment contracts. Computer misuse legislation and data protection laws in many countries forbid unauthorized access to computer systems – where such access is sought, a court order must be obtained.

Privacy law is a minefield, and expert legal assistance or opinion should be sought when conducting or contemplating a computer forensic investigation.

Evidence may also be ruled inadmissible on the grounds of its initial discovery:

> A US federal judge ruled that prosecutors could not submit at trial child pornography found on the work computer of Ronald Kline, a former superior court judge. District Court Judge Consuelo B. Marshall ruled that the child pornography found on Mr Kline's work computer was inadmissible because the warrant obtained by police to search it had been based on intelligence obtained during illegal searches of the judge's *home* and *work* computers by a computer hacker. Bradley Willman allegedly accessed Mr Kline's computers and monitored his online activity. He then forwarded his findings to an Internet watchdog group, which alerted the police. Police used this information to obtain the search warrant. Defence attorneys argued that the evidence found on the office computer was 'the fruit of a poisonous tree' because it was obtained illegally.

Here, the initial discovery of the evidence was judged illegal and unconstitutional. The evidence was inadmissible due to the hacker's actions. In October 2004 a US federal appeals court overturned this ruling, re-admitting the evidence Mr Willman gathered because he acted alone, without police direction. 'No law enforcement agency involved in the case knew or could possibly have known that Mr Willman was illegally searching computers, let alone acquiesced in the practice,' the appeals court concluded.

'The fruit of a poisonous tree' argument is common in law; evidence that might appear unassailable is tarnished because it has been obtained illegally or inappropriately.

The first responder

The 'first responder' to an electronic scene of crime, particularly in a business environment, is likely to be someone from the organization's IT department. Very few information technology training or vocational courses teach the rules of computer evidence. In such circumstances, a little knowledge is a dangerous thing. Ignorance of the most basic rules has led to the serious mismanagement of many computer crime scenes, resulting in the failure to secure exhibits or the loss, destruction or contamination of key evidence.

In probability, the first responder at a computer scene of crime is unlikely to be a computer forensic expert, and may have little or no computer knowledge. This need not, and should not, be a problem, but often is because this person promptly summons the office computer hobbyist or has a friend 'who knows a bit about computers'.

A faulty laptop computer was sent for repair. Upon its return from the manufacturer, a support technician discovered that the machine had been used to view a large number of pornographic websites. This clearly contravened the company's disciplinary code.

Oblivious to established forensic procedure, this technician proceeded to inspect the entire contents of the laptop's Internet cache. He viewed several thousand photographs, video clips and web accesses using the laptop's native operating system and installed browser.

The pornography on the laptop was reported to management and the technician was subsequently instructed to print the offending material as evidence of the assigned user's misconduct. Accordingly, a colour printer was attached to the laptop and suitable printer drivers installed. The printed pictures amounted to several hundred pages, which were submitted as evidence of gross misconduct. The laptop's user was suspended.

In due course, a solicitor representing the suspended employee submitted a report. Prepared by a computer forensic expert, it stated that as a result of a flawed examination more than 1000 files had been created *after* the laptop had been impounded and that a further 9000 native files, including all of the material in contention, had been accessed by the technician. The report stated that the contamination of the material submitted in evidence meant that any conclusions proffered about the laptop, its use, or its owner were baseless.

In this case, the principal assertion of the defence expert witness was that the computer evidence was tarnished because files had been altered and created subsequent to the commencement of the investigation. Computer forensic practitioners can cite dozens of similar cases where evidential integrity is compromised by well-meaning but unqualified examination.

Preserving and processing an electronic scene of crime is a job for professionals requiring the same strict adherence to rules and procedures as any other forensic discipline. Pictorially, it is helpful to think of a computer crime scene as being taped off, demarcated for entry only by authorized and qualified personnel (see Figure 14.3).

Should a non-expert be tasked with securing a crime scene where computers are located, two simple rules should be followed:

- If the computer is switched on, it should not be switched off.
- If the computer is switched off, it should not be switched on.
- Or, more succinctly – DO NOT TOUCH! ANYTHING!

Figure 14.3   If unqualified, do not cross!

Prevent anyone from gaining unauthorized access to the machine, and summon expert assistance. These simple rules apply equally to other electronic data processing devices including mobile telephones.[2]

Preserving the evidence and processing it in accordance with the rules of admissibility are our primary concerns. A fundamental principle applies whenever processing evidential data, in whatever format it is stored:

• Avoid inspecting the original data as this may cause alterations.

Imagine that you are asked to examine an Excel spreadsheet. It is suspected that the formulae used to calculate cells within this spreadsheet have been adjusted fraudulently to increase the volume of sales artificially, and, thereby, inflate commission owed to the sales force. To undertake your analysis, are you going to open the spreadsheet, examine the formulae in the relevant cells and start experimenting by adjusting the sales volumes or commissions payable? The simple act of opening the spreadsheet will change the date of last access, and any more detailed inspection or experimentation is almost guaranteed to result in data within the cells being altered irrevocably. If this original evidential spreadsheet has been changed, its integrity cannot be relied upon, a fact that will not be lost on any halfway astute defence lawyer. In a court of law, this spreadsheet will in all probability be ruled inadmissible. How much safer it is, therefore, to work on a *copy* of the spreadsheet, or better still, to make a *master copy* from which subsequent *working copies* may be generated. If this methodology is adopted, you may experiment to your heart's content, safe in the knowledge that the *original* exhibit remains *exactly* as it was found.

The law in the United Kingdom, the United States and most jurisdictions worldwide stipulates that copied documents, in both paper and electronic formats, are admissible. The expression 'document' encompasses *any* and *all* computer data.

---

2   Be aware, however, that the transportation of a cellular telephone subsequent to its seizure is liable to change the record of the base stations in proximity to the device. This information may be valuable in tracing the whereabouts of the telephone.

To reiterate, examination of evidential data should not be conducted directly. In most instances, this means that the original data storage device is not examined; instead a copy of the data stored on the device is exported.

The objective is to freeze the evidential data by taking backups or copies without altering the source data in any way. It is essential that we do not contaminate the original evidence by introducing any accidental changes as these may seriously undermine the probity and admissibility of any evidence subsequently derived. This rule applies to all evidential data, however stored.

There is also a sound practical reason for not examining original evidential data. Any thorough examination is likely to be *destructive*, in that residual data in unallocated clusters on a disk may be overwritten, particularly if software or other files are copied to an evidential disk.

Potentially destructive and legally inadmissible actions include:

- deletion of evidential files;
- accidental writes to the evidential disk;
- installation of diagnostic software on the evidential disk;
- changes to dates and time stamps;
- relocation of evidential files or directories;
- creation of files or directories;
- recovering deleted files directly on the evidential disk;
- executing native software or applications, batch files or macros on the evidential disk.

All of the destructive actions listed here are also likely to render your evidence legally inadmissible. Even a single *bit* change introduced into the original data area may render evidence inadmissible.

Under *no* circumstances should you ever boot into an original evidential disk.

The temptation to switch any suspect computer on should be resisted. The simple act of booting into a computer causes radical changes to the constitution of the operating system and several hundred files may be altered as a result. This can cause the loss of important evidence, particularly in those areas of the disk where data is temporarily cached from memory.

As an example, evidence in the *swap file* – a temporary cache used by Windows which records significant volumes of data from RAM – may be lost irrevocably if the computer is booted directly.

Conversely, when a computer is processed in accordance with proper evidential methods, evidence may be recovered that otherwise might be destroyed:

> 'You can't have that'. The interviewee's face was ashen and he was clearly shaken. 'Why not?' asked the interviewer, referring to the printed memo that he had just placed on the table. The interviewee shook his head in disbelief, or, perhaps, denial. 'You can't have it ... you can't ... How can you *possibly* have this?' He held his head in his hands as he stared uncomprehending at the damning evidence that had been placed before him. After several minutes of quiet contemplation he broke the silence. 'OK, I admit it. I *did* write this ... but I never saved it, never printed it, never copied it, never filed it, never e-mailed it ... in fact, *I never did anything with it at all*. I wrote it on screen, realized immediately that it was incriminating and immediately switched the computer off ... I didn't even close Windows. I literally pulled the plug. So ... how or *where ... did you find it?*'

In this instance, unbeknown to the suspect, the memo on screen had been cached automatically in the computer's swap file, which has proved an abundant source of evidence and intelligence on many occasions. The key point, however, is that the memo was only found because the computer's resident operating system didn't boot when its hard disk was copied. Had it done so, the memo, in all likelihood, would have been overwritten by other information and lost *forever*.

To reiterate, a computer cannot be powered up and booted without the evidence on its disk changing. It is necessary, therefore, to copy the contents of the computer's evidential hard disk whilst preventing the native operating system installed on this disk from executing and this is achieved by processing the evidential hard disk in a controlled environment.

Record keeping

It is incumbent upon the investigator to keep a record of all evidential exhibits gathered during an investigation. In terms of computer evidence, it is necessary to keep detailed notes about each and every exhibit. For example, in the case of a personal computer it would be necessary to record the manufacturer, the model, the serial number and inventory number of the chassis, the make, model and serial number of any internal hard disk, as well as any other relevant observations, such as whether a modem or a CD writer was installed, and if so the same level of detail should be recorded.

This information will assist the investigator in his analysis and understanding of the data that he copies from the computer's hard disk; it is essential for writing statements (see 'Continuity of evidence' later), and the notation of the system clock is necessary to account for any discrepancy with the real date and time, as this will necessarily impact upon the chronology of the files and directories located on the computer.

When recording these details, do *not* photocopy the information printed onto hard disks or other magnetic media, as this may introduce a potentially damaging electrostatic charge. However, computer equipment may be photographed, as a record of its installation, connectivity and general condition.

If reliable documentation, contemporaneous notes or statements are not produced at trial or in tribunal this may seriously undermine the credibility of the investigator and the probity of any evidence he produces. Under certain circumstances, inadequate documentation can lead to the dismissal of the evidence.

In criminal and civil law in the United Kingdom and some other jurisdictions there is also an expectation of full and frank disclosure by the expert witness or investigator.

In the United Kingdom, for example, the Criminal Procedure and Investigations Act 1996 states that any written statement or report, made at whatever stage in an examination, must be disclosed. A statement or report, made in partial possession of the facts, is equally to be disclosed as a statement made in full possession of the facts. The Act provides a statutory framework for the disclosure of *unused* material.

The computer forensic examiner should also bear it in mind that anything he produces in the course of his examination, be it notes, printouts, electronic copies, is subject to disclosure and there is, therefore, an additional onus on the investigator to *retain, recall* and *reveal* all material gathered during an investigation (the 3 Rs).

An example of a processing checklist used is shown in Figure 14.4.

Processing Checklist

DGI REF: 461   Date: **21/10/04**   Job Start: **16:25**   Job End: **17:40**

Assigned user: **John Smith, Acme Industries**
Machine location: **Accounts area, Block B, Swindon main office**
Address: **123 Bridge End Road, Swindon**

Chassis details: Serial No. / Manufacturer / Model / Inventory **(267)** / Exhibit No. **RWB/1** / Seal No.
B187901

Toshiba Tecra T9100 laptop, MDL PT910E-00DYG-EN, S/N X2074509G

HDD Details: Serial No. / Manufacturer / Model / Inventory **(n/a)** / Exhibit No. **RWB/2** / Seal No.
B187902

IBM TravelStar, MDL IC25N020ATCS04-0, Part No. 07N9317, S/N D2GJW3NB

Peripherals / Dependency Kit / Exhibit No. **RWB/1** / Seal No. **B187901**

(mouse, power pack and cables in laptop bag)

Associated storage media / devices / Exhibit No. **RWB/3** / Seal No. **B187903**

2 CDs and a diskette in bag – copied separately

General layout of desk / Photographs (if covert):   **1 photo each of laptop and hard disk**

Status of power switches (if covert):   **No mains connection**

Chassis Intrusion detection	None

Remove disk, power up, and straight into BIOS menu. Record the following:

BIOS Date and Time	10/3/2004 01:38
Real Date and Time	21/10/2004 16:41 GMT
Boot Sequence	A:\, C:\

(Note attached cables, drives and devices). Photograph internal configuration.

Observations: **Screw missing laptop base-plate, lower left quadrant (see photo)**

System boot diskette removed (covert)	Computer seized – not covert
Target area and system restored	Not covert

Where and when copied	DGI, 18/19 Jockey's Fields, London WC1R 4BW 21/10/2004
Forensic image method	Safeback v.2.18 to hard disk (DGI asset 26)
Audit trail	461RWB1.AUD (printed and attached)
Image file	461RWB1.001 – 461RWB.008
Archive	Awaiting archive to Ultrium LTO tape, safe room, DGI

Completed by   *R Bultitude*   Checked by   *A Stowell*

Figure 14.4 Example of a processing checklist

Technical processing

The computer used to copy the evidential hard disk is configured to boot from a DOS system diskette. The DOS system diskette is the magic object – by booting into a trusted operating system we are effectively in control and can copy the contents of the evidential hard disk safe in the knowledge that the operating system or software stored on it cannot execute. In addition to preserving the evidence on the disk, a controlled processing environment has the added advantage of preventing any nasty surprises in the form of logic bombs or automatic encryption routines from triggering.

The software, configuration files and drivers to execute the controlled download are installed on the system diskette and executed from it.[3]

The choice of backup method used will be dictated by such considerations as speed, flexibility and simplicity while the choice of media will be determined by capacity, reliability, integrity and longevity. A key consideration is whether the chosen backup media may degrade or become unstable over time, thus jeopardizing any evidence that is gathered. This will apply particularly if an extended delay before legal proceedings is contemplated or is likely.

Data may be backed up to rewriteable media such as tape or disk or, preferably, to a non-rewriteable drive, which has the inherent advantage of permanently write-protecting the data recorded to it, thereby preventing any potential alterations to the backup.

At this point it is worthwhile to distinguish between a conventional computer backup and a forensic image copy. A conventional computer backup faithfully duplicates the contents of files and folders as they are stored in the directory tree structure of the system. However, a standard backup will *not* copy many areas on the evidential disk, which are only made accessible using forensic image copying techniques, including:

- unallocated data storage clusters
- file slack space
- disk slack space
- deleted files.

The disadvantage of a standard backup is self evident – large tracts of data are not copied by the process:

> A senior manager had been suspended on suspicion of fraud following the discovery of a number of false invoices. As instructed by management the local IT team had copied the contents of the man's laptop computer, but following inspection had found nothing untoward. A second opinion was sought and the image copy was sent for forensic analysis. It was immediately evident that the copying process was flawed. The documentation with the image stated that the laptop's hard disk was 20 gigabytes in capacity

---

3   A forensic image of a hard disk may also be obtained using a forensically unstable operating system such as Microsoft Windows, provided that a write-protection device is used to prevent the host operating system from altering the data contained on the evidential disk. This is accepted practice by Guidance Software (www.guidancesoftware.com), the manufacturer of EnCase, using its FastBlock write-protection device. A disk image may also be made using the ImageMASSter Drive Lock from Intelligent Computer Solutions (www.ics-iq.com) or with a hardware disk duplication device such as the ImageMASSter Solo also from Intelligent Computer Solutions.

and yet only a single CD-ROM of just 750 megabytes had been submitted for examination. It transpired that the laptop had been processed using Symantec Ghost but that only the *extant* files and folders on the computer had been transferred to the CD, because the IT team overlooked the imaging option within the software (called 'verbose mode'). The forensic examiner subsequently copied the contents of the original laptop hard disk using SafeBack forensic imaging software. The image was inspected and false invoices to the value of $200 000 were extracted from unallocated clusters and file slack space.

By contrast, a forensic image uses bit-stream copying to create an *exact* reproduction of the data located on the evidential disk. Typically, a forensic image will comprise the data stored on a computer's internal hard disk. The backup method used will be non-invasive, that is, it will not alter the constitution of the original data in any way.

Why is the use of forensic disk imaging so important?

By way of simple illustration the grid in Figure 14.5 represents 100 clusters on a disk. Files are stored on disk in file allocation units, or clusters. A file may occupy a number of clusters. Files need not, necessarily, be stored in contiguous clusters but may be allocated in a series of unrelated clusters. For example, in our grid, a file might occupy clusters 1, 2, 6, 33, 46 and 97.

1.	2.	3.	4.	5.	6.	7.	8.	9.	10.
11.	12.	13.	14.	15.	16.	17.	18.	19.	20.
21.	22.	23.	24.	25.	26.	27.	28.	29.	30.
31.	32.	33.	34.	35.	36.	37.	38.	39.	40.
41.	42.	43.	44.	45.	46.	47.	48.	49.	50.
51.	52.	53.	54.	55.	56.	57.	58.	59.	60.
61.	62.	63.	64.	65.	66.	67.	68.	69.	70.
71.	72.	73.	74.	75.	76.	77.	78.	79.	80.
81.	82.	83.	84.	85.	86.	87.	88.	89.	90.
91.	92.	93.	94.	95.	96.	97.	98.	99.	100.

Figure 14.5 Unallocated clusters on disk (in grey)

Files are allocated storage clusters by the computer's operating system, which in turn keeps a record of where each file is stored. This record is called a File Allocation Table (FAT) or a Master File Table (MFT), and it is analogous to an index in a book. If the information recorded in the FAT is destroyed, the data remains on the disk, but the operating system has no method to locate it, because it cannot refer to its index. Because the FAT or MFT is such a crucial reference, there are normally two copies of it; the data between these copies is mirrored and continuously updated as files are saved to disk.

When a file is deleted, the operating system marks the file as deleted and also reassigns the cluster(s) in which the file resided as unallocated, and therefore available to store a new file. Significantly, the operating system does not destroy the data in the deleted file and this information resides in the unallocated cluster(s) until a new file subsequently overwrites it.

In our example grid, the clusters shown in grey are unallocated. They may never have contained data, or they may contain deleted data from a discarded file or files. This deleted data may contain very significant evidence. If, however, we copy the data on the computer disk using a conventional backup program, we are going to lose this potential evidence, because the program will only copy active files and folders and will ignore unallocated clusters.

The grid in Figure 14.6 depicts the net result of copying these 100 clusters using conventional backup software, with the clusters that are *not copied* shown in black. As can be seen, the conventional backup software has failed to copy clusters 7, 8, 9, 13, 14, 26, 27, 48, 58, 62, 64, 65, 69, 70, 82, 83, 84, 85, 86, 87 and 89. As a result of these gaps a mass of potential evidence is missed.

1.	2.	3.	4.	5.	6.				10.
11.	12.			15.	16.	17.	18.	19.	20.
21.	22.	23.	24.	25.			28.	29.	30.
31.	32.	33.	34.	35.	36.	37.	38.	39.	40.
41.	42.	43.	44.	45.	46.	47.		49.	50.
51.	52.	53.	54.	55.	56.	57.		59.	60.
61.		63.			66.	67.	68.		
71.	72.	73.	74.	75.	76.	77.	78.	79.	80.
81.							88.		90.
91.	92.	93.	94.	95.	96.	97.	98.	99.	100.

Figure 14.6   Missing clusters after conventional backup

When a file ends, residual data or data unrelated to that file may also be found at the end of the last cluster allocated to the file. This area, between the end of the file (EOF) and the cluster's end is called *slack space*. Slack space can contain deleted residual data, or it may contain data that has been recorded from random access memory. There are three points about slack space that are noteworthy:

- It is a good source of evidence – particularly where the operating system employs large file allocation units. Cluster sizes of 32 kilobytes may be found on some of the older Windows operating systems, although later releases have reduced cluster sizes to optimize disk storage.
- Slack space represents a potential threat to network and applications security because it can, under certain circumstances, contain plaintext passwords recorded to the hard disk from RAM.
- Slack space is not destroyed when a disk is defragmented. Instead active clusters, including those with slack space, are moved in their *entirety* when defrag is executed. Suspects often defrag their disks in the hope that the constant reading and writing of clusters to different locations on the disk will overwrite incriminating evidence. In fact, defrag will only destroy residual data in unallocated (unused) clusters. The evidence in slack space, however, is simply moved around to different locations and awaits discovery.

Forensic imaging software copies every byte within every cluster within the data partition, and also copies data that may reside on the physical disk that is not contained within an active data partition. We are thus able to access all areas of the suspect's hard disk, including residual data that is deleted as well as physical areas of the disk beyond the active data partitions that may contain information from a previously installed partition.

By reference to a simple graphic in Figure 14.7, the active data partitions in this instance are drives C: and D:, but we can also see the vestigial remains of two previous partitions that have not been overwritten by the new partitions.

C:		Previous partition	
D:		Previous partition	Unused disk

Figure 14.7   Remains of previous partitions

Hiding information outside active data partitions and in areas not addressed by the operating system is a well-known hacker trick. Forensic image copying foils any such attempts at concealment by copying the entirety of the data on the physical disk.

EVIDENTIAL INTEGRITY

It is necessary to establish and demonstrate the evidential *integrity* of the forensic image. How can we be sure that an imaged hard drive is an exact copy of the original evidential disk? Even a seemingly insignificant discrepancy between the original disk and the image copy of it may undermine the probity or credibility of any ensuing evidence.

If required to do so, the computer forensic investigator must be able to demonstrate to a court of law that the image copy upon which his exhibited evidence is based is identical to the original evidential disk. As stated, the forensic imaging methodology is non-invasive and it is an inviolable rule that any software developed for this purpose should not alter or change the data on the original evidential disk in any way.

There are a number of proven forensic software packages available on the market, including Armor Corporation's SafeBack and Guidance Software's EnCase. These products incorporate safeguards based on mathematical principles, which verify the integrity of each image produced. In the case of SafeBack, the software undertakes a Cyclic Redundancy Check and produces a CRC value; any change, however minor, introduced into the image causes the CRC check to fail and the operator is notified at once that corruption has occurred and that the image is invalid.

EnCase adopts a slightly different strategy. During the imaging process, a 'hash value' of the bit-stream copy of the evidential hard drive is calculated using an algorithm called MD5 (Message Digest 5). This algorithm computes a unique value (an acquisition hash) and this is stored in the image file. Upon completion of the imaging process, a verification hash is calculated from the image and compared to the acquisition hash. If the two hash values are the same the image is forensically viable. Following the acquisition of a viable image, EnCase issues the following message:

```
File Integrity:
Completely Verified, 0 Errors.
```

And displays the hash values for the data on the evidential hard drive (the acquisition hash) and on the image (the verification hash).

```
Acquisition Hash:
21DE8CB8D90532C840924E772D76C769
Verification Hash:
21DE8CB8D90532C840924E772D76C769
```

```
SafeBack 2.18 13Feb01 execution started on Oct 13, 2003 14:39.

            202016-01
            Edward W Wilding
            Data Genetics Limited

            14:39:10  Menu selections:
               Function:              Backup
               Remote connection:     Local
               Direct access:         No
               Use XBIOS:             Auto
               Adjust partitions:     Auto
               Backfill on restore:   Yes
               Compress sector data:  Yes

14:39:23  Backup file D:\SMITH.001 created.
          Backup file comment record:
          -------------------------------------------------------------
            MR JOHN SMITH
            HP BRIO
            SN NL12822096 SYS NUM P5819T ABU
            SEAGATE 20 GB HDD
            MODEL ST320413A PN 9R4003-736
            BIOS 13/10/03 14:37
            REAL 13/10/03 12.59
            FDD/CD/HDD/LAN


          -------------------------------------------------------------
14:41:00  Backing up drive 0:
          to D:\SMITH.001 on Oct 13, 2003 14:41
14:41:00  Local SafeBack is running on DOS 7.10
          Source drive 0:
             Capacity........19459 MB
             Cylinders.......2480
             Heads...........255
             Sectors/Head....63
             Sector size.....512
14:41:00  Partition table for drive 0:

             Act Cyl  Hd Sct Rel Sector    MB      Type
             --- ---  -- --- ----------    --      ----
              Y   0   1   1           63  19454  Win95 FAT32 XBIOS

14:54:55  Backup file D:\SMITH.002 created.
15:33:42  Backup file CRC: e594b47e.
15:33:42  Backup of drive 0: completed on Oct 13, 2003 15:33.

          SafeBack execution ended on Oct 13, 2003 15:33.
```

Figure 14.8   Audit trail produced by SafeBack disk imaging software

It has been calculated that the odds of the acquisition hash and the verification hash matching but being generated from different evidential data sets is 1 in 2^{128} (approximately 1 in 340 000 000 000 000 000 000 000 000 000 000 000 000).

Clocks

A common error when evidence from computer systems is processed is for the investigator to fail to make a note of the real date and time and compare this with the evidential computer's clock. Any discrepancies in dates and times should be accounted for, and a determination of the probable chronology of files and directories calculated.

As an intrinsic function, forensic imaging software should produce an audit trail of its operation. The real date and time should be noted by the investigator within the comments section of this audit trail immediately prior to the execution of the copying process.

The forensic imaging software will automatically record the settings of the computer clock, and any discrepancy between the real date and time and the clock may be ascertained by reference to the audit trail.

Most forensic software audit trails will record the computer clock readings and most files are assigned date and time stamps automatically. The common mistake, however, is for the investigator to fail to make a note of the real date and time when he inspects the system and its content.

Regarding the chronology of events, it is essential, therefore, that the investigator records:

- the computer clock date and time;
- the real date and time;
- the international time zone where the computer is located;
- whether daylight saving time (DST) is set (see Figure 14.9).

Figure 14.9   Compare date and times

Pre-dating and post-dating of electronic documents is common in fraud, as is the retrospective amendment of documents to provide alibis. This forgery can only be proved if the investigator can compare the computer clock and calendar reading with the actual date and time:

> The company was in receivership and the administrators suspected that its former directors were channelling assets and funds that should have been declared and repaid to the company's creditors. A mysterious new company had suddenly emerged through which these funds and assets were siphoned. The former MD has sworn an affidavit stating that this new company had been incorporated in 1993 and had been trading for three years. He exhibited a letter of incorporation to support his claim. Suspecting a 'phoenix' fraud, the administrators instructed investigators to report the origin and circumstances of this new company.

> The former MD's computer disk was imaged. The imaging software recorded the date and time of the PC's clock to an audit trail. The clock was accurate. The image of the disk was examined and the disputed letter of incorporation was found. It was a Microsoft Word document dated February 1993. However, the 'document statistics' table within the software showed that the document had been created, modified and printed in December 1996. This indicated forgery, a serious criminal offence.
>
> Witness statements from former employees suggested that the new company was indeed a phoenix and had not existed until late 1996. These statements, combined with the computer expert's report, were submitted in proceedings and resulted in a speedy settlement.

Never take printed documents at face value. The computer clock settings are key in determining the chronology of computer files. See the following example in Figures 14.10 and 14.11.

John Smith Esq.
Derwent Enterprises
Minories
London
EC4

1ˢᵗ August 2001   Ref. FR/as 14.

Dear Mr Smith,

This letter is to advise you that the certificate of incorporation for Derwent-Excel Savior AG has been issued and will be forwarded under separate cover.

I look forward to meeting you again in September.

Yours sincerely,

Frederick Reeves
Attorney at Law

Figure 14.10 Letter dated 1 August 2001

File Name	Short Name	Last Accessed	Last Written	File Created
Derwent Excel Savior AG.doc	DERWEN~1.DOC	21/07/2004	21/07/2004 17:33	21/07/2004 17:26

Figure 14.11 The properties field for the same letter

Cherry picking

The courts are generally averse to cherry picking – a subjective and prejudicial process whereby information is selected from a computer system on the basis that it is incriminating, but where other data on the same system is not disclosed.

Image copying techniques, whereby the entirety of the data on a disk is copied and disclosed, clearly mitigate the risk of an accusation of cherry picking. Image copying, however, while suitable for many microcomputer systems, may prove problematic in cases where evidence is encountered on minicomputers and mainframes. If evidence is located in extant files and directories, a backup of any such system, which should be occurring in any event as part of a sound disaster recovery plan, may suffice for evidential reasons. An individual backup tape may be removed from the cycle, processed and exhibited.

Many systems employ data mirroring and it may be technically possible to obtain a snapshot of the mirrored system at a given time. If the evidence is extracted using specialist disk editing tools, it may be advisable to generate a disk image of the system even if this causes disruption to the business.

The courts tend to favour those who have shown alacrity and best endeavour. The courts are also realistic where business continuity and operations are concerned and will assess whether proportionate and appropriate actions have been taken.

What you see is what you get?

Many computer software packages proclaim that *what you see is what you get* (WYSIWYG). The concept is that information shown on screen reflects exactly the data as it is recorded on disk, in storage, or as printout. In forensic investigations, however, we should never assume that WYSIWYG applies. Often this is not the case.

Printed documents and documents observed on screen (for example, through the Windows operating system interface) do not *necessarily* reflect all relating information within the soft copy. This is a very important fact that is not widely appreciated by the legal profession or the courts.

By way of illustration, continuing with the example correspondence between the fictitious Messrs Smith and Reeves, the screen shot in Figure 14.12 shows a letter written using Microsoft Word as it is displayed through the Windows interface.

However, when the same document is viewed using a hexadecimal editor as shown in Figure 14.13, a different version of the letter appears, revealing a paragraph that has been suppressed by Word on screen but which has been retained within the soft copy document.

This phenomenon occurs when the 'Fast Save' option is invoked within MS Word. It was observed recently when a codicil to a Last Will and Testament was found to contain a key and very incriminating paragraph that could not be seen through the Windows interface and that did not appear in the printed version of the same document.

Continuity of evidence

Ensuring the *continuity of evidence*, also known as the chain of evidence, is a fundamental ordinance, which must be observed. It is necessary to account for an evidential exhibit at all times, including its initial seizure, its subsequent custody, in transit and when transferred between different people. All actions pertaining to the exhibit should be recorded in statements and exhibit receipts should support any transit or transfer.

Defence counsel will seek to exploit breaks in the chain of evidence. If a forensic exhibit is not accounted for at all times subsequent to its seizure there is an innate opportunity for

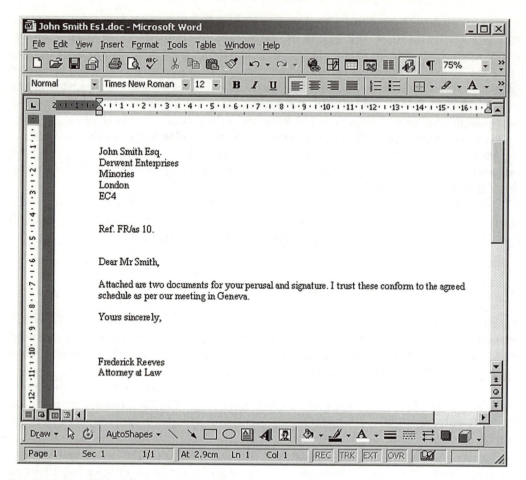

Figure 14.12 Document displayed in Windows

counsel to infer that it has been tampered with or has become contaminated, and as such is not to be relied upon. As we have seen, computer evidence, particularly electronic data, is susceptible to tampering or inadvertent alteration and extra precautions must therefore be taken to ensure each exhibit's evidential integrity.

The legal profession is fully conversant with the concept and practice of evidential continuity and it is not surprising, therefore, that barristers and attorneys will focus on the chain of evidence in preference to exploring complex technical issues with which they are unfamiliar.

Examples of breaks in the chain of evidence, inconsistencies in continuity, and contamination of evidence include:

- an accountant who dutifully placed an evidential backup tape in a signed and sealed evidence bag; unfortunately, the date written on the exhibited tape surpassed the date witnessed on the sealed evidence bag;
- a lost diskette, never retrieved, upon which had been found spreadsheets listing several hundred thousand pounds worth of misappropriated properties;
- a police computer forensic examiner who purged all of the data on an original evidential hard disk and re-issued it for use on an unrelated case;

```
00000600h: 0D 0D 4A 6F 68 6E 20 53 6D 69 74 68 20 45 73 71 ; ..John Smith Esq
00000610h: 2E 0D 44 65 72 77 65 6E 74 20 45 6E 74 65 72 70 ; ..Derwent Enterp
00000620h: 72 69 73 65 73 0D 4D 69 6E 6F 72 69 65 73 0D 4C ; rises.Minories.L
00000630h: 6F 6E 64 6F 6E 0D 45 43 34 0D 0D 0D 52 65 66 2E ; ondon.EC4...Ref.
00000640h: 20 46 52 2F 61 73 20 31 30 2E 0D 0D 0D 44 65 61 ;  FR/as 10....Dea
00000650h: 72 20 4D 72 20 53 6D 69 74 68 2C 0D 0D 41 74 74 ; r Mr Smith,..Att
00000660h: 61 63 68 65 64 20 61 72 65 20 74 77 6F 20 64 6F ; ached are two do
00000670h: 63 75 6D 65 6E 74 73 20 66 6F 72 20 79 6F 75 72 ; cuments for your
00000680h: 20 70 65 72 75 73 61 6C 20 61 6E 64 20 73 69 67 ;  perusal and sig
00000690h: 6E 61 74 75 72 65 2E 20 49 20 74 72 75 73 74 20 ; nature. I trust 
000006a0h: 74 68 65 73 65 20 63 6F 6E 66 6F 72 6D 20 74 6F ; these conform to
000006b0h: 20 74 68 65 20 61 67 72 65 65 64 20 73 63 68 65 ;  the agreed sche
000006c0h: 64 75 6C 65 20 61 73 20 70 65 72 20 6F 75 72 20 ; dule as per our 
000006d0h: 6D 65 65 74 69 6E 67 20 69 6E 20 47 65 6E 65 76 ; meeting in Genev
000006e0h: 61 2E 0D 0D 41 20 74 68 69 72 64 20 64 6F 63 75 ; a...A third docu
000006f0h: 6D 65 6E 74 20 77 69 6C 6C 20 62 65 20 66 6F 72 ; ment will be for
00000700h: 77 61 72 64 65 64 20 75 6E 64 65 72 20 73 65 70 ; warded under sep
00000710h: 61 72 61 74 65 20 63 6F 76 65 72 2E 20 54 68 69 ; arate cover. Thi
00000720h: 73 20 73 68 6F 75 6C 64 20 62 65 20 64 65 73 74 ; s should be dest
00000730h: 72 6F 79 65 64 20 69 6D 6D 65 64 69 61 74 65 6C ; royed immediatel
00000740h: 79 20 66 6F 6C 6C 6F 77 69 6E 67 20 74 68 65 20 ; y following the 
00000750h: 74 72 61 6E 73 61 63 74 69 6F 6E 20 73 63 68 65 ; transaction sche
00000760h: 64 75 6C 65 64 20 66 6F 72 20 74 68 65 20 32 32 ; duled for the 22
00000770h: 6E 64 20 6F 66 20 74 68 65 20 6D 6F 6E 74 68 2E ; nd of the month.
00000780h: 0D 0D 59 6F 75 72 73 20 73 69 6E 63 65 72 65 6C ; ..Yours sincerel
00000790h: 79 2C 0D 0D 0D 0D 46 72 65 64 65 72 69 63 6B 20 ; y,....Frederick 
000007a0h: 52 65 65 76 65 73 0D 41 74 74 6F 72 6E 65 79 20 ; Reeves.Attorney 
000007b0h: 61 74 20 4C 61 77 0D 0D 00 00 00 00 00 00 00 00 ; at Law.........
```

Figure 14.13   The same document viewed using a disk editor

- an investigator who stored his file notes and reports on an evidential diskette intended as a key exhibit in a fraud investigation;
- an insolvency practitioner who used a prime suspect's computer to administer the dissolved company from which the suspect had fled;
- an evidential tape left on a radiator overnight, which melted into an interesting but otherwise useless *objet d'art*.

At court or tribunal, a custody record for each exhibit is required. The custody record provides an audit trail of all actions taken that impact upon the exhibit, or the evidence produced from it. The custody record should be supported by a statement from each and every person involved in the processing of the exhibit, stating the precise details of both the exhibit and the actions taken. The initial statement will be made by the person who first produced the exhibit, and this will detail the circumstances of its discovery or production.

There is rarely ever too much detail recorded in a continuity statement, but there is frequently too little information, or essential details are missed. The details should be written down or typed.

It is necessary to repudiate any accusation that computer evidence has been tampered with. A basic method, but one which is of immense practical value, is for exhibits to be sealed in tamper-proof evidence bags. Each evidence bag is uniquely numbered and access to the exhibit is only possible by physically cutting the bag open, or in the case of larger exhibits, breaking the tamper-proof seal used to secure the bag.

Provided that a record is made each and every time an exhibit is sealed in a bag or removed from it, there can be no sustained accusation that an unauthorized party could have tampered with the evidence. It is important to retain all of the bags that have been sealed and subsequently opened because they, combined, comprise proof of the chain of custody. It is also necessary to seal the evidence in a fresh bag whenever an exhibit is to be left unattended, and to note the unique bag reference number (see Figures 14.14 and 14.15).

WITNESS STATEMENT
(CJA 1967 S9, MCA 1980 S102, MCR 1981 R70)

Statement of   **Noel Bonczoszek**

Age if under 21   Over 21

This statement (consisting of 1 page(s) each signed by me) is true to the best of my knowledge and belief and I make it knowing that, if it is tendered in evidence, I shall be liable to prosecution if I have wilfully stated in it anything which I know to be false or do not believe to be true.

Dated the 26th day of October 2004

Signature ....   Signature witnessed by...........................

I am Operations Manager for Data Genetics International Limited (DGI), 18/19 Jockey's Fields, London, WC1R 4BW, a company specializing in the evidential processing and investigation of computers and digital media.

On Tuesday, 26th October 2004, at 10.05 a.m., at DGI's office, Mr Richard Bultitude, a DGI technical consultant, handed me a Toshiba Tecra 9100 Laptop, Exhibit RWB/1, in evidence bag number B187901.

I removed the computer, serial number X20745096G, from that evidence bag for the purposes of identification. I then resealed the computer including the previous evidence bag B187901, in evidence bag B224444, at 10.15 a.m. and returned it to Mr Bultitude at 10.20 a.m.

I confirm that the computer exhibit RWB/1 was in my possession at all times between 10.05am and when it was returned to Mr Bultitude at 10.20 a.m.

Dated the 26th day of October 2004

Signature ....   Signature witnessed by...........................

Figure 14.14 Continuity statement

Evidence should always be archived in secure storage, ideally in a safe or strong room.

In a commercial context or business setting, it is unlikely that law enforcement standard evidence bags will be readily available. In such circumstances a simple envelope may suffice to secure evidence.

Figure 14.15 Secure archiving of evidence

To secure a computer hard disk evidentially:

1. Discharge static electricity using an anti-static strap.
2. Switch the computer off.
3. Photograph the computer.
4. Note its manufacturer, model and serial numbers and any other identifying data.
5. Remove the cover or any panel.
6. Photograph the internal configuration of the computer.
7. Remove the hard disk from the processor.
8. Photograph the hard disk (but do *not* photocopy the information printed on the disk).
9. Note the hard disk's manufacturer, model, serial number and any other identifying data.
10. Note the setting of the jumper switch on the hard disk.
11. Place the hard disk in an anti-static bag (Figure 14.16).
12. Place the anti-static bag and its contents in an A4 envelope.
13. Seal the envelope.
14. Sign and date each aperture of the envelope (there will normally be three apertures including the seal).
15. A witness signs and dates each aperture of the envelope.
16. The apertures are sealed with transparent Sellotape (Figure 14.17).
17. A photocopy is made of the information at 3, 4, 8 and 9. This is attached to the sealed envelope.
18. The envelope is placed in a safe.

Anyone attempting to gain access to the hard disk must tear the envelope open because the apertures have been sealed and are tamper-proof.

Figure 14.16   A field-expedient evidence bag

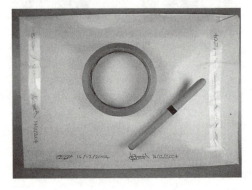

Figure 14.17   The exhibit envelope

Misinterpretation

Misinterpretation of the facts or observed phenomena is a common risk facing the computer forensic investigator. Typically, documentation or evidence is located and its provenance is clear, but the manner in which it came to reside on disk is misinterpreted. This is a common problem with child pornography investigations where, for example, illegal photographs are found on a disk but how and why they came to be on the computer is misconstrued by the forensic examiner. There is always a risk that we attribute an observed phenomenon to an action deliberately taken by a person, when in fact it is the result of an automated process, machine function or software.

An insurance salesman had sent letters to approximately 300 of his clients. The letter stated that he was setting up his own practice. He solicited their custom on the basis that he would provide a more comprehensive set of services than his current employer. Some of the clients returned the letter, not to the salesman, but to his employer.

Lawyers were consulted and suggested that the salesman's computer should be examined for evidence of this and other breaches of contract. A forensic examination of the computer recovered a large number of letters that had been sent to a database of clients, which was the property of the insurance company. Significantly, the letters were deleted and the lawyers were keen to present this as an act of wilful deception. The forensic investigator wrote an affidavit stating that the salesman had deleted the letters, with the inference that he wished to conceal this correspondence from his employer.

In fact, the salesman had undertaken a mail merge using the client database and a template letter. He had executed the mail merge using the diskette drive of the computer in the belief that his actions would not be discovered. However, the operating system could not complete the task using the available space on the diskette and it reverted to the hard disk of the computer as a temporary cache. Upon completing the mail merge, the operating system, not the salesman, automatically deleted the cached data from the hard disk.

This was not a case of intentional deletion by a person, but an automated deletion executed by the operating system. The misinterpretation by the forensic examiner caused him, the lawyers and their client some embarrassment. However, the method admitted to by the salesman to complete the mail merge was clearly furtive.

The examiner needs to be extremely careful in his interpretation of how and why evidence originated. This is particularly important when investigating networked systems or those with Internet access, where information is transmitted between systems, often without any conscious action by the user of a computer and without his knowledge or consent.

Direct examination

Should time considerations or inadequate resources prevent the established methods and procedures to process computer evidence there may be no other option but to examine systems and data directly. There are inherent risks to such a strategy which is best avoided if possible. If such an examination is contemplated, it should only be undertaken by a qualified person with a profound appreciation of the cause and effect of each action taken. Detailed notes of every action and when precisely it was taken should be made. For reasons already explained, it is clearly preferable to undertake any such examination having booted into a trusted operating system controlled by the examiner.

Annotation

There is nothing intrinsically wrong with annotating computer evidence, that is, recording data from screen using a pen and paper. Annotation may be resorted to due to a lack of appropriate resources or opportunity. Should this be the case, the best evidence rule[4] applies.

An illustration of annotation as best evidence occurred in the case of *Regina v Williams*:

Someone at Kingston University, Surrey, England using the user-id cs_d544 had gained access to the JANET[5] network and from there had used various gateways to gain unauthorized access to systems in the United States and elsewhere. This breach of security was reported to the police and computer staff at the university had been watching for cs_d544 to connect to JANET. The activity then ceased for a period and the staff redeployed to other duties.

---

4   The rule by which an original writing must be offered as evidence unless it is unavailable, in which case other evidence, like copies, notes, or other testimony, may be used.
5   Joint Academic Network shared by UK-based universities.

> Then, one afternoon, cs_d544 again became active on the system and the police were summoned. Two difficulties were immediately apparent; first, it proved difficult to identify which room within the campus was being used by cs_d544 and, second, there was no easy way to log the activities of cs_d544 on the system for evidential purposes. The only available quick fix was to add a monitor to the University network and watch cs_d544's activity in real time fleetingly scrolling across the screen.
>
> Police were forced to resort to pen and paper, noting what they could as it flashed across the screen. The information recorded, plus the time it was seen, combined with subsequent verification was sufficient to prove cs_d544's activity. User cs_d544 was found to be a student named Matthew Benjamin Williams who was arrested with a carrier bag full of hacking notes and successfully prosecuted.

However, with respect to annotation, the following story is salutary:

> An electronic organizer had been seized by police investigating a drugs ring and submitted for examination. For expedience, detectives had annotated the names, addresses, telephone numbers and notes stored on the organizer by viewing this information through the machine's interface. The annotated notes had been submitted as evidence. Defence counsel subsequently instructed that the organizer be examined forensically. The detectives' examination of the organizer clearly did not conform with forensic best practice but that fact, in itself, did not necessarily invalidate the evidence. The forensic examiner downloaded the data in solid-state memory to a computer using software manufactured for the purpose. A comparison between the software download and the officers' notes showed that approximately a third of the telephone numbers had been recorded incorrectly as had a number of names and addresses. At trial, the judge ruled all of the annotated information unreliable and it was dismissed from proceedings.

Locard's Principle of Exchange

Edmund Locard was a policeman who served in Lyon, France, in the early twentieth century and he was a pioneer of forensic investigation. Locard asserted that when a crime takes place there is an exchange of physical information between the criminal and the crime scene.

Every contact leaves a trace…

Every contact between individuals or objects results in a transfer of material between them. It is impossible for the criminal to act, and especially to act with the force that a crime demands, without leaving traces of his presence. No one can act with the force that the criminal requires without leaving behind numerous signs of it; either the wrong-doer has left signs at the scene of the crime, or on the other hand, has taken away with him – on his person or clothes – indications of where he has been and of what he has done.

All of forensic science is premised on Locard's Principle of Exchange. The evidence collected from the crime scene represents the individual traces of the offender that he consciously, subconsciously or inadvertently deposits there. Equally, the evidence collected from the offender represents the individual traces absorbed or transferred to him from the crime scene (see Figure 14.18). Forensic techniques identify these divergent forms of evidence so a link may be established between the crime scene, the victim and the offender.

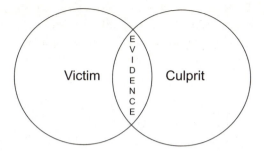

Figure 14.18   Locard's Principle of Exchange

Locard's Principle of Exchange may apply equally to computer forensic investigations, as demonstrated by the following case study:

Private electronic mail correspondence between senior managers at a manufacturing company had been posted to a large number of e-mail addresses by someone who evidently knew the administrative password to the company's electronic mail system. The correspondence included information that was sensitive and intended for restricted circulation.

A CD-ROM containing the electronic web mail logs (see Figure 14.19) recorded at the company's headquarters in the United States played a central role in the ensuing investigation.

```
81.130.170.58 - - [12/Mar/2004:08:39:19 -0800] "GET
/exchange/LogonFrm.asp?isnewwindow=0&mailbox=Bob+Timson HTTP/1.1" 401 0
81.130.170.58 - - [12/Mar/2004:08:39:41 -0800] "GET
/exchange/LogonFrm.asp?isnewwindow=0&mailbox=Tony+Baker HTTP/1.1" 302 121

81.130.170.58 - - [12/Mar/2004:08:45:59 -0800] "GET
/exchange/LogonFrm.asp?isnewwindow=0&mailbox=Tom+Kelly HTTP/1.1" 401 0
81.130.170.58 - - [12/Mar/2004:08:46:35 -0800] "GET
/exchange/LogonFrm.asp?isnewwindow=0&mailbox=Tracy+Simms HTTP/1.1" 302
121

81.130.170.58 - - [12/Mar/2004:08:56:05 -0800] "GET
/exchange/LogonFrm.asp?isnewwindow=0&mailbox=Rod+Smith HTTP/1.1" 302 121

81.130.170.58 - - [12/Mar/2004:09:00:54 -0800] "GET
/exchange/LogonFrm.asp?isnewwindow=0&mailbox=Ted+Chivers HTTP/1.1" 401 0
```

Figure 14.19   Extract of a mail log

These logs recorded the times and dates of each intrusion, the corresponding mailboxes that were accessed and the IP addresses that were dynamically allocated to the intruder's computer on each occasion that he browsed the various managers' mailboxes.

Every contact leaves a trace ...

The company had also received a goading electronic mail message from an unidentified user whom we will call 'bandit_117@yahoo.com'. The company was eager to identify this user.

The web mail logs indicated that the intruder's computer was consistently allocated an IP address in the range 81.130.***.***. Inadvertently, and entirely in accordance with Locard's Principle of Exchange, the intruder had deposited a key element of his identity with his victim.

Every contact leaves a trace…

Using the Ripe 'whois' service (www.ripe.net) it was quickly established that this IP address range was assigned to the intruder's computer by BT Openworld, the Internet Service Provider operated by British Telecom (see Figure 14.20).

```
inetnum:        81.130.72.0 - 81.130.191.255
remarks:
***********************************************************
remarks:        * Please send abuse reports to abuse@btopenworld.com *
remarks:
***********************************************************
netname:        BT-ADSL
descr:          IP Pools
country:        GB
admin-c:        BTOW1-RIPE
tech-c:         BTOW1-RIPE
status:         ASSIGNED PA
mnt-by:         BTNET-MNT
mnt-lower:      BTNET-MNT
mnt-routes:     BTNET-MNT
changed:        preston.dialip@bt.com 20040630
source:         RIPE
route:          81.128.0.0/11
descr:          BT Public Internet Service
origin:         AS2856
mnt-by:         BTNET-MNT
changed:        support@bt.net 20030615
source:         RIPE
role:           BT OPENWORLD OPERATIONAL SUPPORT
remarks:
***********************************************************
remarks:        * Please send abuse reports to abuse@btopenworld.com *
remarks:        *
remarks:
***********************************************************
address:        BT
address:        Openworld
address:        UK
e-mail:         ims.adastral@btopenworld.com
admin-c:        IT337-RIPE
tech-c:         RJG3-RIPE
nic-hdl:        BTOW1-RIPE
mnt-by:         BTNET-MNT
changed:        preston.dialip@bt.com 20030520
source:         RIPE
```

Figure 14.20   Result of the *whois* query

The victim company had a registered user account with BT Openworld and requested the activity logs for this account on the date and time that an intrusion occurred.

The company's web mail logs in the United States showed an intrusion between 08:39 and 09:00 Pacific Standard Time (PST) on a stated day in 2004. The ISP confirmed the use of this account on the stated day between 16:39 and 17:01 Greenwich Mean Time (GMT). The relative timings of the intrusion thus concurred, allowing for the eight-hour time difference between GMT and PST. The assigned IP address in the range 81.130.***.*** was also identical in the two disparate sets of logs.

Again, according with Locard's principle, the intruder had also left evidence of his identity and activity with the ISP.

Every contact leaves a trace...

It transpired that the user assigned the BT Openworld account had given his laptop computer to another employee of the company. With the evidence now obtained, it was decided to retrieve this laptop and examine it forensically.

Using a text search for the self-styled 'bandit_117', it was evident that the laptop had been used to send the anonymous e-mail. Yahoo software was quickly located on the laptop, but more significantly an event log was discovered showing 'bandit_117' entering various Yahoo conference rooms (see Figure 14.21).

```
I 03-211001.434000    5b0 Shutdown/disconnect complete
I 03-211001.444000    dec Create/join conference user=<bandit_117>conf=<ch/Hackers'
Lounge:1::1600390824>)
I 03-211001.554000    5b0 Resolved vc.yahoo.com
I 03-211001.554000    5b0 Start connection to 66.218.70.44
I 03-211001.724000    5b0 Server connected
I 03-211002.295000    5b0 Conference entered
I 03-211002.475000    5b0 Conference ready
```

Figure 14.21   Chat-room event log

Comparative analysis between the IP addresses assigned at the times of the intrusions with the data recorded on the suspect's computer revealed that six IP addresses recorded on the suspect's hard disk exactly corresponded with those that were used to gain unauthorized access to the personal electronic mailboxes.

Every contact leaves a trace...

Moreover, some of the intrusive IP addresses were located on the suspect's hard disk because they had been used as identifying tags by various websites that the suspect had browsed on the days that the intrusions occurred (see Figure 14.22).

```
This site was last updated on <b> Fri Mar 12 10:11:38 2004</b>  </center>
<br>  <hr width="100%" clear="right">  <center><table><tr><td><center><img
src="images/logo.gif" alt="STUD"></center></td><td>  <center><b>SHOP TIL U
DROP</b>br>  Tel: +44 (0)208 322 5271<br>  Fax: +44 ( 0)208 322 5374<br>
</td><td><center><img src="images/logo.gif"
alt="STUD"></center></td></tr></table></center>  </td></tr></table>
<center>  <hr width="100%" no shade size="3" clear="right">  <font size=-
1>Website designed and hosted by website77.com Limited
<ahref="http://www.shopdrop.net"><imgsrc=http://cache.shopdrop.net/images/lo
go.gif border=0 width= 120 alt="logo"></a>  <br>Please visit our <a
href=http://120 alt="logo"></a>  <br>Please visit our <a
href=http://www.support.website77.com>support site</a> for technical
help</font>  </center>  </body>  </html>  <!-- page-stat: process
time:1070036679 - >  <!-- modl-stat: process time:0 -->  <!-- sql-stat:
process time:0 -->  <!-- You are: 81.130.170.58, http://www.shopdrop.net/
```

Figure 14.22   The IP address recorded by a website visited by the suspect

> The IP addresses were located in unallocated disk space on the hard disk of the computer and had been recorded variously by the operating system, the suspect's electronic mail or Internet browser software. The user of the computer would not be prompted to save this information and it is unlikely that he was aware that this incriminating connectivity had been recorded.

This case study exemplifies the interchange and transposition of information that takes place when computer systems communicate. This data interchange, which entirely accords with Locard's Principle of Exchange, is usually unseen and unknown to the user of the computer and has immense forensic, investigative and evidential value.

Locard's Principle of Exchange does not apply invariably. While most computer transactions will leave tell-tale forensic deposits and indications, some actions remain seamless, transparent and undetectable.

The forensic examiner

Computer forensic investigation is increasingly the preserve of specialist practitioners and is generally beyond the ambit of the IT or security professional working day to day in business or industry. Increasingly, the forensic investigator will be an accredited expert witness, qualified in specialist tools and methods and a full-time professional in his field.

The commercial decision to employ a full-time forensic response unit using in-house staff and resources, in preference to contracting this service as and when it is needed, will depend on a number of variables, the most obvious of which are shown in Appendix 4.

Computer forensic investigation is now an established branch of forensic science and there is a diversity of specialist training courses and professional qualifications offered commercially and by vocational and academic institutions. Books and training manuals have been written on the technical forensic examination of computer systems, data and media.

Additionally, a range of specialist hardware and software forensic solutions has recently become available, which far surpass in capability any of the relatively primitive technologies available only a few years ago. Some of the more widely used products are shown in Table 14.1.

If the decision is made to contract the services of a forensic investigator, it is vital that he is briefed properly. 'Print everything out' is the typical instruction of the uninitiated lawyer, which is so vague as to be meaningless, and is usually completely impracticable.

The briefing for the forensic investigator should be written, concise, and comprise:

- a synopsis of what is suspected or known – this may be very concentrated and relate to a specific document or subset of data on the computer, or wider in nature, encompassing a more general review of the system to be investigated;
- the names of the people, companies, organizations, and other entities relevant to the enquiry;
- any telephone or fax numbers, known USERIDs and passwords, e-mail addresses, occupancy or other contact details of the protagonists or their associates;
- bank accounts, vehicles and assets of the protagonists or their associates;
- any specific times and dates relevant to the enquiry, and why;

Table 14.1   Computer forensic software tools

Software	Manufacturer	Functionality
SafeBack v3.0	NTI www.forensics-intl.com	Forensic disk imaging
New Technologies forensic solutions	www.forensics-intl.com/tools.html	A range of investigative software tools
EnCase Forensic Edition V5.04a	Guidance Software www.guidancesoftware.com	Full investigation and disk imaging suite
Forensic Toolkit	AccessData www.accessdata.com	Full forensic investigation suite
PDA Seizure v3.03.86	Paraben Corporation www.paraben-forensics.com	Forensic acquisition and (limited) investigation of PDAs
Cell Seizure v3.00	Paraben Corporation www.paraben-forensics.com	Forensic acquisition and investigation of mobile phones and SIM cards
.XRY v2.6	DataExpert www.dataexpert.nl	Forensic acquisition and investigation of mobile phones and SIM cards
Network E-mail Examiner v2.0.290	Paraben Corporation www.paraben-forensics.com	Investigation of server-based e-mail (Exchange, Lotus Notes)
E-mail Examiner v5.00	Paraben Corporation www.paraben-forensics.com	Investigation of client-based e-mail (Outlook, OE 4/5/6, AOL, Eudora, Netscape)
FINALeMAIL	FINALDATA Inc. www.finaldata.com	Recovers client-based e-mail (Outlook Express 4/5/6, Netscape, Eudora)
R-STUDIO v3.00	R-tools Technology Inc. www.r-studio.com	Search and recovery of previous partitions and data
Recover4all Professional v2.1a	www.recover4all.com	Search and recovery of previous partitions and data
Quick View Plus 8	Avantstar www.avantstar.com	Reviewing of more than 200 file formats
UltraEdit-32 v11.20b	IDM Computer Solutions Inc. www.ultraedit.com	Easy to use Hex editor with binary and text comparison ability
IrfanView v3.98	www.irfanview.com	Graphics viewer
LC5 (Acquired by Symantec)	@stake www.atstake.com	Password recovery
Advanced Password Recovery ToolKit v2.0	NTI www.forensics-intl.com	Password recovery
Password Retrieval Suite	Elcomsoft Co Ltd www.elcomsoft.com	Password recovery

- other details that may assist the forensic investigator, such as known visits by the protagonists overseas, relatives' names and details, and any other data pertaining to the suspected offence;
- any investigative reports, file notes or copies of exhibits or evidential documents relevant to the enquiry.

The spellings of names should be accurate, and numbers should be noted correctly. These will be used to conduct text searches – typically, by running hexadecimal and unicode searches against the data at sector level so that relevant matches are located in residual deleted data as well as in active files. Commonsense applies in choosing search criteria. The more specific and distinct the search string is, the better the results are likely to be. Searches for three letter acronyms are particularly arduous, invariably triggering several hundred thousand false positives on a typical hard disk, and are best avoided if at all possible.

Additionally, the forensic investigator should be told the electronic mail system in use by the organization and its configuration, as this will expedite his examination.

If the investigation is being conducted covertly, the briefing instructions should not be written or transmitted using any computer or mail system accessible to the suspect(s).

Upon the conclusion of his examination, the forensic investigator will present a report with accompanying exhibits and supporting statements of his findings and conclusions.

Excellent results have been achieved when the forensic investigator works in close conjunction with investigators, security and audit personnel in the client organization. Their familiarity with the organization, its personnel, structures and processes is often indispensable when analysing specialist industry data, 'shop talk' and jargon strewn documentation and e-mails. DGI has developed a simple methodology called DRUID (Download Recoverable User Intelligible Data), whereby readily interpretable documents, spreadsheets and e-mails are provided for immediate analysis and assessment by these staff, leaving the forensic investigator to complete the more complex forensic aspects of the investigation.

Conclusion

Where potential evidence is located on computer systems the directive *to do no harm* is fundamental.

Ill-advised actions by unqualified examiners have caused computer evidence to be destroyed, damaged, misinterpreted, overlooked, corrupted and lost.

The instinctive reaction of many organizations in the grip of a crisis is to direct their IT support desks to process any computer evidence identified, despite the fact that these people are usually unprepared and untrained for this task. This has led to numerous cases where the electronic crime scene has been compromised, sometimes irrevocably.

In the UK, the Association of Chief Police Officers (ACPO) has issued a *Good Practice Guide for Computer based Electronic Evidence*. Its four basic principles are:

1. No action taken by law enforcement agencies or their agents should change data held on data storage media which may subsequently be relied on in court.
2. In exceptional circumstances, where a person finds it necessary to access original data held on a computer or storage media, that person must be competent to do so and be able to give evidence explaining the relevance and implications of their actions.

3. An audit trail or other record of all processes applied to computer evidence should be created and preserved. An independent third party should be able to examine those processes and achieve the same results.
4. The person in charge of the investigation (the case officer) has overall responsibility for ensuring that the law and these principles are adhered to.

It is always advisable to process the computer crime scene to criminal prosecution standards. Evidential management is a specialist task, but the correct initial response to securing evidence is key. In achieving this, the following guidelines apply:

- Do not allow the native operating system stored on the hard disk of any microcomputer to execute – clean boot the system from an assured DOS system diskette.
- Preferably, use a trusted processor to copy all media.
- Avoid cherry picking – record the evidence in its entirety and assure its integrity using proven forensic imaging software.
- Work only on forensic copies, from which relevant information may be extracted and annotated.
- Maintain a master forensic copy for each evidential data stream. This should be write-protected and stored securely.
- Avoid contaminating the original data stream – a disparity of a single byte between the original data stream and the copied data stream may be sufficient to render the evidence inadmissible.
- Record the evidence to a reliable and assured media – otherwise the copied data may degrade, become unstable and unreadable.
- Maintain evidential continuity – account for the evidence, its integrity and custody at all times.
- Use evidence bags, forensic audit trails and cryptographic hashes to ensure the integrity of the evidence and to refute accusations of tampering.
- Maintain an exhibits log, showing where, when and by whom the evidence was first found, and who had subsequent access to it.
- Keep contemporaneous notes and report your findings in writing.
- Retain, recall and reveal the evidence and all associated procedures, software, methods, notes, reports and statements.
- Do not speculate – test and prove your theories.
- Your findings must be repeatable and capable of corroboration by an independent inspection of the original evidence by another expert.

Finally, and fundamentally:

- **If in doubt, seek expert assistance.**

15 *Covert Operations*

> **The backbone of surprise is fusing speed with secrecy.**
> Carl von Clausewitz, soldier and strategist (1780–1831)

It is often the case that the best evidence of fraud or wrongdoing is located not on the organization's servers, mainframes or central mail systems but on the hard disks of the local workstation used by the suspect.

Fraudsters and other miscreants often regard their workplace computer or laptop as personal property, which explains why incriminating e-mail and other evidence is so often found on them. Furthermore, the local operating system of a computer tends to cache evidence that will not be located elsewhere in the network infrastructure.

As discussed in Chapters 14 and 17, whenever a computer is implicated in a suspicious transaction or activity it should always be examined forensically. For operational reasons the data on its hard disk may need to be obtained covertly. This chapter discusses the planning and execution of such an investigation.

Right of access and trespass

A fundamental and universal rule is that the investigator shall not trespass or break the law.

In the United Kingdom, unauthorized access to a computer system is a criminal offence under Section 1 of the Computer Misuse Act 1990.

If an employee uses his *own* computer (his property) to connect to the corporate network, a subsequent clandestine inspection of that computer by the employer or his agents is *illegal*, regardless of the employee's own criminality or misbehaviour, or the fact that he is accessing the employer's computer resources, software and data.

- It is always advisable for organizations to own and supply *all* of the equipment that is used in the workplace. This applies equally to laptops, electronic notebooks, PDAs, memory sticks, mobile telephones and any other kit. In most jurisdictions the owner of the equipment has an unequivocal right of access to it. An unambiguous policy on equipment purchase and acceptable usage clarifies the situation for employees and employer alike, and introduces an important element of control.

This control clearly diminishes once contractors, consultants, engineers, outsourced companies and enterprise partners connect to your networks, all using their own systems.

With the ground rules on trespass and the legal right of access established, this chapter proceeds on the principle that an organization has the right to inspect its own computer systems within its own premises.

Operational security

Operational security ('OpSec', see also Chapter 13) is of paramount importance to the successful execution of a covert investigation.

Suspects have adopted several imaginative strategies and tactics to confound the investigator's efforts. These have generally occurred when the suspects were aware that they were under investigation or likely to be placed under surveillance.

The simplest way to confound the forensic examination of a computer is to dispense with its hard disk and associated data storage media. If the suspect is forced to flee at very short notice, the investigator may strike lucky – the hard disks may vanish but incriminating diskettes and CDs are occasionally overlooked and await discovery and ejection from their respective drives or trays. Similarly, the use of positive erasure software and Internet privacy suites will usually be evident to the investigator and may, circumstantially, indicate malpractice – but how much better it is to secure the original data prior to this destruction.

Some 'escape and evasion' tactics to confound investigative efforts if the suspect is alerted are outlined in Table 15.1.

The aim, therefore, should always be to secure computer evidence so that any subsequent destruction or concealment by the suspect is ineffectual. The suspect should be prevented from engaging in escape and evasion tactics until after the evidence has been safely captured.

Paper documents and all the other sources of evidence will also require preservation and processing. Usually the search for documentation and other types of evidence in the suspect's work area takes place concurrently with covert computer download, but by a different investigator or team so as to avoid mission overload.

Objectives

At an early stage it is necessary to outline precisely what is to be achieved. It may be the case that evidence can be retrieved from corporate systems without alerting the suspect. Audit trails, event logs, user directories, mailboxes, telephone billings and other pertinent data may be within easy reach and be downloaded surreptitiously or discreetly. However, the downloading of this data may depend on the assistance of a member of staff or team from corporate IT, particularly if access to areas requires administrative rights. The decision to induct in-house IT specialists is always a judgment call, based on trust and instinct. Obviously, this is unlikely to be an option if the IT department is itself the subject of the investigation.

It is advisable to itemize precisely what potential sources of evidence are available, their location and the required level of access to obtain them, whether physical or logical. This itemization will clarify the nature and extent of any additional specialist expertise or resources that will be required to complete the task (see Chapter 17).

Planning and preparation

The military maxim that time spent on reconnaissance is never wasted applies equally when preparing a covert computer download.

Table 15.1   Escape and evasion tactics

Tactic	Effect and recovery
Format hard disk(s)	From a data recovery perspective a high-level format is relatively innocuous and evidence may be recovered relatively easily. A low-level format is best avoided!
Delete files	Recovering deleted files is usually straightforward.
Alter files to remove incriminating content	Trace evidence of alteration may remain.
Defragment the drive(s)	Residual data in unallocated clusters will be destroyed, but evidence in slack space may be recovered.
Encrypt files, partitions or drives	The encryption will usually be evident upon inspection. The potential to decrypt will depend on the strength of the algorithm used. Many products available for download from the Internet have proved unbreakable.
Sabotage backup tapes	Never allow one person to have unsupervised control of critical backups.
Execute evidence elimination software	Residue of this software and its output will be evident, but the data it destroys is usually irretrievable.
Install destructive software routines, encryption, or 'boobytraps'	Don't touch the computer! Even powering it up may trigger a destructive routine.
Conceal files	Steganography can conceal files – the investigator should remain alert to the use of this method.
Install access control	Modern access control products often employ total disk encryption. Without the key, password or pass-phrase, there is little hope of accessing the data in plaintext.
Smash disk(s)	Data recovery may be possible depending on the severity of the damage, but it will be expensive and time-consuming.
Degauss disk(s)	Subjecting data in magnetic media to high intensity alternating magnetic fields.
Sandpaper the disk substrate	Not a pretty sight or sound when the blasted disk is placed in a drive.
Cut the diskette substrate into pieces	See case study, Chapter 5.
Hide the computer and/or disks and tapes	Not easy to recover the evidence if it is thrown overboard, mid Atlantic.

A covert investigation will always prioritize the capture of the data on the suspect's workstation and/or laptop computer and this usually means gaining *direct access* to these items. It is a fact that evidence is often found on local hard disks that is not located elsewhere – this phenomenon is largely due to the Windows operating system that caches or records data to the locally installed disk by default.

As an example, people use Microsoft's Hotmail messaging service in the belief that it bestows anonymity. In fact, Hotmail communications are frequently to be found in the

Internet cache within a partition on the computer user's local disk. These communications are unlikely to be trapped anywhere else on the corporate network or its gateways. Similarly, deleted documents, spreadsheets and other potential evidence may be found in temporary files, unallocated clusters on the local disk or in file slack space. Residue may also be found in the local disk's swap file.

An abundance of potential evidence may thus be retrieved from local hard disks in workstations and laptops, but accessing this information requires careful planning and preparation.

It is advisable, where possible, to reconnoitre the proposed target area, which in most cases this will be the suspect's immediate work area.

In the planning and preparation phase a profound question applies:

Have you correctly identified the suspect's computer?

If you are confident that the target machine has been correctly identified, consider the possibility that the suspect may also have used other computers – this may be the case if he is trying to conceal his actions from network event logging and other monitoring. These machines, if located, also merit examination.

In planning the operation, the questions in Table 15.2 will apply.

Table 15.2   Planning a covert download

Question	Comment
1. Do you have a legal right of access to the target computer?	Do *not* trespass! Is the computer the organization's property or does it belong to the suspect? If the suspect owns the computer you may be committing a criminal offence of unauthorized access.
2. Is access to the facility guarded and/or video recorded?	Contract security guards have frequently compromised covert investigations by discussing nocturnal or out-of-hours activities with staff.
3. Is movement within the facility monitored on CCTV and/or within access control logs?	Could the suspect access this coverage or view these logs? Who is watching whom? Don't become the hunted.
4. Is the target area a 24/7 operation?	Covert access is problematic – a pretext or diversionary strategy will be required.
5. Is the target area readily accessible or is it behind a locked door or in a restricted area?	A locksmith may be needed.
6. Is the chassis of the computer padlocked?	See 5.
7. Is the keyboard locked using a physical key?	See 5. This problem may be overcome by transplanting the hard disk into a trusted processor (unless 19 applies).
8. Is the diskette drive physically locked?	See 5. This will prevent booting from the diskette drive of the target computer. Not a problem if a trusted processor is used.

9.	What is the make, model and specification of the computer?	Obtain the manual: 'RTFM'.
10.	Is the computer's BIOS information and setup table password protected?	This may prevent you from using the target processor to copy the contents of its disk(s).
		You should be able to obtain the password to the BIOS setup table, as this is an administrative function. If not, the problem may be overcome by transplanting the hard disk into a trusted processor (but see 19).
11.	Does the target computer's BIOS have a chassis intrusion detector?	This presents a serious hurdle. If the BIOS setup table is password protected and the computer will not boot from any device other than its internal hard disk, you will have no option but to remove the chassis in order to remove the hard disk, consequently triggering the chassis intrusion detector. You should be able to obtain the password to the BIOS setup table as this is an administrative function. If not, you need to devise an alternative pretext strategy.
12.	Is the target computer alarmed? Will an audio alarm sound if the chassis of the computer is removed?	
13.	Beware – some systems, particularly servers, may alert the administrator with a text message or pager alert if the machine is re-booted or detects any change to its processing status.	Alarms and alert notifications could jeopardize any operation and require an alternate strategy and possibly specialist tools and tactics.
14.	What is the keyboard escape sequence to access BIOS?	This varies between manufacturer and model – useful to know should you intend to use the target processor to export the data, as you may need to adjust the settings in the BIOS setup table.
15.	What is the boot sequence of the computer?	The computer used to export the data from the target hard disk should be bootable from a system diskette or CD. The target hard disk should not boot at any time.
16.	Does the target computer have a power-on password?	The systems administrator should know this password. Otherwise, the password may be circumvented by transplanting the hard disk into a trusted processor (but see 19).
17.	Is access control software or hardware installed on the target computer?	The administrative password to the access control software should be available to the investigator. If not, this problem may become intractable.
18.	Is the target computer's hard disk encrypted?	An administrative password should be available. If not, this problem may prove intractable.
19.	Is the target computer's hard disk logically accessible only via the machine's installed BIOS?	IBM ThinkPad laptops and certain other computers hard code their internal hard disks to the native processor, thereby preventing the disk from being addressed by any other processor. These hard disks cannot, therefore, be transplanted into a trusted processor.

		The native processor's onboard I/O ports may be used to export the data, typically via Firewire, USB or the LAN.
20.	How many hard disks are there in the target computer?	It is always advisable to check inside the chassis – isolated hard disks unconnected to the bus are often discovered.
21.	Are the hard disks IDE or SCSI?	Be prepared for either eventuality.
22.	What I/O ports or devices are installed on the target computer?	You may need to activate I/O ports in BIOS. See 10, 14.
23.	What passwords are required to bypass or uninstall access control products?	See 16, 17, 18.
24.	Is the target computer a 'hot desk' or used exclusively by the suspect?	There may be a number of user profiles installed on the computer's operating system. When analysing the data it is important to check whether this is the case by identifying all installed user profiles.
25.	What other data storage devices will be located in the target area?	Be prepared to process diskettes, CD-ROMs, DVDs, Zip and Jaz drives, memory sticks and other storage formats.
26.	Is there a software-protection device such as a dongle attached to the computer?	You may need this dongle in order to access information on the computer. Make a note of any manufacturer and model and any production or serial numbers.
27.	Does the suspect have a PDA or personal organiser?	See 1. If company property, be prepared to download these devices.
28.	Are there locked drawers and filing cabinets or a locked briefcase?	See 1 and 5.
29.	Is there an unauthorized telecommunications jack in the target area?	This may enable the suspect to bypass the network firewall and other security measures using an unauthorized modem.
30.	Does the target computer have a modem?	This may not be authorized and transgress company policy.
31.	Does the target computer have a CD writer or DVD writer?	Note the make and model – the suspect may have copied sensitive information to CD or DVD. Check for burned CDs and DVDs in the target area.

Planning a covert computer download in a corporate environment is generally easier than preparing for a search warrant or civil search order because the answers to most or many of these questions may be answered via access to purchase orders, inventory and maintenance records or by the judicious questioning of IT staff (if trusted).

Under these circumstances, we are usually dealing with a known quantity, in contrast to a search order where the exact scale and configuration of the respondent's computer systems is often a mystery until the order is executed. Obtaining this intelligence can save time and money and assists in the preparation of an appropriate technical and operational strategy.

Preserving the target area

In criminology there is a guiding principle of *transposition* whereby the perpetrator of a felony leaves something at the scene of crime whilst concomitantly he takes something away from it.[1]

In a forensic context this exchange occurs unwittingly, as microscopic or minute elements are exchanged. Conversely, in covert operations we must do our utmost to *defy* this principle – the investigator must leave no indication of himself at the scene, nor must he physically remove anything *at all* from it – otherwise he risks compromising the operation. We are not generally talking here of minute traces of hair and fibre or DNA as might be the case in a forensic context. Rather, we are addressing joint obligations:

- Upon completion of the operation, every single item brought to the target area by the covert investigation team must be removed from it;

and

- Every item disturbed in the target area by the covert team must be restored *exactly* as it was prior to the commencement of the operation.

In other words, we must leave the target area in precisely the state that we found it. Absolutely *nothing* must be left behind, or for that matter, removed.

If, for example, a letter is found in the desk drawer that is relevant to the investigation it should be photocopied and the original returned whence it was found. A Post-it™ note with a hand-written password stuck under a keyboard may be crucial – but the original will not be removed from the scene as evidence; instead, it will be photographed *in situ*. Likewise, a diskette found on the desk will be copied and returned to the exact location in which it was found, and so on.

Continuing with the Post-it note, it may be that the handwriting and ink may have forensic value, or that a latent fingerprint or fibre might be discovered that proves its association to an individual. This is physical evidence that will, at some later stage, require forensic processing in a laboratory. Operationally, however, such intrusive forensic testing must be deferred because the removal of the Post-it note, or any other documentation, will surely alert the suspect. Documents and paper-based evidence requires careful handling – cotton gloves should be worn when inspecting originals to prevent contamination.

Following the same principle, the computer evidence must be downloaded in a manner that is completely *non-invasive*. No changes whatsoever are made to the original data on the target computer(s) or to data storage media located in the target area. Effectively, upon completion there will be no indication at all that a computer download has occurred, or that any data storage media has been copied.

The downloaded data will be an exact copy of the suspect's data. Computer hard disks, for example, are copied using forensic imaging software; every single bit of information on the suspect's computer is copied in exact sequence to the downloaded image. In this way, we can replicate the suspect's computer system off-site, and investigate it at our leisure.

---

1   See Locard's Principle of Exchange (Chapter 14).

The operation

In a normal business environment, the operation will take place outside standard working hours. This usually means late at night, at weekends or during national holidays. Obviously, the fewer people on-site the better.

In round-the-clock shift operations where unobserved access is impossible it may be necessary to devise a pretext strategy, perhaps requiring computers to be upgraded or maintenance checked. Any pretext must be credible and appear completely normal and mundane, and if systems maintenance is used as a cover to access the target computer it is advisable that several other machines in the same area are also inspected and 'upgraded'. If a system upgrade is used as a pretext to gain access to the target computer the team must look the part. A systems engineer wearing jeans, T-shirt and Reeboks is both credible and inconspicuous. A systems engineer wearing a pinstriped suit, matching handkerchief and tie makes no sense at all.

On the evening of the proposed covert download it is advisable for a surveillance team to keep track of the suspect following his departure from work. Ideally, the suspect is 'put to bed' (followed home and lights extinguished) prior to the operation commencing. Cost considerations may prohibit such precaution, but it remains best practice nevertheless.

If practicable, it is advisable to post lookouts at entrances and in corridors leading to the target area and in the car park outside the building. The lookouts can warn of any unscheduled or surprise movements or arrivals within these areas. Communication with the central team is by short-range two-way radios.

A SECURE AREA

Upon arrival in the target area it is advisable to establish a secure area. This will be a room that is remote from the target area and which can be locked to avoid casual entry.

TRUSTED PROCESSOR

The secure area is used to house a trusted processor. This is a computer that has been configured by the investigation team specifically to assist the covert download. The method of download is tested and proven prior to the operation and because the team has configured this computer there should be no nasty surprises when it is used to copy the target hard disks.

A key consideration when planning a covert download is speed and efficiency. There is a clear requirement to process the evidence recovered from the target area swiftly. This is not to say that a covert investigation should be conducted with undue haste – far from it – but that the method of copying the data from the target computer's hard disk(s) must be the fastest practicable. The risks of interruption or discovery are ever present and it is always a relief to complete an operation and leave the target area. With covert operations, there is always pressure to get away from the target area as quickly as possible.

Disk-to-disk data transmission rates exceed one gigabyte per minute, a speed that makes this the preferred method of many practitioners to conduct covert downloads, although other storage formats, such as DAT tape, may also be used. The data is copied using forensic imaging software.

The important point is that suitable software and hardware tools are available immediately to hand and the selection of the toolkit is largely determined during the planning and preparation phase. It is always advisable to be flexible and have an array of different methods by which to undertake the download.

BEFORE APPROACHING THE TARGET AREA

Empty trouser and shirt pockets of contents and, if worn, remove jackets and ties. No personal belongings should be allowed into the target area.

All personal belongings are left in the secure area.

AT THE TARGET AREA

Before any disassembly or processing can take place the target area must be photographed using a Polaroid instamatic camera or a digital camera or video. The target computer is photographed from all angles, including the top and the rear of the machine. Everything on the desk is photographed *in situ* and from numerous angles.

It is particularly important to photograph all cables and connections to the PC and also to make a separate note of precisely which cables are connected to which sockets and ports.

These photographs or videos will be used as references to restore the target area to its exact state immediately prior to being processed. Remember, however, to recover the photographs – you do not want the suspect to find a stray Polaroid depicting his desk and computer upon his arrival at work the next morning!

If a digital camera or video is used, remember to take spare batteries – being unable to access your reference shots is both frustrating and unnerving, particularly if the disruption in the suspect's work area is significant and the surgery into the computer traumatic.

No access or disassembly of the target computer may take place until the photography and/or videoing is completed. The more photographs or digital frames of the target computer there are, the better.

Forensic processing of a computer is normally quite disruptive and usually necessitates that the target machine is, at least in part, disassembled in order to gain access to the internal hard disk (or disks). The internal hard disk is typically removed from the target computer and installed in a processor that is pre-configured and controlled by the covert investigation team. Depending on the ease with which cases and access panels are removed, this disassembly can cause quite severe disruption in the target area.

A comprehensive toolkit is a given. This will include screwdrivers, adjustable heads including cross-head (Philips), flat and star bit and a full range of allen keys. It is also recommended that the team has drive bay keys, in case removable drive bays are encountered. Anti-static wrist straps should also be used when removing hard disks.

Prior to removing the target hard disk from the computer it is necessary to photograph the internal configuration of the machine. Make a note of all cable connections. Be sure that you can reconfigure the setup exactly as it is found.

Remember also to search for hard disks that are not connected to the bus. These will also need to be copied. It is also necessary to note the jumper setting of each target hard disk; the setting may need to be changed temporarily during the forensic imaging process, and will need subsequently to be restored.

Once the target disk(s) is removed the cover is replaced on the target computer, making the disk's removal less conspicuous, and the team withdraws to the secure area to commence processing.

PROCESSING

The trusted computer is used to copy the contents of the target computer's hard disk(s), which is transplanted into it. The boot sequence of the trusted processor is set so that it always boots from a system diskette; there is no risk, therefore, that the target hard disk is booted.

The trusted configuration of this computer means that the BIOS configuration of the target computer, however hostile, is irrelevant.

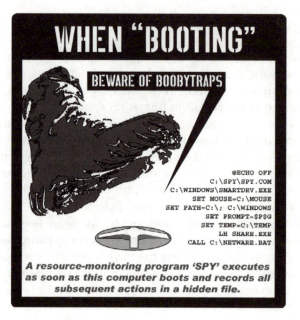

Figure 15.1   Beware of boobytraps

BEGIN	END TIME	LEVEL	PROGRAM	PARAMETERS
2:08	2:08	0:00:01	1	WIN.COM
2:08	2:09	0:00:06	2	WIN386.EXE
2:09	2:11	0:02:54	3	KRNL386.EXE
2:11	2:11	0:00:00	2	WIN386.EXE
2:11	2:11	0:00:00	1	WIN.COM
2:11	2:12	0:00:53	0	<none>
2:12	2:12	0:00:01	1	WIN.COM
2:12	2:12	0:00:07	2	WIN386.EXE
2:12	2:14	0:01:23	3	KRNL386.EXE
2:14	2:14	0:00:00	2	WIN386.EXE
2:14	2:14	0:00:00	1	WIN.COM
2:14	2:14	0:00:05	0	<none>
2:14	2:14	0:00:06	1	NORTON.EXE
2:14	2:14	0:00:23	2	DISKEDIT.EXE
2:14	2:14	0:00:00	1	NORTON.EXE
2:14	2:15	0:00:05	2	NORTON.EXE

Figure 15.2   The perils of going through the front door and snagging a tripwire

Processing the target computer's hard disk using a trusted computer located in a secure area reduces the time spent inside the target area. The trusted computer:

- bypasses any security measures invoked using the target computer's BIOS set-up menu (power-on password, BIOS password, disabled services or drives);
- ensures that the target hard disk does not boot, thereby preserving the evidential integrity of the image and preventing any boobytrap (see Figure 15.1) or harmful software routines from triggering. (The TSR [terminate stay resident] monitor in Figure 15.2 registers the execution times of software and outputs a hidden log. Any attempt to examine the PC directly is revealed to the suspect who will also know precisely what the investigator did, when and for how long);
- is not reliant on the processor on board the target computer. The trusted processor, therefore, can be the fastest available with optimal data transfer speeds;
- reduces the risk of any team member being discovered because less time is spent in the target area;
- instils confidence that the download will process successfully, because the method and configuration are tried, tested and proven and totally under the team's control;
- soothes nerves because no member of the team is in the high-risk target area for a prolonged period.

In addition, the suspect's power-on password (if active) is retained on the target system, so there is no cause for suspicion when the suspect next uses his computer.

This method will work in most instances and may also be used to copy the contents of laptop computer hard disks.

In certain cases, however, where for example the target computer's BIOS is specifically hard-coded to the installed hard disk, it may not be possible to use a trusted processor because the hard disk will not be recognized by it. Similarly, if chassis intrusion detection is active on the target system, the option to remove the disk may not be available and the data will have to be exported via one of the target processor's I/O ports. It is worth devising and testing a number of the technical methods to execute forensic image capture, to include methods to export data using the target computer's onboard I/O ports, with Firewire and USB providing the fastest transmission options.

Serious difficulties tend to occur in circumstances where the administrative passwords to uninstall or disable protective measures are unavailable to the forensic investigator. This re-emphasizes the overriding necessity to store administrative passwords to software and hardware protective systems centrally and securely – otherwise, there is the very real risk that the organization is locked out of its own systems.

The method to bypass or uninstall access control or other protective mechanisms should be devised during the planning and preparation phase. The method adopted should be tested on a machine configuration identical to the target computer and proven to work. There is no room here for trial and error.

The worst approach, to be avoided at all cost, is to engage in guesswork. It is a fundamental rule of covert operations that the investigator should *never*, under any circumstances, guess a password. Many systems, including certain BIOS models, lockout an intruder after three or so failed login attempts. A screen message then appears as shown in Figure 15.3.

```
XXX Invalid password XXX
      Sun 28-03-2004
        23:59:12
    Enter password>
```

Figure 15.3   Intruder lockout

We certainly do not want the suspect to read this message the following morning! The prompt can only be revoked by draining the BIOS battery of power and, of course, if this is done (by removing the battery or the power jumper) all of the BIOS information for the computer will disappear causing the computer to lose its entire hardware configuration, a fact that will not go unnoticed by the user of the computer.

Some BIOS models protest more vigorously should an intruder fail:

 'Sorry to wake you, but I'm in a bit of a fix.' The voice at the end of the line sounded strained. In the background was the high-pitched electronic squeal of a car alarm. 'Stealing cars, George?' 'It's not a bloody car, it's a laptop computer.'

In this instance, the laptop had an on-board capacitor – removing the battery had no effect on the alarm, which continued screeching for several hours.

In situations where the team does not have access to a trusted processor, the suspect's computer itself may be used to process the covert download. This will only be possible if the computer can be configured to boot from a DOS system diskette or CD. The download may be made to tape via a SCSI card or to disk. Any hardware inserted into the machine must, of course, be removed upon completion, and the computer restored to its precise configuration.

If the suspect's computer is used to process the download, care must be made to note:

- all configuration changes are made within BIOS so that these may be reset upon completion;
- the power settings – the computer may be set to power up in a particular fashion and any changes to mains switches or power buttons may alter this, which could alert the suspect;
- the jumper settings on the internal hard disk(s), which again may need to be altered.

And *don't forget* to remove the DOS system diskette!

Figure 15.4   Remove the DOS system diskette

LAPTOP COMPUTERS

The main problem presented by laptop computers is that they are, of course, portable and, therefore, less likely to be found in the suspect's work area after hours.

Suspects are more confident in using their laptops for nefarious deeds, believing the chances of discovery to be minimal. This makes the laptop computer a particularly valuable target for the investigator. However, gaining access can prove difficult, which is where a little lateral thinking comes in handy:

> The investigators were convinced that e-mails and other correspondence pertaining to the hostile management buy-out would be found on the laptop computer belonging to a senior manager. The problem was that this individual never left his laptop unattended and all efforts to isolate the machine and copy its contents were frustrated over a period of many weeks.
>
> The manager was known to be a connoisseur of classical music. What if he received, through the post, some concessionary tickets to Wagner's 'Ring Cycle'? Wagner was a particular favourite of the man and this composer's operas offered an added bonus in that they are extremely long-winded – plenty of time in which to copy the computer. Would the man really take his laptop to the opera?
>
> The tickets duly arrived and the suspect enjoyed an evening of *Die Walküre*. Meanwhile, back in the darkness of his office, the computer ticked merrily away – a forensic bit copy of its hard disk being copied to tape.

Laptop computers, if left in the target area, may be removed to the secure area to be processed. The ease with which access may be gained to laptop computer hard disks varies between manufacturers and models. Some hard disks eject from a bay via a simple panel that clicks open near effortlessly, whilst other manufacturers tortuously embed the hard disk beneath the keyboard, protected by an array of moulded sub-assemblies, each of which must be painstakingly removed, a process that may involve the removal of dozens of tiny screws. Upon contemplating such surgery, it is well worth considering the likelihood of being able to reassemble the laptop at all, and without losing a single component.

Figure 15.5   Reassembly must be exact

Once the laptop hard disk has been extracted it may be connected to a standard IDE bus using an adapter and processed as standard, disk to disk being fastest. Alternatively, the forensic image capture can be made via the laptop computer's onboard Firewire or USB port, but this will depend on whether the computer is password protected or has access control software installed, which again illustrates the importance of knowing the administrative passwords to gain access to these systems. Firewire and USB 2 are relatively fast data transmission methods, faster than the parallel port by an order of magnitude, which should be considered the last resort.

DATA STORAGE MEDIA

Search desk drawers, briefcases, filing cabinets and other areas for data storage media. Data storage media found in the target area should be copied. Photograph any disks *in situ* for reference, before removing them from the scene.

A computer in the secure area should be designated to copy data storage media found in the target area. In most cases, this will comprise diskettes and compact disks, although other devices such as Iomega Zip and Jaz drives may also be encountered. Write protect any diskette prior to copying it and remember to restore the write-protect tag (if altered) before returning it.

Memory sticks are also increasingly common. If possible, these should be write-protected prior to any data being copied.

Upon completion, return all media to the target area and re-position using the photographs for reference.

POWERED-UP COMPUTERS

The team may encounter a target computer that is powered up, logged into a network, or processing proprietary data unattended. Whether to proceed with the operation in these circumstances is a judgment call. If the target computer shows a login prompt, it may be switched off, processed, restored and then rebooted to the same prompt. It may still be possible to proceed by switching off all of the powered-up computers in the target area, and subsequently rebooting them. A localized power cut would explain the resulting login screens or displayed prompts.

If the target computer is processing proprietary data, displays an active document, spreadsheet or file (whether saved or not), or a screen saver has activated, it is advisable not to proceed with the operation. Circumstances will vary. The key is to assess all the consequences of any proposed strategy so that no irrevocable mistakes are made.

RECONSTRUCTION

As stated, it is essential to leave the target area exactly as it is found, and this is facilitated by reference to photographs or video taken immediately prior to disturbing the work area, desk and computer.

Be fastidious when reconstructing the target area. Women, in particular, have a heightened sense of awareness regarding their immediate work environment and the slightest disruption – for example, the movement of objects on the desk – may alert the wary suspect. The desk area, in all its detail, must be restored perfectly. This often involves moving and then restoring ornaments, mementos, postcards, desk diaries, Post-it™ notes and other exotic flora and fauna, all of which can prove extremely time consuming.

If paper documents are to be processed, a photocopier is required. You may require a key card to operate the photocopier, which may also have a counter – do not use any photocopier in the target area, as this action may be traceable by an alert suspect, his colleagues or associates. Remember also, that some photocopiers scan, store and index pages copied – all of which may be of interest to the investigator but the suspect may scour these records too.

Remember to check beneath mouse mats, desk jotters, the keyboard and the desk itself. Interesting scraps and doodles have occasionally been taped or stuck in these places. These may be photographed *in situ*, or photocopied and replaced.

A manufacturing company was fearful that a malign computer programmer had targeted its computer systems. There were rumours that a logic bomb was embedded within a network or that other malicious program routines had been installed to disrupt batch processing and destroy critical databases. A crisis meeting of senior management was held in order to devise a contingency plan and an investigative strategy. Various complex tactics were proposed including the selective use of cryptographic checksumming to protect vital areas of the system as well as exhaustive and time-consuming code analysis and debugging.

A disaffected computer programmer within the IT department was the prime suspect. The head of group security was informed of the potential problem and immediately proposed a covert desk search in the programmer's work area. A computer forensic team was tasked with the backup and analysis of the suspect's computer and diskettes.

During the search a malicious code routine, handwritten on a fragment of graph paper, was discovered hidden under the programmer's mouse mat. The routine enabled the systems administrator quickly to identify which area of the network had been targeted and the precise functionality of the malicious code, a task that might have proved impossible without the culprit's unwitting assistance.

The above case study is not an isolated incident. The quickest discovery of a fraud known to the author occurred within 15 minutes of the investigation commencing – a letter outlining the fraud, the culprit's offshore bank account and his co-conspirators was discovered in his desk drawer.

Remember to look in the waste paper basket. Consider, also, the contents of the shredder bin – line-shredded documents may be recreated.

If the target machine is covered in dust, a possible strategy is to give the entire work area a good dusting and let the cleaners take the credit for it. The computer and work area can then be processed. It is important that all the desks and the computers in the work area are dusted, as a targeted cleaning of only one desk and computer will look suspiciously like favouritism.

Avoid 'other desk' syndrome – this is where the target's desk area is processed meticulously, but neighbouring desks are used to conduct processing, for storage or analysis. Upon his arrival at work, the suspect is alerted to strange activity in the area, not by any adjustments or changes to his own desk or computer, but by his neighbours who have noticed the disruption in their areas.

When preserving the target area, some common mistakes have included:

- allowing untrained people to participate or observe the operation, and failing to control them;
- leaving waste – particularly discarded cellophane wrappers from the image copy tapes – in the target area;
- leaving lights on, or off, which may alert the suspect upon his return. For operational reasons, particularly in areas overlooked by adjacent buildings, it may be necessary to work in darkness;
- opening or closing blinds or windows;
- moving or adjusting the suspect's chair;
- smoking in the target area – believe it or not this really happened and in a non-smokers' office!
- failure to note the exact switch settings on the computer or device to be copied. People power up their computers in various ways – the switches on monitors, processors, printers, mains plugs and power extensions should be noted prior to processing and subsequently restored.

It is strongly recommended that a 'referee' checks the target desk area, computer and all areas that were searched. The referee should sign that all of the team's equipment and belongings (including that all-important system boot disk) have been retrieved, and that the restoration has been satisfactorily completed in accordance with the reference photographs.

FINALLY…

For the uninitiated and seasoned operators alike, this type of work can be quite hair-raising. Even though the actions taken are entirely legal, justifiable and approved, there is always the risk of being discovered by hostile parties or, worse still, the suspects themselves.

The best covert operators have ice blood in their veins:

> The telephone handset was in pieces and Pete was finalizing the necessary adjustments to activate the intercept. Tools were spread across the carpet and wiring sprouted from the access panels in both floor and ceiling. At that very moment the office door flew open and the suspect, an aggressive and overbearing man, strode into the room. It was 2:00 a.m. and Pete had been assured that the area was clear. 'Who the hell are you?' the man roared. Pete didn't bat an eyelid. Feigning weary exasperation, he simply said, 'So, it's you who's been causing all my problems, is it! Your bleeding telephone and the rest of your mates' phones in this part of the building have caused me nightmares. Dragged out three times this week. What are you people *doing* to this system?' With a little further playful banter and cajoling the suspect began to relax, eased into the casual deception that this was a routine maintenance call. He departed after ten or so minutes, having assured Pete that Manchester United would surely win the premiership. The intercept was never discovered and provided vital intelligence for the next three months.

An Oscar-nominated performance.

Needless to say, such sangfroid is rare. This tale illustrates the desirability of always having a convincing cover story if engaged in a covert operation.

16 *Analytical Modes*

> **It requires a very unusual mind to undertake the analysis of the obvious.**
> Alfred North Whitehead, mathematician (1861–1947)

During a fraud or computer crime investigation, the investigator will, without exception, use one or more of these ten analytical modes:

- relational analysis
- transactional analysis
- chronological analysis
- forensic analysis
- contextual analysis
- lateral analysis
- comparative analysis
- behavioural analysis
- statistical analysis
- cognitive analysis.

These analytical modes, if applied appropriately and with judgment, will expedite any investigation. An eleventh mode – the *intuitive* approach – is included, if only to advise against relying upon it.

Relational analysis

Father relates to son, mother to daughter, grandmother to grandson, client to server, head office to subsidiary, chairman to managing director, and so on.

When analysing any structure, system, organization, network, regime or society it is necessary to identify the key players and to understand how the different components relate to each other. In crime investigation this relational analysis is sometimes referred to as link analysis, as the objective is to discern links between entities that might otherwise not be recognized.

At its most basic, relational analysis of a computer crime scene might entail the production of a network topology chart showing the various servers, computers, firewalls and routers involved with their respective connectivity and method of communication.

Alternatively, the investigator may seek to analyse the relationships between front companies, directors, bank accounts and beneficiaries in order, for example, to identify the extent of a money-laundering network.

The purpose of relational analysis is to build a picture depicting the relationships between the various entities involved in an enquiry, including people, computers, bank

TO COUNTER A THREAT WE
MUST UNDERSTAND ITS STRUCTURE
(THIS IS SARIN GAS)

Figure 16.1   Relational analysis

accounts, companies, transactions and assets. An organizational chart showing the management hierarchy and departments within a business is an example of a relational analysis.

When there are complex associations, it is advisable to draw them – even if this takes a large sheet of paper.

Investigators regularly use link analysis on all sorts of enquiries and there are special software packages that have been developed to assist the process.

Transactional analysis

Having established a framework or structure it is then helpful to establish the flow of information within it. Information, in this context, may be data, money, product or other commodity, whether electronic, intellectual or physical in nature.

In a banking transaction, for example, Bank A instructs Bank B to remit funds from its account for the benefit of a beneficiary at Bank C. This is a transaction. Similarly, if A sends an electronic mail to B, that also is a transaction. Likewise, when hacker A breaks into computer C via computer B, this also is a transaction, because data packets have been exchanged as part of the process. Transactions can be quite simple. If A tells B a joke, a transaction has taken place, even if B does not laugh.

A handshake is a transaction. Computers are said to 'handshake' when they communicate. The investigator aims to identify the relevant transactions in the case, their nature and the critical flow of data, information, product, assets or funds.

The point of this exercise is to map the flow of information between people and machines or processes. Arrowed lines are the obvious way to show this information flow. It is important to remember that electronic mail and telephone calls are exchanged between machines and *not* people – do not confuse the *device* with its assigned *user*.

By following the information flow, it may be possible for the investigator to identify all of the people, computers, systems and processes involved in any suspect transaction and thus ascertain the physical and logical locations where possible evidence of the transaction and the identities of those involved may reside.

Chronological analysis

It is necessary to establish the sequence of events (the chronology):

- When did events happen?
- In what sequence did different events occur?
- How do they relate to each other?

For example, A said that he left the pub and walked home at 10:30 p.m. B stated that A left the pub at 10:15 p.m., and that B took a taxi to his girlfriend's flat five minutes later. C stated that she saw B and A in the pub at 11 p.m. There is an obvious discrepancy between these three accounts that is immediately clear from a timeline analysis.

Remember that the computer clock may be wrong, or deliberately reset to backdate or post-date documents or data, or the date-stamp may reflect a different time zone. There are two factors to consider when undertaking a timeline analysis using computer records:

- Are the clocks on the computers accurate?
- Are the clocks on the computers sharing the same time zone?

Computer clocks may be adjusted with little effort to reflect any time or date. Similarly, multi-jurisdictional investigations often require very careful coordination due to the different time zones involved.

Timeline analysis is often of vital importance in computer crime investigation. In which sequence, for example, were documents created, amended or printed? Can activity on the hacker's computer be matched with processes on his victim's computer using a timeline analysis?

The following is an example of a simple timeline analysis:

ⓘ	08:55	CCTV recording shows John Smith entering the building
	08:59	Access control records show 'Smith J' entering room 5A
	09:02	Audit trail shows user account 'smithj' logged in from a workstation in room 5A
	09:00–09:30	Two witnesses report that John Smith was sitting in room 8
	09:04	Call log analysis shows a call to John Smith's home telephone number from an extension in room 8 (Smith states that he telephoned his wife; the witnesses confirm overhearing parts of the call)
	09:09	Telephone call ends
	09:14	Account 'smithj' logs off

It appears that someone is impersonating John Smith using his swipe card, USERID and password. Did Smith gain access to the building without his own swipe card? This should be resolved in interview. If so, whose swipe card did he use? This should show in the access control records. Is the impostor using a cloned swiped card? Is it physically possible to move from room 5A to room 8 within two minutes? Are the witnesses certain that they saw Smith in room 8 at 09:00 or might they be mistaken? Monitoring of access control card 'Smith J' and the computer login account 'smithj' might also ascertain the true identity of the hacker.

Forensic analysis

Forensic analysis comprises the detailed scientific study of objects, materials, substances, phenomena, characteristics or data to establish facts or evidence. A forensic analysis may, for example, encompass the examination of documents, fingerprints or DNA samples.

Forensic analysis in the context of a fraud or computer crime investigation principally encompasses the obtaining of evidence from electronic data processing systems and data storage devices. Computer forensic investigation has evolved into a discrete branch of forensic science.

As a general rule, if a computer or other electronic data processing system or data storage device has been identified as relevant to an investigation or is implicated in an offence, it should always be subjected to a forensic investigation undertaken by a qualified examiner.

The investigator should also consider other forensic methods. In a case of attempted extortion a single diskette was posted to a bank which contained a threat letter processed in ASCII text. Computer forensic examination revealed very little, but physical examination of the diskette and the envelope in which it was posted was undertaken in an attempt to discover latent fingerprints and other potential clues. The production batch number stamped on the diskette also proved useful in this instance.

Computer forensic analysis is distinct from forensic accounting. The latter comprises the detailed study of financial records, often to detect fraud or trace assets.

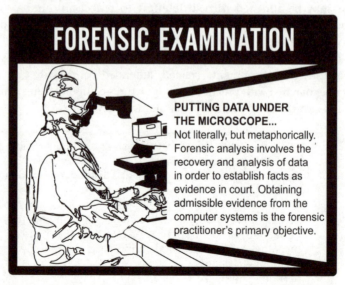

Figure 16.2   Forensic examination

Contextual analysis

What is the context of a piece of information? What does it actually mean? It is necessary to analyse documents, letters, spreadsheets, e-mails or other intelligible data in order to understand the essential meaning of the information conveyed.

It might be presumed that the contextual meaning of messages, reports or other data is self-evident, but this is not necessarily the case. People often don't understand what they are reading, they misinterpret it, they jump to conclusions or they fail to read between the lines.

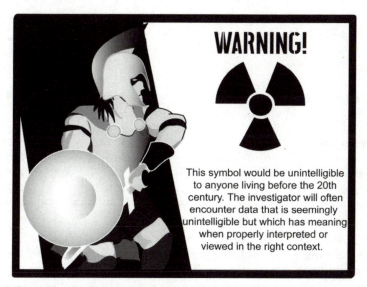

Figure 16.3   Information needs to be assessed in context

A lot of written information is written so abysmally that it is genuinely unintelligible. Then there are wilful deceptions, as well as reports that are deliberately designed to obscure the facts or divert the reader's attention from them.

As an example, consider the following corporate press release:

Total recurring net income increased to $393 million, versus $292 million a year ago.

This upbeat assessment, released on October 16, 2001, supported by a slide (Table 16.1), summarized the income statement for this business for the third quarter of the year.

Table 16.1   Contextual analysis

Executive Summary (millions)	3Q00	3Q01
IBIT:		
Transportation & Distribution	$176	$87
Natural Gas Pipeline	83	85
Portland General	74	−17
Global Assets	19	19
Wholesale Services	589	754
Americas	536	701
Europe and Other Commodity Services	53	53
Retail Services	27	71
Broadband Services	−20	−80
Corp. & Other	−106	−59
Total IBIT	$666	$773
Interest & Other	302	255
Taxes	72	125
Net Income – Recurring	**$292**	**$393**
Non-Recurring Items	0	−1011
Reported Net Income	$292	−618

The bold entry was deliberate. Astute members of the audience noticed the vaguely described 'non-recurring items'. What was actually being reported was a loss for the third quarter of $618 million. The company was Enron.

In computer crime cases, audit trail data is often misinterpreted, or salient points within the audit trails are not identified – this is a failure of contextual analysis. In training exercises, students have regularly failed to analyse audit trail data correctly because they never sought to ascertain what the various fields in the data actually represented. It is imperative that the function or meaning of every field within a given data set is clearly understood. It may be necessary for the investigator to obtain assistance from a technical specialist or refer to a manual. Audit trail data is often confusing at first sight. However, there is no point in staring blankly into space because the data shown is not immediately intelligible – it is clearly advisable to establish what it indicates.

Even simple messages can cause confusion or misunderstanding. There have been many cases where e-mails, letters, memoranda and other communications which were clearly indicative of fraud or wrongdoing failed to raise the alarm because the people reading them failed to interpret them properly. The investigator needs to have a heightened sensitivity to nuance, and be aware of inference, tacit understandings, euphemisms and the other subtleties of language. Documents rarely scream: 'I AM COMMITTING A FRAUD AND I AM RIPPING THE COMPANY OFF – THIS IS HOW I'M DOING IT, P.T.O.'

The letter in Figure 16.4 was written in 2001 and found on a computer used by senior militants close to Bin Laden. It uses a crude code so as to resemble a business communication, lists the benefits of Afghanistan as a base and terrorist training centre and reveals how vital the support of the Taliban (the Omar Brothers Company) was to al-Qaeda operatives. The 'relatives in the South' refers to Sudan, which renounced Bin Laden's militants and the 'international monopoly companies' are the US government and its intelligence agencies.[1]

Similarly, complicit telephone conversations are rarely explicit – people develop subtle codes with which to communicate. This is particularly the case where fraud or wrongdoing is endemic and long term. The investigator needs an attuned ear if listening to telephone intercepts, to be alert to events or situations that are unusual, strange, anomalous or seemingly inexplicable.

> The most important step was the opening of the school. We have made it possible for the teachers to find openings for profitable trade. Our relatives in the south have abandoned the market and we are suffering from international monopoly companies. But Allah enlightened us with His mercy when the Omar Brothers Company was established. One benefit of trading here is the congregation in one place of all the traders who came over from everywhere and began working for this company.

Figure 16.4   Contextual analysis – Al-Qaeda letter

Sound contextual analysis is vital in all investigations. As an observation, people with sharply honed contextual skills appear to be comparatively rare.

Lateral analysis

'Thinking outside of the box' – lateral thought engenders unconventional, original, innovative and ingenious solutions to problems. Lateral solutions are often elegant.

A classic example was Barnes Wallis's bouncing bomb (see Figure 16.5), used to attack the Mohne and Eder dams on the Ruhr in 1943. The cylindrical bomb, spinning at 500 rpm, was dropped onto the surface of the water at 240 mph from a height of 60 feet. The backspin on the bomb caused it to bounce on the surface of the water towards the dam wall at considerable velocity, in a series of arcs. This was a far more precise method of attack than trying to hit the dam wall directly from the air. The bomb exploded at the optimum depth of 30 feet, detonated by three hydrostatic pistols that calculated the water pressure precisely. No altimetre of the time could accurately measure 60 feet. The aircrews maintained this exacting altitude through the use of two spotlights fitted to the undercarriage of the bombers, positioned so that their beams converged on the surface of the water at precisely 60 feet below. Furthermore, the bomb had to be released at a very specific distance from the dam wall. Two pegs were fixed to each end of a wooden rod – when the pegs at each end of the rod were viewed in alignment with the towers on either end of the dam it was time to release the bomb. Simple solutions all round.

---

1   *Al-Qaeda: The True Story of Radical Islam.* Penguin Books, 2003.

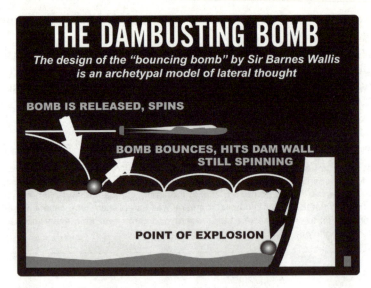

Figure 16.5   The bouncing bomb

Wars tend to engender some of the best examples of lateral thought – the classical example being the Trojan horse of Greek mythology, a seeming gift containing a nasty surprise.

The hacker's tactic of 'dumpster diving' – scavenging through discarded garbage for information – is an example of lateral thinking.

It is often the case that the simplest methods to achieve an objective are the most effective:

> The investigators had identified a firm of accountants suspected of money laundering. The accountants' offices were on a busy thoroughfare in London. A technical team had undertaken a feasibility study to determine whether it was possible to intercept data from the firm's computers using electromagnetic induction or pulse emanation receivers. These tests failed – the signals were completely unreadable due to massive interference from computers and other electronic devices located in the surrounding offices.
>
> The offices across the road from the target building were available for short-term rental and it was apparent from the window of these offices that a computer screen was visible within the accountants' building at a distance of about 40 metres. A powerful spotter scope was used to read every letter, fax, e-mail and other transmission composed on this machine. The observer dictated the contents of the screen to tape, which was transcribed each evening. Within two months, the investigation had ascertained a mass of detail about the offshore trusts, bank accounts and other investment vehicles used by the fraudsters. The method was legal – passive interception of computer data through the use of a telescope or binoculars did not contravene any law.

Comparative analysis

This is the comparison of different data sets. As an example, Smith's telephone log is compared with Jones's telephone log to ascertain those numbers that both men have been in contact with. At its most basic, comparative analysis may be represented by a simple Venn diagram shown in Figure 16.6.

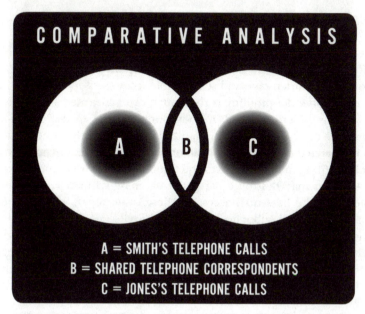

Figure 16.6   Comparative analysis – Venn diagram

Comparative analysis is a very common analytical mode in computer investigations, it often being necessary to compare network event logs, access control records, CCTV recordings, router logs, firewall and remote access and other resource usage in order to ascertain who, when, where, why and how. The investigator aims to determine congruence between these various data sets, particularly in terms of time and place.

DAN JOHNSON	07770 562943	DAN JOHNSON	07770 562943
KEITH ELLIS	01703 571752	TOM SHIPLEY	0171 4291276
JOHN HOWARD	02392 736 227	TOM BARROT	02392 657796
TOMMY NEIL	1714224801	THOMAS JENKINSON	01707 356859
CHARLES JORDAN	01444 146 67	MIKE POWELL	01642 342 282
ANDREW MCCLEAN	01705 153 237	MIKE FINNEY	01895 859391
EDWARD INNES	0171 478 6443	GRAHAM ARMSTRONG	07969 937248
GRAHAM TOMKIN	07970 537652	GERRY ALESFORD	783662657 / 01962 875023
TOBY ROUTLEDGE	370656672	EDWARD INNES	0207 478 6443
TIMOTHY GOLD	860820345	DEAN WINGHAM	01202 587 740
MIKE FINNEY	01895 859391	CHARLES JORDAN	01444 146 67
DANIEL O BRIAN	0976-798325	ANDREW MCCLEAN	01705 153 237

Figure 16.7   Comparative analysis – databases

A comparative analysis may reveal commonalities, indicative of theft or misappropriation. The comparison can be automated – but the trusty highlighter pen remains standard issue. In Figure 16.7 note that an entry is amended in the stolen database (right) to reflect the new London area code. A statistical analysis (see below) will determine the extent of commonality between databases.

Behavioural analysis

The groundbreaking work of the FBI's Behavioural Sciences Unit will be familiar to many readers. Offender profiling is now an established discipline and is regularly applied in the investigation of serial murder, rape and sexual violence, extortion and other serious crimes. The basic premise of offender profiling is that much can be learned about the perpetrator of a crime by observing the crime scene. A body dumped by a roadside with no attempt at concealment may be categorized as a disorganized crime scene. By contrast, a dismembered torso, perhaps incinerated and without a head or hands, is the work of an organized offender.

Behavioural profiling may be of use to the fraud and computer crime scene investigator. For example, a hacker may destroy a particular database while leaving other parts of the system unmolested. If he has equal access to these other areas, why has he targeted this specific database? Does the sabotaged database have some particular relevance to the attacker beyond being the target of an act of casual vandalism? Similarly, if a computer fraud may be committed by simple, expedient means, why has the perpetrator adopted a complex and convoluted method? Does this demonstrate a lack of knowledge or familiarity with the system, or are his actions a 'double bluff' – an attempt to conceal his expertise?

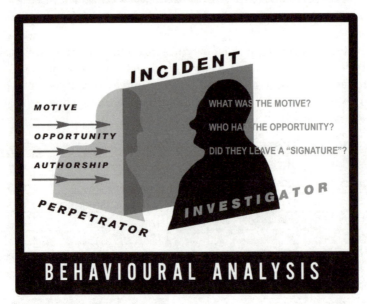

Figure 16.8   Behavioural analysis

The following computer crime scene involving a highly disorganized offender is instructive:

> (i) The PA to the Chief Executive was taking a break, reading her magazine and enjoying a sandwich and a cup of coffee. All of a sudden, the printer beside her desk whirred into action. She watched as five separate printouts appeared; on each one was a single e-mail communication. These electronic mails were all correspondence between the Chief Executive, John Bright, and other employees of the business. All of the e-mails pertained to an investigation that was being conducted into a division of the business.
>
> It appeared that someone had hacked into the Chief Executive's mailbox. Mr Bright was on holiday at the time and did not have any remote access to the e-mail system. The PA had telephoned him on his mobile telephone. He confirmed that he did not print the e-mails.
>
> The PA was the only other person in the business who had access to Mr Bright's mailbox, knowing, as she did, his password. She knew for certain that she had not printed the mails. Had they somehow been delayed in a print queue? She doubted it because she had already printed numerous other documents that morning and had experienced no difficulty or delay.

Investigators were summoned. They read the correspondence shown in Figure 16.9.

	The Printouts
1	**Subj**: Investigation **Date**: 03/09/2000 11:10:40 GMT Standard Time **From**: Steve Good **To**: John Bright Understand things aren't going too well. Legal say they can't allow things to proceed until they've got clearance from external counsel Need to discuss Steve
2	**Subj**: RE: Investigation **Date**: 03/09/2000 12:52:31 GMT Standard Time **From**: John Bright **To**: Steve Good Tell legal to get on with it – I want the monitoring to start tomorrow – we haven't got time to mess about JB
3	**Subj**: Legal issues **Date**: 03/09/2000 14:07:01 GMT Standard Time **From**: Sonia Mayor **To**: John Bright Steve Good has told the investigation company to start placing monitoring equipment and so on. No one has consulted me on the issue. We could end up in serious hot water if we don't get the clearance from the lawyers. Please can we discuss urgently. Sonia
4	**Subj**: RE: Legal issues **Date**: 03/09/2000 15:24:58 GMT Standard Time **From**: John Bright **To**: Sonia Mayor OK – at 6 pm. Suggest Yourself, Steve Good, Joe and myself meet at the Solicitors. Can you let them know and tell them to get a move on. John
5	Subj: Date: 03/09/2000 16:14:08 GMT Standard Time From: John Bright To: Joe Colson ααααααααααααααααααααααααααααααααααααααααα ααααααααααααααααααααααααααααααααααααα Joe Can you liaise with Steve Good about this weekend. I think overnight Saturday would be best. Facilities will need to know that some people will be on site. Give me a call. JB

Figure 16.9   The e-mails in the order they were printed

The context of the correspondence was clear – telephone monitoring was being installed and there were concerns about the technical and legal ramifications of it.

The investigators made some notes:

- The hacker is clearly interested in any correspondence about the departmental investigation and has shown an abnormal determination to obtain information about it.
- The hacker printed these e-mails on the PA's printer when it was possible to print them on a local printer. Did he do this deliberately? Probably not.
- If the hacker did not intend us to have these printouts then he may have made a mistake – not once, but *five* times! This suggests that he is not very IT literate.
- If we believe the PA (there is no reason not to) then the hacker was not using the PA's computer, therefore the e-mails were clearly printed from elsewhere in the building.
- Presumably, the hacker printed the e-mails because he wanted a permanent record of them – perhaps to show to other people? Therefore, he may well be in collusion with others.
- But the hacker has not got these printouts – we have them.
- Why is the fifth e-mail in a different typeface – and why has the format of the black line in this e-mail changed to a row of strange characters?

According to the PA, nobody had come to her office since the e-mails had been printed. It might be presumed that the hacker would appear at her door on some pretext to retrieve the printouts but this had not happened. This suggested a further line of enquiry:

- Does the hacker know that we have these printouts? The evidence suggested that he was unaware that they had appeared on the PA's printer.

The investigators enquired about the abnormal appearance of the fifth printout. A little experimentation with the e-mail system revealed that the strange format and typeface of the fifth printout was the result of the user tapping the PrintScrn key – as a result of doing so the standard character set changed to a default setting and typeface.

- Why had the hacker hit the PrintScrn key to print the fifth e-mail?

It transpired that users were instructed to use the PrintScrn key whenever they had difficulty printing within the normal software applications. This suggested that the hacker had encountered difficulty in printing the e-mails and had resorted to using the print screen facility. This was probably out of frustration because the other four e-mails had not printed to a local printer where he expected to see them.

The hacker's behaviour was now clear. He knew the password to the Chief Executive's electronic mail account and used it to gain access to correspondence that was clearly of great interest to him, probably because he was one of the subjects of the departmental investigation. However, he did not realize that by using the Chief Executive's password, the printout would automatically be routed to the PA's printer and not the local printer where he expected the printouts to appear. The hacker may well have assumed that the e-mails never printed *anywhere*, having just disappeared into the ether. He almost certainly did not know that the investigators now had the printouts and knew when and where they were printed out. All in all, the hacker had demonstrated a very low level of IT literacy or comprehension and considerable clumsiness.

This behavioural profile alone was sufficient to identify the culprit. Collaborative evidence from logs and other sources proved his involvement.

Statistical analysis

There are lies, damned lies and statistics. Arguably, this is the least useful of the analytical modes described but it is included here because statistics often reveal *trends*, and by doing so they can sharpen the focus of our enquiries.

Of necessity, we must differentiate between *meaningful* statistics and *useless* ones.

A MEANINGFUL STATISTIC

Of the 12 security intrusions detected in the last 72 hours, the system has been attacked between 2:30 a.m. and 3:30 a.m. on 11 occasions.

This is useful information that informs us where to concentrate our initial focus and when to maximize our monitoring and tracing efforts. The information also, potentially, discloses one of the hacker's behavioural traits – he may be a nocturnal animal, the proverbial 'night owl'.[2] The information revealed here is relevant and meaningful, particularly should a comparison be conducted between the respective timelines recorded on the violated system and the hacker's own computer, if seized.

Statistical analysis within an investigation or audit can be particularly useful for extrapolating data from a sample or subset of transactions in order to project a quantum of loss.

A USELESS STATISTIC

75 per cent of internal theft is undetected.

Oh really? How can you possibly quantify something that has not been detected? Security surveys bearing ridiculous, utterly illogical statements like this appear with tedious regularity. Alarmist, unverifiable 'statistics' are of little help to the victim of a *real* security intrusion, fraud or other crime.

Cognitive analysis

The dictionary definition of the word cognitive is 'having a basis in or reducible to empirical factual knowledge'. In a nutshell, this means observing the facts and drawing the right conclusions.

A cognitive analysis is the coordination of the analytical methods described in this chapter so that each method and technique is applied appropriately and correctly at each

---

2   Remember, however, the relevance of different time zones.

stage of the investigation. The skill is to apply the right analytical method to the right data set at the right time.

Although the word 'cognitive' is not derived from the word 'cog', there is some value in visualizing a set of intermeshed cogs working in unison. The cognitive analytical mode is crudely analogous to a gear box – just as a car needs to be in the appropriate gear to suit the speed of the vehicle with the road conditions, so must the brain be in the right analytical mode (or modes) to solve the various puzzles that it is presented with.

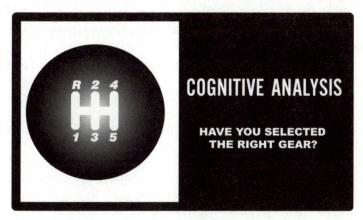

Figure 16.10   Cognitive analysis – question your approach

In classroom simulations of real frauds and computer crimes, students often select an entirely inappropriate analytical method, or scrutinize the wrong data set, or look at the right data set but apply the wrong analytical mode to it.

The investigator should always be in the cognitive mode – asking himself constantly, 'Is this a suitable, sensible, justifiable and potentially productive course of action?' The secret is to select the right analytical mode and tools at each stage of the enquiry.

Intuition

Intuition is:
   a. The act or faculty of knowing or sensing without the use of rational processes; immediate cognition.
   b. Knowledge gained by the use of this faculty; a perceptive insight.
   c. A sense of something not evident or deducible; an impression.

In other words, intuition is having the proverbial hunch – the gut feeling that tells you something isn't right, or that somebody is lying, that things are being hidden, or whatever else it is that 'rings your bell' or causes you unease.

People's intuition is occasionally right, but is also often *wrong*.

The problem with intuition is that it may reflect or be skewed by the investigator's personal prejudices thereby causing the facts to be misinterpreted deliberately. Latent prejudice can cause the investigator, albeit subconsciously, to misinterpret the facts – to bash square pegs into round holes.

It would be foolish to discount intuition altogether as it can be helpful. The subconscious alerts us to potential dangers:

> I had a vivid dream that the suspect, a man that I subconsciously knew was lying to me and was second-guessing my investigation, invited himself to my flat. He then proceeded straight to my bookshelves, of which there are many, and scrutinized every title of every book that I have ever read. He refused my offer of a drink, or to recognize my presence in any way – he just worked his way along the spines of the books.

However, the intuitive approach is not analytical and, of itself, is proof of nothing. It should be applied only with the utmost caution.

17 *Investigative Resources*

It's impossible to move, to live, to operate at any level without leaving traces, bits, seemingly meaningless fragments of personal information.
William Gibson, writer (b. 1948)

At the scene of a suspected fraud, computer misuse or other workplace misdemeanour, there is usually a range of seemingly irrelevant items that may be significant and which merit attention. Many of these potential sources of evidence are unrelated to the computer systems, but they are all worthy of consideration.

In processing different types of evidence, suitable strategies and techniques will be required should the investigation be conducted covertly as shown in Table 17.1.

Table 17.1   Strategies for processing evidence

Evidential source, resource or method	Comments
Documents	
• Purchase orders	Shredded documents may be reassembled.
• Invoices	Do not ignore documents written in foreign languages, programming
• Correspondence	code, shorthand and other material that may be not be readily intelligible.
• Printed e-mails	Consider forensic tests to determine forgery, to recover latent
• Printed faxes etc.	fingerprints and reveal indentations.
Backup tapes	Often overlooked, backup tapes may retain evidence wiped from current systems.
Electronic media	
• Diskettes	Fraudsters use these external devices to misappropriate data, and to
• Memory sticks	conceal correspondence and transactions.
• CDs	Forensic trace evidence of the use of external memory devices may be
• Iomega Zip drives	located by analysing computers.
• DVDs etc.	Deleted files may be recovered.
E-mail	
• Electronic mail	Electronic mail is an abundant source of evidence.
• Deleted e-mails	Latest forensic technology enables deleted e-mail and attachments to
• Attachments	be recovered.
• Hotmail etc.	Hotmail and other 'anonymous' correspondence can be recovered from the Internet cache of the suspect's computer.
Audio recordings	
• Voicemail	Voicemail may be downloaded from the internal telecoms system or
• Answer-phone	computers.

• Tape recordings	Evidential tapes should be write-protected, copied and transcribed.
• Dictaphones	Expert processing is indicated.
• Cassettes etc.	

Telephony

• Mobile telephone	Contact details, last numbers dialled, incoming calls and SMS text
• Itemized telephone bills	messages may be downloaded from mobile phones, but consider your
• Telephone call logs	right of access!
• Interception	Call logs and billing data that is the property of the organization may be reviewed and analysed to establish suspicious contacts or to confirm association between parties.
	Telephone interception must comply with jurisdictional law.
	Where interception is contemplated, expert assistance is indicated.

Computers

• File servers	Expert forensic investigation is indicated for all systems which the
• Minicomputers and mainframes	suspect may have accessed.
• Workstations	Remember that backup and synchronization files from PDAs and
• Laptops and notebooks	personal organizers may be located on laptops, notebooks and desktop
• PDAs, personal organizers	PCs. These should be retrieved and examined.
• Blackberrys etc.	See ground rules for processing computer evidence (Chapter 14).

Fax machine

• Printouts	Printouts will show header information, which makes the sender's
• Call logs	identity traceable, but these can be forged by reprogramming the
• Memory	machine.
• Interception	Depending on the make and model of machine, fax transmissions may be stored in memory and retrieved.
	Interception must comply with jurisdictional law. Where contemplated, expert installation is indicated.

Office search

• Contents of desk, drawers, cabinets	Some of the quickest 'smoking gun' documents have been retrieved from office searches.
• Whiteboards, desk jotter, calendar	Operationally, the search will usually be conducted covertly – take care not to disrupt the search area and to replace everything as found.
• Post-it notes etc.	Original documents should be removed with gloves, photocopied or photographed and returned exactly to the location in which they were discovered. See also Chapter 15.

Audit trails

• Event log	To trace the computers and operators involved in suspicious events or
• Web log	transactions on networks and systems.
• Mail log	Audit trails are essential to resolve many computer crimes – careful
• Router log	consideration is required to assess the appropriate scope, coverage
• Firewall	and level of detail recorded.
• Access control	The period that audit trails are retained also requires consideration – from the investigator's perspective, the longer the better.

CCTV

	To track people's whereabouts on any given day.
	Poor CCTV imagery has seriously hindered many investigations – consider a quality control audit.

Trash

	May be recovered from waste paper baskets, commercial waste and residential locations *but* illegal and inadmissible in some jurisdictions – check local laws!

Typewriter ribbons	Typewriters are still used in many offices.
	Software has been developed that can read and interpret the strike marks on ribbons to recompose letters and other communications.
Transactional records	Transactional records may be downloaded and analysed using data interrogation software.

Covert monitoring	
• Audio monitoring	Any covert surveillance must comply with jurisdictional law.
• Concealed video recording	Video sequences should show an accurate time and date.
• Remote systems surveillance	Covert monitoring technology usually requires specialist
• Keystroke logging	implementation.

The Internet	
• Websites	Google it! The quickest answers to many technical questions and other
• News groups	enquiries is often a mouse click away.
• Discussion groups	Beware that access to a suspect's website or to that of his associates
• Subscriber databases	may be recorded and the browser's identity established – if the
• Libraries	investigation is covert, web searches should be conducted at an
• Other research facilities	Internet café or from a cutout (untraceable) computer.
	Consider also subscriber databases, libraries and other archives as sources of information.

The methods shown in the Table 17.1 are legal in some countries and not others. Telephone interception and trash searches are particularly sensitive. These methods are considered by many to be particularly intrusive. Their deployment, if made public, could cause significant embarrassment for any organization concerned, and the admissibility of any evidence obtained by these methods is likely to be contested.

Whatever methods are contemplated should be assessed by the organization's external legal experts and, if cleared, should be approved at senior level.

Mistaken or ill-advised evidence processing cannot usually be corrected at a later stage. The methods and procedures used to collate and process evidence may be subjected to intense scrutiny at court. In the UK, for instance, the judiciary is increasingly insistent that established procedures are followed and deviations are frowned upon. Counsel for the defence will seek to exploit any mistakes made. For this reason expert advice or specialist expertise should be sought where indicated.

The management and processing of computer evidence is discussed in some detail in Chapters 14 and 15.

The purpose of this chapter is to discuss the processing and use of some of the other resources in Table 17.1 which may not be immediately familiar to the first responder at an electronic scene of crime, or which have more evidential potential than might initially be thought.

Specifically, we will look at:

- documents
- computer audit trails and security logs
- access control records
- call logs
- CCTV

- covert video
- telephone and fax interception.

Documents

It is advisable to inspect paperwork, letters, faxes, desk diaries, invoices, purchase orders and other documents, which may contain incriminating transactions and correspondence. Printouts, transaction reports, Post-it™ notes and other paper documentation have featured in many cases of hacking and computer fraud, and should be collated and preserved as potential evidence. Original copies of all documents relevant to the investigation should be secured as soon as possible.

Documents should be handled with care, preferably only with gloves so as to preserve latent fingerprint evidence and to avoid contamination.

- Never write on original documents, or highlight or annotate them in any way.
- Beware of causing a pressure indentation on an evidential document – typically, caused by a person writing on an overlaid page or pages.
- If forensic analysis is intended, unopened envelopes should not be disturbed.
- Likewise, batches, books, computer printouts, folders and documents should not be separated.
- Staples should not be removed.
- Do not fold, staple, pin or paperclip original documents.

If the investigation is being conducted covertly, original documents should be removed with gloves, photocopied or photographed and returned *exactly* to the location in which they were discovered. See also Chapter 15.

When documents are first obtained they should be catalogued in an exhibits record, detailing who found them, when and where, as these details may be required in legal proceedings. Photocopies of each relevant document should be made, which will serve as master copies for subsequent reproduction and annotation. Original documents may be placed in envelopes, so that latent fingerprints and DNA evidence is not tainted. Remember also, to look for and photocopy any evidence on the reverse side of the document.

The exhibit number for the document should be written on an adhesive label, which should then be attached to the document's envelope.

- The investigator should always use photocopies (never originals) for reference, and to make notes.

Documents may be sent to a laboratory for forensic analysis. Each document should be uniquely referenced with an exhibit number. The questioned documents expert will require a detailed letter of instruction, stating:

- the purpose of the examination;
- the expert opinion required and the facts to be proved or disproved;
- the date by which an opinion is required;

- facts that are relevant to the documents, including any witness statements or confessions.

Forensic analysis, where necessary, will reveal forgery, attempts to tamper with documents, to alter values on cheques or bills, to forge signatures or otherwise distort the contents of written or printed information. It may also determine who touched a document or came into physical contact with it, as fingerprints may be retained by paper indefinitely. See also Chapter 11.

When searching for clues, it is unlikely that the relevance of documents, names and addresses, business cards and other miscellaneous information will be immediately apparent. It is advisable, therefore, to photocopy as much documentation as possible. It is always sensible to photocopy the entire address book and diary where available. Names, addresses and appointments will gradually become relevant as the case progresses.

Audit trails and security logs

The cover illustration of this book shows a sea of people and computers silhouetted in black. These represent the workforce with its corresponding computer terminals. In there amongst this workforce is a single *red person* and a *red computer*. These red elements represent, respectively, the workplace criminal and any computer terminal used to aid or abet his crimes.

The task of the investigator when solving a workplace computer crime is to track down and find these *red* computer terminals and to isolate any *red* culprit or perpetrators amongst the otherwise innocent workforce, and to obtain admissible evidence with which to prosecute them. In a nutshell, we must:

- find the *red computer*, analyse its content, and obtain evidence from it;

and

- identify the *red culprit*.

From here onwards, I refer to the culprit and the computer(s) he uses as the 'red elements'.

A modern workforce may comprise several hundred thousand people, and millions if we include national military forces. The number of computers that potentially may be misused to attack or undermine any given organization nowadays also runs into hundreds of millions, and possibly more than a billion, depending on the latest statistics of computer sales and use worldwide. The task of finding the red elements appears onerous, to say the least.

Methodologies for hunting the computer criminal in the workplace vary – some investigators adopt a process of elimination, by first identifying those people and computers unlikely to be involved in the crime, or provably not involved. In smaller organizations this approach can be productive, but has clear limitations when tracking a miscreant over widely distributed networks or in operations that span numerous jurisdictions. In such cases, audit trails and event logs showing computer usage, access and connectivity have proved invaluable to identify the culprits and the computer(s) used to aid and abet their crimes.

When an incident occurs, it is clearly advisable to identify and secure the relevant audit trails and it may be necessary to do this with some urgency. From an investigator's perspective there can never be too much audit trail data, nor can there be too much detail – the problem is rather the opposite, with many organizations failing to record enough transactional and audit information to support even the most cursory investigation.

Another common problem is that IT professionals may overlook audit trails and event logs or fail to appreciate their significance:

> The investigation proved frustrating and time-consuming. Primarily, the system administrator had discarded the log files and audit trails. On occasions, these had recorded the intrusions, including the misuse of the root account, the precise dates and times of the attacks, the resources manipulated, misused or destroyed and other key indicators, but this information was now irretrievable. Equally dispiriting, the network administrator had made no contemporaneous notes of when the intrusions occurred or how they were executed. He prioritized instead the security of the network and acted swiftly to block and disable the intruder but failed to appreciate the forensic value of this information in identifying and prosecuting a potential culprit. In his haste to combat the intruder, he neglected to preserve this vital evidence.

It is important that the investigator appreciates that the priorities of the IT professional may be at variance to his own. In most situations IT personnel will prioritize the system's security and may be oblivious to the legal, evidential and investigative ramifications that arise as a result of a security breach.

The security of audit trails, transactional records and event logs is also an issue. Typical shortcomings include:

- the failure to activate or maintain the logging of key systems and processes, typically due to perceived or actual constraints on the volume of data storage capacity available for this task;
- logging trivial or peripheral processes that are inconsequential, often due to inadequate or inaccurate risk analysis;
- the failure to record audit trails and logs in sufficient detail to support an investigation, often due to a lack of calibration or bespoke refinement. The level of detail within an audit trail or log is sometimes referred to as its *granularity* – insufficient granularity is a common and debilitating hindrance to investigations;
- inaccurate logging, often because system clocks are not set correctly;
- the failure to record logs for all of the related systems in a processing chain, resulting in insufficient data to conduct a comprehensive, global or complete analysis;
- the accurate logging of chaos. Core systems and processes may be uncontrolled or badly administered and this will be reflected in any audit trail or log. An example would be a network event log showing the same USERID as active on several computers in different locations at the same time;

and, critically…

- the failure to archive audit trail data, records and event logs sufficiently so that past events may be analysed or investigated. Typically, disk space is reallocated or recycled and key transactional or audit data is overwritten before its significance is realized or understood;

- the failure to secure audit trails, records and logs from deliberate sabotage or fraudulent or unauthorized amendment.

Audit trails should be protected at the highest level from physical or logical interference by unauthorized parties. Hackers and fraudsters will usually try to suppress or destroy evidence of their misdeeds, and given the opportunity will target any auditing processes. Two simple preventative measures are as follows:

- Audit trails and processes should be accessible only at system administrator level.
- System administrators should only be able to log on to the network from a select number of workstations, preferably one, in a secure area.

And, to prevent the logging of chaos...

- Consecutive logins on a network by the same user should not be permitted.

Audit trails and event logs are the food and drink of the network investigator, his very sustenance. Time and time again, however, when emergencies occur, there is an alarming shortfall of data to explain what happened, who did it, when they did it, where they did it, why they did it or how they did it. Ironically, lack of disk space is often cited as the reason for this shortcoming, at a time when data storage devices of all sorts are tumbling in cost.

'Sorry, but we can't go back that far' is the predictable, depressing admission from many IT people when audit trail data is requested. The retention of audit data is a key area for review.

Beware also of the tendency for IT people to exaggerate the effort and complexity of retrieving audit trail data and other logs as a blocking tactic to avoid or defer the relative inconvenience of an exercise of no direct interest or obvious advantage to them. Don't be fobbed off with excuses:

> The investigators had flown from London to Hamburg four times in pursuit of the suspect. On each occasion the network administrator at the company assured them that he had exhaustively searched the network for any trace of the suspect's network account or user activity. On this occasion, the investigators explained that they did not believe that no trace whatsoever of the suspect could be found on the network. The suspect was, after all, a principal commercial agent of the company. In light of this apparent failure, they intimated that a comprehensive and truly exhaustive external audit of all the IT systems in the company was being considered at the highest level. The network administrator left the room with a flea in his ear. He returned approximately an hour later with CDs containing the suspect's network event log, his web-mail records, the firewall logs, copies of his e-mail archives and the entire contents of his network directory.

System administrators or other IT staff will usually extract audit trails and other logs to support investigations. Unless there is an overriding operational reason not to do so, it is advisable that the investigator should make it clear to these personnel precisely what it is he is trying to achieve. Wherever possible, the investigator should explain the rationale of his line of questioning or his requests. Very often the IT professional or technician will short-circuit a seemingly laborious task because he fully understands the investigator's reasoning. As an example, consider the following two requests:

1. 'I need the audit trails for last Friday.'
2. 'The router logs show that one of our IP addresses was active and in communication with an IP address belonging to our principal competitor last Friday at 16:27. I need to identify which one of our computers initiated this communication and which USERID was using that PC at the time shown in the router log. Can you advise me how best to do this?'

The first statement is so vague as to be meaningless. If such a request were issued to an IT department it would be unlikely to be acted upon. In real cases where requests such as this were issued they were sidelined and forgotten as operational matters assessed as more critical arose. Consider, also, the consequences if this request *were* acted upon and the information overload that would result (see Figure 17.1).

The second request, however, is clear and precise and contains the crucial intellectual challenge to stimulate interest, and engender a commensurate willingness to undertake and complete the task. Generally speaking, the more involved the technician becomes in the investigative process, the more productive he will be.

IF YOU ASK FOR ALL THE AUDIT TRAILS, EXPECT A BIG CONSIGNMENT!

BETTER TO REMAIN FOCUSED, METHODICAL AND SELECTIVE

Figure 17.1   All the audit trails

Returning to our key concern, the question remains:

Using your current internal resources, could you identify the red elements?

• Any half decent risk analysis should always include a review of audit trail generation, coverage, granularity and retention to determine whether potential breaches of security, particularly those assessed with a severe or catastrophic impact, could be resolved to the point of locating red elements. If red elements are found to be untraceable then the scope and focus of system and process logging and monitoring requires urgent revision.

NETWORK EVENT LOGS

Where logs are used to assist investigations, it is normally the case that they may help us to identify which computers were involved, the USERIDs shown as active on the system at the time(s) of the incident, the actions taken by these USERIDs, connections with other systems and which services were activated and used. For reasons that will become clear, they do *not* show us, definitively, *who* was active on the system.

Many computer networks generate logs of system activity and resource usage. These event logs can be extremely useful for identifying which USERIDs are logged onto the system at any given time. Network event logging typically will show each active USERID on the network, the login and logout times, the duration of the active session, the logical address of the workstation used by each USERID and will highlight any suspicious events such as repeated unsuccessful login attempts.

Audit trail information is usually output into flat ASCII text files. The data can be imported into a word processor or spreadsheet. The investigator may use the text search facilities available to locate suspicious activity, for example, by searching through the audit trail for all instances of 'Invalid USERID/password', 'Account disabled', or other trigger phrases that are standard within the log and which merit scrutiny. Alternatively, he may choose to concentrate his efforts on a known user or group of users, looking, for example, for the activation of USERIDs at times or on dates when the assigned user provably could not have accessed the system.

```
17:23:30 [ 3] Failed login from 00 03 00 20 14 5f 82 15 00 03 00 00 00 00 00 00
        , Reason=STK1028:  User name\password pair is invalid.,
        user=KevinD@CentAdm-Exec@AGL
17:24:06 [ 3] Failed login from 00 03 00 20 14 5f 82 15 00 03 00 00 00 00 00 00
        , Reason=STK1028:  User name\password pair is invalid.,
        user=KevinD@CentAdm-Exec@AGL
17:24:10 [ 3] Failed login from 00 03 00 20 14 5f 82 15 00 03 00 00 00 00 00 00
        , Reason=STK1028:  User name\password pair is invalid.,
        user=KevinD@CentAdm-Exec@AGL
17:24:47 [ 3] Failed login from 00 03 00 20 14 5f 82 15 00 03 00 00 00 00 00 00
        , Reason=STK1028:  User name\password pair is invalid.,
        user=KevinD@CentAdm-Exec@AGL
17:24:52 [ 3] Failed login from 00 03 00 20 14 5f 82 15 00 03 00 00 00 00 00 00
        , Reason=STK1028:  User name\password pair is invalid.,
        user=KevinD@CentAdm-Exec@AGL
17:39:41 [ 3] Login user=KevinD@CentAdm-Exec@AGL, stamp=1529
17:41:38 [ 1] KevinD@CentAdm-Exec@AGL is logging out
Reason -[ End Session], stamp - 1529
17:46:52 [ 3] Login user=KevinD@CentAdm-Exec@AGL, stamp=1530
```

Figure 17.2   An extract from an audit trail

In the example in Figure 17.2, the hacker eventually gained access to 'KevinD's' user account but only after attempting *31* unsuccessful logins between 17:09 and 17:39. Notice that the hacker logs out after approximately two minutes and then, having obtained the password, logs in again at 17:46.52. Most networks are configured to disable accounts after three consecutive failed login attempts — 'three strikes and you're out!' In this instance the exposure was corrected upon discovery.

ACCESS CONTROL LOGS

Comparing the network event log with access control logs for the premises has traced the physical whereabouts and activities of network users on many occasions.

The access control token or card, increasingly used by organizations to secure, monitor and control premises, may be used to trace card owners as they move between departments within a building. The logging software, normally stored on a computer found in the building's reception or security control office, will record:

- the card's ID
- location(s) entered
- location(s) exited
- location(s) denied access
- the date and time of these movements (see Table 17.2).

Access control records are also useful for seeing who was active in a building at unusual times and at weekends or on public holidays.

The main problem with access control records, as with many other types of audit trails and logs, is the immense volume of information recorded and the fact that many organizations do not retain these records for more than a few weeks. Some systems employ 'auto-wrapping' whereby the log is cyclically overwritten – this obviously diminishes the chances of building a historic picture of events.

Table 17.2   Extract from an access control log

Time	Date	ID	Area	Authorize Access = AA Request Exit = RE Access Denied = AD
07:58	27-Feb-03	WILLIAMSON_F	Reception	RE
07:58	27-Feb-03	MARSTON_O	Reception	AA
08:02	27-Feb-03	ROBERTSON_E	Atrium	RE
08:02	27-Feb-03	WILLIAMSON_F	A	AA
08:03	27-Feb-03	MARSTON_O	Reception	RE
08:03	27-Feb-03	MARSTON_O	Vault & FE	AA
08:04	27-Feb-03	ROBERTSON_E	C	AA
08:09	27-Feb-03	CARTWRIGHT_H	ANNEX A & FE	RE
08:10	27-Feb-03	THOMSON_R	Vault & FE	AA
08:12	27-Feb-03	WISE_C	Settlement	AA
08:13	27-Feb-03	BROWN_K	Settlement	AA
08:13	27-Feb-03	RATHBONE_G	ANNEX A & FE	AA
08:13	27-Feb-03	FORSYTH_A	Vault & FE	AA
08:14	27-Feb-03	STANG_J	Settlement	AA
08:15	27-Feb-03	MARSTON_O	Vault & FE	RE
08:17	27-Feb-03	ROGAN_J	ANNEX A & FE	AA
08:27	27-Feb-03	ROURKE_M	C	AA
08:28	27-Feb-03	PRIOR_I	Server	AA
08:31	27-Feb-03	FORD_D	C	AA
08:39	27-Feb-03	WISE_C	Settlement	RE
08:42	27-Feb-03	THOMSON_R	Vault & FE	RE
08:50	27-Feb-03	WILLIAMSON_F	A	RE
08:51	27-Feb-03	PHILLIPS_M	Server	RE
08:52	27-Feb-03	WILLIAMSON_F	Server	AA

Access control cards may be lost, begged, borrowed and stolen and are not, therefore, entirely reliable for ascertaining the movement of individuals. The impostor may use someone else's card to gain entry to a building or department. It is important to understand that the recording of a particular card ID on the system is not a guarantee that its *valid* owner used the card on the date and at the time indicated.

'Tailgating' – where a trespasser follows an authorized user into a controlled area – is also a common phenomenon.

Many organizations that have deployed access control systems maintain a number of unallocated cards (typically for engineer and maintenance purposes), which are often issued to users who have lost or misplaced their cards. The unallocated card, while effective at opening locked doors, will provide no indication of its user and is, therefore, an ideal tool for anyone wanting to roam anonymously.

It is also possible that a systems analyst, programmer or other technician may intentionally edit the access control log such that his or her movements are unrecorded. This may be accomplished using disk editing software or by ascertaining the USERID and master password of the access control software and subsequently tampering with the log-file. Likewise, the fraudster or miscreant may monitor the access control logs to identify other people's movements.

The investigator needs to be aware that the access control software will record his movements and that these may be scrutinized by his quarry. This may particularly apply if the investigation is principally occurring outside normal office hours. If this is the case, it will be necessary for the investigator to seek assistance to edit the records, deleting his entry into the building, his subsequent exit from it, and all movements therein.

It should be borne in mind that evidence provided by access control tokens and keystrokes at the keyboard is *circumstantial*. Without video footage or witnesses, a suspect may plausibly deny his or her involvement in a misdemeanour by claiming that someone else used their token or password to gain access.

Impersonation, commonly called 'identity theft', is probably the commonest form of computer misuse. Impersonation permits the perpetrator of computer fraud or crime to deny his actions by masquerading as another computer user.

For this reason, the investigator should desist confronting any suspect based solely on audit trail data because there is always a likelihood of impersonation, and a premature and mistaken confrontation can jeopardize operational security.

- Where an audit trail implicates a particular computer user in crime or misuse it is always advisable to seek corroborating evidence.

AVOID COMMON PRESUMPTIONS

There are many potential pitfalls that may ensnare the investigator when analysing computer-generated audit trails, event logs and evidence generally, many of which relate to times and dates. For example, an audit trail may be surmised as:

Smith made a call at 9:56 a.m.

It is necessary, here, to reserve judgment, and ask some key questions:

- Was this call ever *actually* made?
- How do we know it was *Smith* who made the call and not someone else?
- Which clock recorded 9:56 a.m.?
- Was this clock *accurate* when the record was produced?
- Which *time zone* was the clock set to?
- Was the call made in this time zone, or another?
- Where was Smith when the call was made?

There is a clear risk that we may presume too much.

If event logs, firewall logs, audit trails, call logs or any other data is used to assist an investigation, it is equally important to note the system time and date of the processor used to log this information, and compare this with the real dates and times.

Regarding misinterpretation, supposition and conjecture, there are three misleading assumptions that regularly feature in computer crime cases:

- The dates and times shown in audit trails or in electronic files are presumed, often wrongfully, to be an accurate reflection of the *real* date and time.
- USERIDs and computer accounts are commonly confused with the actual people to whom the accounts are assigned, for example, 'Smith's account was used to commit the crime, therefore, Smith committed the crime.'
- Similarly, equipment is wrongfully associated with its owner, for example, 'Jones's telephone was used to make the incriminating call. Therefore, Jones made the incriminating call.'

We should remember that many entirely innocent people have been accused of wrongdoing based solely on audit trails and other computer-generated data. We should avoid jumping to conclusions and always seek corroborating evidence from other sources.

FINDING THE RED COMPUTER – AN EXAMPLE

Should an internal security incident occur, the initial priority is to identify and secure the internal resources and information that may assist the investigation. A major focus of the enquiry will be to identify the computer(s) involved in the breach, or those that may store evidence or other information material to it.

A fundamental point when presented with any computer-generated log or audit trail is to understand what precisely the information in the fields shown actually represents. There are millions of different types of transaction that are recorded daily by computer systems worldwide. In all probability, the transaction logs and audit trails produced by these systems will be completely unintelligible to anyone unfamiliar with the processes involved. To the uninitiated, the output of many audit trails is a cryptic, incomprehensible spaghetti of random, unrelated and seemingly chaotic data. Rather than trying to chew his way through this indigestible mess, the investigator should seek clarification from someone suitably qualified to explain the meaning and relative significance of the information presented.

Often, the first indicator in the audit trails as to the identity and whereabouts of the red computer is the IP (Internet Protocol) address that it is assigned to it at the time of the suspected incident. Communication over networks and the Internet is all directed using IP addresses. The IP address is a logically assigned coordinate, and it may be fixed to a particular computer, or, significantly, it may be assigned dynamically.

Table 17.3   Extract from a router log

16/11/04	14h23m04.986s	184.205.72.206	194.15.189.100	80
16/11/04	14h23m05.856s	184.205.72.209	194.15.189.100	80
16/11/04	14h23m08.131s	184.205.72.209	194.15.189.100	80
16/11/04	14h23m09.903s	184.205.72.200	194.15.189.102	80
16/11/04	14h23m12.122s	184.205.72.200	194.15.189.100	80
16/11/04	14h23m13.760s	184.205.72.204	194.15.189.101	61466
16/11/04	14h23m16.005s	184.205.72.204	194.15.189.101	61466
16/11/04	14h23m16.150s	184.205.72.204	194.15.189.101	61466
16/11/04	14h23m18.339s	184.205.72.209	194.15.189.101	25
16/11/04	14h23m19.280s	184.205.72.201	194.15.189.102	25
16/11/04	14h23m20.494s	184.205.72.206	194.15.189.100	80
16/11/04	14h23m22.196s	184.205.72.202	194.15.189.100	80
16/11/04	14h23m24.227s	184.205.72.5	194.15.189.101	80
16/11/04	14h23m25.754s	184.205.72.203	194.15.189.100	53
16/11/04	14h23m26.067s	184.205.72.200	194.15.189.100	80
16/11/04	14h23m26.987s	184.205.72.4	194.15.189.101	80
16/11/04	14h23m27.523s	184.205.72.201	194.15.189.101	80

To illustrate, Table 17.3 shows a brief extract from a router log and it shows us the types of communication that took place between various computers at 2.23 p.m. on November 16, 2004.

The first column is clearly the date.

The second column shows the time when each communication occurs, in milliseconds.

The third column shows computers within our network with their assigned IP addresses. These IP addresses are assigned dynamically – each time the computers are booted they are assigned an IP address, which remains active for each computer shown only for a pre-designated lease period, which may vary from seconds to years. If this lease period is short, a matter of seconds, minutes or hours, dynamically assigned IP addresses may change each and every time the computer is booted.

The fourth column shows communication with IP addresses assigned to computers external to the network, namely, a third party. These IP addresses may equally be fixed (statically assigned), or dynamic.

The fifth column shows the ports in use on the router. Ports are used to convey transactions between computers. There are currently 65 536 ports available to convey different types of transaction or communication between computers, many of which are unassigned.

In the router log we see that port 80 is active – this is the standard port used by the World Wide Web Hypertext Transfer Protocol (HTTP), the underlying service to access the World Wide Web.

Port 25 is the assigned port for the Simple Mail Transfer Protocol (SMTP) used to transmit electronic mail between computers.

Port 53 is used for Domain Name Server (DNS) communication. DNS is an Internet service that translates *domain names* into IP addresses. Because domain names are alphabetic, they're easier for people to remember. At a machine level, however, the Internet is really based on IP addresses. Every time you use a domain name, therefore, a DNS service must translate the name into the corresponding IP address.

Ports 25, 53 and 80 are standard and used in routine day-to-day transactions. They are not, in themselves, suspicious.

Port 61466, however, should be unassigned and not used for any standard or common transaction. Its activation indicates an anomalous transaction that merits further scrutiny.

When seeking answers to technical questions, by far the quickest approach is to 'Google it'.

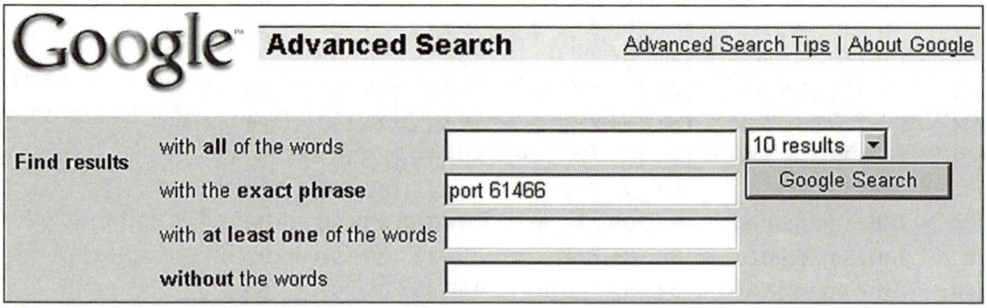

Figure 17.3 When in doubt, Google!

By typing 'port 61466' into an advanced Google search (see Figure 17.3), the probable nature of this suspicious transaction becomes clear.

BLACK CODE TROJAN LIBRARY **www.blackcode.com**
Name: TeleCommando
Aliases:
Ports: 61466
Files: Teleclient.zip - 270,557 bytes Teleclient.exe - 323,538 bytes Teleserv.exe - 211,456 bytes Obdc.exe -
Created: Nov 1998
Requires:
Actions: Remote Access
Versions: 1.5.4,
Registers: HKEY_LOCAL_MACHINE\SOFTWARE\Microsoft\Windows\CurrentVersion\Run\
Notes: Works on Windows.

Figure 17.4 Result of the Google search

The evidence (see Figure 17.4) suggests that a Trojan horse program – TeleCommando – has been activated on this computer. TeleCommando is one of a class of Trojan horses that enables an intruder surreptitious access and remote control of any compromised computer. We do not know at this stage the *direction* of the attack; is it incoming or outgoing?

It is worthwhile, at this stage, to isolate this transaction:

16/11/04	14h23m13.760s	184.205.72.204	194.15.189.101	61466
16/11/04	14h23m16.005s	184.205.72.204	194.15.189.101	61466
16/11/04	14h23m16.150s	184.205.72.204	194.15.189.101	61466

Ideally, we would like to know where the computer on our network assigned the IP number 184.205.72.204 at 2.23 p.m. on November 16, 2004 is located. Its IP address has been assigned *dynamically*. Remember that the IP address is a logical reference to a computer somewhere on our network. The problem is that we do not know which computer, or where it is located.

- Many computer misuse investigations fail because the logical IP address shown as active during a suspicious transaction cannot be cross-referenced to a physical computer. This potential failure applies particularly in network environments that are dynamically addressed, where IP addresses are constantly reassigned.

In order to identify the red computer we need to map its IP address. We can only do this if a log has been recorded showing which computer was assigned this IP address on the day and at the time of the suspicious transaction. Otherwise, the investigation will be severely hindered and may prove intractable.

The IP addresses and the computers to which they are assigned are recorded in the DHCP log. DHCP (Dynamic Host Configuration Protocol) is a communications protocol that automates the assignment of IP addresses on a network. Using the Internet Protocol, each machine that can connect to the Internet requires a unique IP address. When an organization sets up its computers with a connection to the Internet, an IP address must be assigned to each machine. Without DHCP, the IP address must be entered manually at each computer and should a computer be installed in a different location on the network, a new IP address must be entered for it. DHCP allows a network administrator to supervise and distribute IP addresses from a central point and automatically assigns IP addresses as and when computers are attached to the network.

DHCP uses the concept of a 'lease', a period of time that an assigned IP address will be valid for a given computer. The lease time can vary. Using very short leases, DHCP can dynamically reconfigure networks in which there are more computers than there are available IP addresses.

- When conducting a network investigation, the DHCP log is an essential reference because it helps us to convert the logical IP address assigned to our red computer to a physical piece of hardware in the form of a network interface card (NIC), which will reside inside this machine, and which should be traceable.
- If DHCP logging is inactive, you will not be able to locate the red computer.

A NIC is installed in each computer attached to the network. Significantly, each and every NIC has a unique reference, known as a MAC address (see Figure 17.5). The Media Access Controller or MAC address of a network adapter is a unique address assigned to it by its manufacturer. This address is used to ensure that data goes to the right destination on the network. A MAC address consists of 12 hexadecimal digits [0-9 A-F], often written in pairs with colons, spaces or dashes for readability, for example 00-C0-49-B3-5D-B5.

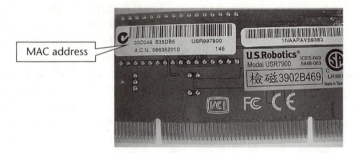

MAC address

Figure 17.5   Network interface card

The following extract from a DHCP log in Figure 17.6 shows us that the computer on our network assigned the IP number 184.205.72.204 on November 16, 2004 is called ALPHA, and contains a network card with the MAC address 00-F0-5A-60-1A-28. The computer was booted at 9.32 a.m.

ID	Date,	Time,	Description,	IP Address,	Host Name,	MAC Address
11,	16/11/04,	09:14:44,	Renew,	184.205.72.203,	FOXTROT,	0070CA056BDB
11,	16/11/04,	09:17:19,	Renew,	184.205.72.205,	GOLF,	007025F9E53A
11,	16/11/04,	09:22:00,	Renew,	184.205.72.219,	ZULU,	0070308A473C
11,	16/11/04,	09:25:34,	Renew,	184.205.72.217,	MIKE,	00E022432F9A
10,	16/11/04,	09:30:01,	Lease,	184.205.72.209,	TANGO,	0020A974F7B3
11,	16/11/04,	09:32:05,	Renew,	184.205.72.210,	DELTA,	00205F53AB27
11,	**16/11/04,**	**09:32:21,**	**Renew,**	**184.205.72.204,**	**ALPHA,**	**00F05A601A28**
11,	16/11/04,	09:34:44,	Renew,	184.205.72.214,	HOTEL,	00805F4373DD
11,	16/11/04,	09:35:18,	Renew,	184.205.72.217,	MIKE,	00E022432F9A
11,	16/11/04,	09:40:09,	Renew,	184.205.72.217,	MIKE,	00E022432F9A
10,	16/11/04,	09:41:41,	Lease,	184.205.72.215,	BRAVO,	006097B78923
11,	16/11/04,	09:42:38,	Renew,	184.205.72.201,	KILO,	006097A7B936
11,	16/11/04,	09:43:48,	Renew,	184.205.72.208,	OSCAR,	00805DFC3DB2
11,	16/11/04,	09:46:38,	Renew,	184.205.72.209,	TANGO,	0020A974F7B3
11,	16/11/04,	09:50:45,	Renew,	184.205.72.211,	LIMA,	00A021943327
11,	16/11/04,	10:12:21,	Renew,	184.205.72.201,	KILO,	006097A7B936
11,	16/11/04,	10:27:30,	Renew,	184.205.72.209,	TANGO,	0020A974F7B3
11,	16/11/04,	10:33:14,	Renew,	184.205.72.210,	DELTA,	00205F53AB27
11,	16/11/04,	17:49:25,	Renew,	184.205.72.219,	ZULU,	0070308A473C
11,	16/11/04,	18:03:26,	Renew,	184.205.72.212,	PAPA,	00500C837591
11,	16/11/04,	18:08:03,	Renew,	184.205.72.212,	CHARLIE,	00F05AD04D2F
11,	16/11/04,	19:50:10,	Renew,	184.205.72.205,	GOLF,	007025F9E53A

Figure 17.6   DHCP server activity log

It is necessary to check that this was the only IP address assigned to computer ALPHA on the day and at the time of the suspicious transaction. Remember that in a dynamically addressed network the IP addresses are leased, and depending on the duration of the lease, the computer may be reassigned a different IP address should it be re-booted. By searching for every instance of the IP address 184.205.72.204 within the DHCP log we can determine that ALPHA was booted only once on the day that the transaction occurred.

- It is essential that all network adapters (NICs) should be registered in a database, so that the computers in which they are installed can be traced in the event of a system malfunction or misuse. The database should show where any computer under investigation or requiring diagnostic attention is located.

Table 17.4 shows the asset registry database entry for machine ALPHA with the MAC address 00-F0-5A-60-1A-28.

Table 17.4   Asset registry database

Computer name	ALPHA
Manufacturer	Hewlett Packard
CPU	Intel P4 2.53 Ghz
Memory	512 Mb DDR
Hard disk	80 Gb, ATA 100
MAC address	00-F0-5A-60-1A-28
IP address	DHCP (dynamic)
Operating system	Windows 2000
Office	Administration Building
Building	Finance Dept, Floor 2
Room number	12
Assigned users	Emily Harris

We have now identified the whereabouts of the red computer ALPHA and know that is assigned to one Emily Harris.

The next stage of the investigation is to ascertain who was using this red computer at the time of the suspicious transaction. This information, recorded as logins and logoffs to the network, will be shown in the network event log (see Figure 17.7).

```
ISC_NT Domain Logon/Logoff filtered 1:00:00 PM to 11:00:00 PM 16/11/04


16/11/04      1:47:18 PM      Security      Success Audit  Logon/Logoff   528      FMORE
        WINNTBACKUP    Successful Logon:
        User Name:      FMORE
        Domain:         ISC_NT
        Logon ID:
        Logon Type:    3
        Logon Process: KSecDD
        Authentication Package:     MICROSOFT_AUTHENTICATION_PACKAGE_V1_0
        Workstation Name:      \\ALPHA
16/11/04      1:51:12 PM      Security      Success Audit  Logon/Logoff   538
        Administrator  WINNTBACKUP    User Logoff:
        User Name:      Administrator
        Domain: ISC_NT
        Logon ID:
        Logon Type:    3

16/11/04      2:05:08 PM      Security      Success Audit  Logon/Logoff   538      SJOYLES
        WINNTBACKUP    User Logoff:
        User Name:      SJOYLES
        Domain:         ISC_NT
        Logon ID:
        Logon Type:    3

16/11/04      2:13:42 PM      Security      Success Audit  Logon/Logoff   528      KWARNER
        WINNTBACKUP    Successful Logon:
        User Name:      KWARNER
        Domain:         ISC_NT
        Logon ID:
        Logon Type:    3
        Logon Process: KSecDD
        Authentication Package:     MICROSOFT_AUTHENTICATION_PACKAGE_V1_0
        Workstation Name:      \\DELTA
```

Figure 17.7   Network event log

Here, we see a successful login to the workstation ALPHA at 1.47 p.m. by the USERID 'FMORE'.

The event log (Figure 17.8) shows FMORE logging out from the network at 2:45 p.m.

```
16/11/04      2:45:04 PM    Security      Success Audit  Logon/Logoff   538
        FMORE   WINNTBACKUP   User Logoff:
        User Name:      FMORE
        Domain:         ISC_NT
        Logon ID:
        Logon Type:     3
```

Figure 17.8   The event log

With the assistance of these audit trails we have been able to establish a number of facts about the red computer:

- It is called ALPHA.
- It is located in the Administration Building, Finance Department, Floor 2.
- It is assigned to Emily Harris.
- It was booted at 9:32 a.m.
- The USERID 'FMORE' was used to login to the network using the computer at 1:47 p.m. and it was logged out at 2:45 p.m. (an active session of 58 minutes).

Circumstantially, it would appear that FMORE was active at the computer when the suspicious transaction occurred at 2:23 p.m. As emphasized, however, we should not presume this to be the case.

Significantly, for the first time in the investigation we have identified a piece of hardware, the computer's internal hard disk, which is likely to have recorded and retained information relevant to the suspicious transaction. It is now incumbent upon us to examine the data on this hard disk *forensically* to determine additional information about this computer, its configuration and operation, any evidence of TeleCommando and port 61466, and, crucially, to identify its user, his actions, methods and motivation.

- Where a memory device, such as a hard disk, is identified as participatory to a suspicious event it should always be processed forensically and the data on it investigated. Not to do so would be negligent.

Having found his machine, the challenge now is to identify the person who was using this computer at the time when the TeleCommando Trojan was executed. This might be accomplished by reviewing CCTV footage of the area in which the computer is located, from the access control logs, or from the forensic investigation of the red computer's hard disk. We also want to determine how and why this Trojan was executed, which again may become apparent from the forensic review.

From this example, based on a real case of IP theft in which a computer was hacked into and proprietary data downloaded, we can see the vital role that audit trails serve when conducting network investigations.

Although incidental, it should also be pointed out that a well-configured firewall would disable all unassigned ports, thereby rendering this particular instance of hacking defunct.

Table 17.5 summarizes the bare minimum level of monitoring that is essential on a network. Far more comprehensive logging than this, particularly of applications and transactions, is clearly advisable.

Table 17.5   Essential audit trail and event logging

Recommendation	Comment
At minimum, networks should generate audit trails that record: • active USERIDs • associated login and logout times • IP addresses of the associated workstations • MAC addresses of the workstations • intruder lockouts.	Minimum information necessary to conduct an internal computer misuse investigation.
DHCP logging should be mandatory in any network environment operating dynamic IP addressing.	Ascertains the physical locations of computers shown in the audit trails.
Server clocks should be accurately set to local times and dates.	Ensures that times and dates are recorded accurately in audit trails.
Firewall monitoring should record port activity, attempts at port scanning and web accesses by users and should also record all communications to and from external IP addresses.	Detects hostile port scanning attempts from external sources. Any attempted exploitation of an unprotected port should be registered and the communication link severed.
Unused port services should be disabled.	External IP addresses and web activity should be recorded as this may show communications with competitors or hostile third parties.
Audit trails should be archived for the longest period feasible and at least four working weeks.	The maximum practicable retention period should be adhered to.

To restate: At minimum, any investigation of network misuse will seek to identify the computer used to perpetrate the crime or misdemeanour, as well as the USERID active on that PC at the time of the offence. In a dynamically addressed network, this will be impossible without properly configured DHCP logging.

AUDIT TRAILS AS EVIDENCE

Computer-generated audit trails, event logs and transaction reports that are to be used as evidence to prosecute a crime or misdemeanour require processing in accordance with best practice.

There is an expectation that the audit trail, log or transaction report will be retained and disclosed. The onus is on the investigator to preserve any trail, log or record in its *entirety*, devoid of any amendment, editing or notation.

It is advisable to write evidential audit trails and logs to a data storage device that can be write-protected, preferably to stable media such as an optical disc, DVD, CD-ROM or

WORM, so that the data is less likely to degrade or become unreadable. Two copies should be made to separate disks, and these should be protected in suitable casings.

A detailed record should be kept of the system date and time when the trail was generated, the real date and time, the process (executable program) that generated the log, the logical location or path of the process (drive and directory), the default location and name of the output log (drive, directory and default name), the physical location and identity of the host machine, and the operator(s) who produced the audit trail or log. The audit trail or log is the operator's exhibit, and he will be required to write a statement detailing his actions, to include all of this detail.

Each audit trail should be produced as an exhibit. Analysis and inspection of data in the audit trails and logs should be conducted only on copies generated from master copies, and should never be undertaken on the exhibited audit trails themselves.

Each discrete audit trail that is produced as an exhibit comprises a vital link in the chain of evidence, and the rules that apply to guaranteeing evidential continuity must be observed accordingly.

In preparing reports, case notes and specific exhibits any relevant entry within a log may be isolated and produced as a succinct extract. Provided that the audit trail or log has been preserved evidentially, any extract exhibited may also be annotated, provided that any such notation is distinct.

Covert video

The investigator may opt to use covert video in cases where systems are being physically tampered with, or on hacking investigations where the suspected perpetrator claims that an unidentified 'impersonator' is consistently breaking into the system using a stolen password. If the hacking attempts are traced to a red computer, the area where this is located can be placed under surveillance.

Fibre-optics, micro-technology and miniature lenses have made it possible to conceal recording efforts:

> (i) The cleaners at a hotel were suspected of a series of cash thefts from the administration office. Someone had tipped them off that this office was being filmed covertly. When investigators reviewed the video coverage of the cleaners at work, they saw them systematically searching every nook and cranny of the office. One of the suspects stared straight into the camera lens, oblivious to its presence, before proceeding with his search for hidden devices.

The recording equipment may be combined with passive infrared (PIR) detectors so that video surveillance commences only when a significant heat source such as a live body enters the area of surveillance. Remember, however, that powered-up computers also generate heat.

All video footage should be programmed so that the accurate time and date are echoed on all recorded video sequences.

Covert video filming has also been used successfully to resolve instances of sabotage where individuals have been recorded disrupting and severing network cabling and connections, and disabling machines. At a more prosaic level, cleaners, assembly-line workers and contractors have regularly been caught on covert video, stealing office supplies, car radios and other items, or committing acts of vandalism.

Video evidence is often compelling, proving problematic only when the suspect has taken elaborate measures to disguise his identity, or is obscured by a hood, balaclava, hat or cap, or when the picture is marred by poor picture quality, inadequate camera adjustment or lighting. It is clearly important to test and maintain surveillance equipment *in situ*, lest key events go unrecorded, or the quality of the recording is too poor to be of use.

Digital video enhancement can be used to enhance picture quality, contrast and lighting. In cases where facial features are obscured or hidden, analytical methods can assist identification using physiognomic and anatomical comparative analysis.

Telephone call logs

Digital call-logging systems are now commonplace in many organizations. The call logs they generate typically show both *outgoing* and *incoming* calls from each extension on the internal telephone network.

In the United Kingdom call-log data is the property of the customer (the custodian) and not the supplier (the telephone company) or anyone else. It may be used, legally, to assist an investigation or for whatever other purpose the custodian sees fit. Be aware that this may not be the case in other jurisdictions.

Call-log data may be archived as a contingency in the event of a billing dispute, as proof that calls were or were not made, to comply with regulatory conditions, to assist telecommunication strategic planning and, where needed, investigations.

Call logs are an extremely useful source of intelligence or evidence. They can be downloaded into a spreadsheet, searchable file or link analysis data-mining program on a computer and analysed to ascertain whether suspicious numbers are being contacted, to identify calls to offshore or unusual jurisdictions, those calls made outside of normal work hours, at weekends or on public holidays and other variables that may merit scrutiny. The investigator may also seek to identify rolling patterns where numbers are dialled in regular succession, for example to a lawyer, then an accountant and then a bank.

By combining call-log information with other data sets, such as the access control records and network event logs, the investigator can start to construct a detailed chronology of events, showing calls made and received, their duration, the contacts, the suspect's movement within the building and his computer activity (see Table 17.6).

Telephone numbers may be reversed (resolved) by a cross-reference with the suspect's contacts database, electronic diary or Rolodex, which may be obtained covertly from his computer, or from photocopies of his address book also made during a covert search (see Chapter 15). Searches of numbers may also be made to see whether they are referenced on websites or elsewhere on the Internet. In some jurisdictions – not the UK – national telephone data is available on CD and numbers may be reversed relatively easily to identify assigned customers.

Frequency analysis identifies the relative volume of telephone traffic. Software packages are available that automatically generate frequency charts. The chart shown in Figure 17.9, generated using RFF Flow from RFF Electronics (www.rff.com), shows outgoing and incoming calls to extension 1058 with the numbers indicated.

Mobile telephone records are equally useful. Beware, however, that billing data is the property of the owner of the mobile telephone – if the suspect uses his own phone there is

Table 17.6   Annotated call log

Extension: 1058   _(Williamson F)_

Time	Date	Destination	Duration	Contact	Comment	Action
10:04	26/02/03	08708509850	03:23	BA	Reservations and general	Ankara? No BA flight to Ankara
10:34	26/02/03	08705511155	01:21	BA	Arrivals and departures	
10:51	26/02/03	02077086912	01:44	Girlfriend		Confirm
11:25	26/02/03	1002	04:01	Thomson		Interview
12:20	26/02/03	00496891013	00:21	Deutsch	Frankfurt Settlements	
12:25	26/02/03	00496891013	00:25	Deutsch	Frankfurt Settlements	
12:30	26/02/03	00496891017	01:50	Deutsch	Confirms payment will be requested	
12:55	26/02/03	08701100300	02:30	DHL	Shipment/package?	Check
16:01	26/02/03	1002	08:03	Thomson		What?
20:25	26/02/03	00903127060121	01:00	Ankara	Unknown Turkish number	Identify
20:35	26/02/03	02087335512	04:13	Pickwick & Co.	Solicitors	His? Why?
20:42	26/02/03	02077086912	02:10	Girlfriend		
08:15	27/02/03	1023	03:01	Robertson	Gets permission to perform system checks	Statement
09:12	27/02/03	1576	01:21	Rourke	Gives spurious reasons to contact Settlements	Statement
09:17	27/02/03	1643	05:01	Stang	Call to Settlements	Interview
12:22	27/02/03	0041844800888	04:30	Credit Suisse	Private banking	Relevance?
12:55	27/02/03	08701100300	03:40	DHL	Tracking – pre 10 a.m.	Check
14:10	27/02/03	1023	02:30	Robertson	Robertson re meeting	statement
15:25	27/02/03	00903124550000	13:01	Hilton Ankara	Reservation? Note fax: 00903124550055	Check for fax.
15:55	27/02/03	1002	05:04	Thomson		What?
16:04	27/02/03	1023	00:20	Robertson	Robertson at meeting	Confirm
16:18	27/02/03	08700100287	03:40	Avis Car hire	Turkey?	Confirm
16:20	27/02/03	00903127060121	01:12	Ankara	Turkish repeat number	Identify
16:33	27/02/03	07904612453	01:14		Unknown mobile	Identify

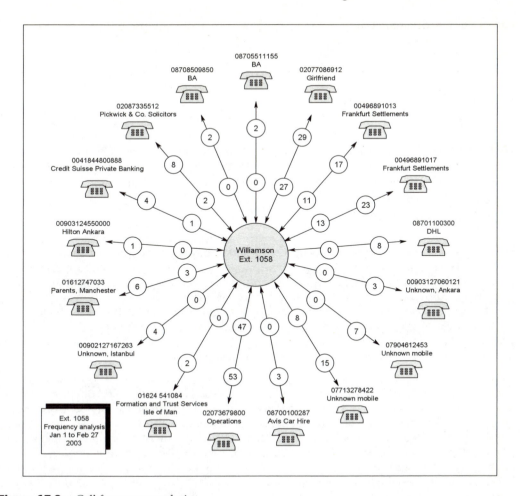

Figure 17.9   Call frequency analysis

no right of access to this information. On one occasion, a suspect was particularly helpful in this regard:

> The investigator had located an itemized telephone bill from British Telecom in the suspect's office desk drawer. Certain numbers had been overwritten with a black ballpoint pen – the numbers were so heavily obscured that they could not be read even when the bill was held up to bright sunlight.
>
> In the laboratory, however, the ink from the ballpoint when subjected to infrared light vanished, as if by magic, to reveal the numbers beneath. The fraudster had expeditiously directed the investigation to the very telephone numbers that he sought to conceal.

Forensic downloads of text messages, numbers, photographs and videos from mobile handsets are also clearly of potential investigative value, but the availability of this data will again be dependent on the right of access. If the suspect uses his own mobile telephone there is no right of audit or inspection unless expressly stated in the employment contract, and access to the data stored in memory or to billing data may only be gained by order of the court.

As always, when analysing call-logs, remember to avoid any presumption:

> *Jones's telephone was used to make the call. But was it in fact him on the line?*

CCTV

Video or digital footage from security cameras and other CCTV networks may assist in identifying people's whereabouts on a given date and at a given time. Unlike security tags, swipe cards and other access control tokens, which may be exchanged randomly, people cannot exchange their physical features, although they may conceal them.

Video evidence may record a crime in progress and assist the identification of the culprits, or it may help to define potential suspects:

> A highly detrimental, litigious, forged and anonymous fax was transmitted from a bank to a third party. The building housed approximately 200 employees and the investigation initially appeared daunting. However, the exact time of the transmission had been ascertained from the fax logs and corroborated with the third party addressee. At that time in the morning, CCTV showed that only 11 employees had entered the building, all of whom were recognizable, which clearly sharpened the focus of the enquiry.

Video evidence may also help to eliminate people as suspects:

> The head of internal audit surveyed the printouts. In total 21 offensive e-mail messages had been transmitted from X's e-mail account to various employees, including members of senior management. Should she call X in and read him the riot act? Her colleague, Steve from security, suggested that they wait. He argued that only a complete fool would use his own e-mail account to send such inflammatory messages.
>
> In the video suite Steve viewed a recording of the day that the first five messages had been sent. He forwarded the tape to a frame showing X leave by the front door of the building. X was a heavy smoker and regularly left the building, a non-smoking office, to indulge his habit.
>
> Steve smiled wryly at his next discovery. The first offensive message was sent within one minute of X's first cigarette break of the day commencing. He smiled again when the tape forwarded to X's next appearance. Surprise, surprise, the second message coincided with X's second nicotine fix later the same morning. Having reviewed the CCTV coverage for each and every incident the pattern that emerged was incontrovertible and by the end of the day Steve had accounted for all 21 messages. Without exception they coincided exactly with X's cigarette breaks. X admitted that he never locked his computer when he left his desk, but was hugely relieved to be conclusively exonerated.

CCTV coverage should be checked regularly to make sure that pictures are properly focused, lit, and date-stamped (see Figure 17.10). Tapes, if used, should also be checked for signs of degraded picture quality, and regularly changed.

Digital recordings are increasingly being stored on hard disk. Where this is the case a suitable backup regime is required. A policy should be set for the retention of CCTV recordings.

If picture quality is poor, forensic video enhancement should be considered.

It is also advisable to make sure that CCTV coverage is appropriate. Apart from toilets, changing rooms and other places where there is an expectation of privacy, there have been

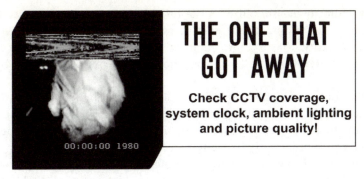

Figure 17.10   A regular audit of CCTV systems is advisable

cases where CCTV has been misused to observe and record sensitive systems and processes, to obtain passwords and access codes from keyboards and entry pads, and to view other objects of interest:

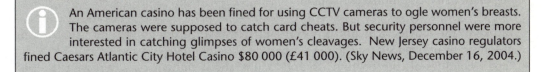

> An American casino has been fined for using CCTV cameras to ogle women's breasts. The cameras were supposed to catch card cheats. But security personnel were more interested in catching glimpses of women's cleavages. New Jersey casino regulators fined Caesars Atlantic City Hotel Casino $80 000 (£41 000). (Sky News, December 16, 2004.)

Telephone and fax monitoring

If the investigation is covert and the suspect does not know that he or she is under investigation, telephone lines and fax transmissions may also be monitored, provided that the monitoring is conducted lawfully.

In many jurisdictions, telecommunications interception is illegal. The product of illegal monitoring is inadmissible, and such criminality clearly may jeopardize an organization's reputation. In the UK, telecommunications interception is legal, provided that certain stipulations are complied with. Guidance on the legality of these techniques is provided in Chapter 13.

Operationally, remote downloading of audio data is now standard procedure on telephone intercepts. On an investigation in 2001, audio data from one such intercept was transmitted daily as a download to a laptop computer operated in a car outside the target building for subsequent review and transcription. This was accomplished without the need to change cassette tapes or batteries on-site. Audio cassettes are gradually being phased out in favour of higher capacity storage media. Nearly all of the information captured, be it audio, visual or data, can be digitally stored and transferred using devices that have immense storage capacity. The MMC/SD memory card for the MBR-64 Micro-Bar Digital Voice Recorder, for example, can store up to 512 hours of audio recording.

The quality of recorded audio data has improved quantifiably with digital technology and mastering, which has enabled improvements in audiotape enhancement methods to reduce background noise or clutter and enhance the clarity of a recorded conversation. Digital recorders have also become more compact and discreet, making them easier to conceal.

Tapes and audio media should be write-protected, dated, exhibited and copied. The tapes are exhibits and should be handled accordingly, observing the rule of evidential continuity and integrity. Master tapes should be retained and the copies generated from them used for transcription. Relevant telephone conversations should be transcribed verbatim.

Provided that RIP (see Chapter 13) or applicable jurisdictional law is complied with, any fax machine suspected of transmitting incriminating correspondence may be monitored. A fax monitor can store the incoming and outgoing fax transmissions on the suspect's fax machine, which can subsequently be viewed and printed out for review.

Operationally, telephone surveillance is resource intensive. Transcription is very time-consuming, and listening to recorded conversations is laborious also. Understanding the actual meaning and relevance of a conversation is just as difficult. The investigator will require an attuned ear to appreciate the subtleties and nuances of what is said. See also Chapter 16, 'Contextual analysis'.

Technical surveillance is a highly specialist area and the installation of telephone and fax intercepts should only be undertaken by trained and qualified experts.

Operationally, commonsense applies:

- Unlike in the movies, it is not generally practicable to record conversations from long distances, or in open spaces such as car parks, shopping malls or woods.
- Tape recordings of conversations in pubs, clubs, social gatherings, any place with loud background music, or where there are crowds or public announcements, are rarely, if ever, audible.

18 *Computer Evidence in Court*

**People who love sausage and people who believe in justice should never
watch either of them being made.**
Otto von Bismark, Iron Chancellor, 1815–1898

Presenting evidence in a court of law is the acid test by which the computer crime
investigator is ultimately judged. Ironically, amidst a plethora of current textbooks
published on the subjects of computer forensics and digital evidence, hardly a word is
mentioned about the credible and intelligible presentation of computer evidence in court.[1]
Emphasis at the moment is often placed on technical minutiae and obscure points of
forensic detail, whilst the ultimate objective of the exercise – a successful criminal
prosecution (or defence) – appears hardly to register at all.

THE MIND OF A JURY

Figure 18.1   The biggest hurdle – the jury

The following brief aide-memoire is based on personal experience, combined with the
observations of expert witnesses, police officers, private investigators, barristers, solicitors

---

1   A very useful handbook is C. Bond, M. Solon and P. Harper, *The Expert Witness in Court: A Practical
     Guide* (1997), Shaw & Sons, ISBN 0 7219 1440 3.

and jury members. It is by no means comprehensive but does provide some practical advice to anyone faced with an appearance at court.[2]

- Refresh your memory; read your notes and study your exhibits and statements before attending court. Your understanding of the evidence that you have obtained should be both profound and detailed. When in the witness box always seek the judge's authority to make reference to your notes and so on.
- Arrive at court ahead of time and familiarize yourself with relevant officers of the court and layout of the building. Panic induces stress and diminishes focus. You can reduce this stress by acquainting yourself with the immediate environment and the personalities involved.
- Dress in a formal and sober manner. Jury members can take irrational exceptions to the slightest eccentricity of appearance, and will inevitably infer much about you from the way you look. The jury should be listening to what you have to say rather than criticizing your choice of tie or staring at the tattoo on your forehead.
- Do not drink alcohol prior to giving evidence. This advice may appear obvious but should be followed if only to prevent extreme discomfort in the witness box in the event of prolonged cross-examination.
- Address the judge by the proper salutation. Find out in advance whether the salutation is 'Your Honour', 'My Lord', 'Sir/Madam' or other title.
- Be polite, respectful and avoid arrogance:

> On swearing the oath, the police officer, a junior member of CID, accelerated the wording to a slurred and unintelligible mumble, as if to imply 'been there, done that'. Casually tossing the Bible onto the shelf of the witness stand he continued his testimony with the same nonchalance – even flippantly glancing at his watch and rolling his eyeballs with clear impatience at Counsel's examination. When the jury eventually retired to consider the evidence they were determined to derail the case. This was successfully achieved by means of a technicality, which the wily foreman of the jury identified and brought to the Judge's attention. The foreman later explained that the police officer's behaviour had undermined the entire prosecution effort; from the moment the officer took the stand he and his fellow jurors were determined to sabotage the prosecution's case.

- Anticipate obvious lines of questioning. Predict, also, those aspects of your evidence that might be contentious and therefore subject to close scrutiny. Forewarn your counsel. You are allowed to brief your counsel about the contents of your report, your observations and findings. Most of the weaknesses in evidence can be easily explained, but their existence and significance need to be accounted for in advance of cross-examination.
- Beyond normal politeness, avoid familiarity or any informal disclosure to the other side. There is a danger of being lured into making unintended comments by wily solicitors, counsel or other expert witnesses. Intelligence gathering of this type is most likely to happen through seemingly friendly approaches outside of the courtroom.
- Avoid any display or indication of partisanship. As an expert witness you are an appointee of the court and answerable to the court. You may be in the pay of a

---

2   This chapter applies to the English legal system. Its recommendations, however, apply equally to adversarial legal systems in other jurisdictions.

particular firm of solicitors that is acting for, or against, the defendant or claimant, but this should not influence the evidence that you produce or your interpretation of it. It is often difficult to remain impartial, but by doing so the expert witness retains credibility.[3]

- Do not confer with any witness following their testimony but prior to, or during, your own. This is an important point of process and objections have been raised by counsel and upheld when such conferring is suspected, or has taken place. Even trivial and seemingly innocuous exchanges have been construed as breaches of the judicial process.

- Answers to questions posed by counsel should be directed to the judge and jury. During cross-examination counsel may try to intimidate or unnerve witnesses using an array of subtle psychological ploys. It is easier to ignore such tactics by avoiding eye contact with counsel as much as possible. It is commonly advised that the witness should point his feet in the direction of the judge so that answers are similarly directed.

- Avoid technical expressions and acronyms that are unlikely to be known to the jury. This is particularly important when discussing or presenting computer evidence because the IT profession is awash with specialist terminology that is completely unfathomable to the layman. The author ill-advisedly broke his own rule, when giving evidence at the Hutton Inquiry in 2003:

> *In testimony Mr Wilding is now describing the internal workings of this device – the evidence is becoming quite complex; for example the word 'hexadecimal' has just been used – here on Sky News we're reaching for our dictionaries.*

- Technical explanations are often best presented using simple analogies and straightforward language. Above all, the expert witness should speak intelligible English and should explain complex systems or processes using simple phrases. Obscure words should not be used and if specialist terminology cannot be avoided it should be explained. Remember also, that there is a fine balance between the need for simplicity and the risk of being perceived as patronizing.

- When being cross-examined by counsel do not volunteer any more information than is strictly necessary. This does not mean that the expert witness should be evasive – far from it – but answers should be thoughtful, well considered and precise. By volunteering further comment unnecessarily, the witness may unwittingly provide counsel with information that he may try to use to undermine or discredit your evidence. Do not be intimidated by counsel using silence as a weapon – the temptation in such circumstances is to 'plug the gaps' by saying more than is necessary, a tendency that can adversely effect your authority and credibility.

- If you do not understand a question asked by counsel, seek clarification. Counsel may use arcane language or complex legal expressions, or pose questions that are intended to confuse. In the following exchange the expert witness, a veteran of many years, clearly prevailed:

---

3   'It is necessary that expert evidence presented to the court should be, and should be seen to be, the independent product of the expert, uninfluenced as to form or content by the exigencies of litigation. To the extent that it is not, the evidence is likely to be not only incorrect but self-defeating.' Lord Wilberforce, *Whitehouse v Jordan* [1981].

	Counsel:	'Is it not the case that my client never wrote this letter?'
	Expert:	'Yes.'
	Counsel:	'So you admit that my client never wrote this letter!'
	Expert:	'No.'
	Counsel:	'But you stated that my client never wrote this letter.'
	Expert:	'I did not. I stated that it was not the case that your client never wrote this letter.'

- Do not attempt to answer any question that extends beyond your area of expertise and do not make statements that you are unqualified to make. For example, you might casually observe, 'The signature looked forged to me' but counsel will quickly retort 'And since when have you been an expert on forged signatures?' This type of retort can be very effective at undermining both your confidence and authority. Facts are best. Do not proffer opinion unless expressly invited to do so and only within your area of competence.

- If you believe your case, state it. Do not be dissuaded by other possible, but improbable, explanations presented by counsel. A suitable reply to this line of questioning is: 'It is possible, but highly unlikely and I do not believe it to be the case.' Counsel may also attempt to force a witness into answering a question with a 'yes' or a 'no'. If such enforced brevity might mislead the court, it is important that you advise the judge accordingly.

- Avoid sarcasm, humour, conceit, pomposity, rudeness, profanity or superciliousness. It is also important that you are not defensive under questioning and under no circumstances should an expert witness enter into an argument with counsel, or resort to personal attacks or vilification.

- Admit mistakes, but do not grovel. It is also important to show reason and flexibility – your credibility will be seriously undermined should you vigorously defend or maintain a position that is untenable.

- If you do not know the answer to a question, say so.

- Do not lie or obfuscate. Lying in court (perjury) is a very serious criminal offence. You are under a sworn oath to tell the truth and it is your duty to do so.

- If possible, keep computers out of the courtroom. Opinions vary as to the advisability of demonstrating computer systems and processes in court. From my own experience, and from discussions with others who have presented computer evidence, I would strongly advise that computers and computer processes should only be demonstrated in court as a last resort. No actor voluntarily chooses to appear with children or animals – likewise, computers are volatile and unpredictable in their operation and you can be assured that on the occasion that you formally demonstrate any given computer, it will misbehave. Judges and juries are prone to impatience and an adjournment caused by a failed computer demonstration will win you no allies.

- If a computer demonstration is genuinely warranted, use high-resolution screen projection and make sure that the demonstration can be clearly seen and understood by the judge, the jury and counsel. Consider also the possibility of video recording any on-screen activity and use the video recording to demonstrate the defendant's computer, its software and processes.

- Never rely on jury members to operate computers or software. It may be tempting to hand out CDs and laptop computers with fanciful demonstrations but you can rest assured that such an exercise will cause vastly more confusion that it seeks to abate. Remember at all times that juries are selected at random from the electoral roll and that whilst a percentage of any given jury will be computer literate there will always be members of a jury who are unfamiliar with computer technology and may even be intimidated by it. You do not want to delay or impede proceedings because you have to instruct jury members on how to operate Windows!

- Printout, screen dumps and relational charts are usually more intelligible than on-screen demonstrations. Printout is tangible, accessible, intelligible and, most significantly, it is *familiar* to barristers, judges and juries. Printout can be exhibited in the exhibits bundle without the requirement for any specialist computer processing.

- Photographs, simple flow diagrams and link analysis charts are more accessible and comprehensible to the court than lengthy technical reports or dissertations, and are usually very effective for conveying complex relationships or situations.[4] Any diagram, chart or other visual aid should contain strictly factual information:

Defence counsel:	'Objection, Your Honour! These charts are highly prejudicial to the defendant's chances of a fair trial and I would request that they be ruled inadmissible.'
Prosecution counsel:	'Your Honour, these charts contain no theory or speculation and are based on verbatim electronic mail extracts from the Bulletin Board operated by the defendant and located in his front room. They simply show the relationships and discussions between the various correspondents and participants of this Bulletin Board.'
Judge:	'On the strict understanding that these charts depict provable relationships and verbatim conversations then I rule them admissible. I also find them extremely helpful. Objection overruled.'

- Try to get prosecution and defence to accept your flow charts, relational diagrams or graphics prior to the trial – it will save a considerable amount of time. Do not swamp the court with graphics or diagrams. Use them sparingly to good effect.

- Be self-reliant; never rely on anyone involved in your case when at court. You are the expert and you should have prepared your papers. Other persons at court are usually preoccupied by a range of concerns and will not necessarily have the time to check your witness statement, affidavit or exhibits.[5] If you have produced a statement, an affidavit or an exhibit then it is your responsibility to make sure that these things are present in the exhibits bundle and that they are ordered and referred to correctly.[6] Always double check statements, affidavits and exhibit bundles and do not let solicitors or anyone else rush you. Seek authority of your defence or prosecution counsel to examine statements, exhibits and so on.

- Take care when giving evidence about events or matters not directly known to you. Hearsay evidence, such as that of a witness who did not see or hear the incident in question but heard about it from someone else, is usually inadmissible.

---

4   An excellent link analysis software package is the Analysts Notebook from I2 Limited. See www.i2.co.uk.

5   Solicitors often delegate exhibit bundles to juniors or paralegals.

6   It is equally important to ensure that relevant procedural documentation is present. Until recently it was necessary in the United Kingdom to produce a Certificate of Evidence from Computer Records (Section 69, Schedule 3 paragraph 8 of the Police and Criminal Evidence Act) when producing computer evidence. Similar procedural documentation is required in other jurisdictions.

- It is always preferable to speak from first-hand experience. In computer crime investigation this normally means that the expert will have had direct access to the systems and processes upon which he is giving evidence. Direct observation is more compelling as evidence than hearsay. It is more credible to assert: 'The password to the system is "Iceberg". I know this because I entered into the system by entering it' than to state: 'I understand that the password to the system is "Iceberg" because Mr Smith told me so.' If you have not examined the systems and processes directly you may not be qualified to comment upon them and this will quickly become apparent under cross-examination. The question that you will be asked is: 'Did you examine the system directly?' If you cannot affirm that you did, your evidence may be contested vigorously.
- The expert should never assert the functionality of any technology or device without first proving the said functionality. For example, the expert may believe that exhibits (hardware and software) seized during a search warrant are capable of being used to forge the magnetic stripe data on payment cards but unless he can demonstrably prove this to be the case he should avoid asserting this capability as fact. The question you will be asked is: 'Have you proved this?' If you have not, your evidence and credibility will appear weak.

Finally, we must be resigned to the fact that absurd and outlandish claims may gain credence in court, even when there is no evidence whatsoever to support them, as the following case from October 2003 demonstrated:

> A 19-year-old accused of launching a denial of service attack on the US Port of Houston's navigation system was acquitted at Southwark Crown Court in the UK's first jury trial for this offence under the Computer Misuse Act 1990.
>
> Aaron Caffrey of Shaftesbury, Dorset, admitted involvement with a group of hackers called Allied Haxor Elite, and that his computer had been used to launch the attack on the Port of Houston's computer network in September 2001.
>
> In his defence, Caffrey claimed that the attack was launched by a Trojan horse program which also planted evidence on his machine. A forensic examination of Caffrey's PC found no trace of any such Trojan horse. However, Caffrey succeeded in convincing the jury that a Trojan could wipe itself completely following its execution, despite vigorous prosecution protests that no such technology existed.

19 *Exit Procedures*

I trust he joins you as he left us – fired with enthusiasm.
Letter, *Daily Telegraph*

Many acts of computer sabotage and vandalism have occurred through negligence or non-existent exit procedures. It is vital that should an employee be dismissed or suspended from the workplace, his access to key systems and processes should be revoked. Similarly, if fraud or wrongdoing is suspected, computer systems and the data on them should be secured so that the suspect cannot hide or destroy evidence.

Exit procedures are necessary to:

- preserve evidence;
- safeguard critical systems and processes from sabotage;
- secure and account for company assets assigned to the departing employee.

It is normally the case that an exit interview will be conducted with the departing employee. Human resources will usually conduct this, although security and audit may also attend should the person involved be suspended or fired for serious wrongdoing. If an employee is to be removed from the workplace, it is essential that they are accompanied at all times, having being notified of their dismissal or suspension, up until the point of their departure from the premises.

Communicate the departure

A typical reason as to why things go awry is that human resources may fail to inform the IT department of an employee's imminent departure – the computer accounts thus remain active on the system providing the opportunity for the ex-employee to regain access. A breakdown in communication between relevant departments, or a failure or absence of procedures, has caused many notable and serious incidents.

CASE STUDY – LACK OF PREPARATION

A solicitor approached a firm of corporate investigators on behalf of his client. The client suspected that an employee had stolen proprietary software, source code, customer databases, methodologies, marketing and business development plans. The employee had been suspended and placed on 'gardening leave'. He had been 'gardening' for six weeks. The solicitor requested advice on how an investigation should proceed in order to prove, or disprove, these suspicions.

His client was facing lengthy legal proceedings on the grounds of unfair dismissal. Neither the solicitor nor his client had any evidence that any information had actually been stolen other than rumours, office gossip and other hearsay.

The information believed to have been misappropriated was stored electronically, so it seemed reasonable to review the suspended employee's laptop computer, his desktop computer in the office, his user directory on the company fileserver and the Compaq personal digital assistant (PDA) with which he had been supplied. All of these devices had been purchased by the company and were its property. The investigators were advised that there were no significant legal obstacles to prevent or impede the examination of the data stored on them.

The investigators recommended that the mobile telephone billings, and the software logs of incoming and outgoing calls from the suspect's office telephone extension should be interrogated. They were informed that the mobile telephone was the property of the company, as were the itemized telephone bills and the software logs. Again, there seemed to be no significant legal hurdles to prevent the analysis of the telecommunications data.

Additionally, the investigators requested an inventory of all items located in the vicinity of the former employee's desk at the time of his suspension and sought assurances that certain vital actions had been taken at the time of the employee's departure.

The scope of the recommended investigation is outlined in Table 19.1 in which evidential sources are itemized and their relevance explained along with a series of recommended actions. Unfortunately, the lack of preparation by HR and its failure to coordinate with the internal IT department confounded virtually every suggested avenue of enquiry.

As can be seen, the actual state of affairs (column 4) was very much at odds with the recommended actions (column 3) and left much to be desired.

The lessons here are self-evident. For some inexplicable reason, departing employees are usually required to return their company cars or to relinquish membership of the company golf club or gymnasium but are often not required to surrender company-owned laptop computers, notebooks, PDAs, mobile telephones or other electronic devices or access tokens.

Revoke access on departure

DGI has investigated dozens of cases where employees have deleted or destroyed system and data files on computers because their access to the systems was not revoked concurrently with their departure from employment. In one such case, a disgruntled programmer knocked out a number of corporate websites administered and developed by his former employer. Having established a simple Telnet connection he proceeded to delete thousands of related files. His USERID and password remained active and valid for more than two months after he had been made redundant, and would probably never have been revoked had the attack not been so blatant.

A similar incident occurred in 1997, leaving the victim organization with no recourse:

Table 19.1 Case study: recommended actions and actual status

Evidence	Relevance	Recommended action	Actual status	Comment
Laptop computer and laptop bag provided to the suspect.	A likely source of evidence to prove misappropriated data and conspiracy to defraud.	An immediate forensic review of the data, documentation and electronic mail on the laptop. The review to comply with criminal prosecution standards. The laptop bag to be searched as it might contain evidential documents, diskettes or other items of interest.	The laptop computer was confirmed as the company's property. However, the laptop and bag were never returned to the company. The suspect retained them after his suspension. They were believed still to be in his possession.	HR should have secured the laptop immediately the employee was suspended and arranged for it to be processed to proper evidential standards. The suspect had ample opportunity to destroy evidence on the laptop using positive erasure software, or to impede inspection using other destructive software or hardware. He could have disposed of the laptop altogether.
Diskettes, CD-ROMs, Zip or Jaz drives, memory sticks etc.	Often overlooked sources of evidence.	Immediate forensic review.	It was rumoured that the suspect had copied files from the server to a CD-ROM.	Intellectual property is often removed on removable media. A forensic review of the laptop or workstation might have proven this to be the case.
Desktop computer used by the suspect in his office.	Data is often stored on the local hard disks of workstations, either intentionally or by default due to the functioning of the operating system.	A forensic review to determine whether misappropriated data was stored or transmitted via the workstation, or whether there were other incriminating documents or communications.	The IT support desk formatted the machine's hard disk, and installed a fresh operating system. It was reallocated to another employee within hours of the suspect being suspended. Other users operated the workstation daily for at least six weeks after the suspect's suspension.	The IT support desk should never have re-conditioned the PC. HR should have secured this computer immediately the suspect was suspended and its contents should have been imaged using forensic software. The subsequent actions on this machine destroyed residual evidence and rendered any recoverable data on it inadmissible. The chain of evidence in this instance was irretrievably broken.

Evidence	Relevance	Recommended action	Actual status	Comment
The suspect's user directory on the fileserver.	Files in this directory might be relevant to the investigation.	The relevant directories should be copied to a CD for review. It might also have been possible to salvage deleted files on the fileserver. Backup tapes should be recovered and their contents reviewed.	The contents of the suspect's directory were deleted and the directory removed two weeks after his suspension. The backup tapes that contained the suspect's directories were subsequently recycled and the data on them was overwritten.	HR should have instructed that the suspect's directories be secured and made available for inspection. Backup tapes for each week should have been retained alongside relevant software. The actions taken effectively denied the investigation the opportunity to review the fileserver directories.
The suspect's e-mail correspondence on the server.	E-mail has proved an excellent source of both intelligence and evidence.	For immediate review.	The suspect had deleted e-mails en masse. Backup tapes had been recycled and the e-mail could not be restored.	The suspect's remote access account was not revoked – he could have deleted these e-mails subsequent to his departure.
Compaq PDA supplied to the suspect by the company.	A probable source of evidence, relating particularly to contacts and the identities of possible conspirators.	An immediate forensic review to extract all contacts and proprietary information.	It was confirmed that the company owned the PDA. However, the suspect retained the PDA after his suspension and was believed to still have it in his possession.	HR should have secured the PDA immediately after the employee was suspended and arranged for it to be examined to proper evidential standards. The suspect had ample opportunity to destroy evidence on the PDA, or dispose of the device.
Documents, faxes, printout, diary entries, calendar entries, contact lists, business cards and other evidence from the suspect's desk and immediate work area.	A desk search will often reveal evidence of malpractice, or will reveal clues and investigative leads.	Material to be reviewed.	The suspect's work area was never reviewed. Documentation and other items were disposed of and the desk and work area reallocated to another employee.	HR should have impounded the suspect's desk and work area upon his departure. Documentation and other relevant items should have been examined and archived securely for subsequent analysis.

Evidence	Relevance	Recommended action	Actual status	Comment
The suspect's cellular telephone	A download of contacts, telephone numbers, SMS text messages and call durations to assist the investigation.	Data to be downloaded forensically and to evidential standards for review.	There was confusion about the ownership of the telephone. It was understood that the suspect owned the cellular telephone. The suspect retained the telephone upon his departure but it was believed that the number had since been disconnected.	HR should have established the ownership of the telephone prior to the suspect's suspension. If it was company property it should have been retrieved immediately. Unauthorized access to the telephone would constitute an unauthorized access offence under Section 1 of the Computer Misuse Act 1990.
Itemized telephone bills (cellular)	To establish contacts, frequency and duration of calls.	Billing data to be reviewed.	It was believed that the suspect paid call charges for the mobile handset directly from a personal account.	The billing data was not the property of the company but belonged to the suspect. A court order, warrant or subpoena would be required to gain lawful access to this billing data.
Voicemail	To review messages that might be relevant.	Voicemail recordings to be copied to CD and relevant messages transcribed with date and time of call.	The voicemail was not reviewed nor was it available from backup tapes.	The opportunity to review the voicemail was wasted. Messages on a telephone answering machine were also not reviewed – the cassette tape was subsequently overwritten.
Fax memory	Transmission numbers in the log may have shown contact to relevant numbers. Fax transmissions may have been recorded in memory.	Retrieve and review.	The fax transmission log covering the relevant period was purged from memory.	

Evidence	Relevance	Recommended action	Actual status	Comment
Photocopier memory	Copies may have been recorded in memory.	Retrieve and review.	This was not the case.	

Other recommended actions

Evidence	Relevance	Recommended action	Actual status	Comment
Check the status of the suspect's remote access account.	To ensure that he was denied remote access to core systems.	The remote access server (RAS) account for the suspect must be revoked and his secure ID authentication card retrieved.	The suspect's RAS account was still active, six weeks after his suspension. The suspect also retained his authentication token.	HR should have directed IT to disable the account when the suspect was suspended. His authentication token should have been retrieved at the same time. Having failed to do this, the suspect still had access to the company's core systems and could have used this access to misappropriate further information, or to access or destroy data, or to plant logic bombs or other unauthorized software or processes.
Ensure that all keys, key cards, swipe cards and other access control devices had been removed from the suspect.	To restrict his access to the company's premises and property.	Check the return of keys and access control tokens. Change PIN numbers on access control keypads.	Keys and swipe cards had been removed from the suspect when he was suspended. However, keypad PINs to sensitive areas had not been changed.	Disgruntled employees have been known to return to premises after hours in order to damage systems. Remember that keys can be duplicated – it may be necessary to change the locks. Do not forget company car keys!

A computer programmer had his contract terminated by a bank on the suspicion that he had leaked confidential client data to a national newspaper. The IT department subsequently revoked the programmer's network access but forgot that he also had a remote access server (RAS) account. The programmer logged in via RAS during the following weekend and wiped a mass of data and processes.

The bank's lawyers were confident that his actions constituted a criminal offence under Section 3 of the Computer Misuse Act 1990. Unfortunately, however, both RAS and network audit monitoring were either inactive or insufficiently attuned to record the attack. A dossier of circumstantial evidence and hearsay testimony was compiled, but the lawyers concluded that without supporting logs and forensic corroboration this was insufficient to support a criminal prosecution.

This case reveals the vital importance of audit trails and event logging. Investigating any incident of computer misuse without these records is virtually impossible (see Chapter 17).

 In another case, a former director of a vehicle accessory supply company retained remote access to its stock control and pricing database for 18 months after his resignation. He had resigned in order to establish a competitive venture – again, nobody thought to revoke his remote access or database account. Within days of component prices being changed, they were subtly undercut by the former director's new venture. The individual even demonstrated how he could still access the database to undercover investigators.

Other incidents have included former employees, contractors and others committing system sabotage, attempted extortion, data misappropriation and the on-line destruction (and, a few instances, the retrospective amendment) of potentially incriminating documents and e-mails. It is also important to remember that current employees have been known to misuse the accounts of other departed members of staff, contractors and temporary staff that were never revoked. The ever-present phenomenon of people and departments sharing passwords only adds to this danger.

These cases are rarely reported, let alone prosecuted, and saboteurs and malevolent IT staff fired from employment are often free to apply for contracts and jobs elsewhere entirely unhindered. Many victim companies mistakenly presume that they are absolved of any civil or criminal liability should these people, having departed their employ, re-offend in the future.

The threat from fired or suspended computer staff is significant, particularly from network administrators. The following recent prosecutions of computer intrusion and sabotage have been reported by the US Department of Justice.[1]

- In September 2004, Neal Cotton, former network administrator of Manhattan-based computer consulting firm Cyber City, Inc. pleaded guilty to attacking the company's computer system. In April 2003, Cotton was told that he would be fired. The following evening, the company experienced a computer intrusion, which wiped out the data of several important clients, rendered computer networks useless and caused irrevocable data loss. Cyber City's direct and consequential losses exceeded $100 000.
- In February 2004, Peter Borghard, 26, a former network administrator of Manhattan-based ISP Netline Services, Inc., pleaded guilty to a felony charge of computer intrusion against his former employer's systems. Borghard left the

---

1   See http://www.usdoj.gov/criminal/cybercrime/cccases.html#INTL.

company abruptly and without explanation in October 2002. Shortly after quitting, he sued for back salary he claimed he was owed. In January 2003, Netline experienced two computer intrusions. The first attack wiped out data and configuration settings on the network and Netline's customers were denied e-mail service for approximately 15 hours. A subsequent attack erased operating systems and configuration settings on other machines.

- In February 2004, Andrew Garcia, a former network administrator at Viewsonic Corporation, a manufacturer of computer monitors, was sentenced to a one-year prison sentence. Approximately two weeks after his contract was terminated, the 39-year-old accessed Viewsonic's system remotely and deleted critical files on one of the servers that he had maintained. The loss of these files rendered the server inoperable and the company's Taiwan office was unable to access important data for several days.

- In April 2003, Alan Giang Tran, 28, a former network administrator at the Airline Coach Service and Sky Limousine Company in California pleaded guilty to a charge of hacking into its computer system and destroying a customer database, shutting down the computer server, Internet-based credit card processing system and website. Consequently, the company was unable to dispatch drivers to pick up clients resulting in the loss of thousands of dollars of revenue. Federal investigators executing a search warrant at Tran's home found a folder marked 'retaliation'.

- In February 2003, Kenneth Patterson, 38, a former employee of American Eagle Outfitters, was charged with trafficking in passwords and information that could have permitted others to gain unauthorized access to his former employer's network. Patterson allegedly posted the usernames and passwords of American Eagle Outfit employees to a Yahoo notice board together with instructions on how to hack into the company's WAN. Patterson was also charged with a series of computer intrusions in November and December 2002, allegedly made to deny computer services to the company's stores in the United States and Canada during the Christmas shopping season.

- In September 2002, Richard Glenn Dopps, 35, pleaded guilty to illegally accessing the computer system of his former employer and reading the e-mails of company executives for the purpose of gaining a commercial advantage at his new job with a competitor. Until February 2001, The Bergman Companies (TBC), a contracting firm, employed Dopps. After leaving TBC to work for a competitor, Dopps continued to access TBC's computer systems on more than 20 occasions. He read e-mail messages of TBC executives to stay informed of the firm's ongoing business and to obtain a commercial advantage for his new employer.

BACKDOORS

It is also important to bear it in mind that IT staff and computer literate employees may implement unauthorized 'backdoors' into the systems that they administer or maintain, which they may use to obtain remote access regardless of whether their official dial-in account is revoked:

In January and February 1999 the National Library of Medicine (NLM) in the United States, relied on by doctors and medical professionals from around the world for the latest information on diseases, treatments, drugs, and dosage units, suffered a series of computer intrusions during which *administrator passwords* were obtained and hundreds of files downloaded. FBI investigators identified the intruder as Montgomery Johns Gray III, a former computer programmer for NLM, whose access to the computer system had been revoked. Gray was able to access the system through a 'backdoor' he had created in the programming code whilst employed at NLM. The FBI arrested Gray within days of the intrusions. Subsequent examination of his seized computers disclosed *evidence of the intrusions*. (Author's italics)

If a backdoor is suspected, a full systems audit should be conducted to identify and disable all redundant or unidentified user accounts. The defensive measures to identify and prevent logic bombs shown in Chapter 7 apply equally to protecting computer systems against backdoors. The independence of computer security and audit staff from the organization's wider IT department is fundamental in this respect, to facilitate autonomous inspection and investigation. IT security and audit staff should be mandated actively to search for and identify unauthorized programs, user accounts and routines on critical systems and dial-in facilities.

Secure all equipment on departure

Former members of staff have often returned laptop computers to organizations with the information stored on them wiped clean. The use of evidence elimination software products is gradually increasing. Of 70 reactive investigations conducted by DGI in a 12-month period commencing February 2002, the concerted use of positive erasure software was observed on four occasions. In certain cases, a subsequent forensic examination of these computers has enabled the forensic examiner to state the manufacturer of the cleansing software used, the date and time of its use and even the names of the files that were eliminated. While an inference may be drawn from these technical observations, they are relatively ineffectual when compared with the probative value of the evidence that might otherwise have been found. This re-emphazises the absolute necessity to secure equipment at the moment of suspension or dismissal:

 The manager disappeared after it was discovered that he had stolen nearly US$1 million through redirecting company cheques. The investigation team arrived on site with the immediate intention of tracking him to an address or hideout.

They sought the whereabouts of his computer and were informed that it had been reconditioned and re-assigned. Eventually, they tracked the machine down. Fortuitously, its hard drive had been formatted at high level, rather than using an unconditional command. The local IT department had installed a fresh operating system onto the computer and it was at first feared that no trace of its former user would be found upon its hard disk. In fact the newly installed operating system had overwritten only a percentage of the available hard disk space, which left a mass of residual data to be discovered. The fugitive's address was located in an unallocated cluster on the disk as was proof of the cheque diversion, including the two banks to which falsified cheques had been submitted. An informant confirmed the address and stated that the fugitive had been seen there on the previous evening. It had been a close call – had the local IT department applied an unconditional format to the PC, the information would never have been recovered.

If personnel are suspended or fired for misbehaviour or suspected impropriety, it is vital that keys, computers, access control devices and any proprietary information are retrieved. Remember also, that keys can be duplicated and that it may be necessary to change the locks on certain doors.

Data from computer systems should be secured in a forensically sound manner. The data need not necessarily be reviewed but it should at least be archived in the event that the employee sues for unfair dismissal or seeks redress through an industrial tribunal. In cases where employees have been allowed to retain their computers they have often attempted to destroy incriminating or embarrassing data. While these attempts have rarely succeeded, they have seriously impeded investigations.

Employees should also be dissuaded from using their own computers, PDAs, mobile telephones or other devices that can connect to company networks. The company will normally only have a legal right of access to these devices if they are its de facto property. In many jurisdictions, the unauthorized inspection of a computer system (for example, one purchased by an employee) constitutes a criminal offence – in the United Kingdom, for example, such inspection constitutes an offence under Section 1 of the Computer Misuse Act 1990.

It is advisable that the company should provide mobile telephones, and all cellular billing should be paid by the company. This will enable the company legally to undertake call-log analysis.

The current fashion for home-working and mobile working imposes additional risks and difficulties. If possible, the organization should stipulate a 'right of audit' to computer systems used by any employee for business purposes at home, as part of the standard employment contract. This right of audit is rarely written into employment contracts, and it is normally not possible to access people's home computers without a court order. This is the case even when the employee is in possession of company data. Obviously, if the company has supplied the computer for home use it has the right to demand the machine's return – but not necessarily a right to enter the user's residence, or to inspect the computer's contents or any other materials in his possession. To prevent disputes about ownership, the organization should always retain its purchase orders, receipts, delivery notices, payment advices and any other documentation showing proof of purchase. The return of any equipment used at home should be done in the presence of the employee at the earliest possible opportunity, and preferably on the day of his being notified of his suspension or dismissal.

The organization should also check whether it is paying for the employee's Internet ISP, T3, ISDN, ADSL or broadband service, as it may wish to terminate any such arrangement. This aspect of exit procedures is often neglected. As a result the accounts payable department, unaware of the employee's departure, does not discontinue the direct debit or payment settlement arrangements with the service providers involved. The employee, particularly if in a managerial position, may have raised standing orders within the accounts payable to various suppliers and these will merit attention.

Company cars should not be driven by the ex-employee but should be collected for return by a trusted member of staff with the appropriate driver's insurance cover. One individual of the author's acquaintance stole his company car upon being fired; another smashed his company car into a bollard causing it to be written off while others have sabotaged or similarly damaged company vehicles or deliberately lost or hidden the keys to them.

Obviously, exit procedures involve more than just securing the computer systems and evidential sources. You wouldn't fire an aircraft mechanic and then allow him to return to the hangars unattended, monkey wrench at the ready! Any heavy plant, critical system, item or process that might be sabotaged requires careful protection:

> The employee was fired in the morning and escorted from the premises. He decided to drown his sorrows in a local pub, which he accomplished with spectacular effect. Later that afternoon, thoroughly inebriated, he returned to the company unchallenged and locked himself inside the main computer suite. In a fit of pique, he threatened to urinate on the servers and telecommunications racks. He was dissuaded from doing so only when the possibility of electrocution and death was brought to his attention.

Security guards, receptionists and others who control access to the premises should be advised of any dismissals or suspensions, so that they may intercept those involved should they attempt to return to the building. In large organizations, it is advisable to distribute photographs to security personnel and receptionists of those deemed *personae non gratae*.

It should also be considered that the departed employee will probably remain in contact with friends and associates within the company, and that he may cajole or otherwise persuade these people to destroy or conceal evidence or to commit other offences on his behalf. DGI has investigated several cases where people dismissed from the workplace have regained access by proxy. We note that secretaries and personal assistants have on occasions remained loyal to their bosses and continued to obey or protect them after their departure. This phenomenon highlights the absolute necessity to secure all potential evidence immediately (see the sample checklist in Table 19.2).

System lockdown

It is clearly vital to secure systems against both physical and logical sabotage, particularly in the event that IT staff and others with systems knowledge are suspended or dismissed. If this is envisaged, it is advisable to assemble a suitably qualified technical response team to take the systems off-line temporarily, whilst they are audited and secured. This exercise is known as a full systems lockdown.

All systems should be taken off-line and secured *before* any dismissal or suspension takes place.

Administrative passwords should be changed on all systems, the accounts of the departed employees should be deactivated, and an audit conducted for each system to identify any obvious vulnerabilities.

Telephone answering systems and voicemail should also be secured against tampering or the unauthorized re-recording of answer messages.

For controlling a full system lockdown it is advisable to prepare a comprehensive schedule of every system in use and its status. The schedule should include systems and websites hosted by third parties. Table 19.3 shows a sample checklist.

FINALLY…

There is an apocryphal story of a disgruntled production line worker in a confectionery factory who was tasked with manufacturing sticks of rock. Following a heated row with the boss during which he was fired, he returned to the programming system that controlled the sugary wording that ran through each stick. Normally, this system dutifully wrote 'Kiss Me Quick', 'I Love You!' or 'Hug Me!' through the continuous tube of sickly pink and white candy. He changed these bland sentiments to read 'FUCK YOU' and then pressed the batch-processing button. The production run measured approximately one and a quarter miles in length, all of which had to be written off.

Table 19.2 Sample inventory of items to be returned

Item	Asset number	Returned	Date/time	Employee signature	Received by	Comments
Laptop computer, bag, port replicator, mouse, power supply	10021	✓	15/08/04	Simon Jones	Tom Smith Manager, HR	Personal documents found in laptop bag returned
Modem and PCMCIA card	PCMCIA – 10046	✓ ✗	15/08/04	Simon Jones	Tom Smith Manager, HR	Modem internal to computer **ACTION** ☛ Recover PCMCIA card
Computer network authentication token	12652	✗	15/08/04	**ACTION** ☛		Deactivate network token
Other authentication tokens – SWIFT/EFT and on-line payment systems	N/A	N/A	N/A	N/A		N/A
Diskettes, CD-ROM, Zip or Jaz drives, memory sticks, other electronic media	Zip – 14673	✓ ✗	15/08/04	Simon Jones	Tom Smith Manager, HR	14 diskettes and two Zip disks secured **ACTION** ☛ Determine status
Computer backups containing any proprietary company data or confidential information	Status unknown	✗	15/08/04	**ACTION** ☛		Determine status
Desktop PC at employee's home address, printer and peripherals, network authentication terminal	PC – 19874 Printer – 12567	✗	15/08/04	**ACTION** ☛		Supplied by the company for 'home working' Recover all equipment that was supplied for home use

Item	Detail		Date	Actioned by	Responsible	Action/Notes
PDA, electronic notebook, personal organizer	Compaq PDA – 10567	✓	15/08/04	Simon Jones	Tom Smith Manager, HR	Damage noted to PDA case
Blackberry		✓	15/08/04	Simon Jones	Tom Smith Manager, HR	Recovered
Mobile telephone with SIM card	10347	✓	15/08/04	Simon Jones	Tom Smith Manager, HR	ACTION ☛ Check for SIM card
Photocopy machine control card	Canon Control Card III	✓	15/08/04	Simon Jones	Tom Smith Manager, HR	Redistributed on 17/08/04
Dictaphone	15436	✗	15/08/04	ACTION ☛	Tom Smith Manager, HR	Recover Dictaphone Recover cassette tapes
Digital camera	10245	✗	15/08/04	ACTION ☛		Recover camera, software and memory card(s)
Keys	126	✓ ✗	15/08/04	Simon Jones	Tom Smith Manager, HR	ACTION ☛ Locker key, gymnasium, is missing – recover and search
Car keys	BMW 7 Series, dark blue Index: R207NET	✓	15/08/04	Simon Jones	Tom Smith Manager, HR	ACTION ☛ Establish location of car and note its condition – check interior, glove compartment and boot
Access control swipe card	578390623592	✗	15/08/04	ACTION ☛		Recover swipe card Deactivate user account
Company confidential reports and hardcopy	Status unknown	✗	15/08/04	ACTION ☛		Determine status
Company credit card	Recover	✗	15/08/04	ACTION ☛		Terminate account

Table 19.3 Sample schedule for a full system lockdown

System	Current status	Revoke user access and audit redundant accounts	Active administrator accounts	Administrator passwords changed?	System secured and reactivated?
RAS	Off-line	✓	2	✓	Scheduled 15/08/04 (a.m.)
VPN	Off-line	✓	2	✓	Scheduled 15/08/04 (a.m.)
Citrix	Off-line	**ACTION**	2	✓	Scheduled 15/08/04 (p.m.)
VMS/Oracle	Off-line	**ACTION**	3	✓	Scheduled 16/08/04
AS/400	Off-line	**ACTION**	2	✓	Scheduled 16/08/04
Exchange	On-line	✓	2	✓	✓
Wi-Fi	Off-line	**ACTION**	2	✓	Scheduled 16/08/04
Voicemail	On-line	✓	2	✓	✓
Telephone system			**SECURED**		
Hosted websites			**DETERMINE STATUS**		
Online subscription services			**DETERMINE STATUS**		

20 *Conclusion*

Know your enemy and know yourself and you can fight a hundred battles without disaster.

Sun Tzu, *The Art of War* (c. 500 BC)

Many of the incidents of sabotage, fraud and other bloody mindedness described in this book could have been defused or prevented altogether through the better management of the people who went on to commit them. Grievances, often entirely justified, have been the root cause of many workplace crimes and misdemeanours. Management that is despotic, bullying, self-serving or corrupt will naturally engender dissent, and will reap what it sows. If people are unhappy, feel persecuted or unfairly treated, they are likely to cause damage or disruption. If you kick a dog for long enough, it will eventually bite you. This is a simple truth.

Proactive and fair management, on the other hand, can nip dissent in the bud, because it is paying attention to what is happening out on the floors. Good managers never bully or intimidate because they do not need to, and they instinctively know how counter-productive these tactics are. They are respected because they are consistently wise, firm and fair. Their judgment is reliable and they have natural authority that is acknowledged by the workforce. There is, then, a fine but very distinct line between *authoritative* management, which leads a willing workforce by example, and *authoritarian* management, which causes resentment, obstruction and inertia.

Things also go wrong when management is weak, aloof, inattentive or disinterested. If a manager doesn't know or care what is happening in his domain, or is frightened to investigate and find out, the opportunity for wrongdoing, error and stupidity increases significantly. Error and stupidity are potentially as dangerous as fraud – arguably more so – and are also more prevalent. By reducing the opportunity for fraud we mitigate the risks of error and stupidity also.

It would be misleading to imply that all workplace crimes and misdemeanours result from poor management. Some people, thankfully a small minority, are plain evil.

The best way to bar the sociopath or criminal from your place of work is not to employ him in the first place. Detective Chief Superintendent Ken Farrow, the head of the City of London Police Economic Crimes Unit, recently reported[1] that his officers see, on average, five cases a week of fraudsters who have been sacked by one firm, only to be taken on by another soon thereafter. DCS Farrow complains that firms are failing to report employees who commit fraud to the police or to flag criminal activity when writing references for disgraced former employees:

---

1   *Sunday Telegraph*, March 13, 2005.

We are very concerned by firms, particularly banks, that do not want the embarrassment of disclosing that they have got a problem with fraud. Therefore what happens is these people are able to move on and get a job with another financial institution and steal a second, third or fourth time. Non-reporting of these crimes is itself a criminal act. Firms who do not do so are running the risk of prosecution and/or a large fine from the Financial Services Authority.

Thorough pre-employment screening is clearly indicated here as a key defensive measure central to the control strategy, and yet only a handful of commercial organizations actually avail themselves of this powerful pre-emptive resource.

A consistent thread that runs through the chapters of this book is the need to impose *control* – over systems, processes and, crucially, people. Where there is a determination to do so, systems and processes may be configured securely. Controlling people, however, is the real challenge. Most IT regimes seek to impose control over people by using technology – strait-jacketing them into specific roles with appropriate levels of access and authority. But this regime, taken in isolation, while ostensibly under control, is really only administered at a machine and process level. If the people who access and use the systems are not themselves controlled, they may find cause or reason to subvert or circumvent the various technical restraints imposed upon them. Likewise, it is absolutely vital that people are properly managed and controlled in the immediate aftermath of a security breach or incident, including those tasked with securing systems and collating evidence, support staff, witnesses, bystanders and, *vitally*, the suspect or perpetrator.

The current fixation with technical controls often means that people are neglected, taken for granted or demeaned. Conversely, managers who engage and interact with the workforce at all levels, attain a significant measure of control because they know what's going on, are listening and reacting all of the time. There are shelves of books about managing people – this book is not one of them, but the effective management of individual human beings is absolutely critical in developing and maintaining a secure and harmonious operating environment.

Achieving 'total control' of the type sometimes promised us in the marketing brochures of the IT security industry is clearly impossible in any environment other than one that is totally stagnant. From an operational, philosophical and ethical standpoint, such total control is probably undesirable also, likely to stifle creativity, suppress character and degrade the sense of personal wellbeing and self-esteem. We must also be realistic and acknowledge that beyond the confines of our own desks and the limits of our immediate computer access, most of us, including even the most competent managers, are often in the dark. We cannot know what is really happening on a 1000 node network – technically it might be possible to look at every PC, every mail message, every document, spreadsheet and web access, but in practice this will never happen. Proclaiming total and absolute control in this ever-shifting environment, as some risk and security managers rashly have, is absurd. At best, we may install tripwire monitoring to alert us to suspicious events. The oft-cited phenomenon of 'information overload' – which in our context is a vast ocean of data in which we find ourselves in danger of drowning – is a major hindrance to our control efforts.

There is much emphasis at the moment on empowerment – giving responsibility and authority to employees, so that decisions may be made quickly and efficiently at the lowest level of management escalation achievable. This is an eminently sensible approach, well suited to any organization that must react quickly and dynamically. But empowerment should not be confused with laissez-faire – empowerment without control descends rapidly into anarchy. The developers of new technologies, operating systems and software emphasize freedom, convenience and personal empowerment when selling to the individual but rarely mention responsibility or personal accountability in the use of systems. This conflict between the need for personal privacy and freedom on the one hand, and the control requirements of corporate or national security on the other, is also apparent in legislation. The dichotomy between satisfying the individual's right to liberty while enforcing law and order is age old. Finding the right balance in the workplace is the trick, and this will depend significantly on the corporate culture and the tolerance of the workforce to restrictions or limitations on its freedom. A control environment that is perceived as unfair or oppressive is likely to cause a rebellion, or engender a sabotage mentality. Great care is required, therefore, when devising controls and implementing them – arbitrarily removing people's privileges, in whatever form, for example, invariably causes conflict.

A key element of managing people, whether empowered or not, is ensuring that they know what is expected of them and the types of behaviour that will not be tolerated. In this respect, a clearly defined, unambiguous policy on the acceptable use of technology in the workplace is essential, because any behaviour, however iniquitous, can be justified or excused in the absence of such rules. A suggested policy is provided at Appendix 2, which underpins any and every other control objective or measure. Remember, however, that rules are not the same as controls – rules provide a formal disciplinary framework only, and cannot, in themselves, prevent people from misbehaving.

The Lord's Prayer intones, 'And lead us not into temptation, but deliver us from evil'. Fraud, criminality and misbehaviour generally are often instigated when people are *tempted*. I was trained that one person in five is inherently honest and will never steal or lie, three are opportunist and will do wrong if they believe their actions will go undetected or unpunished, and one person in five will always submit to temptation, regardless of the consequences. I know of no scientific evidence to support this assertion, but it has always served well as a rule of thumb when conducting investigations or devising controls. Every control weakness that we identify and eradicate from the workplace may alternatively be considered as a *temptation removed*.

Regarding systems and processes, if these are configured so that they cannot be audited, or the people using them cannot be identified, we clearly lose control. In our endeavours to impose order, the importance of correctly identifying the 'red elements' – those computers or other technologies used to initiate or execute an offence or to break the rules – is vital. If we can't find these red elements, perhaps because our logging or documentation are derelict, our investigation will be stymied.

Another consistent theme of this book is that control of systems and processes must extend beyond simple checklist and tick-box auditing. Through subterfuge, the concerted fraudster or computer criminal will, in all likelihood, obtain a copy of your audit procedures, your computer security manual and your incident response plan. He may read your e-mail, download the contents of your computer, use surveillance technology and other devious tactics. He will thus know your control methodology and will determine how best to circumvent it or otherwise subvert it. Remember, that this person does not care about your rules, and is only interested in identifying control weaknesses that may be exploited. To confound his efforts we must do the same.

Auditors sometimes protest, 'We are watchdogs, not bloodhounds!' They are there, they assert, to enforce the rules, but not actively to seek out or investigate any transgression of them. This mantra is sometimes heard at audit and control conferences, raised when the spectre of a proactive, determined and rigorous investigation of workplace wrongdoing is invoked. Many auditors do not consider it their duty or responsibility to detect or investigate fraud. But if the auditor in a company doesn't rise to this challenge, *who will*? If you do not look for fraud or workplace criminality, it will flourish. Ironically, fraud is frequently committed by *managers* – those despotic, bullying, self-serving or corrupt ones already referred to – which may explain this reticence to investigate and confront them.

It is a throwaway cliché, admittedly, but we should prepare for the unexpected, in all its guises. Published surveys consistently state that between 70 and 80 per cent of corporate fraud and computer crime is committed by employees and others who reside *inside* the firewall. The City of London Police Economic Crimes Unit, for example, has reported that 80 per cent of fraud against firms in London's financial and banking district is perpetrated by or with the assistance of the victim companies' own staff.

Why, then, are organizations generally so inept at preventing this threat, identifying it, or responding to it? Is the insider threat really so unexpected? Or do we just refuse to believe or comprehend that our friends, colleagues, associates or employees could do us harm? I believe that many organizations, particularly small and medium enterprises (SMEs), do not take this threat seriously at all, and only do so when their benightedness results in impending calamity. This is not a case of the ostrich putting its head in the sand, because with many SMEs, and a handful of large organizations that really should know better, no threat is even perceived. It is symptomatic, instead, of a potentially fatal combination of arrogance and inexperience often seen in those who manage new and fast-expanding businesses.

In light of this, the prevailing message of this book is that all organizations must:

- acknowledge the insider threat and better understand how and why it arises;
- be proactive and by understanding the insider threat, seek to prevent it;
- always investigate the insider threat when and where it is suspected;
- devise and test contingency plans to respond appropriately, *before* this threat manifests itself.

Technology comes and goes. With technical publications, the information provided is often outdated before the ink is dry on the page. But certain fundamental principles are evergreen. I contend that the ten analytical methods to progress an investigation that are described in Chapter 16 will remain in force until the invention of time travel or equally astonishing advances in psychic or extra sensory perception, while the fundamental principles of incident response and evidence handling discussed within these covers are etched in granite.

Appendices

1 Critical Point Auditing – Identifying the Jugular Vein

Critical point auditing is a risk assessment methodology that aims to identify the systems, processes and people that could expose an organization to those catastrophic risks that threaten its very survival or continuity. These risks, if realized, are analogous to severing the corporate jugular vein or striking the temple; the victim haemorrhages to death or suffers fatal paralysis:

 A manufacturing company was concerned about the security of its mainframe computer, which controlled the shipment of approximately £400 million worth of product annually. The management was particularly worried that the mainframe was vulnerable to attack by computer hackers and that its failure, even for a short duration, would impact heavily on shipments to regional distributors and hence revenues.

A computer security review was commissioned and some improvements were recommended to strengthen logical access control. However, it was clear to the reviewers that a determined attack on the company's computer system could be launched more effectively and speedily using a *hacksaw*. Unprotected trunk cabling transmitting the entire computer and communications traffic of the company could be accessed from a public highway directly outside the company's headquarters. Access to this unprotected cabling was completely open, the area was not fenced, nor monitored by CCTV, flood lighting or in any way guarded.

The assessment methodology uses a 'clean sheet of paper' to identify and quantify these vulnerabilities and exposures. It ignores established audit procedures on the premise that these may be flawed due to presumptions, prejudices or misconceptions reflected in their development, to a lack of applied testing and validation, or because they are obsolete or unsuitable.

Controls and contingency plans are presumed to be *ineffective* until proved otherwise, through inspection and testing in a live operational environment.

The review concluded that anyone with access to the settlements office in London and sufficient knowledge could commit a massive fraud with minimal effort and little or no collusion.

In the event that the electronic fund transfer system was incapacitated, the bank reverted to its contingency plan. Payment instructions were faxed to a standby centre in the United States. The authorizing signatures on each faxed instruction were then compared with a digital specimen book, and a telephone call-back was made from the United States to London to authenticate the instruction.

It became evident that a false instruction faxed from London at the close of business would be executed by the standby centre with minimal authentication. Upon receipt in the United States, the transmitting fax number was never checked and in any event could easily be forged. The telephone call-back from the standby centre was to one of four pre-agreed telephone numbers and named individuals. In practice, this authentication depended on the telephone number only – the individual who answered the call-back was never asked to prove their identity, other than by confirming their name.

This authentication was applied uniformly – a payment instruction for $50 was authenticated in precisely the same way as one for $50 million. Significantly, there was no payment threshold – if sufficient funds were available in the account to be remitted, the payment was executed. The bank was thus exposed to the risk of catastrophic fraud, equal in value to the total credit lines of the total funds under its control.

It is important to assess standby and contingency procedures. The attacker may deliberately knock out a primary system thereby forcing you to invoke a standby system. This may be because he knows of a flaw within the secondary system that may be exploited fraudulently or with criminal intent. Remember also, the risk of redundant and obsolete systems being reactivated and misused – this applies particularly to tested telex machines, which have been superseded by electronic funds transfer systems in many organizations.

The audit intentionally seeks to bypass, circumvent or subvert existing controls in much the same way as the determined fraudster, hacker or saboteur. The objective is to identify simple and efficient ways to destroy an organization, or to inflict high impact damage using a variety of potential methods. Once these exposures are identified and their potential commercial and operational impact is understood they may be closed using appropriate counter-measures.

The risk assessor thinks like a fraudster, a thief, a saboteur, a terrorist, a hacker or a criminal. The methodology dispels cosy assumptions, arrogance or blind faith in protective mechanisms, introducing instead a steely determination to wreak havoc. The analyst will avail himself of the necessary software, tools and equipment to achieve this objective. He will also employ tactics that might be considered 'unfair' or 'below the belt', on the principle that criminals do not abide by the rules, nor do they play fair.

An additional objective of critical point auditing is that it often also identifies debilitating but non-lethal risks, such as low impact employee fraud and embezzlement. These lower impact risks usually become apparent as a by-product of the main exercise, shaken out of the system by virtue of extensive testing and evaluation.

A critical point audit comprises extensive interviewing of key staff, hands-on evaluation of systems and controls, mapping process flows to identify exposed interfaces and junctions, and testing the feasibility of various hypotheses to launch a successful attack on the organization.

2 Computer, Internet and Electronic Mail Policy

Many excruciating embarrassments have been caused by people's negligence, carelessness, foolishness and indiscretion when using the Internet and electronic mail.

We tend to forget the enduring nature of e-mails, and that casual gossip and throwaway remarks may be preserved on backup tapes, or forwarded to unknown correspondents beyond our control, only to reappear at the most inconvenient moments.

Notorious cases from recent history include:

- In 1997 insurance company Norwich Union settled out of court for alleged e-mail defamation against its competitor, Western Provident Association (WPA). Norwich Union staff sent electronic mails falsely claiming that WPA was insolvent. By the time a writ had been issued the e-mail messages had been deleted within Norwich Union. WPA obtained a court order forcing Norwich Union to search their backup systems to retrieve the data. Norwich Union paid £450 000 in damages and costs to settle the case.
- During 1999 and 2000, while bankers at Merrill Lynch enthused about the prospects of high-tech companies to investors, the bank's influential Internet stock analyst Henry Blodget was warning the company's private investment clients to avoid many of the same companies. Unfortunately for his employer, Mr Blodget used e-mail to do so. When regulators discovered these e-mails, some of which described recommended investments as 'junk' and 'a piece of shit', the bank settled, paying $100 million.
- On December 7, 2000, a young lady called Claire Swire responded to an electronic mail message from her friend Mr Bradley Chait, an employee of London law firm Norton Rose. The e-mail, which contained a graphic description of an intimate act between the two, was forwarded by Mr Chait to some of his friends and colleagues and spread worldwide to an estimated 10 million addresses within a matter of hours. It can be found posted on various websites and discussion forums to this day.

In the light of these and many other misfortunes, a comprehensive and transparent policy on the acceptable use of company computer systems is clearly advisable and, in all practicality, mandatory.

Enforcing IT security and best practice without such a policy is impracticable – people cannot obey rules that don't exist or that have never been expressly and unambiguously stated. Disciplining people for contravening non-existent rules is also clearly untenable. A policy is the keystone of the information security regime, because it provides guidance for the most volatile and least predictable element in the security mix – people.

The policy can be sold to the workforce on the truthful basis that its stipulations are designed to protect not only the company but also its employees.

Acceptable usage policy

The following example is typical of a business computer usage policy. It is not intended that the stipulations shown here should be considered mandatory – they serve, instead, to highlight those sensitive issues and areas that organizations need to consider and rule upon.

Each organization is very different and flexibility is therefore essential when devising rules and regulations. In formulating a policy, the organization needs to assess its key operations, its exposure to significant risks and the culture and computing requirements of its workforce. A careful balance must be struck. The objective is to establish a controlled environment that facilitates the efficient running of the business, rather than hinders or impedes it.

An acceptable computer usage policy, in combination with contractual undertakings by the workforce to act responsibly, does not, necessarily, mitigate risk. It does, however, underpin the company's position should an employee act negligently, recklessly or criminally. By issuing a clear and unequivocal computer usage policy, the company serves notice on its employees of what it considers unreasonable behaviour that may subject the employee to disciplinary procedure and possible dismissal. The acceptable usage policy should also outline relevant laws and those actions that may render the employee liable to criminal prosecution.

Policies should be carefully maintained and should at all times reflect current law. An outdated policy that does not account for changes in legislation may prove a severe hindrance to the conduct of an investigation as the following case illustrates:

> Board minutes and other information were being leaked to the business correspondent of a major UK newspaper. An investigation commenced in order to find the mole or moles. It was quickly realized, however, that the company concerned had not accorded with the provisions of the Regulation of Investigatory Powers Act (RIPA).
>
> Specifically, the company had not informed its employees, contractually or otherwise, that the company's computer systems might be subject to monitoring. The duty of an employer to advise employees that company systems may be monitored is a major stipulation of RIPA.
>
> Before the investigation could commence, therefore, a letter drafted by the company's solicitors had to be circulated to the entire workforce advising them that the company's data processing systems were subject to monitoring. Whilst complying with the strictures of the law, this untimely notification alerted the suspect to the investigation and seriously undermined operational security. Had the company complied with RIPA by stating the appropriate clause within its contracts of employment, there would have been no need for such a pronouncement and the investigation could have proceeded in total secrecy.

Ideally, the acceptable computer usage policy should be binding with each employee signing a contract stating that he has both read and understood the policy, and accepts its provisions. The contract should be issued in duplicate, with a copy given to the employee and a copy retained by the company.

The example policy shown here is based on the law of the United Kingdom. Obviously, statute relating to privacy, computer misuse, data protection and other relevant jurisdictional legislation must be accounted for when devising an appropriate computer use policy.

This policy is shown as an example only. It is not to be relied upon as legally valid or enforceable, and is not intended as an alternative or substitution to obtaining qualified legal advice.

COMPUTER, INTERNET AND ELECTRONIC MAIL ACCEPTABLE USAGE POLICY

This policy outlines the acceptable use of computers, electronic mail and the Internet within the company. It applies to all employees. The policy forms part of every employee's terms and conditions of employment.

The policy is to protect the company, its employees, clients, customers, suppliers and other electronic correspondents from the inherent risks associated with computers, electronic mail, the Internet and company intranet and to encourage the responsible and efficient use of the company's systems and software.

The company regards this policy with the utmost importance and compliance with it is mandatory for all employees. Non-compliance, whether wilful or otherwise, may constitute a disciplinary offence, and potentially may constitute a criminal offence. All users should retain this policy and familiarize themselves with it, as well as any periodic updates and amendments deemed necessary. The company reserves the right to amend or replace this policy at its sole discretion without prior notice. The company undertakes to inform all employees of any such changes promptly through a process of formal notification.

Computer and telecommunications systems, comprising hardware, data storage media, data and software (hereafter 'the equipment') are critically important to the company's operations. Only authorized employees may access or use the company's equipment and then, only strictly within set parameters.

Employees authorized to access and operate the company's equipment are entitled to do so for the purposes of fulfilling their duties for the company.

The company complies with the *Regulation of Investigatory Powers Act/ Telecommunications (Lawful Business Practice) (Interception of Communications) Regulations 2000*. Electronic data processing equipment owned and operated by the company, including but not restricted to computers, networks, firewalls and telephones, may be monitored by the company, without prior notification, and data transmitted and stored on these systems may be produced as evidence in disciplinary hearings, civil proceedings, criminal prosecutions or to resolve disputes. Recordings and monitoring may also be made for regulatory purposes, in arbitration, for quality control, for training and other purposes that the company deems necessary.

The company's equipment and its computer networks, the data, electronic mail messages and the information stored in or exchanged through these systems are the property and copyright of the company, unless contractually stated otherwise.

Employees are expected to exercise sound professional judgment whenever sending or receiving electronic mail messages and attachments, faxes and other data transmissions or accessing the Internet or any website, system or network external to the company.

Communication over the Internet, via electronic mail or online systems is usually recorded, stored and may be produced in arbitration, or in legal or regulatory proceedings. It is vital, therefore, that electronic mail and online correspondence is moderate, considered and truthful, and not defamatory, or likely to give rise to litigation or dispute. Sending an unencrypted electronic mail is similar to sending a post card – people other than the intended recipient may read the message. When composing electronic mail, employees are advised to exercise due caution.

When engaged in electronic mail correspondence it is incumbent on all employees to be polite and to use appropriate language, and not to bring the company or fellow employees into disrepute.

To avoid inadvertently sending electronic mail to the wrong addressee, employees must pay careful attention when sending messages to ensure that the intended address is typed correctly. The transmission of company confidential faxes requires commensurate care to ensure that the correct fax number is dialled.

Employees are asked to exercise extreme caution when opening electronic mails and attachments sent by unknown or unfamiliar correspondents, or which require the recipient to execute a program, open an attachment or decompress an archive such as a Winzip™ file. Virus and worm programs typically propagate in this manner, requiring the active assistance or compliance of the unwitting user.

Employees are asked to exercise judgment in their personal use of the company's telephones, electronic mail system and the Internet. Personal telephone calls and electronic mails are permitted using company equipment, in accordance with the strictures of this policy. However, employees should limit the time spent on personal telephone calls or on-line and should use their time efficiently. Due care and consideration should be exercised when transmitting attachments, or any material, however seemingly innocuous, that might cause offence. As stated, the company reserves the right to monitor telephone calls, electronic mails, Internet usage and other data processing that takes place on its equipment.

Managerial consent must be obtained before any message representing the company is posted to the Internet or to any other public computer system or forum. Personal views, opinions or beliefs stated in electronic mails transmitted using company equipment should be clearly differentiated. This policy also applies where an employee refers to his or her employment with the company on a personal or dissociated website. In personal communications and websites where the company is shown as the employer the following disclaimer should appear: 'The views expressed here are the personal views and opinions of [the employee's name] and are not made on behalf of [the company].'

A disclaimer (shown immediately below) is attached automatically to the footer of every electronic mail sent from the equipment:

> The contents of this e-mail (and any attachments) are intended for the named addressee only. It contains information which may be confidential and which may also be legally privileged. If you have received this message in error, please do not copy it, disclose it to any other party or take any action in reliance on it. Please notify us immediately by reply e-mail and then delete it from your system. Any opinion or advice or information contained in this email is not necessarily that of the owners or officers of this company. Please note that neither the company nor the

sender accepts any responsibility for viruses and it is your responsibility to scan the email and attachments if any. This electronic mail and all attachments have been scanned for computer virus infections.

The removal of this disclaimer is strictly prohibited.

The use of the company's equipment to subscribe to mailing lists, to participate in news groups or on-line auctions, sales, merchandising or gambling is prohibited.

Employees must not transmit or disclose USERIDs, passwords, PINs, encryption keys, network or server configuration details, IP addresses, or other information that might assist an intrusion into the company's networks. This is confidential information and its disclosure is a disciplinary offence.

The loss, theft or suspected misappropriation of the company's confidential information or equipment must be reported at the earliest opportunity to the Head of Information Security. Employees must exercise particular care and attention when carrying, storing or using mobile computer systems such as laptops, PDAs, personal organizers, Blackberrys and other portable devices that may contain confidential information and which connect to the corporate computer network. The loss or theft of these devices must be reported immediately.

The company's confidential information and equipment must be surrendered to the company upon demand.

Employees are expected to comply with the laws relating to intellectual property and copyright on the Internet. This particularly pertains to software, games and music that is available online, all of which are prohibited from use on the company's equipment. However, copyright law also pertains to original research papers, articles, reports and other proprietary data that are available for download, but which may not be reproduced without the authors' express permission, the consent of the publishers or other copyright holders. If it is intended that copyright material be reproduced or relied upon extensively for company purposes, permission must be obtained from the relevant copyright holder.

The company complies with the Data Protection Act 1998 and the company is registered with the Information Commissioner. The Data Protection Act 1998 makes provision for the regulation of the processing of information relating to individuals, including the obtaining, holding, use or disclosure of personal information. Any reckless or wilful action by an employee that causes the company to transgress the Data Protection Act 1998 is a disciplinary offence.

Company confidential data may only be transmitted over public communications systems such as the Internet and by electronic mail after it has been encrypted using the company's standard encryption software. Client and customer confidential data, or confidential data owned by a third party, may not be transmitted to any other party unless this is expressly agreed by the data's respective owner. Confidential communications between clients, customers and other parties may also require encryption, and employees should seek suitable arrangements from the company's IT department.

DISCIPLINARY OFFENCES

The following prohibited actions comprise disciplinary offences under the terms of this policy, and may entail gross misconduct leading to dismissal and criminal prosecution under the auspices of the Computer Misuse Act 1990 or other relevant UK legislation.

Specifically, the Computer Misuse Act 1990 comprises three criminal offences:

Section 1   Knowingly to gain unauthorized access to any program or data held in any computer

Section 2   Knowingly to gain unauthorized access to a computer with the intent to commit or facilitate a further offence (for example, fraud)

Section 3   Knowingly to cause unauthorized alteration to any program or data in any computer

So that there should be no misunderstanding, the terms of CMA 1990 are written into each employee's contract of employment, and all employees are expected to understand the basic principles of this legislation.

In cases of gross misconduct, the company will not hesitate in pursuing a criminal prosecution.

The following prohibited actions apply equally, where company equipment is used or where employees identify themselves as associated with the company:

- the theft of the equipment, or unauthorized purchase of equipment through the company's accounts;
- the use of the equipment to participate in any illegal activity, including but not restricted to fraud and forgery;
- deliberate or reckless damage to the equipment, including the wilful or reckless destruction or corruption of data;
- the disclosure of company confidential information or proprietary data to unauthorized parties;
- the possession of company confidential data, unless expressly agreed to and authorized by an officer of the company;
- the use of the equipment by persons unauthorized by the company;
- access to systems or data by an authorized user that extends beyond his or her remit or permitted level of access;
- the use of the equipment to gain unauthorized access to the company's data, computer systems and networks or to any data, computer, system or network used by a third party;
- any reckless or wilful action by an employee that causes the company to transgress the Data Protection Act;
- the use of the equipment to host unauthorized websites, services, newsgroups, forums, displays or data;
- the use of the company's equipment to subscribe to unauthorized mailing lists, to participate in news groups, on-line auctions, sales and merchandising, computer dating services or gambling;
- the use of the equipment to enter into unauthorized contracts or obligations, whether potentially binding to the company or the individual;

- unauthorized tampering with the equipment, regardless of whether this causes damage;
- any attempt to bypass or subvert computer security measures;
- the introduction of any unauthorized software program, code, routine, or unauthorized amendment to any company system, for any purpose is prohibited. This includes, but is not restricted to, fraudulent, malicious and destructive computer mechanisms, and any mechanism to assist unauthorized access to a company system;
- fabricating computer evidence, whether documentation, messages, pictures or other, and planting it on the company's systems or equipment falsely to implicate an innocent party in a crime or misdemeanour;
- the transmission of messages, pictures, attachments or any data that the company deems to be defamatory, offensive, racist, sexist, indecent, obscene, blasphemous or abusive, or any material that is likely to incite hatred or cause offence;
- the transmission of messages, pictures, attachments or any data intended or likely to harass, bully, intimidate, threaten, blackmail or coerce;
- the use of the equipment to 'stalk' – to pursue, spy on, harass or contact another in an unsolicited fashion;
- the transmission or possession of illegal material, or material deemed unacceptable by the company. The company deems the viewing and transmission, downloading or uploading of pornographic and sexually explicit material using its equipment to be unacceptable;
- the intentional or reckless transmission of virus or worm infected files or e-mails, Trojan horses, contaminated or malicious code, attachments, any data or device capable of causing unauthorized modifications to corresponding computers, data or networked systems;
- the misuse of equipment to send junk mail, spam, any solicitation or advert;
- the use of the equipment for personal gain in contravention of the employee's contract of employment, or that constitutes a conflict of interest;
- the use of equipment to spy, snoop or eavesdrop on directors of the company, fellow employees, anyone associated with the company or its operations, or third parties;
- the spreading of chain letters, engagement in gossip or unsubstantiated speculation liable to bring the company into disrepute or legal dispute;
- the disclosure of passwords or access codes, or the unauthorized transfer of any access devices, keys, swipe cards, password generators or security tokens;
- introducing unauthorized changes to the company's data, defacing the company's website or removing legal disclaimers from electronic mails and official documents;
- attaching unauthorized equipment to the company's computer systems or infrastructure, or installing, downloading or uploading unauthorized software;
- the use of personal computers or other equipment that is not the property of the company to process any company data for any purpose;
- the unauthorized use of evidence elimination, security or privacy software;
- downloading or uploading pirated music or video files or reproducing and distributing any material that is copyright;
- downloading, uploading or playing games on the company's computers.

Acknowledgement

I have read the company's policy on the acceptable use of its equipment. I understand the policy and accept its provisions, knowing that if I transgress the policy I may be subject to the company's disciplinary procedure, potential dismissal from the company and possible prosecution.

Signed _____

Date _____

Witnessed _____

3 *Search Orders*

The Search Order is effective in the UK and many Commonwealth countries. It is a powerful remedy to fraud, IP theft and other wrongdoing, providing the legal right for the aggrieved party's lawyers and agents to access and search the records and computers of the alleged wrongdoer, even where these are located in private premises.

In legal terminology, the aggrieved party is known as the Applicant, whilst the alleged wrongdoer is referred to as the Respondent.

The application for the granting of a Search Order is made to the Court by the Applicant's lawyers, after the preparation of affidavits and exhibits. This is a complex and specialist area of the law, requiring the attention of lawyers who are expert in both the preparation and execution of this type of injunctive relief. The application for a Search Order and its subsequent execution is a substantial undertaking involving careful and painstaking preparation, the combined input of specialist lawyers, witnesses and experts, as well as logistical and technical support.

It is also normally the case that an independent solicitor (the Supervising Solicitor) is appointed to oversee the execution of the Search Order so as to ensure that the Order is executed properly in accordance with the law and to safeguard the rights of all those involved.

This Appendix discusses only a limited and clearly defined aspect of this much wider process; namely the search and seizure of computer equipment belonging to the Respondent. If an application is made to the Court, it is necessary that the Order be clear and unequivocal. With regards to computer systems and processes, it is vital that all forms of electronic data processing (EDP) equipment are included for examination, and that any defensive or protective technical measures taken by the Respondent should be revoked by order of the Court.

In a Search Order issued in the High Court of Justice, Chancery Division, Manchester District Registry in July 2004, the following stipulations, **provided here for guidance only**, were issued.

- The Respondent must immediately hand over to the Applicant's solicitors any of the listed items, which are in his possession or under his control, save for any computer or hard disk integral to any computer. Any items the subject of a dispute as to whether they are listed items must immediately be handed over to the Supervising Solicitor for safe keeping pending resolution of the dispute or further order of the court.
- The Respondent must immediately give the search party effective access to the computers on the premises, with all necessary passwords, to enable the computers to be searched and/or imaged. If they contain any listed items the Respondent must provide the Applicant's solicitors with copies of all listed items contained in the computers. The Applicant's solicitors may image the entire hard drive of any computer and take full

forensic copies of any and all electronic processing devices and electronic media. All reasonable steps shall be taken by the Applicant and the Applicant's solicitors to ensure that no damage is done to any computer or data. The Applicant and his representatives may not themselves search the Respondent's computers unless they have sufficient expertise to do so without damaging the Respondent's system. In the event that the Applicant images the Respondent's hard drive and/or takes full forensic copies of any electronic media this shall be done only by the computer experts [as named in this Order] and shall do so in accordance with their undertaking in Schedule G.

Further and in any event the following shall apply:

• The Respondent shall disclose and deliver up to the search party all electronic processing devices and electronic processing and data storage media, including, but not restricted to, computers, disks, tapes, mobile telephones, fax machines, memory devices and any other processing devices and materials.
• The Respondent shall disclose to the search party all passwords, keys, phrases, access codes, software protection devices or other information or equipment necessary to access all data stored on any, and all, of the aforesaid electronic processing and data storage devices.
• The Respondent shall not access any electronic data processing system or data within the control of the Respondent until the completion of the search without the consent of the Supervising Solicitor and subject to such conditions as he may impose. Data for this purpose includes data stored on site and data stored remotely and includes logical, physical and remote access.
• The Respondent shall not remove the electronic processing devices and electronic processing and data storage media including but not limited to computers, disks, tapes, mobile telephones, fax machines, memory devices and any other processing devices and materials from the premises referred to in this order.
• The Respondent shall provide the search party with access to any virtual drives or devices or computer data hosted remotely, wherever it may be, which is under the control of the Respondent.
• In the event that it is, in the opinion of the Supervising Solicitor, not practicable to search the electronic processing and data storage media devices and to image the same and to take full forensic copies given the location of the said devices or media, the devices and media may be removed to the computer experts' offices where two forensic copies shall be made and the devices and media shall be returned to the Respondent within five working days.

SCHEDULE G UNDERTAKING GIVEN BY THE COMPUTER EXPERTS

• The computer experts undertake to take all reasonable care in imaging and taking forensic copies of the devices and not to damage or alter any of the material contained thereon.
• The computer experts undertake to take two copies of each device disclosed or discovered.
• The computer experts undertake not to use the information obtained save in respect of these proceedings.

4 *Internal Response Teams vs External Consultants*

Many big companies and large organizations have trained in-house computer forensic teams and other specialist computer investigators. There may be compelling reasons to establish and maintain such a capability, but the decision to do so should be made only after careful consideration.

One of the key considerations in determining the economic viability of an in-house forensic response team will be the number of investigations that any given organization will conduct in an average year that require computer evidential processing or specialist forensic assistance.

Table A4.1 itemizes the pros and cons of developing an in-house forensic response team or, alternatively, contracting external consultants.

Table A4.1 Internal and external resources – decision matrix

| In-house forensic team | | External forensic expert | |
Pros	Cons	Pros	Cons
Will be familiar with the organization's systems, processes and operations.	Experience is generally limited only to those investigations conducted within the organization.	Extensive, broad experience of many different types of investigation in different commercial environments. The external consultant will have a knowledge of a wide range of operating systems, processors, networks, configurations and devices, encountered in a variety of circumstances.	Will not be conversant with in-house systems or processes, the organizational culture, structure or operations. This may impede the analysis of any information recovered, and may slow the progress of the investigation. The external consultant will necessarily need a period of acclimatization.
The team will be familiar with the organization's culture, management style and structure.	The team's investigative function may be widely known and understood and its members' identities will be known. This awareness amongst the workforce may compromise the team's operations.	The identity of the external team will not be known and there may be greater latitude for covert investigations, undercover or pretext operations.	Unknown individuals are more likely to arouse suspicion if discovered on-site accessing systems or conducting other covert activities. Cover stories need to be credible and properly supported.
Financed internally using salaried employees.	Will require training and the provision of equipment and software which will need regular updating.	There is no ongoing overhead – the consultant arrives with the emergency and departs upon its resolution.	Expensive. Forensic consultants typically charge £1000 a day.
Can deploy as and when required.	There will be a commensurate dilution of focus on core business activities to which staff are principally attached. This is particularly relevant should the team become engaged in prolonged civil proceedings, or criminal prosecutions requiring extensive case preparation and attendance at court.	Commercial forensic teams should be able to deploy anywhere in the world within 24-hours' notice.	A qualified practitioner may be unavailable due to other commitments when most urgently needed. This is particularly true of independent consultants and 'one-man bands'. Some companies offer a retainer, although this is rare.
The team can be assembled from a broad skill set, knowledge base and experience.	There is a risk that the team comprise only IT specialists and will lack the broader knowledge necessary to complete an investigation.	The best independent forensic investigators have a profound working knowledge of corporate fraud and business risk and should add value	Many computer forensic practitioners are technically adept but have little experience of fraud investigation, business risk or commercial malpractice.

In-house forensic team		External forensic expert	
Pros	Cons	Pros	Cons
	Difficult to maintain, equip and train in a state of readiness and as a cohesive unit.	beyond the strict parameters of the computer or IT environment.	There are lots of so-called 'experts' offering consultancy services. The forensic and investigations industry is not regulated nor does it offer professional qualifications. There is a risk of contracting a 'dilettante' or 'wannabe' sleuth who will use the opportunity to learn the basics on your ticket.
Basic procedures and techniques can be regularly disseminated throughout the team.	Experience and knowledge is forfeited through departures and people changing job roles, both internally and externally. This can lead to inconsistency.	The best consultants will remain consistent in their chosen profession and will amass considerable experience accordingly.	The investigator's level of knowledge will be dependent on his commitment and experience. This varies enormously between individuals and companies.
There will normally be good lines of communication within the team.	There is a risk that the team may become insular and will fail to correspond with experts external to the organization. This can lead to blinkered, out-dated attitudes and approaches.	The forensic investigator will normally be involved in the relevant professional associations and will regularly exchange information and ideas with the wider forensic community.	The independent consultant may not know salient facts, background information, gossip or hearsay which might help sharpen the focus of the enquiry, clarify matters or define alternative lines of investigation.
The team should have an innate understanding of what is possible, permissible and acceptable within the organization.	There is a risk that individual members of the team may be subjective in their approach due to personal allegiances or prejudices towards their fellow employees. There also is a risk that the team inadvertently (or intentionally) might leak sensitive information to unauthorized members of staff.	The independent consultant has no vested interest in the matters or the people that are being investigated and is highly unlikely to compromise the investigation. This professional detachment should promote objectivity and reason.	
There will be a clear chain of command and allocation of responsibility within the team.	If the team is subjugated in the wider chain of command, there is a risk that it or its individual members may be	The independent investigator is apolitical and unlikely to be influenced by infighting, or	If the independent investigator reports to corrupt management, or is dependent on the blessing of compromised

| In-house forensic team | | External forensic expert | |
Pros	Cons	Pros	Cons
	subjected to management intimidation, interference or coercion should its findings be considered unpalatable. There is also the ever-present risk of political infighting that is always a possibility in large organizations.	pressurized by coercion. It is relatively easy to control the independent investigator, who is bound by confidentiality and must yield to management decisions.	individuals, it is probable that the investigation will be disabled, impeded or aborted.
The team will normally show a strong allegiance and heightened loyalty to its employer and will act with dedication and commitment and in the organization's interest.	Members of the team may be required to give evidence under cross examination which may result in the disclosure of information, methods and practices which their employer would rather remain generally unknown.	The independent expert is more likely to be perceived by a court or tribunal as impartial even though he is in the pay of his client. Most forensic practitioners undertake defence and prosecution work. This provides them with experience of the criminal prosecution process and the strengths and weaknesses of any evidence submitted into proceedings.	There is a remote risk that the independent investigator will lack passion because the people and processes being examined are of no direct interest to him.
	It is unlikely that the team will have significant or regular experience of presenting evidence in court, or of the legal process. The team may be perceived as lacking independence. Evidence produced by the team may be considered less probative and its testimony may be contested as biased.	The independent consultant will normally have considerable experience of the court process and legal matters because solicitors will comprise a significant proportion of his client base. Many forensic experts are registered as expert witnesses.	Many consultants do not have court experience. A poor performance when giving testimony or under cross examination can seriously impact upon a verdict.
There is a cross-cultivation of skills and knowledge within the team.	Key members of staff engaged in ongoing proceedings or prosecutions may leave the organization.	The contract should state that the consultant or consultancy engaged will commit itself to the formal conclusion of the investigation.	There is a risk that the organization becomes dependent on the testimony and evidence of an individual expert and has no backup in the event that this person is indisposed.

5 *Security Guidelines*

The following guidelines address different aspects of operational security and are designed equally to combat a concerted industrial espionage offensive or to mitigate mundane instances of unwitting information disclosure. The guidelines are issued under different categories, some of which focus upon personnel whilst others are technical in nature. Clearly, the decision to follow these guidelines, fully or partially, will be based on a risk assessment.

Travel

Employees are vulnerable to pretext approaches and social engineering when overseas and in unfamiliar territory.

Table A5.1   Travel

	Recommendation	Comment
1	Do not plug laptops into on-board power supplies or docking ports whilst travelling on aircraft.	Certain intelligence agencies reportedly have devices that may be installed upon national airline carriers in first-class and business cabins to record information from laptop computers.
2	Beware that some national airline carriers may bug seats on their aircraft.	This applies mostly to first-class and business-class cabins.
3	Beware of shoulder surfing if using a laptop during a flight.	Agents can be placed in neighbouring seats to
4	Beware of shoulder surfing if reading sensitive documentation during a flight.	observe and read screens and documents.
5	Do not send sensitive e-mails using airport business facilities and Internet connections.	These can be monitored.
6	Do not send sensitive faxes from hotel machines.	These can be intercepted.
7	When travelling do not put company labels on baggage and hand luggage, and do not wear company-branded clothing or accessories.	Executives and other employees should not be readily identifiable, as this may lead to pretext approaches.
8	Do not engage in conversation with strangers in aircraft, hotel bars, restaurants and so on.	These conversations may be the start of a pretext approach or trap.
9	Do not discuss sensitive issues with colleagues whilst travelling together.	There is a risk of being overheard by a planted agent travelling alongside.
10	Travel itineraries, bookings and ticket purchases should be made using a trusted agency.	This reduces the opportunity for agents to plan surveillance, pretext approaches or traps.
11	Be careful if flying with national carriers (airlines).	To reduce the exposure to pretext approaches or surveillance.

| 12 | Do not use in-cabin telephones on aircraft for calls relating to sensitive information. | These systems may be monitored. |
| 13 | If hire cars are booked in advance, do not discuss any sensitive information in them. | Cars can be wired for audio transmission or recording. |

Hotels and restaurants

Employees staying in hotels should be made aware of the types of blackmail attempt to which they may be exposed. Education and awareness training are the best defences against such approaches.

The organization should also ensure it is aware of any of its own employees more at risk to subversion than others.

Table A5.2   Hotels and restaurants

	Recommendation	Comment
14	Do not send sensitive e-mails from hotel business centres or from connection ports in hotel rooms (if provided).	These can be monitored.
15	Do not send sensitive faxes from hotel machines.	These can be intercepted.
16	Consider *everything* you do in your hotel room can be seen and recorded.	Hotel rooms may be covertly monitored by video cameras or recording devices. Assume that this is the case.
17	Do not discuss anything of a sensitive nature in your hotel room.	
18	Do not entertain or hold any meeting in your room you would not wish to be recorded.	
19	Do not leave any sensitive material in your hotel room (even if placed in a safe).	Assume everything can be accessed, viewed and copied. Cleaners and chambermaids may be bribed to access information left in hotel rooms.
20	If you have to carry it, keep sensitive material with you at all times.	As above.
21	Do not discard any sensitive material in hotel rubbish bins.	This can be collected.
22	Do not leave sensitive documents for collection at a hotel reception.	These can be viewed and copied.
23	Where conference or meeting rooms are booked by third parties, do not discuss sensitive material in them.	They can be wired for audio recording or transmission.
24	Where more than one employee is staying in a hotel, ensure rooms are booked side by side.	Employees can act as witnesses for each other if any blackmail approaches or false accusations are made.
25	Be aware of blackmail attempts: honey traps (sex and prostitution), money traps (where a sum of money is left in a room – should you keep it you will be blackmailed), people offering information, political access and so on. If anyone	All these can be used for blackmail. They are often initiated in public meeting places.

approaches in this manner refuse to talk to them and contact a colleague (if one is in the hotel). Report the matter to the hotel reception.

26	Where third parties book restaurants, do not discuss sensitive material at the table or bar.	The restaurant can be wired for audio transmission or recording.
27	Do not engage in conversations with strangers.	An unsolicited encounter may be a pretext approach.
28	Any gifts given to the office or a person, such as statues, lighters, pens, pictures and so on. should be swept for listening devices.	This is a favoured tactic to covertly plant bugs and other electronic surveillance into an office or residence.

Telecommunications

Table A5.3   Telecommunications

	Recommendation	Comment
29	Do not discuss sensitive material on landline telephones.	These are easily monitored, either officially or with bugs.
30	Conduct regular (bi-annual) electronic sweeps of telephones, frame rooms and internal exchanges.	Management offices and boardrooms should be swept regularly particularly during major upheavals, crises or commercial developments.
31	Use a trusted electronic surveillance counter-measures team to sweep for bugs and taps. Do not use a resident team if located overseas from your head office.	Boardrooms and general meeting areas are often targeted.
32	Do not discuss sensitive material on mobile phones.	Many governments have the capability to monitor mobiles. In certain circumstances, an eavesdropper tuning in to the correct frequency from a neighbouring office or room can also monitor analogue cellular telephones.
33	Do not use e-mail to transmit sensitive material (unless heavily encrypted).	Electronic mail can be intercepted and monitored. An encrypted electronic mail methodology should be devised and implemented.
34	Offices should be equipped with encrypted fax systems of a suitable cryptographic strength.	Encrypted fax should be the preferred method for transmitting sensitive documentation between offices. The encryption and hardware should be tested and standardized for all operations.
35	Beware of using conference microphones and personal address systems in meeting rooms and so on.	These can be intercepted from a distance.
36	Consider using a covert recording device (briefcase, memory stick and so on) in meetings with local partners, sponsors, third parties and so on.	The recording can be translated later to determine what was said. You should take take legal advice on this point.

Office and work

Table A5.4   Office and work

	Recommendation	Comment
37	Assume anything in the office can be viewed and copied by the authorities.	Government agents will have complete access to any premises.
38	Implement effective access control and maintain usable logs of access to important and sensitive areas of the operation.	Deters unauthorized entry and maintains a record of people's movement within the building.
39	Ensure effective CCTV coverage of key areas (entry/exit, R&D and so on). Test equipment regularly to ensure its effectiveness.	Poor CCTV coverage may confound investigative efforts.
40	Operate random searches of personnel entering and leaving the premises.	This will require advice from legal counsel.
41	Ensure personnel are aware of items specifically banned from the premises (cameras, recording devices and so on).	Prominent notices should be displayed at the entrances to sensitive facilities.
42	Maintain effective control of keys.	Deters unauthorized access.
43	Do not attach company key rings/logos to key sets. Do not attach an address or identifying label to keys.	If lost they will be easily identified and could provide an opponent with an opportunity to gain unauthorized access.
44	Conduct an electronic counter-measures sweep of the office (especially key meeting rooms) before important meetings.	Counter-surveillance. The counter-measures should search for line taps, electronic bugs and transmitters, hidden cameras, recorders and vibration[1] monitors.
45	Consider holding sensitive discussions out of the office, in open spaces (parks and so on).	Counter-surveillance – listening in is much more difficult.
46	Maintain a clear desk policy.	Documents, diskettes, and other materials may be stolen or copied by cleaners or other unauthorized persons.
47	Lock all sensitive information in secure cabinets.	All locks should be sufficiently strong to prevent them being picked.
48	Ensure passwords are not written on Post-it™ notes and attached near to the computers they relate to.	Approximately 3 per cent of computer systems have passwords written down in their immediate vicinity – a major security risk.
49	Ensure computer screens do not face windows and that their contents are not visible from outside the building.	The contents of computer screens can be easily read from overlooking buildings. This technique is often used.
50	Attach blinds to windows where necessary.	
51	Use a cross-cut shredder to dispose of all confidential information.	Line shredders are insecure and allow documents to be reconstructed. They should not be used.
52	Do not place diskettes or other electronic media in the waste bins for disposal – they should be consigned to the IT controller.	They can be recovered and read.

---

1   A laser device that calibrates vibration on windowpanes caused by air movement, and allows an eavesdropper to hear conversations inside rooms. This monitoring is feasible over distances of up to 500 metres.

53	Only put non-confidential waste in the waste bins.	Consider shredding all waste – this is a 'catch all' strategy.
54	If interesting or sensitive articles are removed from open source publications such as journals, magazines or newspapers, do not dispose of the remainder of the publication using a waste bin.	A copy of the original can be located and compared to identify what was removed and retained.
55	If a third party is used for secure waste disposal, check that it carries out its duties properly.	Such companies can be targeted or used to gather intelligence.
56	Industrial or development scrap materials should be destroyed in a controlled manner where their destruction can be observed.	Scrap items are highly useful in intelligence gathering and are often overlooked.
57	Take care when using recycling companies – be aware of the potential for recycling companies to be a front for intelligence collection, especially for technical items.	In one case microfiche was 'recycled' to enable the recovery of silver nitrate content. In fact the microfiche was read and analysed by a competitor.
58	Consider using in-house, company-employed cleaners. They will have more loyalty and accountability than a professional cleaning firm.	Cleaners may be used to gather intelligence.
59	Do not leave Dictaphones, tape recordings, PDAs, memory sticks or other devices out overnight.	These devices can be stolen or downloaded.
60	Ensure strict controls over production runs and examine any cast-offs or defective product.	Production lines may manufacture in excess of the agreed production run and claim that the over-production was due to defects and breakages. The over-production is sold on for analysis or reverse engineered off site.
61	Shorthand notes and memos are often overlooked because most people cannot read shorthand. PAs and secretaries use shorthand and they should be aware that their notes should be secure from prying eyes.	Shorthand memos, notes and transcriptions have revealed significant information once transcribed.
62	Typewriter ribbons should be disposed of by incineration.	The strike indentations on typewriter ribbons can be read and interpreted using specialist software.
63	Do not send sensitive materials or documents using the postal service or local couriers.	Packages and letters may be intercepted and their contents copied.
64	Packages sent for international despatch or being received from abroad may be X-rayed, inspected and copied by customs officials.	Judgment should be made about the content and sensitivity of international despatches.
65	Implement access control on photocopiers (many models are equipped with swipe card controls and page counters).	Photocopiers, if uncontrolled, offer the opponent a traceless way to copy sensitive documents.
66	Consider the overt or covert monitoring of photocopy machines using CCTV or video.	Overt to deter misuse, covert to record and investigate misuse.
67	Control flatbed scanners and optical character recognition devices in the same ways as photocopiers.	They can be used to make illicit copies of sensitive material.
68	Do not allow printers that can also scan and/or photocopy.	These will bypass any controls on the photocopiers and scanners.

| 69 | Ensure the control, collection and destruction of papers, graphics, visual aids, presentations and so on. Do not leave these in rooms after meetings. Ensure all drawings, notes, plans and so on are removed from pads, whiteboards, blackboards or flipcharts after meetings close. | There have been numerous cases where sensitive information was overlooked following meetings and presentations. |

Documents

The key to document control in any environment is to identify, prioritize and safeguard those documents deemed highly sensitive.

Table A5.5   Documents

	Recommendation	Comment
70	All sensitive documents to be clearly marked with the relevant level of sensitivity on every page.	
71	The printing and distribution of sensitive documents should be strictly controlled. Numbered copies should be signed out and in of a register maintained under strict control. Sensitive documents should be clearly marked 'Company Confidential'.	Minimizes the risk of loss and assists any subsequent investigation if leaks occur.
72	Sensitive documents should be destroyed (shredded) under supervision and signed as such in the register.	See 51.
73	Consider 'seeding' highly valuable documents (making subtle but specific changes to different copies that are distributed to different recipients).	This is a subtle and effective way to trace the unauthorized disclosure of information.
74	All sensitive documents should be marked as 'Page 1 of 20', 'Page 2 of 20' and so on.	Helps to ensure pages do not get removed and that the document is produced in its entirety.
75	Distribution of sensitive documents should be kept to a strictly need-to-know basis.	Avoids unnecessary distribution and risk.
76	The need-to-know distribution list for a document should be printed on the document itself so that it can be confirmed at any point by those people that should have had access to it.	This clarifies the distribution list and is useful when investigating leaked information.

Glossary

3COM US company, which produces network routers amongst other products.

Access control Logical access control is the process by which computer systems and software is restricted only to those authorized to use them. Physical access control is a process by which buildings, rooms and other areas are entered only by authorized personnel.

ACF2 ACF2 (more formally, CA-ACF2; the ACF stands for Access Control Facility) is a set of programs from Computer Associates that enable security on mainframes.

Active attack An attack on a computer system, whereby the attacker modifies or inserts information, malicious code or corrupts data or software. See also **Passive attack**.

Affidavit A written statement made on oath.

Algorithm Set of rules specifying a method by which a task may be completed (e.g. an encryption algorithm).

AS/400 Minicomputer system manufactured by IBM.

ASCII American Standard Code for Information Interchange. A standard system for representing letters, numbers and symbols.

ATM Automated Teller Machine. Typically, a high street cash-point machine

Audit trail Records various details about the use of resources on a computer network or other data processing system and may be of assistance in determining how, when and where a security violation occurred.

Authentication Establishes the identity of the user of a computer, network, system or process to permit only those with authorized access.

AUTOEXEC.BAT Special batch file, executed when a computer running the DOS operating systems or early versions of Windows is switched on and which may be edited to configure the computer to the user's requirements.

Backdoor Undocumented means of bypassing software or hardware access control measures. Many manufacturers of systems intentionally include backdoors as a contingency in case the authorized user of the system loses a token or forgets a password.

Backup Copy of computer data, which may be used to restore the system in the event that data is lost, mislaid, corrupted or destroyed.

BACS Banks Automated Clearing System. A method by which payments between parties in the UK are automated using electronic funds transfer.

Bad sector When a disk is formatted, the operating system checks sectors to determine their usability. Unusable sectors are labelled as bad and are not used by the operating system to store data.

Biometric access control Access control technique, which authenticates a user by a unique physical characteristic such as a retinal pattern or fingerprint.

BIOS Basic Input/Output System. Firmware stored in a ROM chip which interfaces directly with a microcomputer's hardware. The BIOS stores essential configuration information about the computer, which may be altered by accessing the BIOS menu.

Bit copying Technique for copying a disk by reading every bit on each track of the disk and writing each bit in sequence to another disk. A bit copying program has no concept of the file or directory structure of its target disk. The method is sometimes referred to as disk imaging.

Bit stream A bit stream is a contiguous sequence of bits, representing a stream of data, transmitted continuously over a communications path, serially (one at a time).

Blackberry A handheld device principally used for wireless e-mail receipt and transmission.

Blade technology Computers housed or stacked at a central data centre. End users access or connect to the blade device from either a PC or from a thin client device with no onboard data storage capacity or external communications channels.

Boot protection An access control technique, which prevents an unauthorized user from using a system diskette to boot a PC in order to access the data on it.

Boot sector Part of the operating system, which is first read into memory from disk when a PC is switched on. The program in the boot sector is then executed, which in turn loads the rest of the operating system into memory from the system files stored on disk. This process is known as 'booting' the computer.

Cache Data storage in memory, which precludes the need for data to be continually read from and written to disk.

CAD/CAM Computer aided design/manufacturing.

Call log Record of telephone calls, which usually shows the time and date of each call, the numbers dialled, their duration, and the extensions from which calls were made. Many logging systems include a record of incoming calls.

Chain of evidence The factual matrix, which proves or disproves a particular assertion and the evidence, which supports the factual matrix.

CHAPS Clearing House Automated Payments System – an electronic funds transfer system used in the UK.

Checksum Value calculated from data, which can be used to verify that data or code is not subsequently altered. Checksums are commonly used to check the integrity of computer software.

Cipher Encryption algorithm.

Ciphertext Encrypted text or data.

Circumstantial evidence Facts that are strongly indicative of an event but not proof.

CISCO US company, which produces network routers and other Internet backbone products.

Cluster Windows allocates disk space in clusters. A single cluster is the smallest unit of disk space, which Windows can manage. Typical cluster sizes are 4 KB, 16 KB or 32 KB.

CMOS Complementary Metal-Oxide Semiconductor is a technology to manufacture computer chips with a very low power consumption. CMOS chips are used for the non-volatile storage of configuration parameters and set-up information in PCs (see also **BIOS**).

Compiler Program, which translates programs written in a high-level language interpretable by users into low-level instructions, which may be executed by a computer's CPU.

Control environment Regime where control over people, systems and processes is emphasized.

COPINE Combating Paedophile Information Networks in Europe – a project founded in 1997, originally based at the University College of Cork, Ireland, and since transferred to Interpol.

Copy protection Hardware and/or software designed to make it difficult or impossible to copy computer programs, smart cards, integrated circuits or other technology.

CPU Central Processing Unit – the device in a computer, usually a micro-processor, which takes instructions from memory and executes them.

Cracker Program, mechanism or person who breaks passwords or system security.

CRC Cyclic Redundancy Check – mathematical method to verify the integrity of data.

Cryptanalysis Study of encrypted data (ciphertext) or of an encryption algorithm, usually with the intention of detecting cryptographic weaknesses, which might be exploited by an attacker.

Cryptographic checksum Checksum calculated using a cryptographic algorithm. The theory is that it should be impossible to 'engineer' changes to data in such a way as to leave a cryptographic checksum of its contents unchanged.

DAT Digital Audio Tape – used for data archiving and storage.

Data mining Interrogating large volumes of data, usually by using specialist software, in order to determine patterns or associations.

Data protection 1) Preserving the confidentiality, integrity and availability of information; 2) Legal term relating to personal information held by third parties on computer, hence the Data Protection Act.

Decryption Process of transforming encrypted data (ciphertext) into plaintext. Decryption is the reverse process of encryption.

Defrag PC computer program which rearranges clusters on a disk so that file content remains contiguous rather than disrupted. The operating system need not allocate clusters contiguously, which impairs the speed of disk access. Defragmentation thus enhances the speed with which the contents of a disk may be read or written to by the operating system.

Degauss Destroying information contained in magnetic media by subjecting that media to high-intensity alternating magnetic fields, following which the magnetic fields slowly decrease.

Deleted files Files which are no longer accessible to the operating system but which may be recoverable using specialist tools.

Denial of service A denial-of-service (or 'DoS') attack is the targeted transmission of extremely heavy network traffic to cause a server computer or network to crash. In a DoS attack, the server is typically so busy processing useless traffic that it cannot respond to legitimate requests.

Disassembly Process, similar to reverse engineering, whereby a computer program is analysed in order to understand its coded instructions and functionality.

Disk image Bit copy of a disk.

Diskless workstation Networked PC, which does not contain a local disk drive.

DNA Deoxyribonucleic Acid – Genetic information, which may be used to identify a person or living thing.

Dongle Hardware copy-protection device. The device, which is typically inserted into the parallel or USB ports of a PC, must be present before a program associated with it will run.

DOS DISKCOPY Simple sector-by-sector disk copy utility.

Dpi Dots per inch – a term used to describe the clarity and definition of printed output.

DRUID Download recoverable user-intelligible data – a download of readily interpretable files and directories from a computer for immediate review, prior to a low-level forensic examination.

DTP Desktop publishing – producing camera-ready copy using a PC and software.

Dumpster diving Hacker term used to describe the process of obtaining information from rubbish and discarded waste.

EBCDIC Extended Binary Coded Decimal Interchange Code – IBM's data interchange format.

EFTS Electronic Funds Transfer System – a generic term for technology used in inter-bank funds transfers.

Encryption Process of rendering data unintelligible to an unauthorized person by scrambling it. The data is subsequently decrypted by an authorized person, usually by means of a password, or a digital key.

ESDA Electrostatic Detection Apparatus – equipment used to read indentations on documents and letters caused by a person writing on an overlaid page or pages, by franking machinery or other pressure.

Ex parte Law. From or on one side only, with the other side absent or unrepresented: testified *ex parte*; an *ex parte* hearing.

False negative Existent event reported as non-existent, for example, a computer virus remaining undetected by detection software.

False positive Non-existent event reported as existent, for example, a virus being reported by detection software where no virus is present.

FAST Federation Against Software Theft – British organization, which investigates and prosecutes software pirates and illegal software users on behalf of major software companies.

FAT File Allocation Table – term used by PC operating systems to describe the table, which outlines the location of all of the files on disk. There are two FATs, and in a 'healthy' computer both will be identical.

Fax monitor Software, which copies facsimile transmissions to the hard disk of a PC for subsequent inspection or printing.

File compression Software process whereby a file is compacted by recoding so that space may be saved on disk, or for backup or transmission purposes. WinZIP is a compression utility for the PC.

File server Central data repository for a network, which may provide centralized services. File servers on microcomputer networks are usually powerful PCs with large storage capacities.

Fingerprinting Cryptographic checksumming, whereby data is said to be 'fingerprinted'.

Firewall Set of related programs, located at a network gateway server, that protects the resources of a private network from users from other networks. (The term also implies the security policy that is used with the programs.)

FireWire IEEE 1394 high performance serial bus standard, for connecting devices to a personal computer. FireWire provides a single plug-and-socket connection on which up to 63 devices can be attached with data transfer speeds of up to 400 Mbps (megabits per second).

Firmware Computer program stored in non-volatile memory.

Force majeure Unexpected and uncontrollable event.

Forensic image copy Exact and complete bit-by-bit copy of computer media.

FSA Financial Services Authority – an independent non-governmental body that regulates the UK financial services industry.

Gigabyte (GB) 1 Gigabyte = 1024 Megabytes. A gigabyte is a measure of memory capacity.

Google Free, powerful Internet search engine, with a hosted e-mail facility.

Grep Unix command and also a utility available for Windows and other operating systems, used to search one or more files for a given character string or pattern and, if desired, replace the character string with another one.

GUI Graphical User Interface – uses icons instead of a command line to invoke software.

Hacker (1) An individual who produces a prodigious amount of software or demonstrates considerable systems expertise; (2) A person who breaks into computer systems or software without authorization to do so.

Handshaking In networking, handshaking is the exchange of information between two systems and the resulting agreement about which protocol to use that precedes each communication.

Hard disk A hermetically sealed magnetic disk, fixed within a computer, which stores data.

Hate mail Offensive or abusive electronic mail.

Hexadecimal Number base 16 used to represent binary information stored on computers.

Hotmail Free Internet-hosted electronic mail service from Microsoft Corporation.

HTTP Hypertext Transfer Protocol – set of rules for transferring files (text, graphic images, sound, video, and other multimedia files) on the Internet.

I/O port Used by a computer to communicate with its peripheral devices.

IDE Integrated Disk Electronics – interface standard for data storage devices.

Intaglio Incised or engraved printing often used to deter forgery.

Interpreter Program that executes instructions written in a high-level programming language. The advantage of an interpreter, however, is that it can immediately execute high-level programs saving the time necessary to compile the code. For this reason, interpreters are often used during software development when sections of code require testing quickly.

ISO 17799 ISO/IEC 17799: Code of Practice for Information Security Management is a generic set of best practices for the security of information systems for all organizations, no matter what their size or purpose. ISO 17799 was previously published in the United Kingdom as BS 7799.

ISP Internet Service Provider – company that sells access to the Internet via telephone or cable line to your home or office.

JANET Joint Academic Network in the UK.

Jaz drive Removable disk drive developed by Iomega Corporation storing up to 2 Gigabytes of data.

Kilobyte 1024 bytes – a 'K' is often used as an abbreviation for a data capacity of 1000 bytes.

LAN Local area network – computer or data communication network distributed over a limited area up to several kilometres in radius.

Legacy system Old or inherited system, which may be integrated with a more modern system.

Link analysis Technique used in crime analysis to depict the relations between various parties diagrammatically.

Logic bomb Program, which is triggered when certain processing conditions are met causing damage or unauthorized alteration to software or data.

MAC address Unique identifier for a network adapter, typically a network interface card. Also known as hardware or physical addresses, they are 12-digit hexadecimal numbers (48 bits in length).

Magnetic remanence Magnetic representation of residual information that remains on a magnetic medium after the medium has been erased or overwritten.

Malware Software designed and written for malevolent purposes.

Mareva injunction Law. A legal redress whereby suspect bank accounts or assets are frozen by order of the court.

MD5 hash Digital signature of a data set calculated using an algorithm created in 1991 by Professor Ronald Rivest. When this algorithm is applied to a data set it creates a unique value. Changing the data in any way will cause any subsequently generated MD5 hash to change and thus conflict with the original value generated. The MD5 hash thus serves as a control to ensure the integrity of digital evidence.

Megabyte 1048576 bytes – a 'Mb' is often used as an abbreviation for a data capacity of 1 000 000 bytes.

Melissa Notorious computer virus that spread by electronic mail in April 1999 and overwhelmed commercial, government and military computer systems.

Memory stick Highly portable solid-state data storage device with a capacity in the order of 1 gigabyte.

MFT Master File Table – file and directory index used by some operating systems. See also **FAT**.

Mirroring Process whereby data is written simultaneously to two (or more) disks of equal configuration. Commonly used on file servers as a contingency in case a disk should fail.

Money laundering Immersing funds obtained illegally into legitimate banking and financial channels in order to conceal their origin, and render the funds 'respectable'.

Non-invasive Diagnostic or investigative operation that causes no alteration or damage.

Non-volatile memory Integrated circuits, which retain information even when the computer is switched off.

OCR Optical Character Recognition – a process which can scan typed and handwritten documents and convert their text to ASCII data files.

Operating system Series of computer programs usually combined with a command interpreter which perform basic housekeeping functions and provide the environment within which other programs may run.

OpSec Operational Security – controlling and securing a covert investigation through 'the need to know'.

Optical disk Storage device, which uses a laser to read and write data from a rotating disk.

Packet interception Interception of data packets as they are transmitted over a network, sometimes to obtain authentication passwords or to read unencrypted data. See **Sniffer**.

Parallel port I/O port which is usually used to print output from a computer but which may also be used to transfer data between computers or to an external device.

Partition In personal computers, a partition is a logical division of a hard disk created so that you can have different operating systems on the same hard disk or to create the appearance of having separate hard drives for file management, multiple users, or other purposes.

Passive attack Attack on a computer system whereby sensitive data or software is copied or accessed without authorization but where no modifications or corruption are introduced by the attacker.

PDA Personal Digital Assistant – pocket-sized machines typically holding phone and address lists, diaries, basic business software and usually include network and e-mail functionality.

Penetration testing The security-orientated probing of a computer system or network to seek out vulnerabilities that an attacker could exploit.

PGP Pretty Good Privacy – software used to encrypt, authenticate and protect the integrity of electronic mail and other data. PGP is available worldwide and has contravened the US government's embargo on the export of encryption products.

Phish Internet scam designed to trick the recipient into revealing personal information.

TCP/IP Transmission Control Protocol/Internet Protocol – basic communication language or protocol of the Internet. It can also be used as a communications protocol in a private network (either an intranet or an extranet). When you are set up with direct access to the Internet, your computer is provided with a copy of the TCP/IP program just as every other computer that you may send messages to or get information from also has a copy of TCP/IP.

Telnet Terminal emulation program for TCP/IP networks such as the Internet. Telnet runs on your PC and connects it to a server on the network. You can then enter commands through the Telnet program and they will be executed as if you were entering them directly on the server console. This enables you to control the server and communicate with other servers on the network.

TEMPEST Transient Electromagnetic Pulse Emanation Standard – investigation, study and control of compromising emanations from telecommunications and automated information systems equipment. The Tempest standard sets forth the official view of the US government on the amount of electromagnetic radiation that a device may emit without compromising the information it is processing. A device, which conforms to this standard, is referred to as Tempest certified.

TIFF Tagged image file format – for storing bit-mapped images on personal computers.

Time bomb Logic bomb set to trigger at a specific date and time.

Timeout Access control feature available in many operating systems, which automatically logs out those user accounts, which show no sign of activity after a pre-determined period has elapsed.

Trojan horse Computer program which purports to be beneficial or harmless but which contains malicious code or a 'hidden agenda' unknown to the user.

Trusted processor Computer that has been configured by a forensic investigation team to assist the download of data storage media, independently of any host system. The method is tested and proven prior to the download and because the team has configured the trusted processor there should be no nasty surprises when it is used to copy target hard disks or other storage media.

TSR Terminate stay resident – program, which, once executed, remains active in RAM but transparent to the user unless it is programmed to intervene, or the user invokes it.

Unallocated data Residual data in a cluster or sector of a disk that is not allocated by the FAT or MFT.

Unicode Standard for representing characters as integers. Unlike ASCII, which uses 7 bits for each character and is limited to 128 unique characters, Unicode uses a 16-bit set, allowing up to 65 536 unique characters. This is superfluous for English and Western-European languages, but it is necessary for some other languages, such as Greek, Russian, Chinese and Japanese.

USB Universal Serial Bus – plug-and-play interface between a computer and add-on devices (such as memory sticks, audio players, joysticks, keyboards, telephones, scanners and printers). With USB, a new device can be added to a computer without having to add an adapter card or turn the computer off.

USERID User identification assigned to a network user. Security on most network systems relies on the user knowing two pieces of information, his unique USERID and a password.

Virtual drive Term used when a computer drive is emulated in some fashion. The drive being emulated could be a hard drive, floppy drive, CD or DVD drive among others. A virtual hard drive can be created from RAM for fast read/write access.

WAN Wide area network – computer network that spans a relatively large geographical area. Typically, a WAN connects two or more local area networks (LANs). Computers connected to a wide area network are often connected through public networks, such as the telephone system. They can also be connected through leased lines or satellites. The largest WAN in existence is the Internet.

WEP Wired Equivalent Privacy – security protocol, specified in the IEEE Wireless Fidelity (Wi-Fi) standard, 802.11b, that was designed to provide a wireless local area network (WLAN) with a level of security and privacy comparable to what is usually expected of a wired LAN. It has since been superseded by WPA.

Wi-Fi 'Wireless fidelity' is a term for certain types of wireless local area network (WLAN). The term Wi-Fi was created by the Wi-Fi Alliance, which oversees tests that certify product interoperability. A product that passes the tests is given the label 'Wi-Fi certified' (a registered trademark).

WLAN Wireless local area network.

WORM Write once read many – information recorded on a WORM drive cannot be altered, which enables the forensic technician to refute potential allegations of evidence tampering.

WPA Wi-Fi Protected Access – a system to secure Wi-Fi networks, created to patch the known security exposures in WEP. Transmission is encrypted using the RC4 stream cipher with a 128-bit key. By increasing the size of the key, the number of keys in use, and adding a secure message verification system, WPA significantly enhances WLAN security. WPA2 is a further enhancement certified in May 2005 that employs a message authentication code that is considered fully secure.

ZIP Popular data compression format. Files that have been compressed with the ZIP format are called ZIP files and usually end with a .ZIP extension.

ZIP Drive 3.5-inch removable disk drive with capacities ranging variously from 100 to 750 Megabytes.

Index

About the author

Edward Wilding has investigated several hundred cases of computer fraud, sabotage and misuse in many jurisdictions. He has served as an expert witness for the prosecution and the defence in criminal cases, at employment tribunals, in civil litigation and at other hearings including the Hutton Inquiry. His previous book, *Computer Evidence: A Forensic Investigations Handbook*, published by Sweet & Maxwell in 1996, was one of the first to discuss computer forensic investigations. The author has lectured worldwide on forensic methods and investigative techniques to law enforcement agencies, law firms, government bodies and IT security and audit professionals. He has trained incident response teams for a number of multinational companies, and has conducted security and risk reviews for a wide range of corporate clients. In 2002 he co-founded Data Genetics International Limited (DGI), a company specializing in all aspects of computer crime investigation, incident response and forensic evidence.